The War with Turkey, 1914–18
Volume 1

The War with Turkey, 1914-18
Volume 1
The Campaigns in Mesopotamia and the
Dardanelles During the First World War

ILLUSTRATED

John Buchan

The War with Turkey, 1914-18
Volume 1
The Campaigns in Mesopotamia and the Dardanelles During the First World War
by John Buchan

ILLUSTRATED

FIRST EDITION

Leonaur is an imprint of Oakpast Ltd

Copyright in this form © 2021 Oakpast Ltd

ISBN: 978-1-78282-990-4 (hardcover)
ISBN: 978-1-78282-991-1 (softcover)

http://www.leonaur.com

Publisher's Notes

The views expressed in this book are not necessarily those of the publisher.

Contents

Turkey Enters the War	7
The Situation in Egypt	25
Mesopotamia	38
The Problem of the Dardanelles	44
The Attack on the Dardanelles by Sea	50
The Battle of the Landing	65
Appendix to Chapter 6	82
The Struggle at Gallipoli	108
Appendix to Chapter 7	124
The Deadlock at Gallipoli	151
Appendix to Chapter 8	175
The War in Mesopotamia	199
The New Landing at Gallipoli	214
Appendix to Chapter 10	240
The New Situation in the Near East	301
The Baghdad Expedition	317
The Situation in Egypt	331
The Evacuation of Gallipoli	337
Appendix to Chapter 14	353

CHAPTER 1

Turkey Enters the War

On 29th October, 1914, Turkey's many breaches of international etiquette, of which her behaviour in regard to the *Goeben* and *Breslau*, (two German warships which had evaded the Royal Navy in the Mediterranean and had fled to Turkey where they were immediately put into service), and her summary abolition of the Capitulations (essentially Ottoman contracts of diplomatic and trading priviledge) were the chief, culminated in definite acts of war. A horde of Bedouins invaded the Sinai Peninsula and occupied the wells of Magdala, and three Turkish torpedo boats raided Odessa, in the Ukraine, sank and damaged several ships, and bombarded the town.

On the 30th the ambassadors of the Allies had interviews with the *grand vizier*, which Sir Louis Mallet described as "painful." The *Sultan*, the *grand vizier*, and Djavid Bey were in favour of peace, but Enver, the Minister of War, responsible for the Turco-German alliance, and his colleagues overruled them. The Odessa incident was justified by a cock-and-bull story of prior Russian hostilities, and nothing remained for the ambassadors but to ask for their passports and withdraw. On 1st November Sir Louis Mallet left Constantinople, and the century-old friendship of Britain and Turkey was rudely broken.

The Turkish Army was based nominally on a universal conscription, but in practice only the Mussulman population was drawn upon; not all of that, indeed, for the Arabs were more usually opposed to than incorporated in the Turkish ranks. The conscript served for twenty years—nine in the First Line (Nizam), nine in the Active Reserve (Redif), and two in the Territorial Militia (Mustafiz). The major unit was the army corps of three divisions, each division embracing ten battalions. The artillery, which had suffered severely in the Balkan wars, was patchy and largely out of date, though in recent months

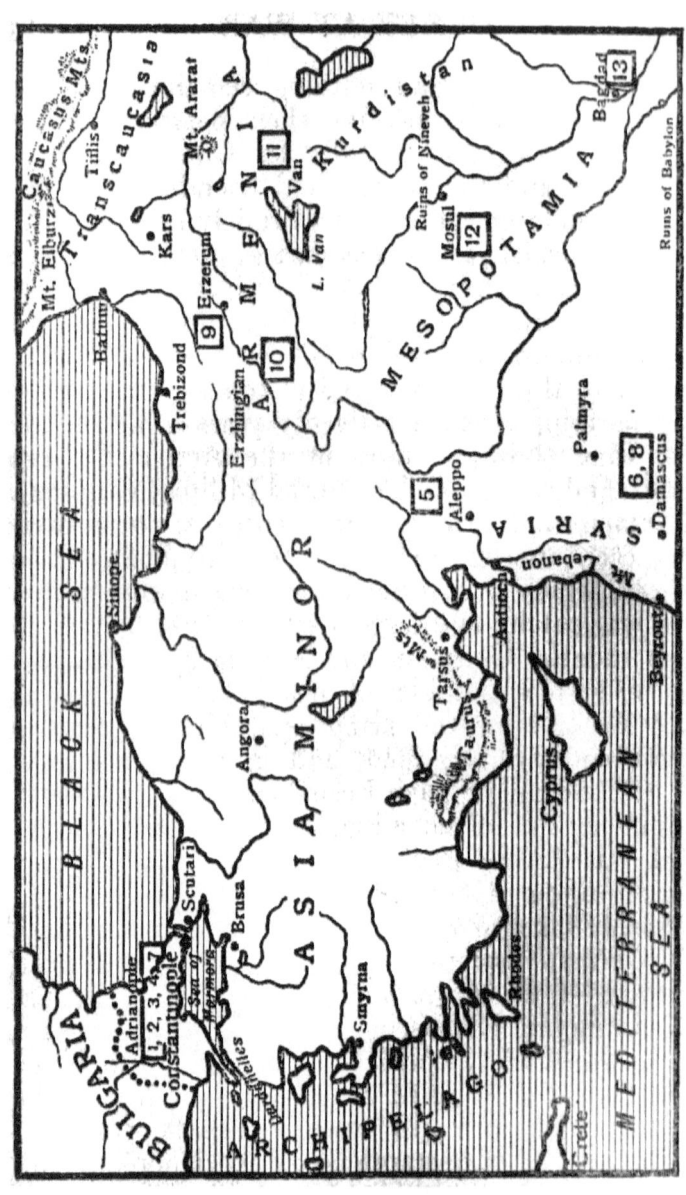

Peace Distribution of Turkish Army Corps.
(The 14th Corps has no Territorial Base.)

Germany and Austria had strengthened it with a number of heavy batteries.

The peace strength of the army was, roughly, 17,000 officers and 250,000 men, and in war some total like 800,000 might have been looked for, provided equipment was forthcoming. The commander-in-chief was Enver Bey, and the German Military Mission under General Liman von Sanders had practically taken over the duties of a General Staff. The German system of "inspections" had been instituted—four in number, with headquarters at Constantinople, Damascus, Erzhingian, and Baghdad. The fourteen army corps were distributed in peace throughout the Empire at strategic points.

The 1st, 2nd, 3rd, and 4th were nominally stationed in Europe—at Constantinople, Adrianople, Kirk Kilisse, and Rodosto; but they drew most of their reserves from Asia Minor. The 5th, 6th, 7th, and 8th belonged to the Damascus "inspection;" the 9th, 10th, and 11th were in Armenia and the Caucasus, the 12th at Mosul, and the 13th at Baghdad, while the 14th Corps had no territorial basis. On the outbreak of war these corps were reshuffled, six apparently having been concentrated around the Sea of Marmara.

The Turkish infantryman had for many years a high reputation as a soldier—especially, as he showed at Plevna, (during the Russo-Turkish War of 1877-8), in a stubborn defensive. His physique was good, his nerves steady, and his power of endurance incredible. But in recent wars his fame had suffered a certain eclipse. He had been badly led and badly armed, the commissariat and transport had been rudimentary, and successive defeats were believed to have shaken his morale. The truth seems to be that Turkey had fallen between two stools. Her ill-provided levies in the past had fought desperately under brilliant officers, because they were inspired by a simple trust in their religion and their leaders and a genuine patriotic devotion.

An attempt had been made to engraft upon this tradition the mechanical perfection of the German system. But the Turk is not meant by Providence to be a soldier of the German type, and the seed of Marshal von der Goltz and General Liman von Sanders was sown in barren soil. The consequence was a machine without precision and without motive power. The Turk had been at his best when he fought for Islam and the Padishah; but Islam was inconspicuous in the ideals of the new committee, the old Padishah was somewhere in exile, and the new one too patently a cypher. In addition, he could have little confidence in men who had already led him to disaster, and who had caused him to endure needless and horrible privations.

A perfect machine is a mighty thing, but an imperfect machine is so much scrap iron. The Turkish soldier was now an incomplete German, which is like a gun lacking the breech-block. It is impossible to withhold our sympathy from a brave race going out to battle in a cause which they neither liked nor understood, from an army in the grip of an unfamiliar and imperfect machine, from a nation sacrificed to a muddled *Weltpolitik*. Disaster loomed large in its horoscope, but courage never failed it; and the time was to come when the machine went to pieces, and, amid the snows of the Caucasus or the sands of the desert, the children of Osman, fighting once more in the old fashion, died without fear or complaint.

The beginning of war found Turkey with a curious strategical problem before her. Europe was the chief interest of her leaders. She hankered to recover the lost provinces of Thrace, and there she looked for her reward when her allies emerged victorious. But, so long as Greece and Bulgaria remained neutral, there was no room for an offensive in Europe and no need of a defensive. Accordingly, she was free to move the bulk of her corps to those frontiers where she faced directly the belligerents.

The chief was Transcaucasia, where, in a wild cluster of mountains, she looked across the gorges at Russia. An offensive in Transcaucasia was what Germany and Austria urgently desired. Russia, they knew, had none too many equipped men, and a diversion on her flank would draw troops from that thin line, a thousand miles long, which she held from the Niemen to the Dniester. Against Britain, too, Turkey might use her armies with effect. An attack upon the Suez Canal would precipitate the long-expected Egyptian rebellion, and would at the worst detain the Australian and Indian troops now training there, and at the best compel Britain to send out as reinforcements some of her still scanty reserves. Further it would bar the short road to India, and give the flame of Indian insurrection time to kindle.

But the great chance of fermenting Indian trouble, in the certainty of which Germany still firmly believed, lay in the scheme now coming to a head on the Persian Gulf. German agents had been busy among the Gulf traders, and elaborate preparations had been made for undermining the virtue of the Amir of Afghanistan, and for preaching a *Jehad* among the Mussulman tribes of the Indian north-west. Turkey believed that she had little to fear in the way of attack. The Russians were too busily engaged elsewhere to penetrate the far west front: the frosty Caucasus, while Britain had enough to do in Flanders without attempting an advance into Syria or Mesopotamia. The one serious danger-point in a war with a great naval power was the Dardanelles; but Enver and his colleagues were confident that the penetration of these Straits, long ago pronounced by experts a task of the utmost difficulty, had been rendered impossible for all time by the heavy guns which Krupp and Skoda had so diligently provided.

The doings in the Dardanelles and the fighting on the Suez Canal must be reserved for later chapters. Here we propose to consider only the campaign on Turkey's eastern frontier—in Transcaucasia and in Persia. The latter comes first in order of time. Turkey had shown her hand since the last week of August, and Russia and Britain had anticipated the events of 30th October. On the Persian Gulf the Ottoman troops found their offensive forestalled by a British invasion.

The Persian Gulf is one of the oldest of Britain's fields of activity. Englishmen, looking for trade, visited it in the reign of Elizabeth. In its early days the East India Company established a party at Bundar Abbas, and fought stoutly with Dutch and Portuguese rivals for the better part of two centuries. The Indian Navy first began the survey of the Gulf, and looked to its lighting. For fifty years we hunted down the pirates and cleared out their strongholds on the Pirate Coast. We protected Persia against those who would have deprived her of a seaboard, we policed the waters, we suppressed slavery and gun-running, we wrestled with the plague, and introduced the rudiments of sanitation in the marshy estuaries.

For three hundred years we did this work for the benefit of the shipping of all nations, since we claimed no monopoly and desired no perquisites. All we took in return was a fraction of an island for a telegraph station. One thing, indeed, we asked, and that was a matter of life and death, on which compromise was impossible. No other power should be allowed to seize territory, and no other flag should dominate those land-locked waters. For with our prestige in the Persian Gulf was bound up the future of India and of the Empire.

Before ever the Turkish crescent appeared on the shore of Arabia, Britain had shown her flag in the Gulf. In the sixteenth century Suleiman the Magnificent had captured Baghdad, but it was not till 1638 that the conquest was confirmed, and not till 1668 that Turkey reached Basra and the seacoast. For the next two centuries the writ of Constantinople ran haltingly on the western shores or not at all. The rise of the Wahabis threatened the Turkish power, and all through

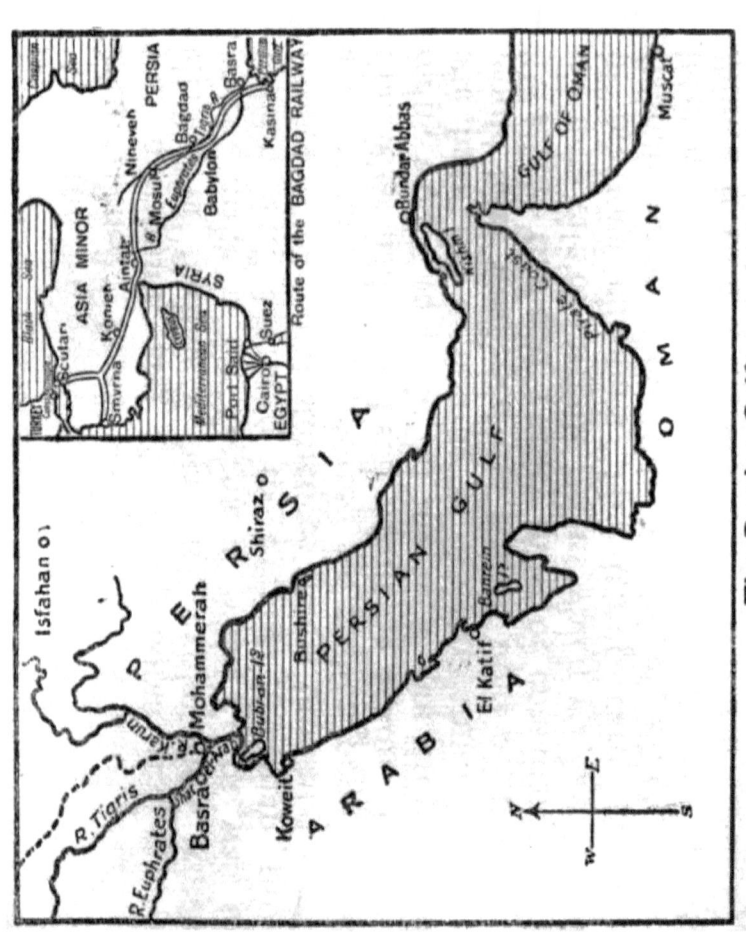

The Persian Gulf.

the nineteenth century Eastern Arabia was the scene of a rivalry between the great Wahabi houses of Ibn Saud and Ibn Rashid, a rivalry in which the Khalif did not dare to interfere. At Kuwait and at Bahrein lived independent *sheikhs*, and not all the efforts of Midhat Pasha could turn that coast into a Turkish province. The Gulf shores, baked and barren, and hot as a furnace, were a museum of types of incomplete sovereignty and *de facto* rule. But out on the waters lay British warships which kept the peace.

To this happy hunting-ground the eyes of Germany turned. Persia was a decrepit state, Turkey was moribund, and in Mesopotamia she saw a chance of finding a field for exploitation which would make it for Germany what Egypt was to Britain and Morocco to France. German professors told excited audiences that a thousand years ago the land had supported six million people, and that what had once been might be again. If Germany won a foothold on the Gulf, not only would she have the exploiting of Mesopotamia, but she would have weakened the British hold upon India. To secure this end Turkey must be conciliated, and the long tale of intrigue began.

Her trump card was the Baghdad railway. In 1899 a German company, backed by the Deutsche Bank, obtained a concession from the Porte to build a railway from Konieh, then the terminus of the little Anatolian railway, to Baghdad and Basra on the Persian Gulf. The concession was made valuable by a Turkish guarantee of the interest on the cost of construction at the rate of £700 per kilometre *per annum*. Britain awoke somewhat late in the day to the political purport of the new railway, and a diplomatic conflict began which was still in progress at the outbreak of war. Germany had followed the practice of that Lord of Breadalbane who built his castle on the extreme confines of his land with the avowed intention of "birsing yont." Her "yont" was Kuwait, on the actual Gulf shores, and she persuaded Turkey into various pretensions to *suzerainty*, which the watchful eyes of the British agents detected in time and frustrated.

Meantime she was busy at her old game of "peaceful penetration." A certain firm, Wonckhaus by name, played here the part which Woermann played in West Africa and Luderitz in Damaraland. A simple, spectacled gentleman in white ducks and a *topi* appears on the beach in quest of pearl shells. From a modest shanty on the foreshore he directs his operations, and spends freely money which cannot come out of his profits. Presently arrives a German consul, and soon there are little tiffs between the employees of the shell merchant and the natives, which give the consul something to do. Quickly the business grows, but not on commercial lines. Then comes the Hamburg-Amerika line, playing national airs and dispensing sweet champagne, and the spectacled gentleman is revealed as its accredited agent.

Very soon the innocent traders go concession hunting, and call upon Turkey to ratify their claims under a pretence of *suzerainty*. Then Britain interferes, reveals the hollowness of the business, and puts her veto on the game. But next week it begins all over again elsewhere. Colonel Sir Percy Cox, the British Agent and Consul-General on the Gulf, had a task scarcely less difficult than that of Lord Cromer in the early days in Egypt, and he performed it with a patience, judgment, and resolution which deserved well of his country.

By the beginning of November, the British in the Gulf were ready for the offensive. The Government of India had sent the Poona Brigade, under Brigadier-General W. S. Delamain, to Bahrein.

★★★★★★

The brigade contained the 2nd Dorsets, the 20th (Punjab) Infantry, the 104th (Wellesley's) Rifles, the 117th Mahrattas and the 23rd (Peshawur) and 30th Mountain Batteries.

★★★★★★

On 7th November the force reached the bar of the Shat-el-Arab, where the village of Fao, with its Turkish fort, lies among the flats and palm groves. The gunboat *Odin* bombarded the fort, and troops landed and occupied the village. The brigade then sailed thirty miles up the estuary, passing the refinery of the Anglo-Persian Oil Company at Abadan, and disembarked at Sanijeh, on the Turkish bank, where it prepared an entrenched camp, and sat down to wait for the rest of the British force. Here, on the 11th, there was some fighting with the Turks from Basra, who were dislodged from a neighbouring village by the 117th Mahrattas and the 20th Punjabis. Two days later Lieutenant-General Sir Arthur Barrett arrived with the rest of the Indian contingent—the Ahmednagar Brigade and the Belgaum Brigade.

★★★★★★

The Ahmednagar Brigade (Brigadier-General W. H. Dobbie) contained the 1st Oxford Light Infantry, the 119th Infantry, and the 103rd Mahrattas. The Belgaum Brigade (Brigadier-General C. I. Fry) contained the 2nd Norfolks, the 110th Mahrattas, the 7th Rajputs, and the 120th (Rajputana) Infantry. There were also the 48th Pioneers, the 3rd Sappers and Miners, and the 33rd Light Cavalry.

★★★★★★

On the 15th the disembarkation of the remainder began—no light task on the soft, muddy banks of the Shat-el-Arab. Meanwhile General Delamain with the Poona Brigade was busy with a force of 2,000 Turks, who held the village of Sahain, four miles to the northward. The action was meant only as a reconnaissance in force, and Sahain and the date plantation beyond it were not entirely cleared. During that day the landing was completed, and on the 16th the British force rested. News arrived that the Basra garrison was advancing to give battle; and since there were Europeans in the city whose fate might depend upon a speedy British arrival, General Barrett ordered the advance for the early morning of the 17th.

Sahain was found to be deserted, and we moved on for nine miles to a place called Sahil, near the river, where was the main Turkish force. The ground was open plain, and heavy rains in the morning had turned the deep soil into a marsh. The fight began with an artillery preparation, both from the British field guns and from gunboats on the river. The Turkish fire was bad, but they were screened by a date grove, and the country over which we advanced was as bare as a billiard table.

Under a punishing fire our men never wavered, the Dorsets especially behaving with admirable coolness and decision. The enemy did not wait for the final bayonet charge, but broke and fled. Pursuit was well-nigh impossible, partly because of the heavy ground, and partly owing to a mirage which, fortunately for the enemy, appeared to screen his flight. Our losses were 353, of which 130 were in the Dorsets. Our killed were 38. The Turkish casualties were estimated at over 1,500. The action decided the fate of Basra.

On the 21st, while the bulk of our force lay at Sanijeh, news came that the Turks had evacuated Basra, and that the Arabs had begun to loot the place. Accordingly, General Barrett embarked certain troops on two river steamers, and ordered the rest of his forces to take the direct road across the desert. The Turks had sunk three steamers at one point in the Shat-el-Arab, and had a battery to command the place, but after silencing the battery the river expedition managed to pass the obstruction early on the morning of the 22nd. About ten o'clock General Barrett reached Basra, where the Turkish Custom House had been set on fire, and the British flag was flown on the German consulate. The desert column, after a thirty-mile march, came in about midday. Next day the British formally entered the city of Sindbad the Sailor.

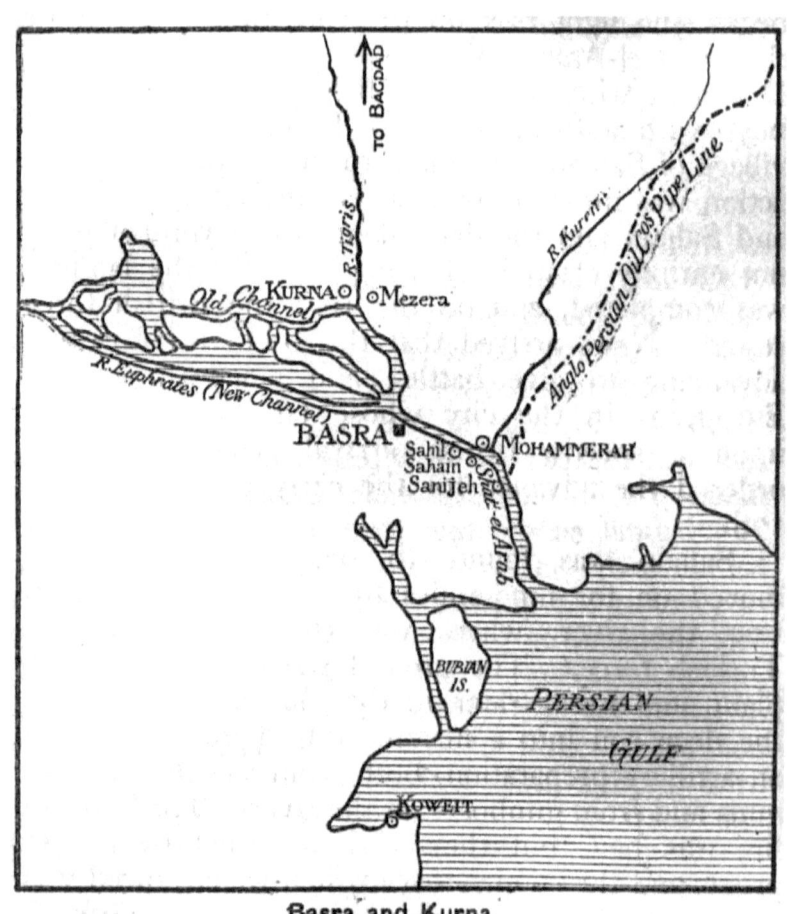

Basra and Kurna.

During the remainder of the month we were occupied in preparing a base camp. Our position was secure, but it was certain that we would be subjected to further attack. The enemy had fled at Sahil, but he would return, and the great military station of Baghdad was little more than three hundred miles distant. Fifty miles above Basra, at the point where the former channel of the Euphrates joins the Tigris, lies the town of Kurna—a position now of less strategical importance than in former days, for the old Euphrates is little use for traffic, Kurna is the point where ocean-going steamers can no longer ascend the river. On 2nd December we heard that the Turks had reassembled there, and next day a small force of Indian troops, with a detachment of the Norfolks under Lieutenant-Colonel Frazer, was sent upstream to deal with them, accompanied by three gunboats, an armed yacht, and two armed launches.

Kurna proved to be a more difficult business than was expected. The British force landed on the eastern bank four miles below the town early on the morning of the 4th, while the gunboats went ahead, shelled Kurna, and engaged the Turkish artillery on the east bank of the Tigris near Mezera, about ten miles above the town. Meanwhile the British column advanced, and about midday came abreast of Kurna, which was clearly held in force. Our men were subjected to a heavy fusillade, and since the Tigris is there three hundred yards wide, and Kurna is screened in trees, we could do little in reply. Accordingly, Colonel Frazer led his troops back to the original camp, which he had strongly entrenched, and sent a message to Basra for reinforcements.

Nothing happened on the 5th, and on the 6th General Fry appeared with help—the 7th Rajputs and the rest of the Norfolks. On the 7th we advanced against Mezera, which the Turks had again occupied, took it, and drove the defenders across the water to Kurna, while our naval flotilla was busy on the river. It was now decided to take Kurna in the rear; so, early on the 8th, the 104th and 110th were marched some miles up the Tigris. A body of sappers swam the stream with a line, and with the aid of a *dhow* a kind of ferry was established and our men crossed. By the evening the force was close to Kurna, entrenched among the trees north of the city.

But there was to be no assault. That night Turkish officers approached the British camp downstream and asked for terms. General Fry insisted upon an unconditional surrender, and just after midday next day the Turkish garrison laid down their arms. We had now obtained complete control of the whole delta, and we made entrenched camps at Kurna and Mezera on each side of the Tigris, to hold off any possible attack from the north. Turkish troops from Baghdad hovered around, and in January there were 5,000 of them seven miles from Mezera; but they offered no serious attack. We had achieved our purpose, and established a barricade against any advance upon the Gulf which might threaten India.

Farther north on Turkey's eastern frontier the war was with Russia alone. A glance at the map will show that the Russian Caucasian border has on the south Persia for two-thirds of its length and Turkey for one-third. Since Persia was a negligible military power, this meant that North-western Persia gave each of the belligerents a chance of turning the flank of the other. The Persian province of Azerbaijan had, therefore, during the recent troubled years been occupied in parts by both Russian and Turkish troops, and when war broke out it was certain that this locality would be a scene of fighting. South of Lake Urmia the Turks took the offensive.

A Kurdish force advanced by way of Suj Balak upon Tabriz, and meeting with no resistance from the Persian governor, took that city in the beginning of January, and moved some way northwards towards the Russian frontier. Russia who had left no troops to speak of in Tabriz, soon repaired her omission, and having heavily defeated the invaders at Sufian, reoccupied Tabriz on 30th January.

In this unimportant section of the campaign we have to chronicle two other movements where Russia was the invader. Early in November a Russian column, assisted by the tribesmen of Maku, crossed the Turkish frontier from the extreme north-west corner of Persia, and occupied on 3rd November the ancient town of Bayazid, which lies under the snows of Ararat, on the great trade-route between Persia and the Euxine. Other columns entered Kurdistan from the east, and a movement was begun against Van. Farther north, and fifty miles west from Bayazid another Russian column from Erivan crossed the frontier in the neighbourhood of the Alashgird valley. The town of Kara Kilisse was taken, but the Turks under Hassan ed Din Pasha—part of the Baghdad 13th Corps—showed a vigorous defensive, and held the invaders on the borders. The struggle died away towards the beginning of January when the disaster in the Caucasus compelled a general retreat of the Turkish frontier guards upon Erzerum.

We come now to the vital part of the Eastern campaign—the struggle in Transcaucasia, upon which Germany built all her hopes and Enver expended all his energy. The main features of the district are

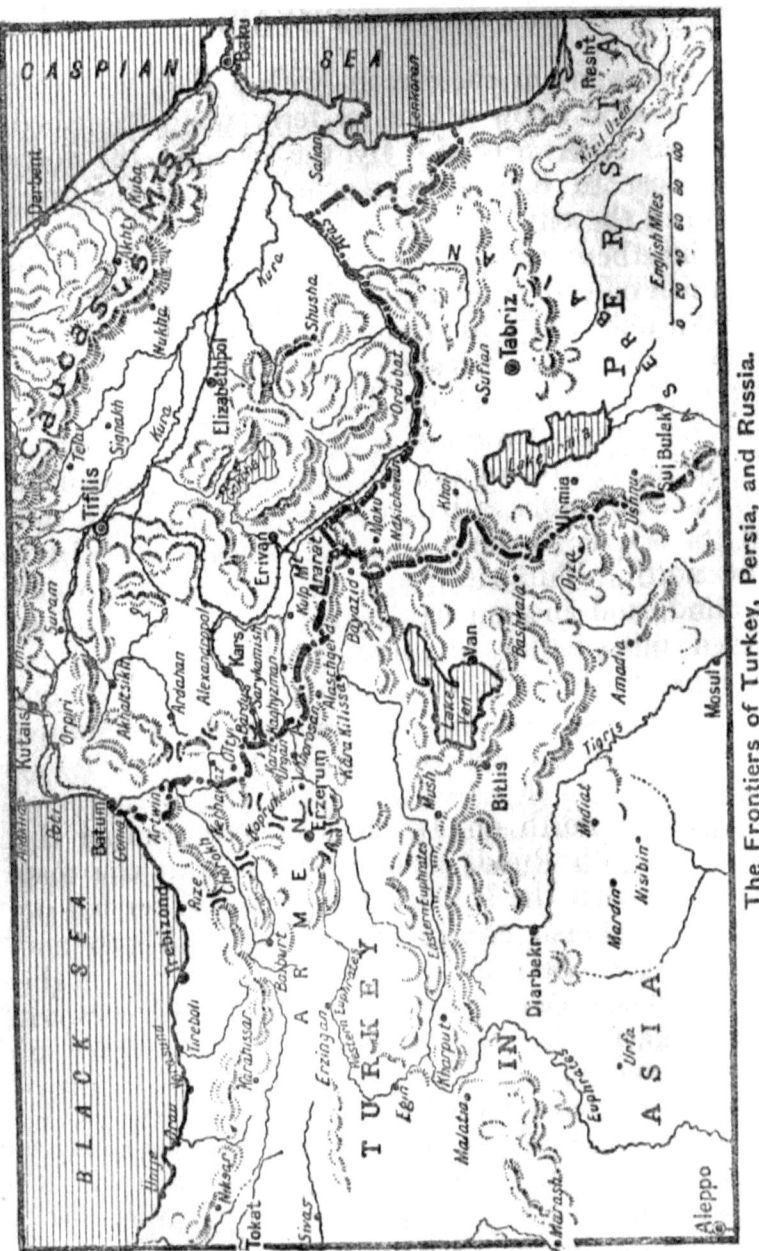

The Frontiers of Turkey, Persia, and Russia.

sufficiently familiar. The great range of the Caucasus, which contains the highest of European mountains, runs from the Black Sea to the Caspian, blocking the isthmus much as the Pyrenees block the neck between the Bay of Biscay and the Mediterranean. South-west of the range is a huge trough running nearly all the way to the two seas. Here stands Tiflis, the ancient capital of Georgia, and through it runs the main railway of those parts, from Batum on the Black Sea to Baku on the Caspian. On the south-west side of the trough lies the mountain tangle of Transcaucasia, midway in which comes the Russian frontier.

A railway runs from Tiflis past the fortress of Kars to a terminus at Sarikamish, fifteen miles from the Turkish border, while another line runs from Alexandropol by Erivan to the Persian frontier. Erzerum, the Turkish fortress, stands about the same distance from the frontier as Kars, but it is on no railway, and has none nearer than about five hundred miles. The mountain ranges extend north to the shores of the Black Sea, and south into Persia and Kurdistan. The whole district is one vast upland, most of the villages and towns standing at an altitude of 5,000 and 6,000 feet, and the hills rising as high again. All the passes are lofty, and in winter well-nigh impassable; none of the roads are good, and, as we have seen, there is no railway on the Turkish side, and but one that matters on the Russian. Winter campaigning there was likely to be as desperate as Xenophon's Ten Thousand had found it in 399 B.C.

It is an old theatre of war since the days of Cyrus and Alexander, and whenever Russia and Turkey have faced each other it has been the cockpit of the struggle. There, in 1853, Shamyl led his mountaineers. There, two years later, Fenwick Williams held Kars against Muraviev in one of the greatest stands in modern history. There, in 1877, Loris Melikov and Mukhtar met, and Kars and Ardahan and Bayazid were the scenes of desperate conflicts. If Kars could be seized, the way would be open to Tiflis and the Caspian oil fields—perhaps even across the great Caucasus itself to the levels of Southern Russia. To the leaders of a race which have always been famous as mountain fighters the offensive in the Caucasus seemed the easiest way of effecting that diversion which Germany had commissioned.

Enver's strategy was ambitious to the point of madness, but it was skilful after a fashion. He resolved to entice the Russians from Sarikamish across the frontier, and to hold them at some point as far distant as possible from the railhead. Then, while thus engaged, he would swing his left centre in a wide enveloping movement against Sarikamish, and with his left push round by Ardahan and take Kars in the rear. The device has been generally described as the ordinary German enveloping movement, but it has also affinities with the Napoleonic "pivoting square." To succeed, two things were necessary. The force facing the Russian front must be strong enough to hold it while the envelopment was going on; and the operative part, the left wing, must be correctly timed in its movements, for otherwise the Russians would be able to destroy it piecemeal. It was this "timing" which formed the real difficulty. The swing round of the left must be made by a variety of mountain paths and over necks and valleys deep in snow, where progress in winter must be tardy and precarious. To "time" such a plan accurately was beyond the wits of any mortal general staff.

For the Caucasian campaign Turkey had the 9th, 10th, and 11th Corps— stationed in peace respectively at Erzerum, Erzhingian, and Van—which had been concentrated at Erzerum about the middle of October. To reinforce the 11th Corps, the 37th Arab division had been brought up from the 13th Baghdad Corps. For the movement on the extreme left two divisions of the 1st Corps had been brought by sea from Constantinople to Trebizond. Turkey could obviously get no reserves in case of disaster.

The nearest corps, the 12th, at Mosul, had gone to Syria, and the remainder of the Baghdad Corps had its hands full with the British in the Persian Gulf. The nominal commander of the Caucasian Army was Hassan Izzet Pasha, but Enver was present as the real *generalissimo*, and he had with him a large German staff. A German, Posseld Pasha, was appointed Governor of Erzerum. The total Turkish strength was not less than 150,000, and they had against them the army of General Woronzov, which cannot at the outside have been more than three corps strong—say 100,000 men.

Fighting began in the first fortnight of November, when the Russians crossed the frontier and reached Koprikeui on the Erzerum road, which after a great deal of trouble they occupied on 20th November. The time was now ripe for Enver's plan. The 11th Corps was entrusted with the duty of holding the Russian advance on Erzerum. The 10th Corps at Id was to advance in two columns over the passes by Bardus against the road between Kars and Sarikamish, with the 9th Corps wheeling between it and the 11th. At the same time the 1st Corps, which had landed at Trebizond, was to move up the Choruk valley across a pass 8,000 feet high, take Ardahan, and advance over somewhat easier country to the railway between Kars and Alexan-

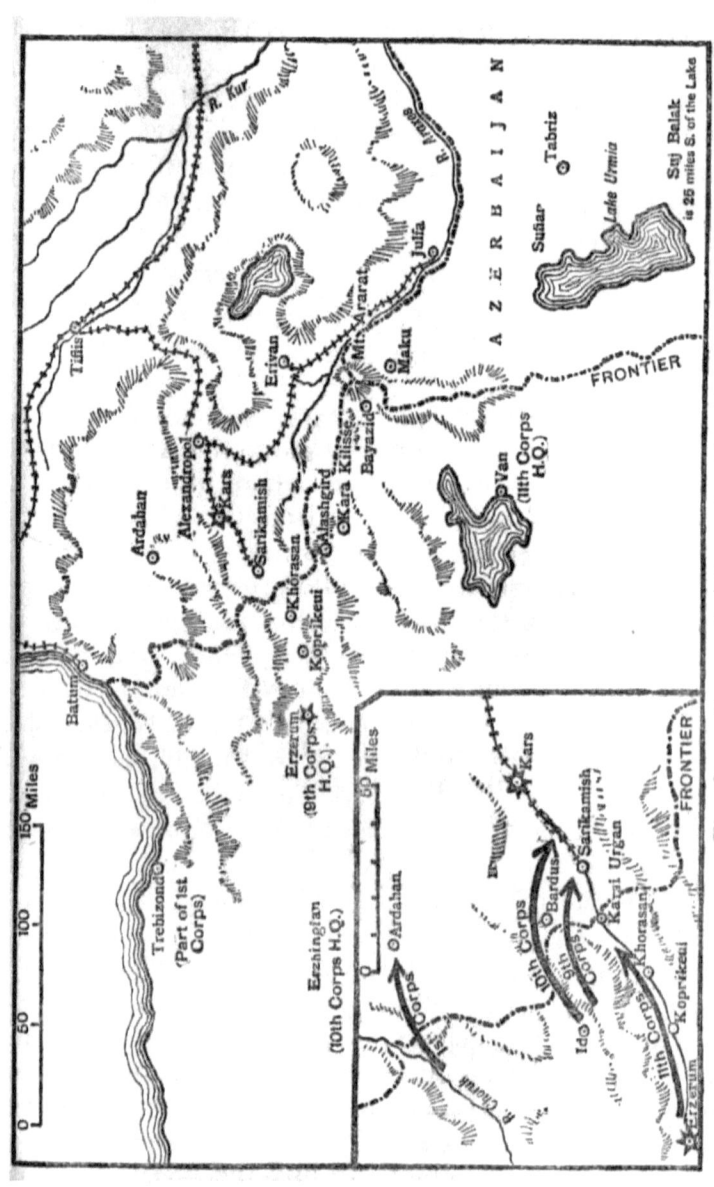

The Campaign on the Caucasian Frontier.
(Inset—The Turkish Advance.)

dropol. The difficulty about the whole scheme was the roads. The only real way for an army through the Armenian heights is by the high trough in which lie Kars and Sarikamish, and thence westwards to the upper valleys of the Araxes and Euphrates. Everywhere else the paths were tracks, now blind with snow, and hopeless for artillery.

The Turkish offensive began about the middle of December. The 11th Corps pushed the Russians out of Koprikeui and forced them back a dozen miles to Khorasan, where, on Christmas Day, the retreat halted. The Russian Army was now strung out along the thirty miles of the road from Khorasan to Sarikamish. Meanwhile, in desperate weather, the 9th and 10th Corps forty miles north had struggled over the high watersheds, and by Christmas Day had descended upon Sarikamish and on the railway east of it. The 1st Corps on the extreme Turkish left was crossing in a blizzard the steeps at the head of the Choruk, and already looking down through the pauses of storm on where Ardahan lay in its deep pocket of hills. If we take 28th December as a view-point, we find the Russian van held by the 11th Turkish Corps at Khorasan, the 9th Corps at Sarikamish, and the 10th east along the Kars railway, threatening to pierce the Russian front, and sixty miles north-east the 1st Corps descending upon Ardahan. It looked as if Enver's ambitious project had succeeded.

But the attacking force was worn out, half starved, and short of guns and ammunition, for no transport on earth could cope with such a breakneck march. The Russian general dealt first with the 10th Corps. From 28th December to 1st January there was a fierce struggle on the railway, which late on New Year's Day resulted in the defeat of the Turks and their retreat into the hills to the north. This withdrawal isolated the 9th Corps at Sarikamish, which was now enclosed between the Russian right, flung well forward in pursuit of the 10th Corps, and the Russian vanguard at Khorasan. That corps was utterly wiped out. Its general, Iskan Pasha, with all his staff, Turkish and German, surrendered after a gallant and fruitless stand. The Turks fought with their old stolidity till hunger and cold were too much for them, and they surrendered as much to the Russian field kitchens as to the Russian steel. Meanwhile the 1st Corps, which had entered Ardahan on New Year's Day, found that it could go no farther. On 3rd January a detached Russian force drove it out of the town, back over the ridges to the Choruk valley, whither the flight of the 10th Corps was also heading.

The 11th Corps at Khorasan did its best to redeem the disaster. It could not save the 9th Corps, but it might cover the retreat of the 10th, and accordingly it pushed back the Russian van from Khorasan, and advanced as far as Karai Urgan, some twenty miles from Sarikamish. It achieved its purpose, for the pursuit of the 10th Corps was relaxed, and the bulk of the Russian Army went westwards to reinforce the van. At Karai Urgan a three days' battle was fought among snowdrifts, and by the 17th the 11th Corps had been broken also, and, with heavy losses in men and guns, was retreating upon Erzerum. Meanwhile the 1st Corps and the remnant of the 10th were cleared from the Choruk valley by the Russian right, and driven towards Trebizond. The Turkish navy, which attempted to send stores and reinforcements by sea, was no more fortunate, for the several transports and provision boats were sunk along the coast by Russian warships, and the *Breslau* and the *Hamidieh* were hunted home by the Black Sea Fleet. The *Goeben* had been for some weeks out of action.

So, ended Enver's bold diversion. It had failed signally because his reach exceeded his grasp, as has happened before with adventurers. The three weeks of desperate conflict amid snowdrifts and blizzards—for the battlefields were scarcely less than 8,000 feet high—must have accounted for not less than 50,000 of Turkey's strength. Badly led and ill equipped, the starving Turkish levies had fought like heroes, and their sufferings were among the most terrible of the war. The Battle of Sarikamish—to localise the series of engagements—made certain that Russia would not be menaced from the Caucasus. Turkey must look elsewhere to find the joint in the armour of the Allies.

Chapter 2

The Situation in Egypt

In 1517, forty-eight years before the Turkish invasion of Europe spent itself on the fortifications of Malta and the gallantry of the Knights of St. John, the Sultan Selim acquired Egypt by conquest; and in spite of many vicissitudes, of the weakness of Turkish rule, the ambitions of Napoleon, and the boldness of Mehemet Ali, the *suzerainty* of Constantinople continued.

The misgovernment of Ismail and the precarious position of the Egyptian bondholders brought in the Western Powers, France and Britain, and a dual control was established over administration. Then came the deposition of Ismail, followed by the Nationalist rising under Arabi, the bombardment of Alexandria, and the Battle of Tel-el-Kebir, (1882). To Britain fell the task of restoring order, and that British occupation began which has never ceased. There succeeded the menace from the Sudan, the devastating advance of the Mahdi and his fanatical armies, the loss of the southern provinces, and the death of Gordon, (1885). *Quae caret ora cruore nostro?* is more true of Britain than of Rome, and the sands of the Nile have had the best of our British blood.

From 1885 onwards the task of the *de facto* rulers of Egypt was twofold—the reconquest of the Sudan, and the elevation of the Nile valley from bankruptcy to prosperity. The first was accomplished in 1898, when Lord Kitchener, at the Battles of the Atbara and Omdurman, shattered the Dervish levies. The second, in the wise hands of Lord Cromer, progressed yearly, in spite of international bickerings, Court intrigues, and a preposterous dualism in finance. In a multiplicity of problems there is usually, as Lord Cromer saw, one master question, the settlement of which involves the others. In the case of Egypt this was finance; and with infinite patience and perfect judgment the greatest of modern administrators first of all reduced taxation, then

Massed Turkish machine-guns, Sinai

from his scanty balances spent wisely on reproductive works, till he had given Egypt the water which is her life, and raised the peasants from a condition of economic slavery to a comfort unknown in the Nile valley since the days of the Pharaohs. In 1904 the British occupation was formally recognised by the Powers of Europe, and the Egyptian finances were released from the bondage of international control.

On 17th December the Khedive Abbas II., having thrown in his lot with Turkey, ceased to reign in Egypt, which, with the assent of France, was formally proclaimed a British Protectorate. Lieutenant-Colonel Sir Arthur Henry MacMahon, a distinguished Indian political officer, was appointed High Commissioner. The title of *Khedive*, first adopted by Ismail, disappeared; and the throne of Egypt, with the title *Sultan*, was offered to Prince Hussein Kamel Pasha, the second son of Ismail, and therefore the eldest living prince of the house of Mehemet Ali—an able and enlightened man, who had done great services to Egyptian agriculture. The change thus made was the smallest which the circumstances permitted. There was no annexation; the shadowy *suzerainty* of Turkey disappeared; but otherwise things remained as before. Apparently, the tribute to Constantinople still continued, since that tribute had been ear-marked for the interest on the Ottoman debt, and was paid direct to the bondholders.

Protectorate is the vaguest of political terms, and may involve anything from virtual sovereignty to an almost complete detachment. In this case it meant that Britain was now wholly responsible for the defence of Egypt and for her foreign relations. The very vagueness of the arrangement had its merits, for nothing was laid down as to the order of succession to the *sultanate*, and the hands of the British Government were left free for some future revision of the whole arrangement. In the meantime, it regularised an anomalous international status.

The first object of a belligerent Turkey would naturally be the Suez Canal. The Turkish force in Syria in peace time consisted of the 8th Corps of three divisions, whose headquarters were Damascus. But during November there was a large concentration in Syria, which included the bulk of the 12th Corps from Mosul, part of the 4th Corps from Adrianople, and apparently the Anatolian division normally stationed at Smyrna. Out of this force, which cannot have been less than 90,000, an Expeditionary Army of 65,000 men was created.

Its commander was Djemal Pasha, the Turkish Minister of Marine, a vehement Pan-Islamist, and an inveterate enemy of Britain. The seizure of the two Ottoman Dreadnoughts building in England

Muster of Turkish troops before Sinai attack

had embittered his mind, and he burned to wipe off the score by a blow at the Suez Canal, one of the channels by which Britain exerted her naval supremacy. He had been Governor of Baghdad and of Basra, and had been at the head of an army corps in the Balkan war. He had no particular military reputation, having won his power rather as an energetic leader of the Committee of Union and Progress than as a general in the field.

The advantages of a blow at the Suez Canal were obvious. If the eastern bank could be held the use of the canal by shipping would be endangered, and Britain cut off from one of her most vital sea routes. If the Canal could be crossed in force, then there was the chance of that Egyptian rising for which the faithful of Turkey and Germany hoped. But the difficulties were no less conspicuous. To reach the Canal from Syria an all but waterless desert had to be traversed, a stretch varying from 120 to 150 miles in width. Across this tract of rock and sand there were three routes, all of them hard. The first, which we may call the northern, touched the Mediterranean coast at El Arish, and ran across the desert to El Kantara, on the Canal, twenty-five miles south of Port Said. It was 120 miles long, and had on its course only a few muddy wells, quite insufficient to water an army.

The southern road ran from Akaba, at the lead of the gulf of that name on the Red Sea, across the base of the peninsula of Sinai to a point on the Canal a little north of Suez. This route was the old Pilgrims' Road from Egypt to Mecca; it was 150 miles long, and, like the other, ill supplied with wells. Between the two was a possible variant which we may call the Central Route. Leaving the Mediterranean coast at El Arish, it ran up the dry valley called the Wady el Arish to where the upper part of that depression touched the Pilgrims' Road. Now, from the Turkish bases of Gaza and Beer-sheba there was no railway to assist an advance, and no route for motor transport; and, since an army must carry its own water, it seemed impossible for the invaders to move in force unless they laid down some sort of light railway, or so improved the roads as to make them possible for motors.

The Mecca Railway, which ran to the east of Akaba, gave them no help, for between it and the escarpment of the Sinai Peninsula lay two rugged limestone ridges, enclosing a trench 3,000 feet deep. The best route—indeed the only possible—for a light railway was up the Wady el Arish, but this had the disadvantage that at its debouchment on the coast it would come under fire from the sea.

The difficulties of Turkey's strategical problem were enhanced by

Sinai 1916, Turkish Cavalry

Turks entrenched in Sinai

the nature of her object of attack The Suez Canal is not only the equivalent of a broad and deep river, but it is navigable for warships and its banks provide superb opportunities for defence. It cannot be turned, for it runs from sea to sea. It has a width of over 200 feet, and the banks in most places rise at an angle of thirty degrees to a height of 40 feet. On its western shore a lateral railway runs the whole way from Port Said to Suez connecting at Ismailia with the line to Cairo, and a fresh-water canal follows the same bank for threequarters of its length, from Suez to El Kantara. Again, most of the ground to the east is flat, and offers a good field of fire to the defenders on the west bank, or to ships in the channel. In a few places there are dunes on the east side which might give cover to an invader.

Such a place is just south of El Kantara, several others are to be found south of Ismailia, and there is a small rise south of the Bitter Lakes. Any Turkish attack might therefore be looked for in the Ismailia-Bitter Lakes section. The British forces in Egypt then included certain detachments of Indian cavalry and infantry, the Australian and New Zealand contingents under Major-General Birdwood, a number of British Territorials among them the East Lancashire Division, as well as the regular Egyptian Army. The whole force was under the command of Major-General Sir John Maxwell, a soldier with a long experience of the Nile valley wars.

At the end of October, it was reported that a force of 2,000 Bedouins was marching on Egypt, and on November 21st there was a skirmish at Katiyeh, east of the Canal, between this force or a part of it, and some of the Bikanir Camel Corps under Captain Chope. Previous to this the Anglo-Egyptian posts had been withdrawn from El Arish and from the Sinai Peninsula. Nothing more was heard of the invasion for more than two months. There were many rumours that Djemal Pasha was having difficulties with his Syrian command, and was impressing for his expeditionary force a variety of unwarlike Syrians from peasants in the Jordan valley to cab drivers in Jerusalem.

On January 28, 1915, small advanced parties had crossed the desert. One coming by the El Arish route reached Katiyeh, and was beaten back by a Gurkha post east of El Kantara. Another party coming by the Akaba route was driven back at Kubri, just east of Suez. The desert was well scouted by British airmen, and about that time we landed a party at Alexandretta Bay, in North Syria, and cut the telegraph wires. On the 29th it was announced that the Turks had occupied Katiyeh, and had several posts to the west of that place. Four days later, on 2nd

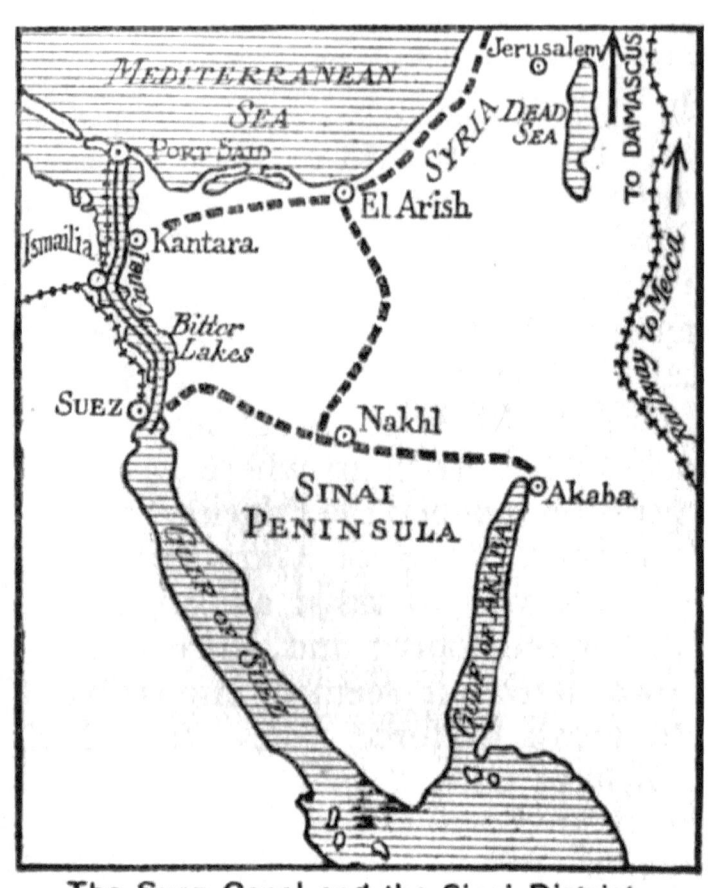

The Suez Canal and the Sinai District.

February, came the main attack, for which these proceedings had been reconnaissances.

The Turks officially described the main attack as a reconnaissance, and we may accept the description, for it cannot be regarded as a serious invasion. But it seems likely that it was a reconnaissance, not of design but by compulsion, and that Djemal Pasha found, when he began the attempt, that to transport even one army corps across the desert was wholly beyond his power, and that of his German Chief of Staff, von Kressenstein. The troops seem to have numbered about 12,000, and to have advanced by the central route up the Wady el Arish. Four hours' journey from the Canal they split into two detachments. One moved against Ismailia, to the south of which the east bank gives a certain cover. A second, and much the strongest, advanced to a point opposite Toussum, just south of Lake Timseh, where a patch of ground on the east is high and broken. A small flanking attack was made from the northern route against El Kantara. The Mosul and Smyrna divisions had been left behind, and the troops were the 25th or Damascus division of the 8th Corps, with a few of the 4th (Adrianople) Corps, a remnant of the old Tripoli field force, a few Turkish soldiers, and a number of Bedouin irregulars under Mumtaz Bey.

The first movement was made on the night of 2nd February. A feint against Ismailia that evening had been spoiled by a dust storm, but in the darkness our sentries on the Canal saw and fired at shadowy figures on the side opposite Toussum. The Turks had brought a number of pontoon boats in carts across the desert, and these they attempted to launch, along with several rafts made of kerosene tins. They never had a chance of succeeding. Crowded on the shore, with a high, steep bank behind them, our men mowed them down with rifle fire and Maxims. A few of the vessels were launched, but they were soon riddled and sunk. The enemy then lined the high banks, and tried to silence our fire, and the duel went on till morning broke

With daylight the battle became general all along the stretch from Ismailia to the Bitter Lakes. We had a small flotilla on the Canal—several torpedo boats, the old Indian Marine transport *Hardinge*, and the French guardships *Requin* and *d'Entrecasteaux*. The Turks had a number of field batteries and two 6-inch guns, which one of the French ships promptly silenced. The torpedo boats made short work of the remaining pontoons, and the crew of one landed on the eastern bank, and raided a trench of the enemy. A few Turkish soldiers had got across in the night—a score, perhaps, in all—and sniped our men in the rear;

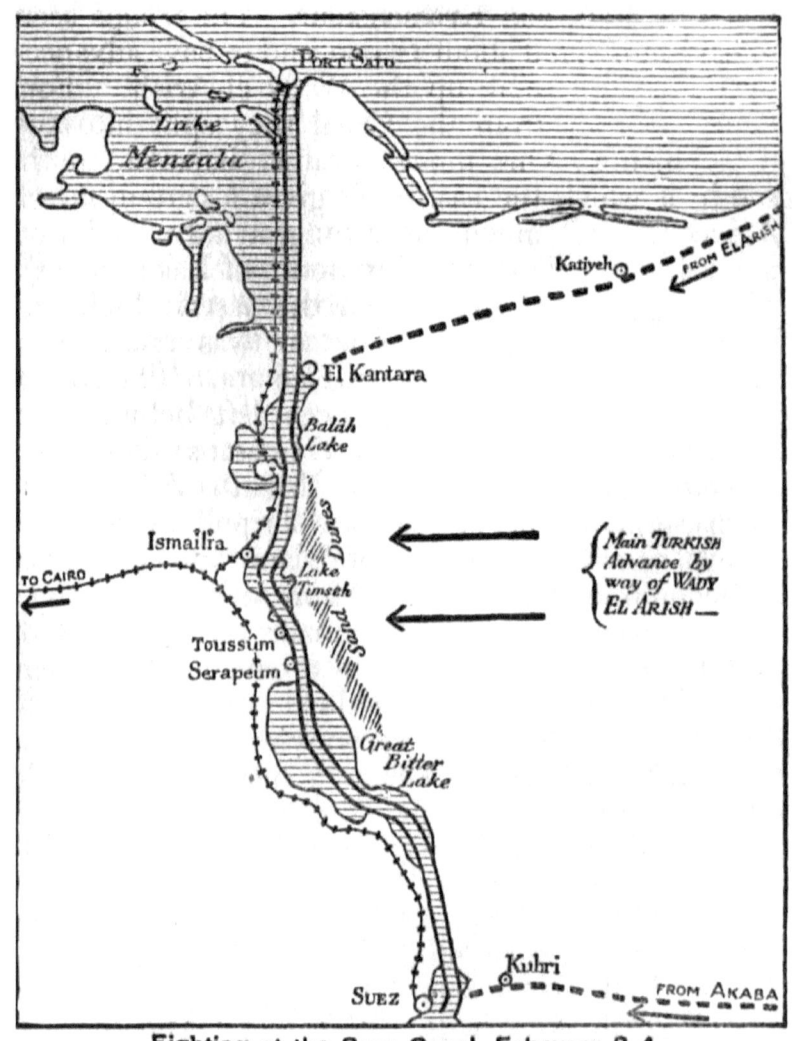

Fighting at the Suez Canal, February 2-4.

but they were speedily disposed of, and those who swam over later were deserters.

In the afternoon our Indian troops from Serapeum and Toussum took the offensive, and, admirably supported by artillery, drove the enemy from a large part of the eastern bank. Meanwhile the Ismailian garrison also moved forward, and cleared their front. About the same time the half-hearted attacks on our flank near El Kantara and Suez had also failed. By the evening of the 3rd the fiasco was over, and early next morning we crossed the Canal in force and began the work of rounding up the enemy. We counted 400 killed and made 600 prisoners during the two days' fighting, so we may estimate the total Turkish casualty list for the Battle of the Canal at well over 2,000. The list grew rapidly in the succeeding days, as deserters began to drift in.

By 8th February there were no Turks within twenty miles of the Canal, and beyond that only a few scattered rearguards, the main force being in full retreat for the borders. It should never have been allowed to return. With 130 waterless miles to cover, there was no reason why a beaten and dispirited force should ever succeed in reaching Beersheba. That it did, and with all its guns, detracts considerably from the British success. The cause of this escape seems to have been a heavy sandstorm, which made it impossible to use our camel corps. It is believed, however, that the Turks suffered heavily in the retreat from their Bedouin allies, who, baffled of the plunder of Egypt, took what they pleased from their friends.

It remains to notice one or two further incidents in the Turkish campaign. Cyprus, which had been administered by Britain since 1878, was formally annexed to the British Empire. The town of Akaba on the Red Sea, which was apparently being used as a station for mine-laying, was visited by H.M.S. *Minerva*, who found the place occupied by soldiers, including one German officer. The *Minerva*, being unable to get satisfaction, shelled the fort and destroyed the barracks and government buildings, but did no harm to private dwellings. A British cruiser, with a landing party of Indian troops, captured the Turkish fort at Sheik Said, opposite Perim, at the southern end of the Red Sea. In South-Eastern Arabia our Indian troops had some fighting around Muscat, but this was only indirectly traceable to the war with Turkey. The Sultan of Oman had for two years been at strife with certain of his lieges, and since all men were fighting, the rebels were resolved to follow the fashion.

Suez Canal, 1915

TURKISH TROOPS MARCHING TO THE SUEZ

NIGHT ATTACK ON THE SUEZ CANAL

CHAPTER 3

Mesopotamia

The defeat at Sarikamish had broken utterly the cohesion of the Turkish Army, and the Russian troops were engaged during the subsequent weeks in driving the remnants across the frontier. The chief sweeping movement was down the Choruk valley, whither, it will be remembered, the 1st Turkish Corps had retired after the disaster at Ardahan. One Russian column moved from Ardahan through the passes, while another, supported by vessels of the Black Sea Fleet, operated along the coast from Batum. By the end of March, the whole frontier region was empty of the enemy. Farther south, from Sarikamish, there were a number of insignificant conflicts. Turkish stragglers united with the local professionals to form *banditti*.

Villages, the strongholds of the enemy, had to be cleared, and the brigands driven to the snowy hills. In all this there was no serious Turkish defensive, and presently the Turkish and Persian borders were as quiet as they are ever likely to be in a world-wide upheaval. The Russian commander made no attempt to advance to Erzerum, though from all accounts the defences of that fortress were strong only on paper. Russia's object was merely to hold the gate. The vital blow at Turkey must come from another quarter.

In the Persian Gulf area, the British force was at the beginning of the year securely entrenched on both sides of the Tigris at Kuma and Mezera, a strong position commanding the highway to the sea. The situation, however, was not without its anxieties. In spite of Turkey's rebuffs in Transcaucasia and her diversions towards the Suez Canal, she had sufficient troops left in the Baghdad command to outnumber gravely the small British Army on the Shatt-el-Arab. Further reinforcements were brought from India, under Lieutenant-General Sir John Nixon, who, on his arrival at Basra, took supreme command of the operations.

Early in January, 1915, we discovered that the Turks were occupying a strong position on the banks of a canal some eight miles north of Mezera, and on 20th January we organised a reconnaissance to ascertain their strength and dispositions. Supported by our gunboats from the Tigris we shelled their camp, and drove them back with some fifty casualties to our own troops. The Turkish force was estimated at over 5,000 men, with six guns. The enemy next appeared near Ahwaz, on the Karun River, the scene of an engagement between Sir James Outram and the Persians during the short war of 1857. There we had placed a small garrison to protect the pipe line of the Anglo-Persian Oil Company. West of Ahwaz a Turkish force of three regiments and a number of Arab tribesmen were reported, and on 3rd March we made an attempt to reconnoitre this position. The enemy was discovered to be 12,000 strong, and our small expedition of 1,000 men were in imminent danger of being cut off. Our retirement was not effected without heavy fighting, in which we severely punished the enemy, but lost five officers and fifty-six rank and file killed, and about 130 wounded, mostly from the 4th and 7th Rajputs.

The sight of the red and white flags of the Arabs, whom we had hoped for as allies in breaking the Turkish rule, was disquieting, and it presently appeared that the enemy was clustering in strength round our whole area of occupation. On the day following the operations near Ahwaz, our cavalry, reconnoitring towards Nakaila, twenty-five miles north-west of Basra, had an encounter with 1,800 mounted Turks, and lost four of their officers. But the great attack did not mature till a month later. Three places, Kurna, Ahwaz, and Shaiba, a few miles west of Basra, were selected for the assault. On 11th and 12th April Kurna was bombarded at long range, but beyond the destruction by a floating mine of one of the Tigris bridges, no damage was done, and the attack was not pressed home. A number of Turks in boats suffered severely from the guns of H.M.S. *Odin*. The bombardment of Ahwaz was no more effective, and we saw nothing of the enemy but clouds of horsemen.

Kurna and Ahwaz were only feints, and the real blow was directed against Shaiba and the possession of Basra. The action began on 12th April, and lasted for three days, and even in a war of this magnitude it deserves the name of a battle. The invading force was estimated at 18,000 men, of whom 11,000 were regulars of the Baghdad Corps, accompanied by at least twenty guns. The British position around

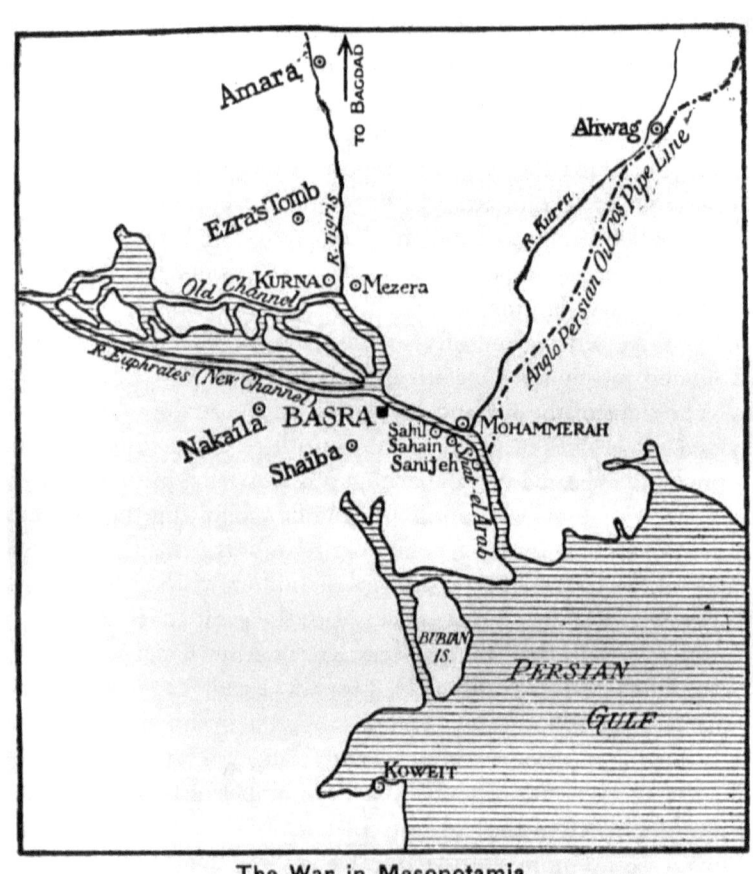

The War in Mesopotamia.

Basra was protected on the east by the river, so the Turkish assault was directed from north, west, and south. Early in the morning, under cover of a heavy artillery preparation, the Turkish infantry advanced from three sides, and when their gun fire slackened, set to work to dig themselves in. The attack was resumed in the afternoon from the south, where we succeeded in beating it back.

During the night there was a steady fire from rifles and machine-guns, and in the morning, we found the Turks in possession of some houses and rising ground to the north of us, from which it was imperative that we should oust them. Our advance was completely successful, and a simultaneous counterattack by the Turks from the west was easily repulsed, with the loss of several hundred prisoners.

That afternoon we observed a new concentration of over 5,000 Turkish troops to the south, where a strong position had been entrenched some four miles from the British lines. On the morning of 14th April we moved in force against these entrenchments, which contained the bulk of the enemy's army, at least 15,000 strong. We carried their advanced position, and in the afternoon swept them from their main trenches in spite of a heavy machine-gun and rifle fire. A final charge with the bayonet put the whole enemy force to flight. The British casualties amounted to about 700 officers and men, and the Turkish loss was not less than 6,000 killed, wounded, and prisoners. We captured several machine-guns and large quantities of stores and equipment, including motorcars and ammunition wagons. As usually happens, the routed Turks were set upon by their former Arab allies, who completed what the British had begun.

The victory of Shaiba meant the end of a serious Turkish offensive for the present. Suliman Askeri, the Turkish general, fell back to Nakaila, but he could not stay there, and we occupied the place on the 17th. By the 20th the enemy was more than a hundred miles from Basra.

On the river twelve of his boats were either captured or sunk. April is the season of floods in Mesopotamia, and our pursuit was much impeded by the swollen waters. The reconnoitring parties whom we dispatched found no sign of the enemy in all the countryside except abandoned positions and derelict stores. Sir John Nixon's brilliant action had cleared the delta of Turkish troops, rendered the pipe line secure, and, it was hoped, had convinced those shrewd trimmers, the Arab tribesmen, that for once they had erred in their forecast of the winning cause.

During May there was a general cessation of hostilities, save that, about the middle of the month, we were compelled to give the Arabs a sharp lesson in the neighbourhood of Ahwaz. But on 31st May the enemy was threatening again north of Kurna, and it was resolved to disperse him. Starting at 1.30 in the morning, our troops, partly by boat and partly wading, surprised his position on the heights two miles from the town. Our artillery, especially our naval guns, silenced his batteries, and by midday we had cleared the heights, taking 250 prisoners and three fieldpieces. Next day as we advanced, we found him in full retreat. He stayed not upon his going, for he had left the tents standing in his camps at Barhan and Ratta. That evening we were north of Ezra's Tomb, thirty-three miles from Kurna, and our naval flotilla was in pursuit of the steamers and native boats by which the Turks had fled.

One steamer, the *Bulbul*, was overtaken and sunk, and we captured two large lighters, carrying field guns, ammunition, and mines, and some 300 prisoners. The pursuit was continued by moonlight, and on 3rd June Amara, an important military station, seventy-five miles from Kurna, was captured, together with 30 officers and 700 men. The rest of the invading forces dispersed among the marshes of the Tigris.

In Egypt, after the fiasco of the Canal attack in February, there were only affairs of outposts. On 22nd February the French cruiser *Desaix* landed marines at Akaba, and her guns cleared the Turkish troops from the town. On 31st March a British cruiser bombarded Mowilah, another place at the head of the Red Sea. Patrols and aircraft along the Suez Canal reported that the nearest enemy posts were four days' march distant, and from other sources we learned that their main army was still quartered in Palestine.

But on 22nd March there was another attempt to force the Canal. An enemy force, mainly infantry with guns, but including a few cavalry squadrons, was located near El Kubri, in the neighbourhood of Suez. Shots were exchanged, and the Turks retired to a point eight miles from the Canal. Next day the British, under Lieutenant-General Sir George Younghusband, fell upon their camp and drove them to Nakhl, seventy miles inside the desert. A few stray Turks still haunted the Canal banks, and on 8th April shots were exchanged between patrols close to El Kantara. A few days later the French warship *St. Louis*, assisted by several hydroplanes, bombarded a large Turkish camp near Gaza. Camps were bombarded during the month at El Arish and El Sirr, and the Bikanir Camel Corps on 28th April had a brisk skirmish with a detachment of the enemy. These, however, were minor incidents: it was clear that the Turkish Army destined for the invasion of the Canal was thoroughly impotent and disheartened; and Egypt was used as a base for our Dardanelles operations without any anxiety as to its eastern frontiers.

CHAPTER 4

The Problem of the Dardanelles

If Constantinople fell Turkey would fall, and the doom of the capital was sealed so soon as the Allied battleships entered the Sea of Marmara.

The strategic importance of the forcing of the Dardanelles in a war with Turkey was therefore clear. But in how far would the fall of Constantinople influence the decision of the main European conflict? In the first place, it would to some extent simplify Russia's problem, and release troops for Poland and Galicia. To a limited extent only—for there was reason to believe that the loss of Constantinople might be followed by a continuance of the campaign in Transcaucasia. At the same time there was the possibility that a mere threat to the capital might lead to a revolution which would overthrow the shaky edifice of Enver's rule. The bulk of the Turkish people did not share the passion for Germany felt by the Committee of Union and Progress, and advices from Constantinople during these days seemed to point to the imminence of a rising which would make a clean sweep of the Young Turk party, and restore the *Sultan* to his old place at the side of France and Britain.

Again, the opening of the passage between the Black Sea and the Aegean would give Russia a channel for exporting her accumulated wheat supplies. The lack of these was increasing the cost of bread in Western Europe, and the restriction of Russian exports had made the rate of exchange set violently against her, so that she was paying in some cases thirty times the normal price for her foreign purchases. She also stood in sore need of a channel for the entrance of war munitions. Archangel had been closed since January, the trans-Siberian line was a costly and circuitous route for all but her imports from Japan, while entries by Norway and Sweden were at the best precarious.

She needed especially rifles and ammunition, and though the Western Powers had little to spare in the way of the finished articles, they could send her the raw materials. Certain chemicals especially, which she badly wanted, could be imported in large quantities if the Straits were open.

But the main strategic value of the Dardanelles lay in its effect upon hesitating neutrals. Italy at the moment was still in the valley of decision, and the downfall of Turkey and its influence upon the Balkan States would impel her to action. Turkey's defeat would have an effect upon the Balkan position like the addition of a new chemical to a compound—it would leave none of the constituents unaltered. A volume would be required to riddle out the intricacies of the situation in the Balkans.

Suffice it to say that Greece, Rumania, and Bulgaria had national interests and purposes which compelled them to keep a watchful eye on each other, and which made it difficult for any one of them to move without its neighbour. Bulgaria, who had borne the heavy end of the Turkish campaign, had lost the prize of victory. Three compacts had been violated to her hurt, and she was deeply distrustful of all the great powers, and especially of Russia. German financiers had befriended her in 1913, when France and Britain had stood aside, and her Stambolovists had always looked to Austria as their ally. With Greece and Serbia—especially with the latter— she had a bitter quarrel over the delimitation of territory after the Balkan wars, and she had little cause to forget Rumania's intervention.

At the same time her geographical position made it highly perilous for her to join the Teutonic League. A victorious Turkey would be a bad neighbour for a state of her antecedents, and the fate of Belgium, and the grounds on which Germany had justified it, were not encouraging for a small nation. Her attitude was therefore a circumspect neutrality. But the first Allied guns that spoke in the Sea of Marmara would compel her to a decision, and there was little doubt what that decision would be.

With Bulgaria decided, Greece and Rumania would follow suit. We have already glanced at Rumania's position, a complicated one which was slowly disentangling itself under the pressure of events. If her southern frontiers were safe it seemed likely that she would make her choice, and her geographical situation and her well-equipped army of more than half a million would make her an invaluable ally. With Turkey out of action and the Balkans united on the Allies' side, the most critical part of the main campaign—the long front of Russia—would be greatly eased. When the Italian guns sounded on the Isonzo and the Rumanian force could take the Austrian right wing in flank, the balance against Russia's arms might be redressed.

In a speech made just after he relinquished the office of First Lord of the Admiralty, Mr. Churchill discussed the strategic purpose of the Dardanelles expedition, he told his hearers:—

> You must not forget the prize for which you are contending. The army of Sir Ian Hamilton, the fleet of Admiral de Robeck, are separated only by a few miles from a victory such as this war has not yet seen. When I speak of victory, I am not referring to those victories which crowd the daily placards of many newspapers. I am speaking of victory in the sense of a brilliant and formidable fact, shaping the destinies of nations, and shortening the duration of the war. Beyond those few miles of ridge and scrub on which our soldiers, our French comrades, our gallant Australian and New Zealand fellow-subjects are now battling, lie the downfall of a hostile Empire, the destruction of an enemy's fleet and army, the fall of a world-famous capital, and probably the accession of powerful allies. The struggle will be heavy, the risks numerous, the losses cruel; but victory, when it comes, will make amends for all. *There never was a great subsidiary operation of war in which a more complete harmony of strategic, political, and economic advantages has combined, or which stood in truer relation to the main decision which is in the central theatre.* Through the Narrows of the Dardanelles and across the ridges of the Gallipoli peninsula lie some of the shortest paths to a triumphant peace.

The contention in the words we have italicised seems to be in its strictest sense justified. The Dardanelles expedition directly subserved the main object of the war. There remain for the reader's consideration the questions whether the right way was taken to ensure success, and whether the forces employed in it weakened the efforts of the Allies in the main European theatre.

NOTE ON ADMIRAL HORNBY'S EXPEDITION, FEBRUARY 1878.

Admiral Hornby's correspondence, including his confidential communications with the Admiralty, has been published (*Life of Admiral Sir Geoffrey Phipps Hornby*, G.C.B., by his daughter; Blackwood,

The Dardanelles Campaign—General sketch map of the scene of the operations.

1896), and it throws much light upon the whole problem of operations in the Dardanelles. The defences of the Straits at the time are described in a telegram from the British Ambassador at Constantinople, dated January 20th. "Torpedoes" was then used as a term to describe submarine mines.

> Consul at Dardanelles reports that he thinks a further series of torpedoes have been laid at the entrance to the Straits between Castles Kum Kale and Seddul Bahr, and also at the northern extremity of the Narrows between Forts Nagara and Bokali. ... Connecting wires to mines placed last summer on Asiatic shore have been led probably into old fortress, Sultanieh Kalessi (Chanak). About sixty heavy rifled guns are mounted now in the four principal forts in the Narrows. The 50-ton Krupp gun at Sultanieh Fort may be called ready for service.

Hornby's ships were the *Alexandra* (flagship), *Agincourt, Achilles, Swiftsure, Téméraire, Sultan,* and *Salamis*. They left Besika Bay on the morning of the 13th February in an easterly gale, with thick snow squalls, and at once cleared for action. It was known that the forts at the Narrows had been greatly improved under the supervision of the German engineer, Blum Pasha, and that a number of modern guns from Armstrong and Krupp had been mounted, and submarine mines laid in the channel. The danger from these last was not considered serious, for the mines of 1878 were somewhat primitive affairs. The Turkish gunners and their officers were believed to be badly trained, and it was anticipated that the naval guns could silence the land batteries. Landing-parties were ready on board each vessel to be put ashore to attack the works in the rear.

There was no occasion to test these arrangements in actual conflict, for at the last moment the Turkish officer in command of the Narrows decided to let the fleet pass. This, however, was not known to the ships, and they steamed up the Narrows against a strong current and in the face of a blinding snowstorm, with the men at their guns watching for the flash from the forts which would be the signal for battle. There was an anxious moment when the *Alexandra*, leading the line, was closing in to Chanak at the narrowest part of the Straits. For some minutes the snow became so thick that all guiding marks were lost, and the flagship got aground on the Asiatic side within easy range of the big guns at Sultanieh Kalessi. She was hanging on the edge of a bank, with twenty fathoms of water only two ships' length away. The

Sultan stood by her to help her off, a piece of work which took four hours, and meanwhile the other ships steamed on to Gallipoli. On being rejoined by the *Alexandra* and the *Sultan* the whole squadron entered the Sea of Marmara.

It is useless to speculate on what might have been in naval or military operations. The conditions of the Dardanelles in 1878 were very different from what they were in 1915. Though the armament of the forts had been improved, the number of guns mounted was comparatively small. There was no elaborate mine defence, and there were no drifting mines. Most important of all, the batteries were only those of the old forts on the low ground at the water's edge. There was not a single gun on the heights, which in many places overhang the Straits in lines of cliff. Had there been a fight, Hornby would not have been exposed to the fire of mobile guns and howitzers on the higher ground, hidden in positions where it would have been practically impossible to silence them.

He had, in fact, a comparatively easy task against an incomplete scheme of defence directed by half-trained officers of the old Turkish Army. But even so, if there had been any resistance, it seems certain that the Narrows would not have been passed without considerable loss. Had the Turks opened fire as the snow squall passed away and showed the Alexandra lying bow on under their guns in a position in which most of her armament was useless, the flagship might have been destroyed.

CHAPTER 5

The Attack on the Dardanelles by Sea

The true beginning of Turkey's naval war was the arrival of the *Goeben* and *Breslau* at Constantinople in the second week of the campaign. They were speedily followed by a liner, once employed in the German East African trade, which slipped through the patrols of the Allies, and brought a large cargo of mines and explosives sufficient to improvise a naval base. To her we owe the construction of the first minefield in the Dardanelles. Meanwhile quantities of war stores were reaching Constantinople overland through Rumania, and presently Admiral Limpus and his British Staff, who had been employed to reorganise the Turkish Navy, found the work passing into other hands. Early in September both the navy and the army of Turkey were under German control, and the sea-gates were being prepared for defence against that war with the West which daily became more certain.

Our warships had been watching the outlet of the Dardanelles since early August, and when war broke out with Turkey it was easy to establish an effective blockade. Hostilities began at daybreak on 3rd November, when the combined French and British squadrons bombarded the entrance forts at long range. Our ships suffered no injury, only one shell falling anyrwhere in their vicinity. The operation appears to have been a mere reconnaissance, intended to draw the fire of the forts and ascertain if they possessed long-range guns. It was admitted in the Admiralty report that no safe estimate could be made of the damage we inflicted.

Thereafter for some weeks this section of the war languished. On 18th November there was a sea fight off the Anatolian coast of the Black Sea, in which the *Goeben* was badly damaged. On 10th December the same ship attempted to bombard Batum, and was hunted back to the Bosphorus by the Russian fleet. The Allies maintained their Dardanelles blockade, and on 13th December Lieutenant Holbrook took a submarine into the Straits through five lines of mines, and torpedoed the old Turkish warship, the *Messoudieh*, which was guarding the minefields. For this gallant exploit, performed under difficulties which seem on paper insuperable, he received the Victoria Cross. But the incident had no sequel. The end of the year came, and still no attempt was made upon the Straits, where week by week the German and Turkish officers were elaborating their schemes of defence.

By this time, however, the Admiralty had decided that our ample margin of naval strength and our clear superiority in gunnery, of which proof had been given in several cruiser actions, made it safe to detach a number of our older ships for operations against the Dardanelles. It may be that the *Formidable*, which was sunk in the Channel by a submarine on New Year's morning, was one of a squadron destined for this purpose. By the end of January, the blockading squadrons off the Straits had been reinforced by French and British vessels from various stations, and had grown into a powerful combined fleet. We had seized the island of Tenedos, which was still Ottoman territory, and Greece tolerated the use of Lemnos, which she only nominally held, and in which the bay of Mudros supplied a useful advanced base for naval operations.

These began in earnest with the attack on the forts at the entrance to the Dardanelles on Friday, 19th February. A month later came the attack on the forts at the Narrows. All the operations from 19th February to 18th March were part of a general plan. They represented an attempt to destroy the defences of the Dardanelles, and force a passage into the Sea of Marmara, by naval power alone. Before describing these movements in detail, it will be well to examine with some closeness the strategical and tactical conditions of the problem, for on our view of them depends our judgment of the possibility of success, and, therefore, of the justification of this subsidiary operation.

A naval attack on the Dardanelles without the co-operation of a military force would be a battle of ships against forts, and it had long been widely held by experts that in such a contest the advantage would lie with the forts.

It may be said, however, that though ships are not likely to silence forts, forts cannot prevent ships running past them. The argument is not relevant to the case of the Dardanelles, where in the long run not only a passage, but the occupation of the passage, is necessary, as Hornby found in 1878.

Such being the accepted doctrine among naval and military students of the question, it may well be asked why the scheme of forcing the Dardanelles by a naval attack alone was ever accepted by the British Government. It is known that very high naval authority was opposed to it; it is equally true that certain naval authorities approved of it. On what grounds? Probably because there was an idea abroad that new conditions had been introduced into the problem. There is always a tendency to begin by exaggerating the effect of a new weapon. The Dreadnought, the long-range gun, the submarine, have each been hailed as about to revolutionize warfare.

It was presumed that the huge high-explosive shells of the modern warship would make land batteries untenable, not by silencing their guns one by one, but by acting like flying mines, the explosion of which would shatter the defences and produce a panic among the gunners. Once the forts were thus temporarily overcome, landing-parties would complete the task, the minefields would be cleared, and the passage be won. It was also anticipated that with the long range of the newest naval guns the forts could be bombarded from a distance at which their own armament would be ineffective. The notion was that the outer forts at the entrance to the Straits could be silenced by the converging fire of a number of ships from the open sea, while the attack on the inner forts would be carried on by individual fire from ships in the Gulf of Saros, which, with aeroplanes to direct them, would send their shells over the hills of the Gallipoli peninsula.

These two factors—aerial reconnaissance and the increased range of naval guns—were believed to have changed the whole conditions of the enterprise.

It would be unfair to say that there was no colour for this forecast. But it erred in strangely neglecting and underestimating other factors in the situation, and in unduly simplifying the problem. It was not a mere question of a duel between the guns of the fleet and those of the permanent fortifications. Had it been, there would have been much to be said for the optimistic view. But the defences of the Dardanelles had been organised on a system which took the fullest advantage of natural features, and was based on past experience and a scientific knowledge of modern warfare. It was no improvised Turkish expedient, but the work of the German general staff. It contemplated an attack, not only by a fleet, but by a large military force acting in conjunction. When, therefore, the Allies, to the surprise of their enemies, decided upon a mere naval attack, the problem of defence was exceedingly simplified.

To appreciate the Allies' difficulties, we must consider briefly the topography of the Straits. Their northern shore is formed by the peninsula of Gallipoli, a tongue of land some fifty miles long, which varies in width from twelve to two or three miles. The country is a mass of rocky ridges rising to a height of over 700 feet from the sea. The hills are so steep and sharply cut that to reach their tops in many places is a matter of sheer climbing. There is little cultivation, few villages, and no properly engineered roads. Most of the land is covered with a dense scrub from three to six feet high, with stunted forests in the hollows. Communications are so bad that the usual way from village to village is not by land, but by boat along the inner or outer coast. At the head of the Dardanelles, on the European side, is the town and harbour of Gallipoli, the headquarters of the naval defence of the Straits.

The southern shore is also hilly. Near the entrance on the Asiatic side there is the flat and marshy plain of Troy, which is bounded on the east by hills running to 3,000 feet. On both sides the high ground overhangs the sea passage, and on the north side for about twelve miles the hills form a line of cliffs, with narrow half-moons of beach at the base, and here and there a stream making a gully in the rampart. As everywhere in the Mediterranean, there is practically no tide, but a strong current sets continuously down the Straits from the Sea of Marmara. Its speed varies, but it often rises to four knots an hour. North-easterly winds are prevalent, and before the days of steam these often closed the passage for weeks at a time to ingoing traffic. In the spring bad weather is not infrequent. Sudden gales with driving showers of rain, and long spells of mist in calmer weather, are a bar to naval operations.

There are two groups of forts. The first is at the entrance—on the north side, Cape Helles and Sedd-el-Bahr, with one or two adjacent batteries; on the opposite shore, Kum Kale and Orkanieh, None of these forts were heavily armed, for it was recognised that in any case they would be at a disadvantage against a long-range attack from a fleet in the open sea. The entrance forts were merely the outposts of the real defensive.

The second group is at the Narrows. Fourteen miles from the mouth the Straits close in to a width of about three-quarters of a mile. Up to this point their general course has been from south-west to north-east, but now the channel makes a short turn directly northward before resuming its original direction. There is thus within a distance of a few miles a sharp double bend, and guns placed in position at the water's edge can cross their fire against ships ascending the Straits, which can also be brought under end-on fire from guns at the top of the Narrows.

At the entrance to the Narrows are the forts of Chanak, or Sultanieh Kalessi, on the Asiatic side, and Kilid Bahr, on the European. The slopes above the latter were studded with batteries, some commanding the approach to the Narrows, others commanding the seaway towards Gallipoli. Along both sides, but especially between Chanak and Nagara, the low ground was lined with batteries. It was possible to attack the forts at the entrance to the Narrows at fairly long range from the wider channel below the bend, but there was no room to bring any large number of ships into action at the same time. Once the entrance was passed all fighting must be at close range, but the strength of the defence did not depend only on the batteries. An attacking fleet had other weapons to face besides the guns.

There was first the obstruction of the channel by submarine mines. To get rid of these by sweeping was probably impossible, for the light vessels, which alone could be employed, had to face not only the fire of the forts but that of mobile guns on the higher ground. Further, at various parts in the Narrows, torpedo tubes were mounted in concealed positions, and the land torpedo tube is a formidable weapon. It can fire a more powerful missile than those discharged from ships, and since its station is fixed it can make good shooting. Again, the descending current could be used to send down drift mines upon the attacking ships. The artillery defence was further supplemented by howitzer batteries on the heights, difficult to locate, easy to move if located, and therefore almost impossible to silence.

It is clear that a fleet endeavouring to force a channel thus defended was at the gravest disadvantage. There was only one way to complete success—the co-operation of a land army. By that means there was a chance of gaining possession of the heights behind the forts, attacking them in reverse, assisting the fleet to silence them, and then destroying the mine-field. Only a landing force, too, could deal with the mobile batteries. Such an army would be met by many difficulties. The country, all ridges and pockets, was hard to operate in, and the Turks, who when acting on the defensive are among the best soldiers in the world, were certain under German leadership to take advantage of every natural feature.

They had, in fact, converted the Gallipoli peninsula and the hill country on the Asiatic side into two vast fortresses manned by powerful armies. At the outbreak of war there were 200,000 Turkish soldiers in the Constantinople area, and this number, in spite of Caucasian and Egyptian adventures, was not allowed seriously to dwindle. The garrison of Constantinople alone was kept up to 180,000 men, and by February, when the Turkish offensive elsewhere had failed, there was probably well over half a million of men available for the Straits defence. They had no railway communication to speak of, both the Adrianople and the Anatolian lines being too distant, but they had an uninterrupted water route from Europe and Asia through the Sea of Marmara. We cannot tell the number of guns which they had mounted on the shores, but we know something of their calibre.

At the Narrows forts there were 14-inch Krupp guns, which threw a shell of 1,366 pounds. They had a number of 11-inch guns, and at the outer forts some of 10.2-inch. Lighter guns of from 6- to 9-inch calibre were in all the forts. They had besides a number of field howitzers, which do not seem to have been higher than the 8-inch variety. The defect of Turkey in the past had been shortage of munitions, but in this case her German masters saw that she was well supplied. Large stores of Krupp shells had been accumulated in Constantinople during the winter, and when the struggle began there was no slackening of the Turkish fire.

It is a simple matter to be wise after the event, and it is easy to judge a military problem pedantically, without allowing for the chances of war. Every operation is to some extent a gamble, even after all the unknown quantities seem to have been determined. History showed a clear verdict on the handicap of a contest between ships and forts, without the assistance of a land army. History, too, showed that to pass the Dardanelles was a perilous achievement, unless the invader held the Gallipoli peninsula, and so could secure his supplies and his retreat. But it is permissible sometimes to go in defiance of history and create new precedents—laudable if the attempt succeeds, excusable if it fails.

It is time to turn to the details of the first phase—the Attack by Sea.

The first step was comparatively easy. By the middle of February, a considerable naval force, French and British, had been concentrated at the entrance to the Dardanelles. With two exceptions, the larger British ships belonged to the pre-Dreadnought class; but there were also present the *Inflexible*, which had been in the Battle of the Falkland Islands, and the new super-Dreadnought, the *Queen Elizabeth*. The latter belonged to the most recent and most powerful class of battleship in the world. She was one of a group of five which, when war began, were still in the builders' hands, and in the ordinary course she would not have been commissioned till the late summer of 1915. Her main armament was made up of eight 15-inch guns, so mounted as to give a fire of four guns ahead or astern, and of the whole eight on either side.

The operations against the outer forts began on Friday, 19th February. The ships engaged were the *Inflexible*, *Agamemnon*, *Cornwallis*, *Vengeance*, and *Triumph*—British; and the *Bouvet*, *Suffren*, and *Gaulois*—French; covered by a flotilla of destroyers.

★★★★★★

Inflexible—17,250 tons, eight 12-inch guns, sixteen 4-inch guns; *Agamemnon*—16,750 tons, four 12-inch guns, ten 9.2-inch guns; *Cornwallis*—14,000 tons, four 12-inch guns, twelve 6-inch guns; *Vengeance*—12,950 tons, four 12-inch guns, twelve 6-inch guns; *Triumph*—11,980 tons, four 10-inch guns, fourteen 7.5-inch guns; *Bouvet*—12,200 tons, two 12-inch guns, two 10.8-inch guns, eight 5.5-inch guns, eight 4-inch guns; *Suffren*—12,730 tons, four 12-inch guns, ten 6.4-inch guns; *Gaulois*—11,260 tons, four 12-inch guns, ten 5.5-inch guns.

★★★★★★

The naval force was under the command of Vice-Admiral Sackville Cardan, and the French squadron was under Rear-Admiral Guépratte. Behind the battle-line lay the new mother-ship for seaplanes, the *Ark Royal*, named after Howard's flagship in the war with the Spanish Armada. From her aircraft were sent up to watch the fire of the battleships and signal the result.

The action began at 8 a.m. It was clear that the forts at Cape Helles, on the point of the peninsula, and at Kum Kale, on the opposite shore, were frequently hit, and at times seemed to be smothered in bursting shells. It was harder to make out what was happening to the low earthworks of the batteries about Sedd-el-Bahr. All morning the bombardment continued; it was like target practice, for not a single shot was fired in reply. Admiral Carden came to the conclusion that the forts had been seriously damaged, and at a quarter to three in the afternoon gave the order to close in. What followed shows that aerial observation of long-range fire is no easy matter.

As the ships steamed nearer, the hitherto silent and apparently destroyed forts began to shoot. They made bad practice, for no one of the six ships that had shortened range was hit. By sundown the European batteries were quiet again, but Kum Kale was still firing, when, on account of the failing light. Admiral Carden withdrew the fleet.

For some days there was bad weather, but by the morning of Thursday, 25th February, it had sufficiently improved for operations to be resumed. At 10 a.m. on that day the *Queen Elisabeth, Agamemnon,* and *Irresistible,* (15,000 tons, four 12-inch and twelve 6-inch guns), and the French battleship *Gaulois,* renewed the long-range bombardment of the outer forts.

It was clear that these had not been seriously damaged by the action of the 19th, and what injury had been done had been repaired in the interval. Once again, the four forts, Sedd-el-Bahr, Cape Helles, Kum Kale, and Orkanieh, were attacked. We know from the Admiralty report that of these the first mounted six 10.3-inch guns, the second two 9.2-inch, the third four 10.2-inch and two 5.9-inch, and the fourth two 9.2-inch. Against the sixteen heavy guns of the forts the four ships brought into action twenty pieces heavier than anything mounted on the land, including the 15-inch guns of the *Queen Elizabeth,* the most powerful weapon ever used in naval war. The forts were thus greatly outmatched, and the long range of the *Queen Elizabeth's* guns enabled her to come into the fight at a distance where nothing from the land could possibly touch her.

In an hour and a half, the *Queen Elizabeth* had silenced the Cape Helles guns, but not before they had hit the *Agamemnon,* a shell fired at a range of six miles bursting on board her, with a loss of three men killed and five wounded. This was the only casualty we suffered during the first stage of the bombardment. At 11.30 a.m. the *Vengeance* and *Cornwallis* came into action, and, running into close range, silenced the lighter armament of the Cape Helles battery. The attack on the Asiatic forts was at the same time reinforced by two of the French ships, the *Suffren* and the *Charlemagne,* which poured in a heavy fire at a range of only 2,000 yards. Early in the afternoon the *Triumph* and the *Albion,* (12,950 tons, four 12-inch guns, twelve 6-inch), attacked Sedd-el-Bahr at close range. It says much for the courage and discipline of the Turkish artillerymen that, though they had to face overwhelming odds, their last gun was not silenced till after 5 p.m.

Little daylight remained, but, covered by the battleships and destroyers, a number of North Sea trawlers at once set to work to sweep for mines in the entrance. The work was resumed next morning at sunrise, and the minefield was cleared for a distance of four miles up the Straits. Then the *Albion, Vengeance,* and *Majestic,* (the oldest battleship type in the navy; 14,900 tons, four 12-inch guns, twelve 6-inch), steamed in between the headlands, and opened a long-range fire on Fort Dardanos, a work on the Asiatic side some distance below the Narrows. It was not heavily armed, its best guns being four 5.9 Krupps. As the battleships opened fire, a reply came not only from Dardanos but from several unlocated batteries at various points along the shore. The Turkish fire, however, did little harm, and we were able to attack the rear of the entrance forts, and drive off several bodies of Turkish troops. One party near Kum Kale was driven across the bridge near the mouth of the River Mendere (the ancient Simois), and the bridge itself destroyed by shell fire.

We believed that by this time the Turks had everywhere been forced to abandon the defences at the entrance, and landing parties of Royal Marines were sent ashore with explosives to complete the destruction of the guns in the forts. This they successfully accomplished, but near Kum Kale they encountered a detachment of the enemy, and, after a hot skirmish, had to fall back to their boats with a few casualties. On this slender basis the Turkish bulletins built up a report of landing parties everywhere repulsed with heavy loss.

The result of the day's operations was that we had cleared the entrance to the Straits. This was the easiest part of the problem, and only the beginning of the formidable task assigned to the Allied fleets. The real defence of the Dardanelles—the forts at the Narrows—had not been touched. Nevertheless, with that misleading optimism which has done so much to paralyze national effort, the Press of France and Britain wrote as if the fall of the outer forts had decided the fate of Constantinople. In that city at the moment there was undoubtedly something of a panic among civilians, but the German and Turkish Staffs were in the best of spirits.

They were greatly comforted by the time it had taken the powerful Allied fleet to destroy the outer forts, and they believed that the inner forts were impregnable. There long-range attacks would be impossible; no large number of ships could be brought simultaneously into action, and drifting mines and torpedoes could be used to supplement the artillery defence. Enver, not usually partial to the truth, was for once in a way correct when he told a correspondent:

> The real defence of the Straits is yet to come. That lies where the difficult waterway deprives ships of their power to manoeuvre freely, and obliges them to move in a narrow defile commanded by artillery and mines.

German view of the naval attack on the forts

For a few days there were strong northerly winds, but in spite of the rough weather the minesweepers continued their work below the Narrows.

On Thursday, 4th March, the battleships were again in action. Some attacked the forts inside the Straits, probably Dardanos and Soghandere, and a French cruiser in the Gulf of Saros demolished a look-out station at Cape Gaba Tepe. The published casualty lists show that among the ships engaged were the *Ocean* and the *Lord Nelson*, (a sister ship of the *Agamemnon*—16,500 tons, four 12-inch guns, ten 9.2-inch). A landing-party of Royal Marines near Kum Kale were driven back to their boats by a superior Turkish force with the relatively large loss of 22 killed, 22 wounded, and 3 missing. On 5th March there was a demonstration against Smyrna, a British and French detachment, under Vice-Admiral Peirse, bombarding the outer forts. As the attack was not pushed, it was probably only intended to induce Enver to keep a considerable force in that neighbourhood.

On 6th March the weather was again fine, with a smooth sea, and a preliminary attempt was made on the Narrows forts. On the preceding day some of the ships had entered the Straits and drawn the fire of the forts at Kilid Bahr. There was an explosion in one of them, and after that it ceased firing. On the morning of the 6th the *Vengeance, Albion, Majestic, Prince George*, (a sister ship of the *Majestic*), and *Suffren* steamed into the Straits and attacked the forts on both sides just below the Narrows. The fire was chiefly directed against Dardanos on the Asiatic, and Soghandere on the European shore—works which may be regarded as the outposts of the main Narrows defence. The attacking ships were struck repeatedly by shells, but no serious damage was done, and there was no loss of life.

This attack from inside the Straits was, however, a secondary operation. The main attack, from which great results were expected, was made by the *Queen Elizabeth, Agamemnon*, and *Ocean* from the Gulf of Saros, on the outer side of the Gallipoli peninsula. Lying off the point of Gaba Tepe, they sent their shells over the intervening hills, with aeroplanes directing their fire. Their target was two of the forts at Chanak, on the Asiatic side of the Narrows, about twelve miles off. These forts had a very heavy armament, including 14-inch guns, and it was hoped to destroy them by indirect fire, to which they had no means of replying. The Turks replied from various points on the heights of the peninsula with well-concealed howitzers and field guns, and three shells struck the *Queen Elizabeth*.

Next day, 7th March, the attack was renewed. Four French battleships, the *Bouvet, Charlemagne, Gaulois,* and *Suffren,* attacked the forts from inside the Straits and engaged Dardanos, which they succeeded in silencing. Behind them, farther out, lay the *Agamemnon* and *Lord Nelson,* firing at a range of from 12,000 to 14,000 yards at the forts at the Narrows entrance. Chanak, which the *Queen Elizabeth* had been trying to demolish the day before, brought its heavy guns into action. The *Gaulois, Agamemnon,* and *Lord Nelson* were hit several times, but we believed that we had put the Chanak forts, the strongest of the Narrows, out of action. Subsequent experience showed that it was a difficult matter permanently to silence the forts.

Reports of German officers made it clear that under the heavy fire of the ships it was hard to keep the guns constantly in action, not so much on account of any serious damage, but because the batteries were flooded with stifling vapours from the shells, and it was necessary to withdraw the men until the air cleared. Further, the defenders had been ordered to economize ammunition, and to reserve their fire for the closer attack which they believed would follow. The fact, therefore, that a fort ceased firing was no proof that it had been really silenced. Again, and again during these operations we heard of forts being silenced, which next day or a few days after could bring most of their guns into action.

The following week saw nothing but minor operations. On the 10th an attempt was made to shell the Bulair defences at long range, and the British warships shelled some new batteries of light guns which the Turks had established near Morto Bay, on the European side of the entrance to the Straits. The Turkish Government sent out a report that the Allied fleets had been unsuccessfully bombarding the defences at Sedd-el-Bahr and Kum Kale. The British Press treated this as an impudent fiction, and pointed out that the forts there had been destroyed many days before. But the Turkish *communiqué* had a basis of fact. We had destroyed the forts, but we had not occupied the ground on both sides of the entrance.

The Turks had accordingly entrenched themselves strongly near the ruins, and mounted guns, and these we attacked on 10th and 11th March. At that time, misled by the optimism of the newspapers, the ordinary man in France and Britain counted with certainty on the speedy news that our fleet was steaming through the Sea of Marmara on the way to Constantinople. When tidings came that the light cruiser *Amethyst* had on 15th March actually made a dash into the

Narrows, he believed that the Turkish defence had collapsed.

The *Amethyst's* enterprise was, apparently, part of a mine-sweeping expedition, and also, perhaps, a daring reconnaissance in which the little ship drew the fire of the upper forts. She seems to have got but a short way, and to have lost heavily in the attempt. But her exploit, magnified through Greek channels, made us believe that the Narrows defences had been seriously damaged, and that the time was ripe for a determined effort to force a passage. The combined fleet had now grown to a formidable strength, and included a Russian cruiser, the *Askold*, (our sailors called it "The Packet of Woodbines," from its five thin funnels), which appeared from somewhere or other on 3rd March, Vice-Admiral Carden had been compelled by ill health to relinquish the command, and Vice-Admiral John Michael De Robeck succeeded him.

The great effort was made on Thursday, 18th March. It was a bright, clear day, with a light wind and a calm sea. At a quarter to eleven in the forenoon the *Queen Elizabeth, Inflexible Agamemnon, Lord Nelson, Triumph,* and *Prince George* steamed up the Straits towards the Narrows. The first four ships engaged the forts of Chanak and the battery on the point opposite, while the *Triumph* and *Prince George* kept the batteries lower down occupied by firing at Soghandere, Dardanos, and Kephez Point. After the bombardment had lasted for an hour and a half, during which the ships were fired upon not only by the forts but by howitzers and field guns on the heights, the French squadron, *Bouvet, Charlemagne, Gaulois,* and *Suffren*, came into action, steaming in to attack the forts at short range. Under the combined fire of the ten ships the forts once more ceased firing.

A third squadron then entered the Straits to push the attack further. This was made up of six British battleships, the *Albion, Irresistible, Majestic, Ocean, Swiftsure,* (a sister ship of the *Triumph*—11,980 tons, four 10-inch, fourteen 7.5-inch guns), and *Vengeance*. As they steered towards Chanak the four French ships were withdrawn in order to make room for them in the narrow waters. But in the process of this change all the forts suddenly began to fire again, which showed that none of them were seriously damaged. According to Turkish accounts, only one big gun had been dismounted.

Then came the first disaster of the day. The French squadron was moving down to the open water inside the Straits, being still under fire from the inner forts. An officer on a British destroyer, who was watching its movements, reported that he saw three large shells strike the *Bouvet* almost simultaneously, and that immediately after there was a loud explosion, and she was hidden in a cloud of smoke. The first impression was that she had been seriously damaged by shell-fire, but her real wound was got from one of the mines which the Turks were now sending down with the current. They had waited to begin this new attack till the narrow waterway was full of ships. As the smoke cleared, the *Bouvet* was seen to be heeling over. She sank in three minutes, in thirty-six fathoms of water, carrying with her most of her crew.

The attack on the forts continued as long as the light lasted. The mine-sweepers had been brought up the Straits in order to clear the passage in front, and to look out for drift-mines. An hour and a half after the *Bouvet* sank, the *Irresistible* turned out of the fighting line with a heavy list. She also had been struck by a mine, but she floated for more than an hour, and the destroyers took off nearly all her crew—a dangerous task, for they were the target all the time for Turkish fire. She sank at ten minutes to six, and a quarter of an hour later another drift-mine struck the *Ocean*. The latter sank almost as quickly as the *Bouvet*, but the destroyers were on the alert, and saved most of her crew. Several of the other ships had suffered damage and loss of life from the Turkish guns. The *Gaulois* had been repeatedly hit, her upper works were seriously injured, and a huge rent had been torn in her bows. The *Inflexible* had been struck by a heavy shell, which killed and wounded the majority of the men and officers in her fire-control station, and set her on fire forward.

As the sun set most of the forts were still in action, and during the short twilight the Allied fleet slipped out of the Dardanelles. The great attack on the Narrows had failed—failed, with the loss of three battleships and more than 2,000 men.

For more than a month the sea attack languished. Almost every day one or more ships entered the Straits and opened fire to prevent the Turks repairing the entrance forts, or establishing themselves in new positions. Mine-sweepers were also constantly at work, and had to be protected. On 28th March there was some activity at the other end of the passage, the Russian Black Sea fleet having bombarded the outer forts of the Bosphorus. On 6th April we again bombarded the Smyrna forts. Meantime our submarines had been busy, and on Saturday, 17th April, *E15* had the misfortune to ground in the Straits near Kephez Point. There was some danger of her falling into the enemy's hands in a serviceable condition, so on the Sunday night two picket-boats of the *Triumph* and the *Majestic*, under Lieutenant-Commander Eric

Robinson, carried through a brilliant "cutting-out" expedition.

The boats were under heavy fire from the forts 200 yards off, and from numerous small guns at close range. Notwithstanding this, the submarine was torpedoed and destroyed. The *Majestic* picket-boat was sunk, but the crew were saved by the other boat, and the only casualty was one man, who died of his wounds. During these weeks the naval attack was not pushed because the Allies had decided upon a different strategy. The events of 18th March had convinced the most optimistic that ships alone could never force the passage, and a combined movement by sea and land was now in train.

CHAPTER 6

The Battle of the Landing

The world first heard of the Dardanelles Expeditionary Force on 9th April, 1915, when the French Government, in an official note, announced that the French contingent had been ready since 16th March, and was then in Egypt waiting to be used. It may be assumed that at first only a small expedition was contemplated, sufficient to secure the ground which the victory of the fleets would have made untenable by the enemy. But the failure of the great naval attack on 18th March, 1915, had produced a wholly new situation. What we needed now was not a contingent to occupy but an army that might conquer.

The French Staff rightly and properly declined to detach for a secondary field of operations even a single division of the armies organised for the main theatre of war. General Joffre had none too many men to hold the long front in the West, and he would not permit his carefully-prepared strategical plans to be dislocated by any side show. But France, as we have seen, was able to draw upon forces which did not belong to her regular army. The navy could furnish Fusiliers Marins. The Colonial Department had its Armée Coloniale, and there was the Foreign Legion, good fighting material, enlisted for service anywhere. From these various sources a detachment was got together, and put under the command of General d'Amade, one of the soldiers who had most distinguished himself in the first months of war.

★★★★★★

His place was taken on May 10th by General Gouraud, a man of forty-seven, who had had a unique experience of French Colonial war. During the winter he had done brilliant work in the Argonne, and was the youngest *Général de Division* in the French Army.

★★★★★★

The bulk of the Expeditionary Force had to be provided by Britain. Originally there had been hopes of aid from Greece, but M. Venezelos failed for the moment to carry through his policy of intervention. It was our aim in the business to avoid entrenching upon the new service armies which were destined for Sir John French's command. The nucleus of our contribution was the 29th Division, composed almost wholly of regulars, and under the command of Major-General Hunter-Weston, who had originally commanded the 11th Brigade of the Third Corps on the Western Front. It embraced the 86th Brigade of infantry—2nd Royal Fusiliers, 1st Lancashire Fusiliers, 1st Royal Munster Fusiliers, and 1st Royal Dublin Fusiliers; the 87th Brigade—2nd South Wales Borderers, 1st King's Own Scottish Borderers, 1st Royal Inniskilling Fusiliers, and 1st Border Regiment; the 88th Brigade—and Hampshires, 4th Worcesters, 1st Essex, and a Territorial battalion, the 5th Royal Scots. For divisional cavalry it had a squadron of the Surrey Yeomanry, and in its artillery force were included two batteries of the 4th (Highland) Mountain Brigade.

The Naval Division was also available. It had been at Antwerp, and since then had had six months of training, while the gaps in its ranks had been filled. As before, it consisted of two Naval Brigades and a brigade of Royal Marines. There was, further, a considerable army already existing in Egypt. The Australian and New Zealand divisions, under Lieutenant-General Birdwood, between them made the strength of a corps; there was a large number of seasoned Indian troops; and a Territorial division, the East Lancashire, under Major-General Douglas, had been in training there during the winter.

******

This division had volunteered as a unit for foreign service. Its infantry comprised the Lancashire Fusiliers Brigade—5th, 6th, 7th, 8th Lancashire Fusiliers; the East Lancashire Brigade—4th and 5th East Lancashires, 9th and 10th Manchesters; and the Manchester Brigade—5th, 6th, 7th, and 8th Manchesters.

******

Egypt was now reasonably safe, the more so as the Turkish Army which had threatened it from Syria was being largely moved to the shores of the Sea of Marmara. Its defence was, therefore, left to part of the Indian troops, the Native Army, and some regiments of British yeomanry, and the Australasians, the Territorials, and some of the Indian troops were added to the Dardanelles force.

The total strength thus created was the equivalent of three corps. It was placed under the command of General Sir Ian Hamilton, who had previously been nominated to command the Fourth Army which was being formed at home. Sir Ian Hamilton had been Commander-in-Chief in the Mediterranean and Inspector-General of Oversea Forces since 1910. For nearly forty years he had served with distinction in every British war, and had been present with the Japanese forces in Manchuria. He was a soldier of a type rare in modern armies. A man of wide general culture, an accomplished writer, and something of a poet, he had proved himself one of the most gallant of regimental leaders, a brilliant staff officer, and an efficient administrator. In a high command in the field his reputation was still to make. The commander-in-chief on the Turkish side was the German General Liman von Sanders, the former Chief of the Military Mission at Constantinople. On 29th March the *Sultan* issued a decree appointing him to the post and constituting the Dardanelles forces the Fifth Army.

The inception of the Land Expedition raises the last of the questions by which we have tested the justification of a "subsidiary" operation. Did it weaken the Allied strength in the vital Western theatre? The 120,000 men who were assigned to it can scarcely—with the exception of the 29th Division—be said to have included any troops who had been definitely relied upon for France and Flanders, D'Amade's Colonials were a special effort of the North African depots; our Naval Division was an Expeditionary Force for Admiralty purposes; our Australasian and Indian troops and the Lancashire Territorials had already been set apart for work in Egypt, and, but for the collapse of Djemal's invasion, might still have been engaged on the Canal.

We may, therefore, regard at any rate the bulk of the Expeditionary Force as being composed of the loose fringes of our military strength, of troops not ear-marked for France and Flanders, but specially reserved for such expeditions as the Dardanelles. But were 120,000 men sufficient, and, if not, how could reinforcements be supplied except by drawing upon those new service armies, on which General Joffre and Sir John French were relying?

This question is in reality the crucial point in any criticism of the Dardanelles policy. It is difficult to see how any commander could hope to force a position of the utmost natural difficulty in the face of an enemy amply supplied with guns, with forces numerically inferior to that enemy's. Yet such was the situation to be faced. More men would be needed, and for such further troops our potential strength on the Western Front must be weakened. It is possible to argue that at this point the Dardanelles Expedition ceased to be a legitimate subsidiary, and became an illegitimate divergent operation.

As we have seen, its strategical purpose was vital to the main issue of the war. The attempt to force a passage by ships alone had at least a colour of reason—what is called a "sporting chance"; and if it failed did no irrevocable harm. But the land attempt was begun with forces which were patently insufficient, and adequate reinforcements would be apt to involve a weakening of the main efforts of the Allies in the West. The whole business might have been broken off with ease after the failure of 18th March. But so soon as the first landing was effected the die was cast. Thereafter there could be no looking back until, at whatever cost, our end was attained; and that, it may be argued by critics of the enterprise, is the very opposite of the true character of a subsidiary operation.

Let us examine briefly the military elements of the Gallipoli Peninsula. One of the difficulties of the task before us was that it was impossible to surprise the enemy. Surprise is the essence of most schemes of invasion. If Britain lost command of the sea and our coast lay open to attack, the enemy could count upon surprise as his chief asset. It is true that the attack would be expected, but there are so many possible landing-places on our coasts that no man could tell where the blow would fall. Our plan of defence would necessarily be a careful watch along our shores by a great chain of outposts, while our main forces were held in reserve at points inland where they could easily be moved to the zone of invasion. If, however, the attack were well directed, it might for long be doubtful where the chief effort was being made. There would be feints at several places, and troops landed only to be withdrawn, till the defence was in that condition of nervous confusion which gives the chance to the enemy with the bold initiative.

But in the Dardanelles expedition there was no room for such ingenuities. From the start the element of surprise was wholly eliminated. This was nobody's blame; it was due, not to the premature naval enterprise of February and March, but to the nature of the Gallipoli peninsula. The possession of that peninsula was essential to the control of the Straits, and this was clear to the Turco-German staff before the first shot was fired on 3rd November. To master Gallipoli meant an assault from the Aegean, and the possible landing-places were few in number, small in extent, and clearly defined by the nature of the ground. Gaps must be found in the screen of yellow cliffs which fringe the sea. If we take the peninsula west of the line drawn north and south across the upper end of the Narrows, there were only two places where troops could be disembarked. One of these was the various beaches round about Sedd-el-Bahr and Cape Helles. The other was on the Gulf of Saros, near Gaba Tepe, where the sandstone hills leave a narrow space at the water's edge. Neither was good, and both were believed by the Turkish staff to be wholly impracticable. Nevertheless, they left no stone unturned in their defence.

The mere landing of the Expeditionary Force would not effect much. The hills of the Gallipoli peninsula may be said to form a natural fortress defending the rear of the Narrows forts. It will be seen from the map that behind the point of Kilid Bahr a rocky plateau, which is more than 600 feet high, extends inland for some five miles. Its highest ridge runs up to the summits known to the Turks as Pasha Dagh. These hills are a salient with the point towards the Gulf of Saros, and the sides curving back to the Dardanelles above and below Kilid Bahr. North the high ground continues, and is pierced by a pass, through which a rough track runs from Krithia to the town of Maidos, on the channel opposite Nagara.

But to an invader coming from the west and aiming at Maidos the Pasha Dagh is not the only obstacle. West of it and south of Krithia rises the bold peak of Achi Baba, nearly 600 feet high, which sends out rocky spurs on both sides to the Dardanelles and the Gulf of Saros, and forms a barrier from sea to sea across the narrow western point of the peninsula.

The problem before Sir Ian Hamilton was, therefore, simple enough in its general lines. He must effect a landing at the apex of the peninsula and at Gaba Tepe, in the Gulf of Saros. It would then be the business of the force landed at the first point to fight its way to Krithia, and carry the Achi Baba ridge, while the second force would advance from Gaba Tepe against the pass leading to Maidos. It might then be possible for the left wing of the first to come in touch with the right wing of the second, and together to force the Pasha Dagh plateau. If that movement succeeded the battle was won. We could bring up artillery to the plateau, which would make the European forts untenable. Moreover, we would dominate at short range the enemy's positions on the Asiatic side, and a combined attack by land and sea would give the Narrows to our hands.

The Expeditionary Force was assembled in Egypt during the first half of April. Sir Ian Hamilton had arrived at Tenedos on March 17th, but he found that the transports had been wrongly loaded, and had to send them back to Alexandria. Lemnos was chosen as the advanced base, and by the middle of the month the expedition began to arrive in the Bay of Mudros. Part of the force was landed on the island, and the rest remained on board the ships, where day and night, under the direction of naval officers, they practised the landing of men, horses, and guns. Germany was well aware of our intentions, and on 22nd April published an announcement that 20,000 British and French troops had landed at Enos at the mouth of the Maritza, a place some sixty-four miles from Bulair by a bad road. This was a legend, but we experimented during these days in small landings and bombardments in the Gulf of Saros as feints to distract the enemy. Meanwhile, by the 20th of April Sir Ian Hamilton had perfected his plans, and the first attack was fixed for Sunday, 25th April,

That Sunday morning was one of those which delight the traveller in April in the Aegean. A light mist fills the air before dawn, but it disappears with the sun, and all day there are clear skies, still seas, and the fresh, invigorating warmth of spring. A glance at the map will show the nature of the place chosen for the attempt, Gaba Tepe, on the north side of the peninsula, we have already described. Round about Cape Helles there are five little beaches. Beginning from the left, there is Beach Y, and, a little south of it, Beach X. Rounding Cape Tekke, we come to Beach W, where a narrow valley opens between the headlands of Tekeh and Helles. Here there is a broad, semi-circular stretch of sand. South of Helles is Beach V, a place of the same configuration as Beach W, but unpleasantly commanded by the castle and village of Sedd-el-Bahr at its southern end.

Lastly, inside the Straits, on the east side of Morto Bay, is Beach S, close to the point of Eski Hissar. The landing at Gaba Tepe was entrusted to the Australian and New Zealand troops; that at the Helles beaches to the 29th Division, with some units of the Naval Division. It was arranged that simultaneously the French should land on the Asiatic shore at Kum Kale, to prevent the Turkish batteries from being brought into action against our men at Beaches V and S. Part of the Naval Division was detached for a feint farther north in the Gulf of Saros.

Let us assume that an aeroplane, which miraculously escaped the enemy's fire, enabled us to move up and down the shores of the peninsula and observe the progress of the different landings. About one in the morning the ships arrive at a point five miles from the Gallipoli shores. At 1.20 the boats are lowered, and the troops line up on the decks. Then they embark in the flotillas, and the steam pinnaces begin to tow them shorewards in the hazy half-light before dawn. The Australians destined for Gaba Tepe are carried in destroyers which take them in close to the shore. The operations are timed to allow the troops to reach the beaches at daybreak.

Slowly and very quietly the boats and destroyers steal in towards the land. A little before five an enemy's searchlight flares out. The boats are now in shallow water under the Gaba Tepe cliffs, and the men are leaping ashore. Then comes a blaze of rifle fire from the Turkish trenches on the beach, and the first comers charge them with the bayonet. The whole cliff seems to leap into light, for everywhere trenches and caverns have been dug in the slopes. The fire falls most heavily on the men still in the boats, who have the difficult task of waiting as the slow minutes bring them shoreward

The first Australians—the 3rd Brigade, under Colonel Sinclair Maclagan—do not linger. They carry the lines on the beach with cold steel, and find themselves looking up at a steep cliff a hundred feet high. In open order they dive into the scrub, and scramble up the loose yellow rocks. By a fortunate accident the landing is farther north than we intended, just under the cliffs of Sari Bair. At Gaba Tepe the long slope would have given the enemy a great advantage in defence; but here there is only the forty-foot beach and then the cliffs.

He who knows the Aegean in April will remember the revelation of those fringed sea walls and bare brown slopes. From a distance they look as arid as the Syrian desert, but when the traveller draws near, he finds a paradise of curious and beautiful flowers—anemone, grape hyacinth, rock rose, asphodel, and amaryllis. Up this rock garden the Australians race, among the purple cistus and the matted creepers and the thickets of myrtle. They have left their packs at the foot, and scale the bluffs like chamois. It is an achievement to rank with Wolfe's escalade of the Heights of Abraham. Presently they are at the top, and come under the main Turkish fire. But the ground gives good cover, and they set about entrenching the crest of the cliffs to cover the boats' landing. This is the position at Gaba Tepe at 7 a.m.

As we journey down the coast, we come next to Beach Y. There at 7 a.m. all is going well. The three cruisers, *Dublin, Amethyst,* and *Sapphire,* have covered the landing of the King's Own Scottish Borderers and the Plymouth battalion of the Naval Division, who have without difficulty reached the top of the cliffs. At Beach X things are even better. The *Swiftsure* has plastered the high ground with shells, and the landing ship, the *Implacable,* has anchored close to the shore in six

The Bombardment of the Dardanelles.

fathoms of water. Without a single casualty the Royal Fusiliers have gained the cliff line. There has been a harder fight at Beach W, between Tekke and Helles, where the sands are broader.

The shore is trenched throughout, and wired and mined almost to the water's edge, and in the scrub of the hinterland the Turkish snipers are hidden. The result is that, though our ships have bombarded the shore for three-quarters of an hour, they cannot clear out the enemy, and do not seem to have made much impression on the wire entanglements. The first troops landed to the right under the cliffs of Cape Helles, and reached the top, while a party on the left scaled Cape Tekke. But the men of the Lancashire Fusiliers who landed on the shore itself had a fiery trial. They suffered heavily while still on the water, and on landing came up against unbroken lines of wire, while snipers in the valley in front and concealed machine-guns and quick-firers rained death on them. Here we have had heavy losses, and at 7 a.m. the landing has not succeeded.

But the case is more desperate still at Beach V, under Sedd-el-Bahr. Here, as at Beach W, there are a stretch of sand, a scrubby valley, and flanking cliffs. It is the strongest of the Turkish positions, and troops landing in boats are exposed to every type of converging fire. A curious expedient has been tried. A collier, the *River Clyde*, with 2,000 men of the Hampshires and Munster Fusiliers onboard, as well as eight boat-loads towed by steam pinnaces, approached close to the shore. The boat-loads—the Dublin Fusiliers—suffered horribly, for when they dashed through the shallows to the beach they were pinned to the ground by fire. Three lines of wire entanglements had to be forced, and a network of trenches.

A bank of sand, five or six feet high, runs at the back, and under its cover the survivors have taken shelter. In the steel side of the liner doors have been cut, which opened and disgorged men, like some new Horse of Troy. But a tornado of shot and shell rained on her, and few of the 200 gallant men, who leaped from the lighters to the reef and from the reef to the sea, reached the land. Those who did have joined their fellows lying flat under the sand bank on that beach of death.

At Beach S, in Morto Bay, all has gone well. Seven hundred men of the South Wales Borderers have been landed from trawlers, and have established themselves on the cliff tops at the place called De Totts Battery.

Let us go back to Gaba Tepe and look at the position at noonday. We are prospering there, for more than 10,000 men are now ashore, and the work of disembarking guns and stores goes on steadily, though the fire from inland is still deadly. We see a proof of it in a boat full of dead men which rocks idly in the surf. The great warships from the sea send their heavy shells against the Turkish lines, seaplanes are "spotting" for them, and wireless stations are being erected on the beach. Firing from the ships is not easy, for the morning sun shines right in the eyes of the gunners. The Royal Engineers are making roads up the cliff, and supplies are climbing steadily to our firing line.

On the turf on the cliff top our men are entrenched, and are working their way forward. Unfortunately, the zeal of the Australians has outrun their discretion, and some of them have pushed too far on, looking for enemies to bayonet. They have crossed three ridges, and have got to a point above Eskikeni within sight of the Narrows, in that "pocket" country such an advance is certain death, and the rash attack has been pushed back with heavy losses. The wounded are being brought in, and it is no light task getting them down the cliffs on stretchers, and across the beach and the bullet-splashed sea to the warships. Remember that we are holding a position which is terribly conspicuous to the enemy, and all our ammunition and water and food have to be dragged up those breakneck cliffs. Still the first round has been won, Indian troops are being landed in support, and we are firmly placed at Gaba Tepe.

As we move down the coast, we find that all goes well at Beaches Y and X, and that the troops there are working their way forward. The *Implacable* has knocked out of action a Turkish battery at Krithia which gave much annoyance to our men at Beach X. At Beach W we have improved our position. We have cleared the beach and driven the Turks out of the scrub at the valley foot, and the work of disembarking men and stores is proceeding. Our right wing—Worcesters and Lancashire Fusiliers—is working round by the cliffs above Cape Helles to try and enfilade the enemy who are holding Beach V, where our men are still in deadly jeopardy.

The scene at Beach V is strange and terrible. From the deep water the *Cornwallis* and *Albion* are trying to bombard the enemy at Seddel-Bahr, and the 15-inch shells from the *Queen Elizabeth* are screaming overhead. The Trojan Horse is still lying bow on against the reefs, with her 2,000 men unable to move, and the Turkish howitzers playing on her. If a man shows his head he is picked off by sharpshooters. The troops we have landed lie flat on the beach under cover of the sand ridge, unable to advance or retreat, and under a steady tornado of fire.

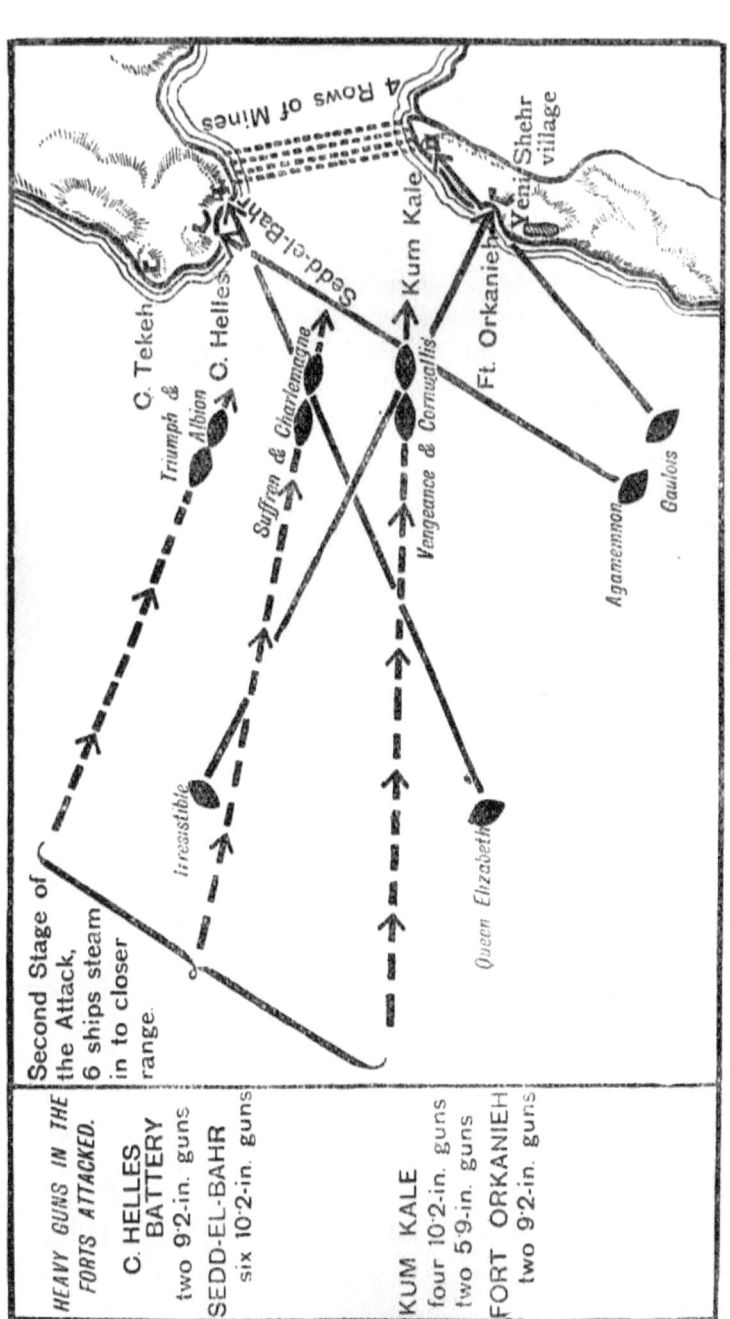

Attack on the Outer Forts (Dardanelles).

Brigadier-General Napier has fallen, and Lieutenant-Colonel Carrington Smith, commanding the Hampshires.

At Beach S things are satisfactory. Meantime the French landing at Kum Kale has achieved its purpose. Originally timed for 6 a.m., it did not take place till 9.30. They had a skirmish with the Turks, partly on the height at Kum Kale, and partly on the Trojan plain. Then they advanced along the swell of ground near the coast as far as Yenai Sheri. Next evening, they re-embarked, and joined our right wing at Beach S. They took 500 prisoners, and could have taken more had there been room for them in the boats. The Turk, who showed himself a dauntless fighter when fighting was the order of the day, surrendered with great complaisance and good humour when the game was up. He had no crusading zeal in the business.

As darkness fell on that loud Sabbath, the minds of the Allied Staff may well have been anxious. We had gained a footing, but no more, and at the critical point it was but a precarious lodgement. The complexity and strength of the enemy's defence far surpassed our expectation. He had tunnelled the cliffs, and created a wonderful and intricate trench system, which took full advantage of the natural strength of the ground. The fire from our leviathans on the deep was no more effective against his entrenched positions than it had been against the forts of the Narrows.

Let us resume our tour of the beaches about 10 a.m. on the morning of the 26th. At Gaba Tepe the Australians are facing a counterattack. It lasts for two hours, and is met by a great bombardment from our ships. A correspondent on one of the battleships has described the scene:—

> The noise, smoke, and concussion produced was unlike anything you can even imagine until you have seen it. The hills in front looked as if they had suddenly been transformed into smoking volcanoes, the common shell throwing up great chunks of ground and masses of black smoke, whilst the shrapnel formed a white canopy above. Sections of ground were covered by each ship all around our front trenches, and, the ranges being known, the shooting was excellent. Nevertheless, a great deal of the fire was, of necessity, indirect, and the ground affords such splendid cover that the Turks continued their advance in a most gallant manner, whilst their artillery not only plastered our positions on shore with shrapnel, but actually tried to drive the ships off

the coast by firing at them, and their desperate snipers, in place of a better target, tried to pick off officers and men on the decks and bridges. We picked up many bullets on the decks afterwards. . . . On shore the rifle and machine-gun fire was incessant, and at times rose into a perfect storm as the Turks pressed forward their attack. The hills were ablaze with shells from the ships and the enemy's shrapnel, whilst on the beach masses of troops were waiting to take their places in the trenches, and the beach parties worked incessantly at landing stores, material, and ammunition. (*Times*, May 7th.)

The end comes when the Australians and New Zealanders counterattack with the bayonet, and drive back the enemy. But all that day there is no rest for our troops, who are perfecting their trenches under a deluge of shrapnel.

At Beach Y things have gone badly. Our men there had advanced during the Sunday afternoon, and had been outflanked and driven back to the cliff edge. The Scottish Borderers lost their commanding officer, Lieutenant-Colonel Koe, and more than half their men. It was decided to re-embark there, and as we pass the retreat is going on successfully under cover of the ships' fire. At Beach X there has been a hard struggle. Last night we were strongly attacked there, and driven to the very edge of the cliffs, where we hung on in rough shelter trenches. This morning we are advancing again, and making some way.

At Beach W, too, there has been a counterattack. Yesterday afternoon our right wing there, which tried to relieve the position on Beach V by an enfilading attack on the enemy, got among wire, and were driven back. During the night the Turks came on in force, and we were compelled to fling our beach parties into the firing line, bluejackets and sappers armed with whatever weapons they could find. This morning the situation is easier, we have landed more troops, and are preparing to move forward.

At Beach V the landing is still in its first stage. Men are still sheltering on the deadly beach behind the sand bank. We have gained some positions among the ruins which were once Sedd-el-Bahr, but not enough to allow us to proceed. Even as we look a final effort is beginning, in which the Dublin Fusiliers and the Munster Fusiliers distinguish themselves, though it is hard to select for special praise among the splendid battalions of the 29th Division. It continues all morning, most gallantly directed by Lieutenant-Colonel Doughty Wylie of the

FRENCH CRUISERS IN THE NARROWS

Headquarters Staff, and Captain Welford of the Royal Artillery, (both officers received the Victoria Cross, and both fell in the moment of victory), and about 2 p.m. it is successful.

The main Turkish trenches are carried, the debris of the castle and village are cleared, and the enemy retreat. The landing can now go forward, and the men, who for thirty-two hours have been huddled behind the sand bank, enduring torments of thirst and a nerve-racking fire, can move their cramped limbs and join their comrades.

By the morning of Tuesday, the 27th, all the beaches—except Beach Y, which had been relinquished—were in working order, and the advance could proceed. On that day the *Queen Elizabeth* was informed by a seaplane that a Turkish transport was coming down the Straits. She sank it in three shots, fired over a range of hills at a distance of nine miles. That day the Turkish gunners attempted to put a barrage of fire between the ships and the shore, but in spite of it the work of landing supplies went on swiftly. To quote the same correspondent:—

> The whole scene on the beach irresistibly reminds you of a gigantic shipwreck. It looks as if the whole army with its stores had been washed ashore after a great gale or had saved themselves on rafts. All this work is carried on under an incessant shrapnel fire which sweeps the trenches and hills. The shells are frequently bursting ten or twelve at the same moment, making a deafening noise and plastering the foreshore with bullets. The only safe place is close under the cliff, but everyone is rapidly becoming accustomed to the shriek of the shells and the splash of the bullets in the water, and the work goes on as if there was not a gun within miles.

That night our position on the peninsula ran from Eski Hissarlik on the Straits north-west to a point on the Gulf of Saros, 3,200 yards north-east of Cape Tekke. The dispositions from left to right were the 29th Division, four French battalions, and the South Wales Borderers. There was too little room for so large a force, and an advance was ordered for the 28th.

Our main objective was Krithia village, and we found our road stoutly opposed. Our front was the 87th Brigade on the left, the 88th Brigade in the centre, and the French brigade on the right, with the 86th Brigade in reserve. In such a country a line has a tendency to "bunch" and become too thin in places. The result was that our progress was irregular, and under the strong Turkish counterattacks we were too weak to hold all we won. The 87th Brigade advanced two miles, and this was the maximum we were able to make good, though parties of the 88th Brigade got within a few hundred yards of Krithia village, and the French to within a mile. Still, by that evening we had securely won the apex of the peninsula, and our front ran from three miles north-west of Cape Tekke to a mile north of Eski Hissarlik.

An incident of that fight deserves to be recorded. A Turkish attack was made on our left, at a point which the nature of the ground hid from the threatened troops. It was observed by the *Queen Elizabeth* far out on the sea, and a 15-inch shell was dropped right in the midst of the attacking party. It was a shrapnel shell weighing 1,800 pounds and holding 13,000 bullets. The attack was literally blotted out, 250 Turks being killed.

So ended the first stage in the Gallipoli campaign—the Battle of the Landing. It is a fight without a precedent. There have been landings—such as Abercromby's at Aboukir—fiercely contested landings, in our history, but none on a scale like this. Sixty thousand men, backed by the most powerful navy in the world, attacked a shore which nature seemed to have made impregnable, and which was held by at least twice that number of the enemy, in positions prepared for months, and supported by the latest modern artillery. The mere problem of transport was sufficient to deter the boldest. Every rule of war was set at nought.

On paper the thing was impossible, as the Turkish Army Order announced. By the textbooks no man should have left the beaches alive. In Sir Ian Hamilton's words, it "involved difficulties for which no precedent was forthcoming in military history." Remember that we were fighting against a gallant enemy who was at his best in defence and in this unorthodox type of battle. All accounts prove that the Turks fought with superlative boldness and courage—with chivalry, too, as their treatment of our wounded showed. (Some atrocities were committed by an Arab battalion, but all the evidence shows that the Turks were punctilious in observing the etiquette of war towards the wounded). That our audacity succeeded is a tribute to the unsurpassable fighting quality of our men—the Regulars of the 29th Division, the Naval Division, and not least to the dash and doggedness of the Australasian Corps. Whatever be the judgment of posterity on its policy or its consequences, the Battle of the Landing will be acclaimed as a mighty feat of arms.

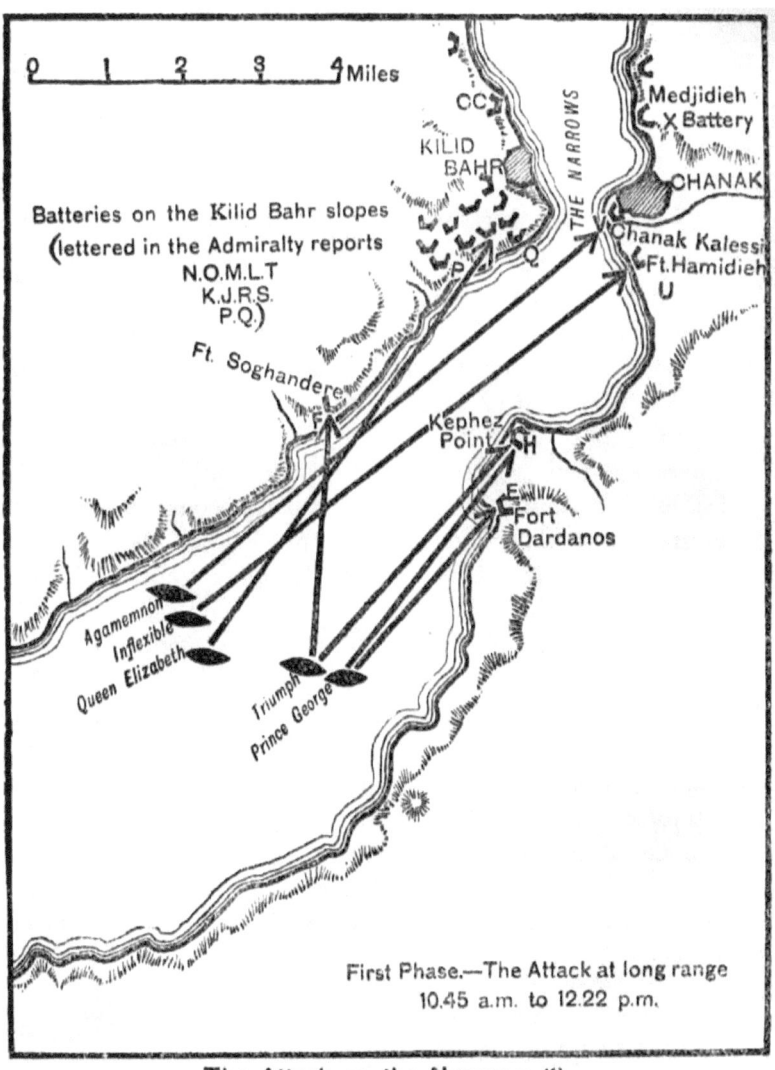

The Attack on the Narrows (1).

Appendix to Chapter 6

THE BRITISH FLEET AT GALLIPOLI.
Admiral de Robeck's Dispatch.
Admiralty, August 16, 1915.

The following dispatch has been received from Vice-Admiral John M. de Robeck, reporting the landing of the army on the Gallipoli Peninsula, 25-26 April 1915:—

Triad, July 1, 1915.

Sir,

I have the honour to forward herewith an account of the operations carried out on the 25th and 26th April 1915, during which period the Mediterranean Expeditionary Force was landed and firmly established in the Gallipoli Peninsula.

The landing commenced at 4.20 a.m. on the 25th. The general scheme was as follows:—

Two main landings were to take place—the first at a point just north of Gaba Tepe, the second on the southern end of the peninsula. In addition, a landing was to be made at Kum Kale, and a demonstration in force to be carried out in the Gulf of Xeros near Bulair. The night of the 24th-25th was calm and very clear, with a brilliant moon, which set at 3 a.m. The first landing, north of Gaba Tepe, was carried out under the orders of Rear-Admiral C. F. Thursby, C.M.G. His squadron consisted of the following ships:—

Battleships.	Cruiser.	Destroyers.	Seaplane Carrier.	Trawlers.	Balloon Ship.
Queen London Prince of Wales Triumph Majestic	Bacchante	Beagle Bulldog Foxhound Scourge Colne Usk Chelmer Ribble	Ark Royal	15	Manica

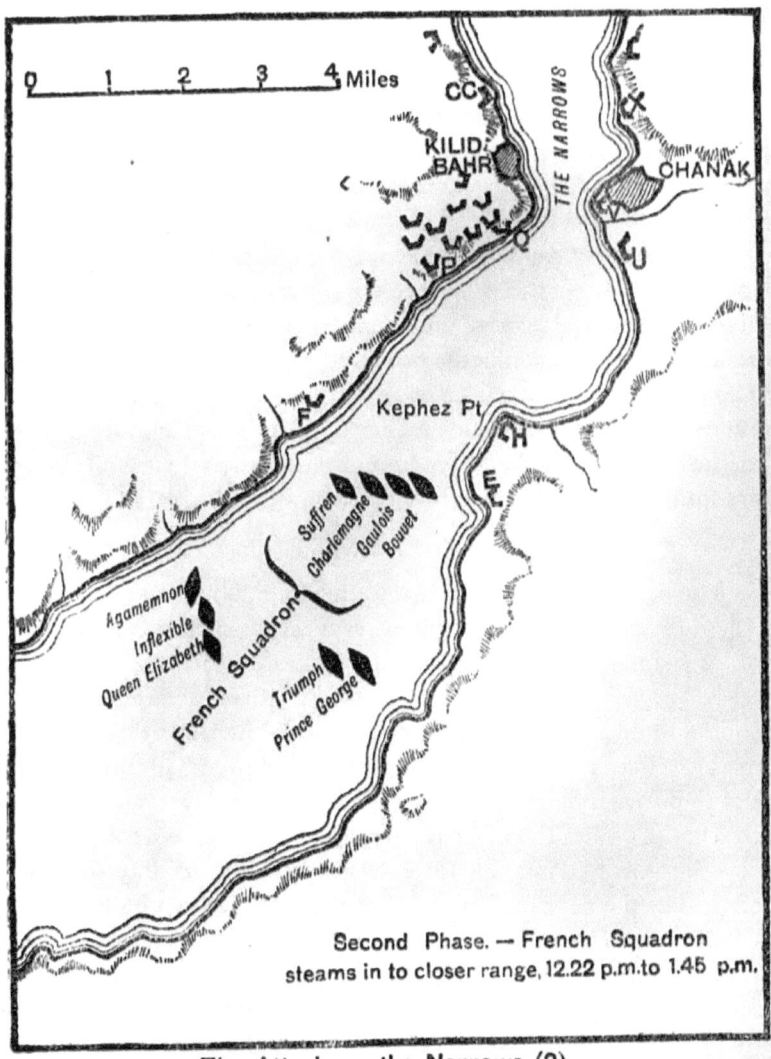

The Attack on the Narrows (2).

To *Queen, London,* and *Prince of Wales* was delegated the duty of actually landing the troops; to *Triumph, Majestic,* and *Bacchante* the duty of covering the landing by gunfire.

In this landing a surprise was attempted. The first troops to be landed were embarked in the battleships *Queen, London,* and *Prince of Wales.*

The squadron then approached the land at 2.58 a.m. at a speed of 5 knots. When within a short distance of the beach selected for landing the boats were sent ahead. At 4.20 a.m. the boats reached the beach, and a landing was effected.

The remainder of the infantry of the covering force were embarked at 10 p.m., 24th.

The troops were landed in two trips, the operation occupying about half an hour; this in spite of the fact that the landing was vigorously opposed, the surprise being only partially effected.

The disembarkation of the main body was at once proceeded with. The operations were somewhat delayed owing to the transports having to remain a considerable distance from the shore in order to avoid the howitzer and field gun fire brought to bear on them, and also the fire from warships stationed in the Narrows at Chanak.

THE LANDING AT GABA TEPE.

The beach here was very narrow and continuously under shell fire. The difficulties of disembarkation were accentuated by the necessity of evacuating the wounded; both operations proceeded simultaneously. The service was one which called for great determination and coolness under fire, and the success achieved indicates the spirit animating all concerned. In this respect I would specially mention the extraordinary gallantry and dash shown by the 3rd Australian Infantry Brigade (Colonel E. G. Sinclair Maclagan, D.S.O.), who formed the covering force. Many individual acts of devotion to duty were performed by the personnel of the navy; these are dealt with below. Here I should like to place on record the good service performed by the vessels employed in landing the second part of the covering force; the seamanship displayed, and the rapidity with which so large a force was thrown on the beach, are deserving of the highest praise.

On the 26th the landing of troops, guns, and stores continued throughout the day; this was a most trying service, as the enemy kept up an incessant shrapnel fire, and it was extremely difficult to locate the well-concealed guns of the enemy. Occasional bursts of fire

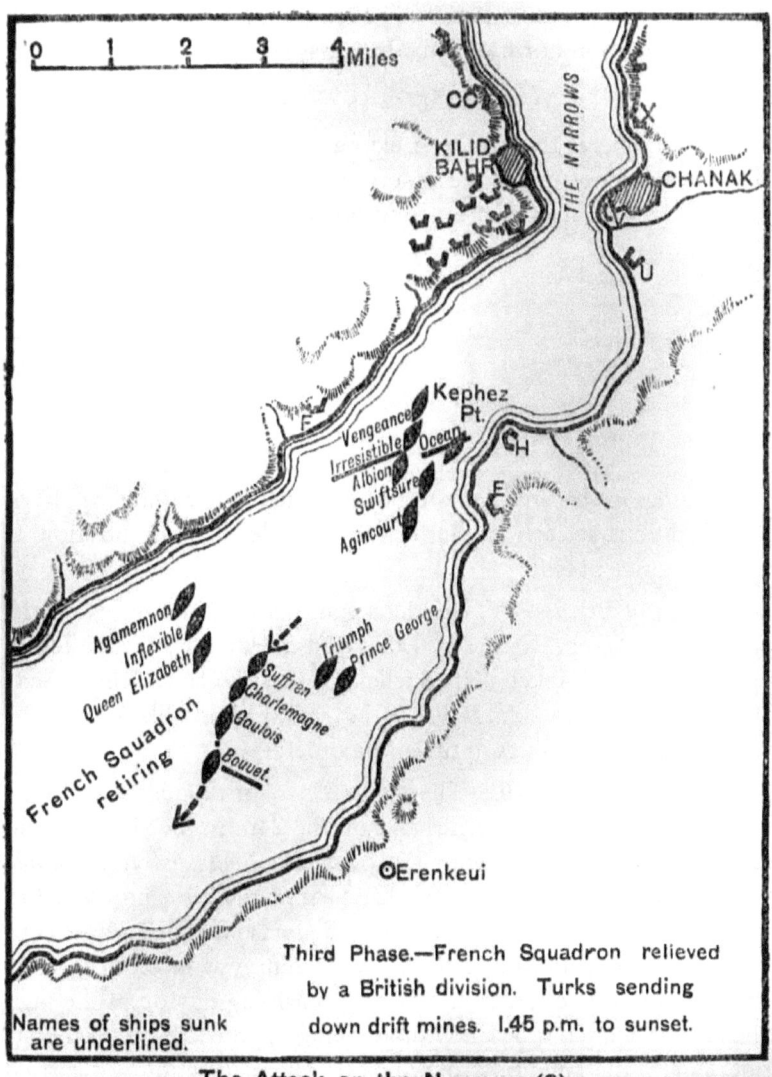

The Attack on the Narrows (3).

from the ships in the Narrows delayed operations somewhat, but these bursts of fire did not last long, and the fire from our ships always drove the enemy's ships away.

The enemy heavily counterattacked, and though supported by a very heavy shrapnel fire he could make no impression on our line, which was every minute becoming stronger. By nightfall on the 26th April our position north of Gaba Tepe was secure.

Landing at Beaches "Y" and "X".

The landing at the southern extremity of the Gallipoli Peninsula was carried out under the orders of Rear-Admiral R. E. Wemyss, C.M.G., M.V.O., his squadron consisting of the following ships:—

Battleships.	Cruisers.	Fleet Sweepers.	Trawlers.
Swiftsure *Implacable* *Cornwallis* *Albion* *Vengeance* *Lord Nelson* *Prince George*	*Euryalus* *Talbot* *Minerva* *Dublin*	6	14

Landings in this area were to be attempted at five different places; the conditions at each landing varied considerably. The position of beaches is given below.

Position of Beach.—"Y" beach, a point about 7,000 yards north-east of Cape Tekeh. "X" beach, 1,000 yards north-east of Cape Tekeh. "W" beach, Cape Tekeh Cape Helles. "V" beach. Cape Helles—Seddul Bahr. Camber, Seddul Bahr. "S" beach, Eski-Hissarlik Point.

Taking these landings in the above order:—

Landing at "Y" Beach.—The troops to be first landed, the King's Own Scottish Borderers, embarked on the 24th in the *Amethyst* and *Sapphire*, and proceeded with the transports *Southland* and *Braemar Castle* to a position off Cape Tekeh. At 4 a.m. the boats proceeded to "Y" beach, timing their arrival there at 5 a.m., and pulled ashore covered by fire from H.M.S. *Goliath*. The landing was most successfully and expeditiously carried out, the troops gaining the top of the high cliffs overlooking this beach without being opposed; this result I consider due to the rapidity with which the disembarkation was carried out and the well-placed covering fire from ships.

The Scottish Borderers were landed in two trips, followed at once by the Plymouth Battalion Royal Marines. These troops met with severe opposition on the top of the cliffs, where fire from covering

Waiting to disembark

Landing of the 25th

ships was of little assistance, and, after heavy fighting, were forced to re-embark on the 26th. The re-embarkation was carried out by the following ships: *Goliath*, *Talbot*, *Dublin*, *Sapphire*, and *Amethyst*. It was most ably conducted by the beach personnel and covered by the fire of the warships, who prevented the enemy reaching the edge of the cliff, except for a few snipers.

Landing at "X" Beach—The 2nd Battalion Royal Fusiliers (two companies and M.G. Section) embarked in *Implacable* on 24th, which ship proceeded to a position off the landing-place, where the disembarkation of the troops commenced at 4.30 a.m., and was completed at 5.15 a.m.

A heavy fire was opened on the cliffs on both sides. The *Implacable* approached the beach, and the troops were ordered to land, fire being continued until the boats were close into the beach. The troops on board the *Implacable* were all landed by 7 a.m. without any casualties. The nature of the beach was very favourable for the covering fire from ships, but the manner in which this landing was carried out might well serve as a model.

Landing at Beach "W."

The 1st Battalion Lancashire Fusiliers embarked in *Euryalus* and *Implacable* on the 24th, who proceeded to positions off the landing-place, where the troops embarked in the boats at about 4 a.m. Shortly after 5 a.m. *Euryalus* approached "W" beach and *Implacable* "X" beach. At 5 a.m. the covering ships opened a heavy fire on the beach, which was continued up to the last moment before landing. Unfortunately, this fire did not have the effect on the extensive wire entanglements and trenches that had been hoped for, and the troops, on landing at 6 a.m., were met with a very heavy fire from rifles, machine-guns, and pom-poms, and found the obstructions on the beach undamaged. The formation of this beach lends itself admirably to the defence, the landing-place being commanded by sloping cliffs offering ideal positions for trenches and giving a perfect field of fire.

The only weakness in the enemy's position was on the flanks, where it was just possible to land on the rocks and thus enfilade the more important defences. This landing on the rocks was effected with great skill, and some Maxims, cleverly concealed in the cliffs and which completely enfiladed the main beach, were rushed with the bayonet. This assisted to a great extent in the success of the landing; the troops, though losing very heavily, were not to be denied, and the beach and the approaches to it were soon in our possession.

The importance of this success cannot be overestimated; "W" and "V" beaches were the only two of any size in this area on which troops, other than infantry, could be disembarked, and failure to capture this one might have had serious consequences, as the landing at "V" was held up. The beach was being continuously sniped, and a fierce infantry battle was carried on round it throughout the entire day and the following night.

It is impossible to exalt too highly the service rendered by the 1st Battalion Lancashire Fusiliers in the storming of the beach; the dash and gallantry displayed were superb. Not one whit behind in devotion to duty was the work of the beach personnel, who worked untiringly throughout the day and night, landing troops and stores under continual sniping. The losses due to rifle and machine-gun fire sustained by the boats' crews, to which they had not the satisfaction of being able to reply, bear testimony to the arduous nature of the service.

During the night of the 25th-26th enemy attacked continuously, and it was not till 1 p.m. on the 26th, when "V" beach was captured, that our position might be said to be secure.

The work of landing troops, guns, and stores continued throughout this period, and the conduct of all concerned left nothing to be desired.

Landing at Beach "V."

This beach, it was anticipated, would be the most difficult to capture; it possessed all the advantages for defence which "W" beach had, and in addition the flanks were strongly guarded by the old castle and village of Seddul Bahr on the east and perpendicular cliffs on the west; the whole foreshore was covered with barbed-wire entanglements which extended in places under the sea. The position formed a natural amphitheatre with the beach as stage.

The first landing here, as at all other places, was made in boats; but the experiment was tried of landing the remainder of the covering force by means of a collier, the *River Clyde*. This steamer had been specially prepared for the occasion under the directions of Commander Edward Unwin; large ports had been cut in her sides and gangways built whereby the troops could reach the lighters which were to form a bridge on to the beach.

"V" beach was subjected to a heavy bombardment similarly to "W" beach, with the same result—*i.e.*, when the first trip attempted to land they were met with a murderous fire from rifle, pom-pom, and machine-gun, which was not opened till the boats had cast off from the steamboats.

A landing on the flanks here was impossible, and practically all the first trip were either killed or wounded, a few managing to find some slight shelter under a bank on the beach; in several boats all were either killed or wounded; one boat entirely disappeared, and in another there were only two survivors. Immediately after the boats had reached the beach the *River Clyde* was run ashore under a heavy fire rather towards the eastern end of the beach, where she could form a convenient breakwater during future landing of stores, etc.

As the *River Clyde* grounded, the lighters which were to form the bridge to the shore were run out ahead of the collier; but unfortunately, they failed to reach their proper stations, and a gap was left between two lighters over which it was impossible for men to cross. Some attempted to land by jumping from the lighter which was in position into the sea and wading ashore. This method proved too costly, the lighter being soon heaped with dead; and the disembarkation was ordered to cease.

The troops in the *River Clyde* were protected from rifle and machine-gun fire, and were in comparative safety.

Commander Unwin, seeing how things were going, left the *River Clyde* and, standing up to his waist in water under a very heavy fire, got the lighters into position; he was assisted in this work by Midshipman G. L. Drewry, R.N.R., of H.M.S. *Hussar*; Midshipman W. St. A. Malleson, R.N., of H.M.S. *Cornwallis*; Able Seaman W. C. Williams, O.N. 186774 (R.F.R. B.3766), and Seaman R.N.R. George McKenzie Samson, O.N. 2408A, both of H.M.S. *Hussar*.

The bridge to the shore, though now passable, could not be used by the troops, anyone appearing on it being instantly shot down, and the men in *River Clyde* remained in her till nightfall.

At 9.50 a.m. *Albion* sent in launch and pinnace manned by volunteer crews to assist in completing bridge, which did not quite reach beach; these boats, however, could not be got into position until dark owing to heavy fire.

It had already been decided not to continue to disembark on "V" beach, and all other troops intended for this beach were diverted to "W."

The position remained unchanged on "V" beach throughout the day, men-of-war and the Maxims mounted in *River Clyde* doing their utmost to keep down the fire directed on the men under partial shelter on the beach.

During this period many heroic deeds were performed in rescuing wounded men in the water.

During the night of the 25th-26th the troops in *River Clyde* were able to disembark under cover of darkness and obtain some shelter on the beach and in the village of Seddul Bahr, for possession of which now commenced a most stubborn fight.

The fight continued, supported ably by gun fire from H.M.S. *Albion*, until 1.24 p.m., when our troops had gained a position from which they assaulted Hill 141, which dominated the situation. *Albion* then ceased fire, and the hill, with old fort on top, was most gallantly stormed by the troops, led by Lieutenant-Colonel C. H. H. Doughty-Wylie, General Staff, who fell as the position was won. The taking of this hill effectively cleared the enemy from the neighbourhood of the "V" Beach, which could now be used for the disembarkation of the Allied armies. The capture of this beach called for a display of the utmost gallantry and perseverance from the officers and men of both services; that they successfully accomplished their task bordered on the miraculous.

OTHER LANDINGS.

Landing on the Camber, Seddul Bahr.—One half-company Royal Dublin Fusiliers landed here without opposition, the Camber being "dead ground." The advance from the Camber, however, was only possible on a narrow front, and after several attempts to enter the village of Seddul Bahr this half-company had to withdraw after suffering heavy losses.

Landing at "De Totts" "S" Beach.—The 2nd South Wales Borderers (less one company) and a detachment 2nd London Field Company R.E. were landed in boats, convoyed by *Cornwallis*, and covered by that ship and *Lord Nelson*.

Little opposition was encountered, and the hill was soon in the possession of the South Wales Borderers. The enemy attacked this position on the evening of the 25th and during the 26th; but our troops were firmly established, and with the assistance of the covering ships all attacks were easily beaten off.

Landing at Kum Kale.—The landing here was undertaken by the French.

It was most important to prevent the enemy occupying positions in this neighbourhood, whence he could bring gunfire to bear on the

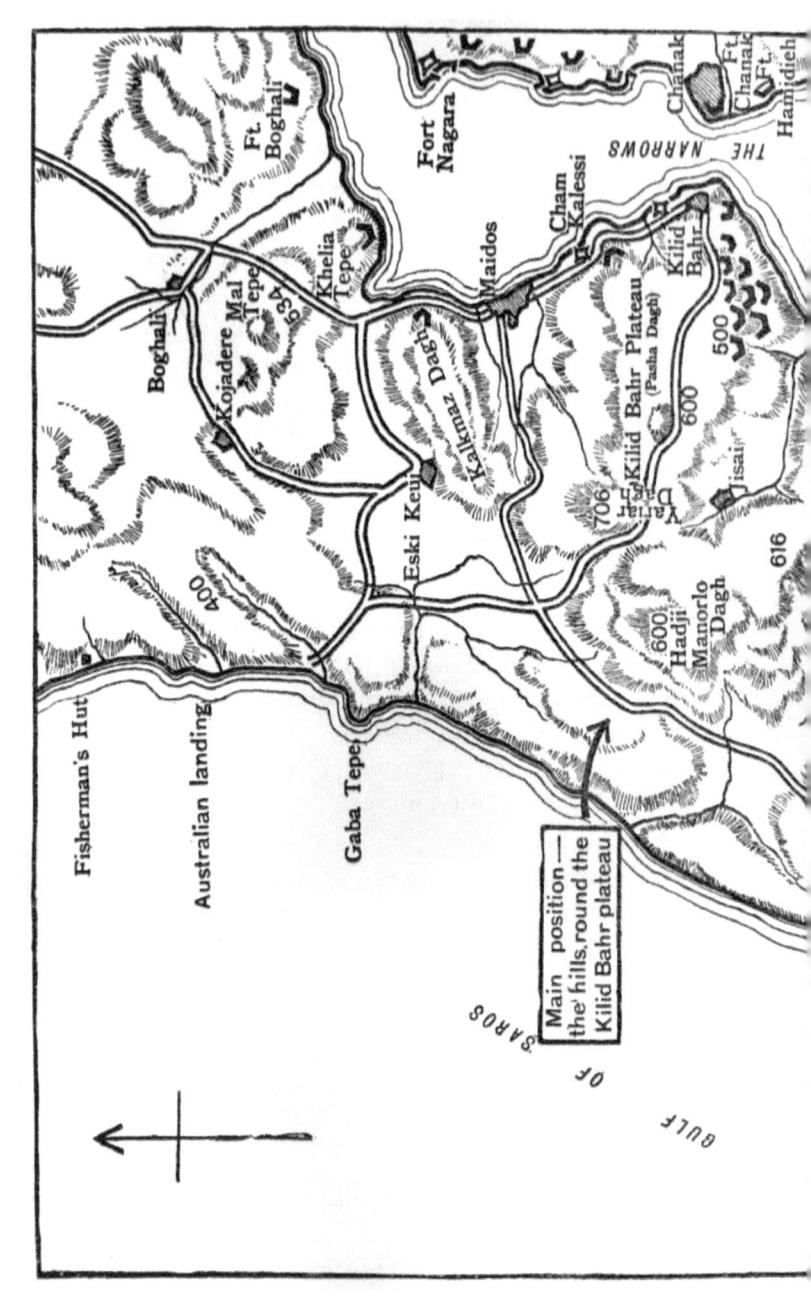

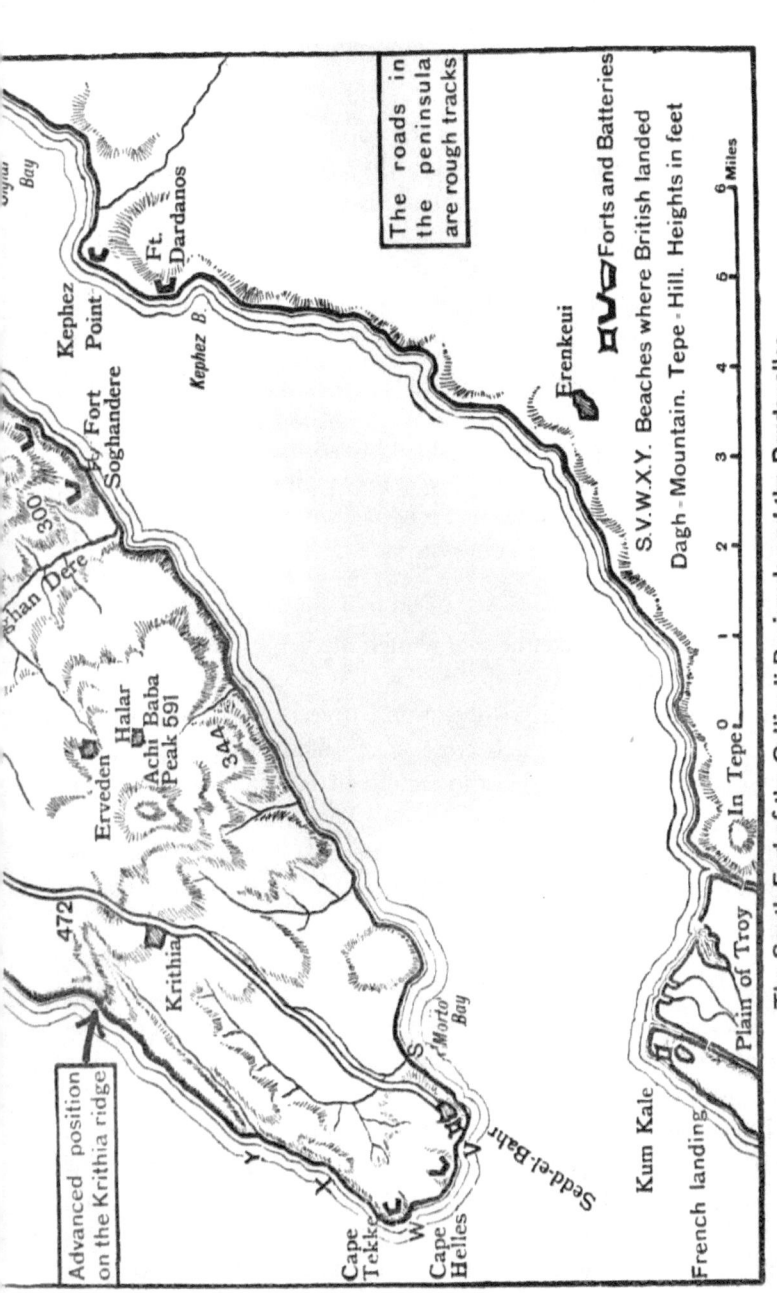

The South End of the Gallipoli Peninsula and the Dardanelles.
(Showing the landing places and the Turkish positions.)

transports off Cape Helles. It was also hoped that by holding this position it would be possible to deal effectively with the enemy's guns on the Asiatic shore immediately east of Kum Kale, which could fire into Seddul Bahr and De Totts.

The French, after a heavy preliminary bombardment, commenced to land at about 10 a.m., and by the afternoon the whole of their force had been landed at Kum Kale. When they attempted to advance to Yeni Shehr, their immediate objective, they were met by heavy fire from well-concealed trenches, and were held up just south of Kum Kale village.

During the night of the 25th-26th the enemy made several counterattacks, all of which were easily driven off; during one of these 400 Turks were captured, their retreat being cut off by the fire from the battleships.

On the 26th, when it became apparent that no advance was possible without entailing severe losses and the landing of large reinforcements, the order was given for the French to withdraw and re-embark; which operation was carried out without serious opposition.

Allies' Co-operation.

I now propose to make the following more general remarks on the conduct of the operations.

From the very first the co-operation between army and navy was most happy; difficulties which arose were quickly surmounted, and nothing could have exceeded the tactfulness and forethought of Sir Ian Hamilton and his staff.

The loyal support which I received from Contre-Amiral E. P. A. Guepratte simplified the task of landing the Allied armies simultaneously.

The Russian fleet was represented by H.I.R.M.S. *Askold*, which ship was attached to the French squadron. Contre-Amiral Guepratte bears testimony to the value of the support he received from Captain Ivanoff, especially during the landing and re-embarkation of the French troops at Kum Kale.

The detailed organisation of the landing could not be commenced until the Army Headquarters returned from Egypt on the 10th April. The work to be done was very great, and the naval personnel and material available small.

Immediately on the arrival of the Army Staff at Mudros, committees, composed of officers of both services, commenced to work out

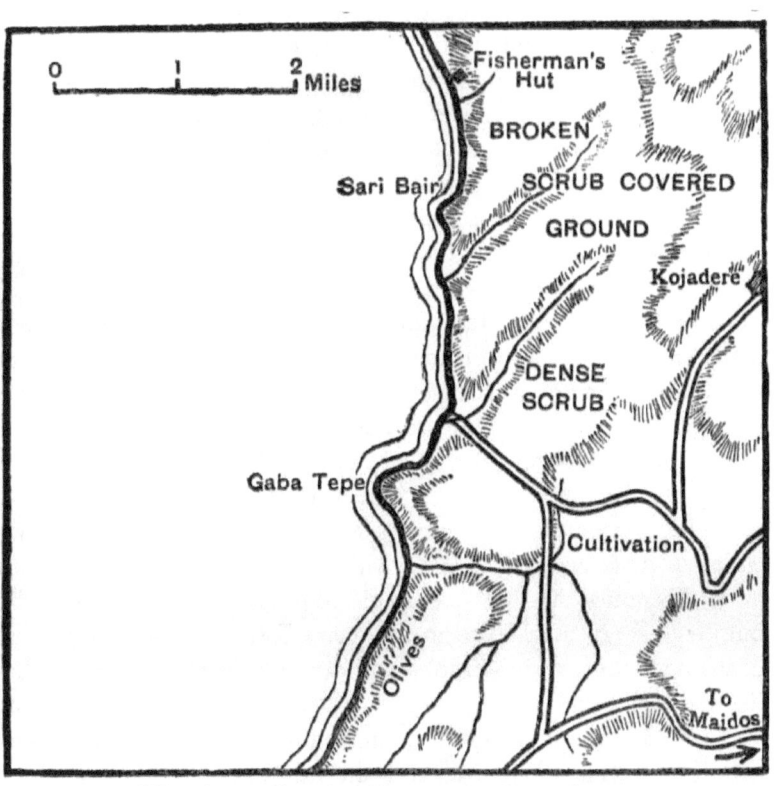

The Australian Landing near Gaba Tepe.

the details of the landing operations, and it was due to these officers' indefatigable efforts that the expedition was ready to land on the 22nd April. The keenness displayed by the officers and men resulted in a good standard of efficiency, especially in the case of the Australian and New Zealand Corps, who appear to be natural boatmen.

Heroism of the Enterprise.

Such actions as the storming of the Seddul Bahr position by the 29th Division must live in history for ever; innumerable deeds of heroism and daring were performed; the gallantry and absolute contempt for death displayed alone made the operations possible.

At Gaba Tepe the landing and the dash of the Australian Brigade for the cliffs were magnificent; nothing could stop such men. The Australian and New Zealand Army Corps in this, their first battle, set a standard as high as that of any army in history, and one of which their countrymen have every reason to be proud.

In closing this dispatch, I beg to bring to Their Lordships' notice the names of certain officers and men who have performed meritorious service. The great traditions of His Majesty's Navy were well maintained, and the list of names submitted of necessity lacks those of many officers and men who performed gallant deeds unobserved and therefore unnoted. This standard was high, and if I specially mention one particular action, it is that of Commander Unwin and the two young officers and two seamen who assisted him in the work of establishing communication between *River Clyde* and the beach. Rear-Admirals R. E. Wemyss, C.M.G., M.V.O., C. F. Thursby, C.M.G., and Stuart Nicholson, M.V.O., have rendered invaluable service. Throughout they have been indefatigable in their efforts to further the success of the operations, and their loyal support has much lightened my duties and responsibilities.

I have at all times received the most loyal support from the commanding officers of His Majesty's ships during an operation which called for the display of great initiative and seamanship.

Captain R. F. Phillimore, C.B., M.V.O., A.D.C., as principal Beach Master, and Captain D. L. Dent, as principal Naval Transport Officer, performed most valuable service.

Deeds of Conspicuous Merit.

Commander Edward Unwin, R.N.
While in *River Clyde*, observing that the lighters which were to

Royal Munster Fusiliers of the *River Clyde*

form the bridge to the shore had broken adrift, Commander Unwin left the ship and under a murderous fire attempted to get the lighters into position. He worked on until, suffering from the effects of cold and immersion, he was obliged to return to the ship, where he was wrapped up in blankets. Having in some degree recovered, he returned to his work against the doctor's order and completed it.

He was later again attended by the doctor for three abrasions caused by bullets, after which he once more left the ship, this time in a lifeboat, to save some wounded men who were lying in shallow water near the beach. He continued at this heroic labour under continuous fire, until forced to stop through pure physical exhaustion.

Midshipman George L. Drewry, R.N.R.

Assisted Commander Unwin at the work of securing the lighters under heavy rifle and Maxim fire. He was wounded in the head, but continued his work and twice subsequently attempted to swim from lighter to lighter with a line.

Midshipman Wilfred St. A. Malleson, R.N.

Also assisted Commander Unwin, and after Midshipman Drewry had failed from exhaustion to get a line from lighter to lighter, he swam with it himself and succeeded. The line subsequently broke, and he afterwards made two further but unsuccessful attempts at his self-imposed task.

Able Seaman William Chas. Williams, O.N. 186774 (R.F.R, B.3766).

Held on to a line in the water for over an hour under heavy fire, until killed.

Seaman R.N.R. George McKenzie Samson, O.N. 2408A.

Worked on a lighter all day under fire, attending wounded and getting out lines; he was eventually dangerously wounded by Maxim fire.

Lieut.-Commander Ralph B. Janvrin, R.N.

Conducted the trawlers into Morto Bay, for the landing at "De Totts," with much skill.

This officer showed great judgment and coolness under fire, and carried out a difficult task with great success.

The Gallipoli Landings

The Landings at Anzac Cove

Lieut. John A. V. Morse, R.N.
Assisted to secure the lighters at the bows of the *River Clyde* under a heavy fire, and was very active throughout the 25th and 26th at "V" beach.

Surgeon P. B. Kelly, R.N., attached to R.N.A.S.
Was wounded on the foot on the morning of the 25th in *River Clyde*. He remained in *River Clyde* until morning of 27th, during which time he attended 750 wounded men, although in great pain and unable to walk during the last twenty-four hours.

Lieut.-Commander Adrian St.V. Keyes, R.N.
General Sir Ian Hamilton reports as follows :—

Lieutenant-Commander Keyes showed great coolness, gallantry, and ability. The success of the landing on "Y" beach was largely due to his good services. When circumstances compelled the force landed there to re-embark, this officer showed exceptional resource and leadership in successfully conducting that difficult operation.

I entirely concur in General Hamilton's opinion of this officer's services on the 25th-26th April.

Commander William H. Cottrell, R.N.V.R.
This officer has organised the entire system of land communication; has laid and repaired cables several times under fire; and on all occasions shown zeal, tact, and coolness beyond praise.

Mr. John Murphy, Boatswain, *Cornwallis*.
Midshipman John Saville Metcalf, R.N.R., *Triumph*.
Midshipman Rupert E. M. Bethune, *Inflexible*.
Midshipman Eric Oloff de Wet, *London*.
Midshipman Charles W. Croxford, R.N.R., *Queen*
Midshipman C. A. L. Mansergh, *Queen*.
Midshipman Alfred M. Williams, *Euryalus*.
Midshipman Hubert M. Wilson, *Euryalus*.
Midshipman G. F. D. Freer, *Lord Nelson*.
Midshipman R.V. Symonds-Taylor, *Agamemnon*.
Midshipman C. H. C. Matthey, *Queen Elizabeth*.
Lieut. Massy Goolden, *Prince of Wales*.

Recommended for accelerated promotion:—
Mr. Charles Edward Bounton, Gunner, R.N., *Queen Elizabeth*.

The following officers are "Commended for service in action":—
Capt. H. A. S. Fyler, *Agamemnon*, Senior Officer inside the Straits.
Capt. A. W. Heneage, M.V.O., who organised and trained the mine-sweepers.
Capt. E. K. Loring, Naval Transport Officer, Gaba Tepe.
Capt. H. C. Lockyer, *Implacable*.
Capt. C. Maxwell-Lefroy, *Swiftsure*.
Capt. the Hon. A. D. E. H. Boyle, M.V.O., *Bacchante*.
Capt. A. V. Vyvyan, Beach Master, "Z" beach.
Capt. C. S. Townsend, Beach Master, "W" beach.
Capt. R. C. K. Lambert, Beach Master, "V" beach. Commander the Hon. L. J. O. Lambart, *Queen*.
Commander (now Captain) B. St. G. Collard, Assistant Beach Master, "W" beach.
Commander C. C. Dix, Assistant Beach Master, "Z" beach.
Commander N. W. Diggle, Assistant Beach Master, "V" beach.
Commander H. L. Watts-Jones, *Albion* (acting Captain).
Commander I. W. Gibson, M.V.O., *Albion*.
Lieut.-Commander (now Commander) J. B. Waterlow, *Blenheim*.
Lieut.-Commander H. V. Coates, *Implacable*.
Lieut.-Commander E. H. Cater, *Queen Elizabeth*.
Lieut.-Commander G. H. Pownall, *Adamant* (killed in action).
Lieut. A. W. Bromley, R.N.R., *Euryalus*.
Lieut. H. R. W. Turnor, *Implacable*.
Lieut. IT. F. Minchin, *Cornwallis*.
Lieut. Oscar Henderson, *Ribble*.
Lieut. Kenneth Edwards, *Lord Nelson*.
Major W. T. C. Jones, D.S.O., R.M.L.I., Beach Master, "X" beach.
Major W. W. Frankis, R.M.L.I., *Cornwallis*.
Tempy. Surgeon W. D. Galloway, *Cornwallis*.
Mr. Alfred M. Mallett, Gunner T., *Ribble*.
Mr. John Pippard, Boatswain, *Sapphire*.
Midshipman Eric Wheler Bush, *Bacchante*.
Midshipman Charles D. H. H. Dixon, *Bacchante*.
Midshipman Donald H. Barton, *London*.
Midshipman A. W. Clarke, *Implacable*.
Proby. Midshipman William D. R. Hargreaves, R.N.R., *Sapphire*.

Midshipman F. E. Garner, R.N.R., *Triumph*.
Midshipman George H. Morris, R.N.R., *Lord Nelson*.
Midshipman the Hon. G. H. E. Russell, *Implacable*.
Midshipman D. S. E. Thompson, *Implacable*.
Midshipman W. D. Brown, *Implacable*.

Work of the Destroyers.

The work accomplished by the destroyer flotillas fully maintained the high standard they have established in these waters.

On the 25th and 26th *Wolverine* (Commander O. J. Prentis) (killed in action), *Scorpion* (Lieut.-Commander (now Commander) A. B. Cunningham), *Renard* (Lieut.-Commander L. G. B. A. Campbell), *Grampus* (Lieut.-Commander R. Bacchus), *Pincher* (Lieut.-Commander H. W. Wyld), and *Rattlesnake* (Lieut.-Commander P. G. Wodehouse), carried out minesweeping operations under Captain Heneage inside the Dardanelles in a most satisfactory manner, being frequently under heavy fire. On the 26th the French sweepers *Henriette* (Lieut. de Vaisseau Auverny), *Marius Chambon* (Lieut. de Vaisseau Blanc), and *Camargue* (Lieut. de Vaisseau Bergeon), assisted them, *Henriette* doing particularly well.

Beagle (Commander (now Captain) H. R. Godfrey), *Bulldog* (Lieut.-Commander W. B. Mackenzie), *Scourge* (Lieut.-Commander H. de B. Tupper), *Foxhound* (Commander W. G. Howard), *Colne* (Commander C. Seymour), *Chelmer* (Lieut.-Commander (now Commander) H. T. England), *Usk* (Lieut.-Commander W. G. C. Maxwell), and *Ribble* (Lieut.-Commander R. W. Wilkinson) assisted in the disembarkation at Gaba Tepe.

Rear-Admiral Thursby reports as follows on the work accomplished by these boats:—

> The destroyers under Captain C. P. R. Coode (Captain 'D') landed the second part of the covering force with great gallantry and expedition, and it is in my opinion entirely due to the rapidity with which so large a force was thrown on the beach that we were able to establish ourselves there."

I entirely concur in Admiral Thursby's remarks on the good work performed by this division.

Petty Officers and Men.

P.O. John Hepburn Russell, O.N. F.839, of the Royal Naval Air Service.

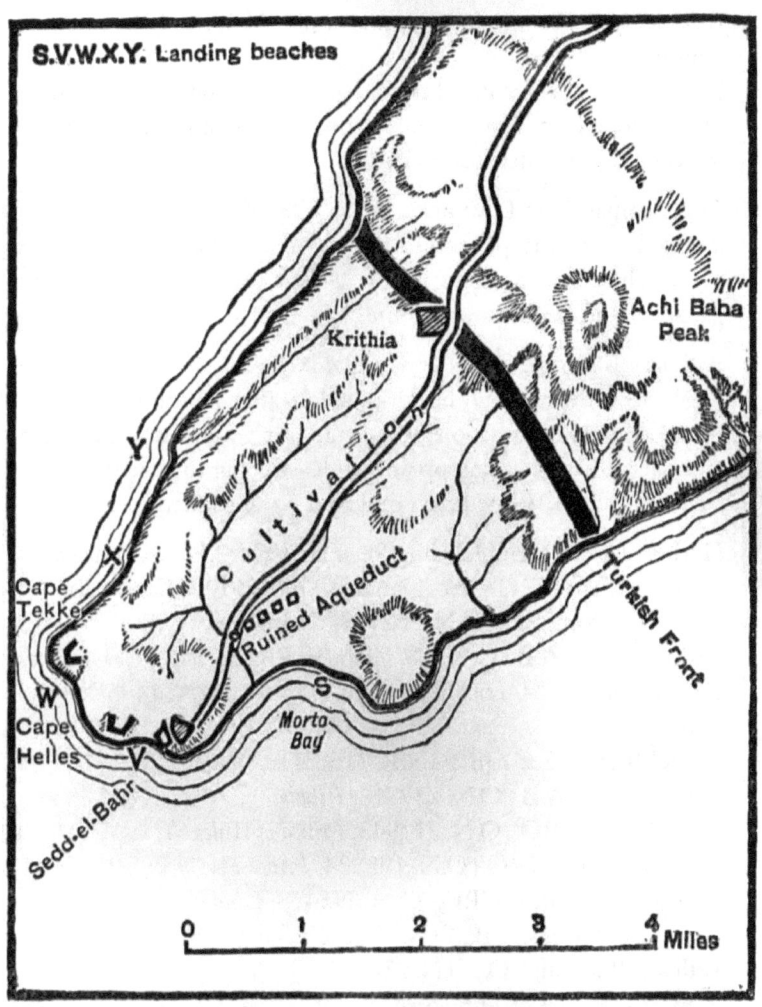

The Landing Beaches.

Was wounded in gallantly going to Commander Unwin's assistance.

P.O. Mech. Geoffrey Charlton Paine Rummings, O.N. F.813, Royal Naval Air Service.
Assisted Commander Unwin in rescuing wounded men.

P.O. Sec. Cl. Frederick Gibson, O.N. 191025, R.F.R. 6.3829, *Albion*.
Jumped overboard with a line and got his boat beached to complete bridge from *River Clyde* to shore. He then took wounded to *River Clyde* under heavy fire.

Ord. Seaman Jesse Lovelock, *Albion*, J.28798.
Assisted in getting pontoon in position; also helped wounded on beach and in boats to reach River Clyde, displaying great gallantry and coolness under fire.

A.B. Lewis Jacobs, O.N. J.4081, *Lord Nelson*.
Took his boat into "V" beach unaided, after all the remainder of the crew and the troops were killed or wounded. When last seen Jacobs was standing up and endeavouring to pole the cutter to the shore. While thus employed he was killed.

Herbert J. G. Morrin, Leading Seaman, O.N. 236225, *Bacchante*.
Alfred J. Chatwin, Ch.Yeo. Signals, O.N. 156109, *Cornwallis*.
Albert Playford, P.O., O.N. 202189, *Cornwallis*.
Arthur Roake, A.B., O.N. S.S. 1940 (R.F.R. B.8843), *Cornwallis*.
Henry Thomas Morrison, Seaman, R.N.R., O.N. 1495D., *Albion*.
Daniel Roach, Seaman, R.N.R., 1685D., *Albion*
David S. Kerr, A.B., O.N. 239816, *Ribble*.
Albert Balson, P.O., O.N. 211943, *Prince of Wales*.
William Morgan, P.O., O.N. 193834, *Prince of Wales*.
James Getson, Stoker, P.O., O.N. 295438, *London*.
Edward L. Barons, A.B., O.N. J.7775, *London*.
William Putman, P.O., O.N. 236783, *Queen*.
Robert Fletcher, Leading Seaman, O.N. 213297, *Queen*.
Samuel Forsey, A.B., S.S. 2359 (R.F.R. B.4597), *Albion*.
Henry J. Anstead, Acting C.P.O., 179989, *Implacable*.
Kenneth Muskett, Leading Seaman, J.1325, *Implacable*.
Thomas P. Roche, Ch. P.O. (Pensioner), O.N. 165533, *Prince George*.

John Maple, Leading Seaman, O.N. 171890 (R.F.R., Chat., B.2658), *Euryalus*.
Henry Williams, Leading Seaman, O.N. 176765 (R.F.R., Chat., B.1326), *Euryalus*.
William F. Hoffman, A.B., O.N. 195940 (R.F.R., Chat., B.2650), *Euryalus*.
Henry G. Law, A.B., O.N. 195366 (R.F.R., Chat., B.8261), *Euryalus*.
Henry Ridsdale, Stoker, R.N.R., O.N. 1136U, *Euryalus*.
Colin McKechnie, Leading Seaman, O.N. 157509, *Lord Nelson* (killed).
Stanley E. Cullum, Leading Seaman, O.N. 225791, *Lord Nelson* (killed).
Frederick T. M. Hyde, A.B., O.N. J.21153, *Lord Nelson* (killed).
William E. Rowland, A.B., O.N. 3.17029, *Lord Nelson* (wounded).
Albert E. Bex, A.B., O.N. J.17223, *Lord Nelson* (wounded).

The above men from *Lord Nelson* were part of boats' crews landing troops on "V" beach, a service from which few returned.

Commended for service in action:—

Harry E. Pallant, P.O., O.N. 186521, *Implacable*.
Jesse Bontoft, P.O., O.N. 193398, *Implacable*.
Thomas J. Twells, Leading Seaman, O.N. 232269, *Implacable*.
Richard Mullis, Leading Seaman, O.N. 220072, *Implacable*.
Matthew B. Knight, Leading Seaman, O.N. 230546, *Implacable*.
John E. Mayes, Leading Seaman, O.N. 196849 (R.F.R. B.8581), *Implacable*.
William J. White, P.O.I., O.N. 142848, *Albion*.
Frederick G. Barnes, P.O., O.N. 209085, *Swiftsure*.
Henry Minter, P.O., O.N. 163128, *Queen Elizabeth*.
Harry R. Jeffcoate, Sergeant, R.M.L.I., Ch. 10526, *Cornwallis*.
Frank E. Trollope, Private, R.M.L.I., Ch. 19239, *Cornwallis*.
George Brown, Ch. P.O., 276085, *Sapphire*.
Bertie Sole, Leading Seaman, 208019 (R.F.R. 8.10738), *Sapphire*.
Charles H. Soper, Signalman, J.9709, *Sapphire*.
Frank Dawe, A.B., 231502, *Albion*.
Samuel Quick, Seaman, R.N.R., 3109B., *Albion*.
James Rice, Seaman, R.N.R., 519D., *Albion*.

William Thomas, Seaman, R.N.R., 2208B., *Albion*.
William H. Kitchen, Seaman, R.N.R., 4330A. *Albion*.
Francis A. Sanders, A.B., 221315 (R.F.R., Chat., B.8199), *Euryalus*.
William F. Hicks, A.B., S.S. 4795, *Euryalus*.
William F. Hayward, A.B., 235109, *London*.
George Gilbertson, A.B., 207941 (R.F.R. B.4910), *London*.
Andrew Hope, A.B., S.S. 2837 (R.F.R. B.5847), *London*.
Charles A. Smith, A.B., J.27753, *Lord Nelson* (wounded).
Basil Brazier, A.B., J.6116, *Lord Nelson* (wounded).
Charles H. Smith, A.B., J.28377, *Lord Nelson*.
Henry A. B. Green, A.B., 238024, *Lord Nelson* (wounded).

Work of Staff.

No officer could have been better served by his staff than I have been during these operations. The energy and resource of my Chief of Staff, Commodore R. J. B. Keyes, was invaluable, and, in combination with Major-General Braithwaite—Chief of the General Staff—he established a most excellent working agreement between the two services.

Captain George P. W. Hope, of *Queen Elizabeth*, acted as my flag captain. His gift of organisation was of the greatest assistance in dealing with the mass of details inseparable from an operation of such magnitude.

Commander the Hon. A. R. M. Ramsay has used his sound practical knowledge of gunnery to great advantage in working out, in connection with the military, the details of gun-fire from the covering ships.

Captain William W. Godfrey, R.M., a staff officer of great ability, has given me invaluable assistance throughout the operations.

I would also mention my secretary, Mr. Basil F. Hood, Acting Paymaster, and secretarial staff, whose good services under the direction and example of Mr. Edward W. Whittington-Ince, Assistant Paymaster, will form the subject of a later separate report.

Also, Lieutenant-Commander James F. Sommerville (Fleet Wireless Telegraph Officer), and Flag Lieutenants L. S. Ormsby-Johnson, Hugh S. Bowlby, and Richard H. L. Bevan, who have performed good service in organising with the military the intercommunication between the Allied Fleets and Armies.

I have, etc.,

J. M. de Robeck, Vice-Admiral.

The Secretary of the Admiralty.

Admiralty, August 16, 1915.

The King has been graciously pleased to approve of the grant of the Victoria Cross to the undermentioned officers and men for the conspicuous acts of bravery mentioned in the dispatch:—

Commander Edward Unwin, R.N.
Midshipman Wilfred St. Aubyn Malleson, R.N.
Midshipman George Leslie Drewry, R.N.R.
Able Seaman William Chas. Williams, O.N. 186774 (R-F.R. B.3766) (since killed).
Seaman R.N.R. George McKenzie Samson, O.N. 2408A.

The king has been graciously pleased to approve of the grant of the Victoria Cross to Lieut.-Commander (now Commander) Eric Gascoigne Robinson, R.N., for the conspicuous act of bravery specified below.

Lieutenant-Commander Robinson on the 26th February advanced alone, under heavy fire, into an enemy's gun position, which might well have been occupied, and destroying a four-inch gun, returned to his party for another charge with which the second gun was destroyed. Lieutenant-Commander Robinson would not allow members of his demolition party to accompany him, as their white uniforms rendered them very conspicuous. Lieutenant-Commander Robinson took part in four attacks on the mine fields—always under heavy fire.

CHAPTER 7

The Struggle at Gallipoli

The Allied forces, after the first movement against Krithia on 28th April, were extended on a line running from a point on the Gulf of Saros, three miles north-east of Capa Tekke, to a point one mile north of Eski Hissarlik, whence it bent back a little to the shore of the Dardanelles. For the next months the story of the campaign is concerned with a slow and desperate struggle for Krithia and the Achi Baba heights, which were the first step towards the conquest of the peninsula. Before we enter upon the details of that struggle it may be well to glance at the problem of the Turkish communications, for it had a direct bearing upon the Allied strategy of the campaign.

General Liman von Sanders had in the butt-end of the peninsula not less than 200,000 men and a lavish provision of artillery. To feed his troops and supply his guns he needed ample communications, and these could not be found in the narrow road from Rodosto across the Bulair isthmus, a road bad at the best, and now commanded by the fire of the Allied ships in the Gulf of Saros. His true communications lay by water down the Sea of Marmara to the ports of Gallipoli and Maidos. If this water transport could be hampered, the only remaining plan was to bring his reserves and supplies along the Asiatic coast to Chanak, and have them ferried over in the darkness of the night. This was a practicable route, but slow and circuitous. If he wished for free and speedy transport, he must keep the Sea of Marmara inviolate.

It was the object of the Allies to make that sea impossible. The only means at their disposal was the submarine. An attempt was made by the Australian submarine *AE 2*, but on 30th April it was unfortunately sunk in a bold effort to enter the Marmara. On 27th April, *E* 14, under Lieutenant-Commander Edward Courtney Boyle, dived under the minefields, entered the Marmara, and for some days operated brilliantly in those waters right up to the entrance to the Bosphorus.

It was hunted hourly by Turkish patrols, and had many difficulties with currents, but it contrived to sink two Turkish gunboats and one large transport full of troops. A few days later, *E* 11, under Lieutenant-Commander Eric Naismith, followed the same course, and sunk one large gunboat, two transports, one communication ship, and three store ships, and drove a fourth store ship ashore. It exploded a torpedo right under the wharves of Constantinople. On its return it was well down the straits when another Turkish transport was discovered astern, and it returned and torpedoed it. It became entangled with a floating mine, and towed the thing behind it to the mouth of the Straits, where it managed to cast it off.

These brilliant feats, for which Lieutenant-Commanders Boyle and Naismith received the Victoria Cross, were performed with signal humanity. They involved a prolonged risk and tension which it would be hard to parallel from the annals of war. Their results, too, were singularly fruitful. The Sea of Marmara was no longer regarded as safe, and the Turkish supplies began to travel by the Asiatic shore and the ferries of the Narrows. This involved a certain dislocation and delay which were of inestimable service to the Allied troops which faced the formidable batteries of Achi Baba and Kilid Bahr.

On 30th April two further battalions of the Naval Division disembarked, and next day came the 29th Brigade of Indian Infantry. By that evening the French corps on our right had landed all their troops and all but two of their batteries. These were just in time, for the night had scarcely fallen when the Turks attacked in force. They began with a bombardment, and then, as the moon rose, their infantry charged. Their German officers had issued an invocation to a counter-crusade:—

> Attack the enemy with the bayonet and utterly destroy him. We shall not retire one step, for, if we do, our religion, our country, and our nation will perish. Soldiers! the world is looking at you! Your only hope of salvation is to bring this battle to a successful issue or gloriously to give up your life in the attempt!

The plan of the attack was for the Turks to crawl forward under cover of their artillery fire till the time came for the final rush. They came on in a three-deep formation, and the first line had no ammunition, so that it might be forced to rely on the bayonet.

The Allied front from left to right was held by the 87th, 86th,

THE GREATEST OF MODERN BATTLEFIELDS: ACHI BABA, A "NATURAL BASTION" DEFENDING THE ROAD TO CONSTANTINOPLE

and 88th Brigades, and on the right was a French division, with the Senegalese in the first line. The bombardment had fallen most heavily on the right of the 86th Brigade, and this part suffered also the chief impact of the Turkish charge. A gap opened up in our line, which was promptly filled by the 5th Royal Scots, the Territorial battalion of the 88th Brigade. They faced to their left flank, and with the bayonet cleared the enemy from the trenches he had occupied. The 1st Essex came to their assistance, and presently our front was restored.

The attack now swung against the French left, where were the Senegalese. Here ground was lost, and some British gunners and the 4th Worcesters came up in support. All night long we maintained our position here with difficulty, and at two in the morning a battalion of the Naval Division was sent to strengthen the French right.

The counterattack was ordered for dawn. At 5 a.m. the whole line advanced, and on the British left and centre progressed fully 500 yards. The Senegalese on the French left were able to conform to this movement, in spite of their heavy fighting during the night, but the French right were held up by barbed wire and cunningly-concealed machine-guns. The result was that the advance was enfiladed upon the right, and about 11 a.m. had to withdraw to its former line. At one moment the Turkish retirement looked like a rout, and Sir Ian Hamilton was of opinion that but for the barbed wire and the machine-guns on the right we should have carried Achi Baba.

That afternoon the enemy buried his dead under a flag of truce. In the evening the French front was again assailed, and the following night the attack was repeated and repulsed. On the 4th, part of the French line was taken over by the 2nd Naval Brigade, and on the 5th the East Lancashire Territorial Division arrived, and was added to the reserves. Since the 25th of April the British losses had been just short of 14,000, of whom no less than 3,593 were prisoners. In attack in such a country, where the movement is not uniform, troops which lead the advance are in great danger of being cut off. From the 3rd to the 5th we were busy readjusting our line in preparation for a fresh offensive.

What may be called the Second Battle of Krithia began on the morning of Thursday, 6th May, and lasted for three days. The Allied dispositions at the beginning of the action were as follows:— On the extreme left the 87th Brigade held the hollow, down which a small stream flows to Beach Y, and was entrenched on the heights above it. Then came the 88th Brigade and a Naval Brigade, and then the

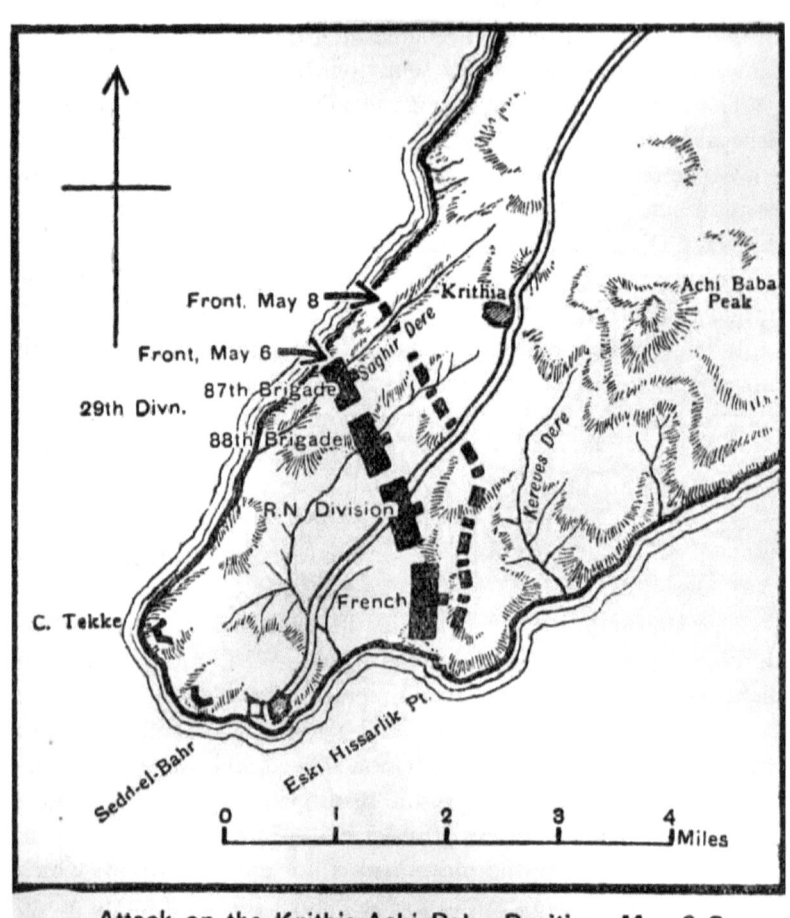

Attack on the Krithia-Achi Baba Position, May 6-8.

French to the Straits. In reserve were the 86th Brigade, the 29th Indian Brigade, a brigade of Australians and New Zealanders brought down from Gaba Tepe, and the East Lancashire Territorial Division.

Our plan of attack was for the left and centre to attempt to occupy the Krithia ridge, while the French should assault the high ground on the right across the valley of the Kereves Dere—the small stream which enters the Dardanelles just beyond Eski Hissarlik. The French were to begin the movement, since, until they had made some progress, the British advance on Krithia would be enfiladed by the Turkish left.

The French 75-mm. guns opened fire from the neighbourhood of Sedd-el-Bahr about eleven in the morning, aiming at the southern spur of Achi Baba and the broken ground in front of it towards the Krithia road. At the same time the battleships in the Straits, among which were the *Agamemnon*, plastered the upper slopes of Achi Baba and the Turkish trenches in the Kereves valley. After half an hour of artillery preparation the Senegalese attacked in open order, while their field guns dropped shells fifty yards in front of them. As they reached the top of the slope overlooking the Kereves Dere they came suddenly upon Turkish trenches skilfully concealed behind the crest. This compelled part of the line to wheel to the left, where they advanced by a bridle path which traverses the upper end of the Kereves hollow. Part of the Naval Brigade was sent forward to reinforce the French left, but they too fell in with concealed Turkish trenches.

The ships' guns and the French field artillery rained shrapnel and high-explosive shells on the Turkish position, but could not check its fire. Again, and again through the afternoon the Senegalese struggled to advance, but the place was too strong, and with heavy casualties they had to be withdrawn and their place taken by a brigade of Colonial infantry. At 5.30 p.m. the fighting died away. The result of the day was that the French had pushed forward a mile, and had dug themselves in on the slopes above the Kereves Dere, but had failed to carry the Turkish trenches on the reverse slope or the redoubt at the top of the valley. That night the Turks counterattacked between 10 p.m. and 2 a.m., but the French held their ground.

Next day, 7th May, about ten o'clock, the ships began a bombardment of the Turkish right on Achi Baba. They directed special attention to the ground at the head of the ravine leading to Beach Y. A quarter of an hour later the British left attacked, the 87th and 88th Brigades towards the slopes between Krithia and the sea, and the Naval Brigades in the centre towards Krithia village. They carried the

British soldiers go on the attack

front Turkish trenches, but the second line held them up, and their supports were heavily shelled by Turkish guns from the heights. One battalion got well ahead of the rest, but at 1.45 p.m. was caught by machine-gun fire, and forced to retreat. By 2 p.m. we seemed to have reached an *impasse*.

Meantime the French on the right had lain quiet till noon. Then they began an elaborate bombardment, and at 3 p.m., supported by part of the Naval Brigade, attacked over the same ground as the day before. During the afternoon they made some progress, but about 5 p.m. their advanced infantry was caught on the slopes by such a hail of shrapnel that the line wavered and broke. The Turks counterattacked and took the French trenches on the crest. D'Amade flung in his reserves, and after an hour's severe fighting they recovered the lost ground, and held it till nightfall under a heavy fire.

During the afternoon the British had done little. At 3.15 p.m. we strengthened our left, and at five a second time bombarded the Turkish position. Our infantry advanced, and about six attempted to carry the hill between Krithia and the sea. It proved too strong, but as a result of the day we had got our front entrenched within 800 yards of Krithia. It was desperately costly fighting. Our artillery fire seemed to have no effect upon the enemy, who had trench lines cunningly hidden over the whole position.

Next day, 8th May, the battle was renewed at ten o'clock. Again, the ships in the Gulf of Saros bombarded the Turkish right and the ground behind it, and after half an hour's "preparation" the British left and left centre attacked. The 87th and 88th Brigades gained further ground in the broken bush country between Krithia and the sea. The 86th Brigade and the Australian and New Zealand supports were then pushed in to strengthen the line. Nothing happened on the right of our front, and during the afternoon there was a lull. We were reorganising our forces, with a view to a last attempt upon Krithia valley.

At 5.15 p.m. all the available ships and the shore batteries united in a terrific bombardment. From the report of an observer, the Turkish position was smothered in flame and smoke.

According to all preconceived theories of artillery fire, the enemy should have been wiped out and so stunned by the exploding lyddite that he would not be capable of resisting the advance of our infantry. Not a Turk was to be seen, and their artillery had not fired a shot.

A French soldier at Gallipoli

Once again, we were to learn the strength of scientifically-prepared entrenchments. At 5.30 our advance began, and no sooner did we move than the Turks opened fire along the whole front with artillery, machine-guns, and rifles. On the left we, moved a little way towards Krithia, but soon reached our limit. The French on the right carried the first Turkish trenches, and there stuck fast. Confused fighting continued till 7.30 p.m., when night put an end to the battle.

The result of the three days' struggle was that our front had been advanced over a thousand yards, but we had not touched the enemy's main position. We had realised its unique strength, and all idea of rushing it was abandoned.

We must turn to the doings of the Australasian Corps at Gaba Tepe.

★★★★★★

This corps comprised the Australian Division (General Bridges) 1st, 2nd, and 3rd Australian Infantry Brigades; the New Zealand and Australian Division (General Godley) 4th Australian Brigade, New Zealand Brigade, and Composite Mounted Brigade.

★★★★★★

During the battles of 6th-8th May they were persistently attacked; but though they had lent part of their forces to the Krithia front, they held their ground at all points. On the morning of 9th May the 15th and 16th Battalions of the 4th Australian Brigade stormed with the bayonet three lines of trenches on Sari Bair. Next day, at dawn, the Turks counterattacked and retook the trenches, but were repulsed with heavy losses when they continued their attack against the main Australian position. After that nothing of importance occurred till the night of 18th May. The Australian line lay in a semicircle, with the enemy's trenches close up to it in some places as near as twenty yards except in that part adjoining the shore where the ships' guns kept him off.

A wide hollow, which our men called Shrapnel Valley, divided the position into two sections. On the northern section the Turkish trenches were on much higher ground than ours. The curious alignment may be seen from the attached sketch, which gives a rough plan of the main situation. Our position at Gaba Tepe was of great strategical value, for it divided the enemy's efforts. He could not attack or defend at Achi Baba in full force, since he was compelled to leave a large part of his army to hold the Australian Corps.

On the night of 18th May General Liman von Sanders brought fresh troops from Constantinople, and drew off part of his Krithia garrison. About midnight a heavy fire from rifle and machine-guns broke

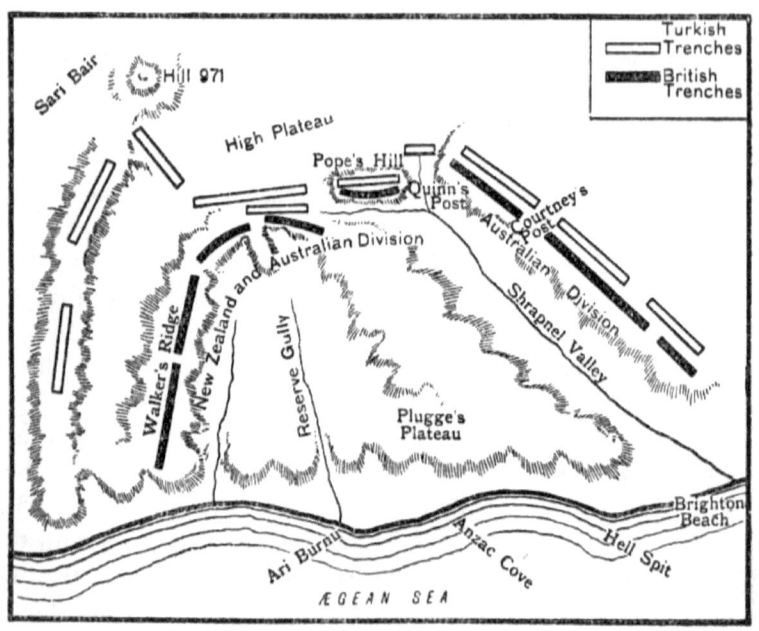

Position of Australian and New Zealand Corps at Gapa Tepe.

out against the Australian trenches, and at various points attacks were made which crumbled away before our defence. At 5 a.m. on the 19th the Turkish artillery began, and all morning the enemy attempted to rush our lines. The cool and steady shooting of the Australians kept him at bay, and by eleven o'clock the battle died down. In the evening there were renewed attacks, in one of which Lance-Corporal Jacka of the 14th Battalion retook a trench occupied by seven Turks, killing all seven single-handed—a deed for which he received the Victoria Cross. On that day, the 19th, the Turks were believed to have lost over 7,000 men, while the casualties of the Australians were only some 500. An observer who saw the action thus described the field:—

> The ground presents an extraordinary sight when viewed through the trench periscopes. Two hundred yards away, and even closer in places, are the Turkish trenches, and between them and our lines the dead lie in hundreds. There are groups of twenty or thirty massed together as if for mutual protection, some lying on their faces, some killed in the act of firing, others hung up in the barbed wire. In one place a small group actually reached our parapet, and now lie dead on it, shot or bayoneted at point-blank range. Hundreds of others lie just outside their own trenches.

To return to the main front in the south. Little happened between 9th and 12th May. On the night of the 12th Major General Hunter-Weston, with some troops of the 29th Division and a double company of Gurkhas, operating close to the sea, drove in the extreme Turkish right, and won some ground. On the 17th the 29th Division advanced their trenches 200 yards, and next day the French on the right, supported by a Naval Brigade, made some progress. During the following fortnight there was nothing to record, except small local advances. On the night of 28th May the Turks had a slight success, and advanced in some force to press it further. But our guns caught their supports, and demoralised them, and their bombers threw their grenades into their own first-line trenches. The Turkish casualties were estimated at about 2,000. That same night the French carried the redoubt, which they had named "*Le Haricot*," at the head of the Kereves Dere, that same redoubt which had held up their advance with its machine-guns in the battle of 6th-8th May.

The third great attempt upon Krithia and Achi Baba was made on 4th June. Our front was formed by the 29th Indian Brigade on the left, the 29th Division on the left centre, the East Lancashire Territorial Division in the centre, the Naval Division on the right centre, and the French 2nd Division on the right. After a preparation by all our shore batteries and ships' guns, the advance began at noon. The Indian Brigade at first made good progress, and captured two lines of trenches. Unfortunately, on their right a part of the 29th Division had found itself faced with a heavy wire entanglement which our artillery had not cut. This checked their progress, and the Indians were compelled by enfilading fire to retire to their original line.

The rest of the 29th Division captured a redoubt and two trench lines beyond it, and advanced the front by 300 yards. The Territorials in the centre captured three lines of trenches, and advanced 600 yards, but they were too far beyond the rest for comfort, and after holding an advanced captured trench for a day and a night, had to fall back to the second trench. The Naval Division progressed for 300 yards, taking a redoubt and a line of trenches, but was obliged to yield its gains owing to the position on its right. There the French, charging with desperate gallantry, retook for the fourth time the redoubt of "*Le Haricot*," but were driven out of it by shell fire. Their right was more fortunate, and captured a strong trench line, which they were able to hold.

There were many counterattacks during the night, which forced us out of one of the captured trenches. At the same time General Birdwood attacked from Gaba Tepe, in order to divert reinforcements which were coming from Maidos, and carried a trench line, inflicting heavy losses upon the enemy. The fruits of this third attempt on Achi Baba were an advance of some 500 yards on a front of three miles, and the occupation of two lines of Turkish trenches.

It was after the battle of 4th June that the need for large reinforcements became too urgent to be denied. After five weeks' struggle, in which the fighting had been as desperate as any in the war, we had not yet touched the outer Turkish position. The German engineers had turned the *terrain* to brilliant defensive uses, and even when long lengths, of trenches were carried by our infantry attacks, there remained redoubts, like the *fortins* on the Western Front, to make a general advance impossible. It may be questioned whether a more abundant supply of high explosives would have greatly altered the case.

Our bombardments had been lavish enough, but they had scarcely touched the enemy. The Gallipoli campaign had revealed itself as a slow and deadly frontal attack, in which yard by yard we should have to fight our way across the ridges. Such warfare was costly beyond all

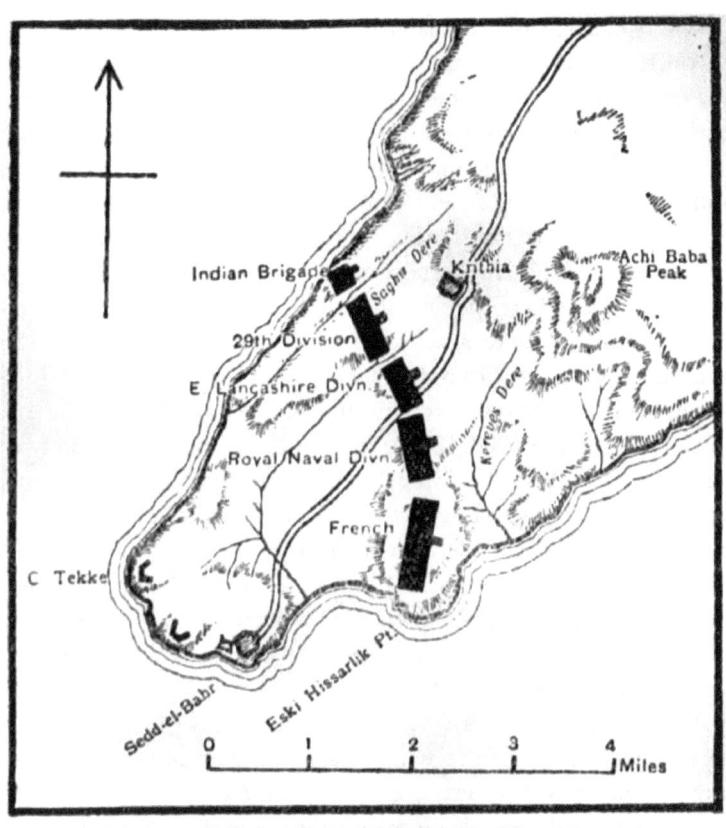

Attack on the Krithia-Achi Baba Position, June 4.

reckoning. Up to 31st May the casualties in the Dardanelles—exclusive of the French—reached a total of 38,636, of whom 1,722 were officers. The battle losses for the three years of the South African War were only 38,156. This figure, it will be noted, covers only the landing and the first two attempts on Achi Baba. The Turkish losses were estimated at some 60,000.

The Allied Fleets had shared in every land attack, and the *Goeben*, on the Turkish side, from farther up the Straits, took part in at least one engagement. These large vessels, stationary or moving very slowly along the coasts, were a superb target for underwater assault, and presently news came that some of the large ocean-going German submarines, which had been commissioned early in the year, were on their way to the Mediterranean. About the middle of May, one was reported near Malta, and there were many spots on the long indented Anatolian coast where they could find a base.

This possibility gave much anxiety to the Allied admirals. Meantime, on the night of 12th May, a Turkish destroyer performed a singularly bold feat on its own account. It found the old British battleship, the *Goliath*, (built in 1900, 12,950 tons, 19 knots, four 12-in. and twelve 6-in. guns), protecting the French flank just inside the Straits, sunk it by torpedo fire, with a loss of the captain, 19 officers, and 500 men, and managed to return safely. Such an exploit was only possible under cover of darkness, and the risk of it did not interfere with the daylight operations of the fleet. But presently a far more formidable foe arrived, a foe whose presence made naval support so far at least as concerned the great battleships a very doubtful and costly undertaking.

About midday on 26th May the *Triumph* was moving slowly up the northern shore of the peninsula in support of the Australasian troops. Apparently, her nets were out, and there were destroyers close at hand. A torpedo from a German submarine tore through the nets, struck the vessel amidships, and sank her in nine minutes. Nearly all the officers and men were saved, and the submarine was chased unsuccessfully by the destroyers. Here was an incident to give serious thought. The enemy in broad daylight, in water full of shipping, had broken through all our safeguards, and destroyed a battleship. The hunt for the submarine there seems at the moment to have been only one was vigorously conducted, but nothing was heard of it till next day, when the *Majestic*, steaming very close to the shore, was sunk in the same fashion.

The Allied Fleets, compelled by the necessities of gunnery to move slowly, were obviously at the mercy of an enemy under water. From this date, therefore, the larger vessels began to withdraw. The *Queen Elizabeth* returned home, and there remained only a few of the older battleships, a number of cruisers, French and British, like the *Euryalus, Minerva, Talbot, Phaeton, Amethyst,* and *Kleber,* and a flotilla of destroyers, including the *Scorpion, Wolverine, Pincher, Renard,* and *Chelmer*. In addition, we had the *Humber,* one of the monitors which had operated in October off the Flanders coast a type of vessel whose shallow draught made it most suitable for coast bombardment and least vulnerable to submarine attack.

The strength of the Gallipoli position and the menace of the German submarines had turned the operations in the Eastern Mediterranean into some of the most difficult of the war.

Appendix to Chapter 7

THE GALLIPOLI LANDING
Sir Ian Hamilton's First Dispatch.
From the General Commanding the Mediterranean Expeditionary Force.
To the Secretary of State for War, War Office, London, S.W.

General Headquarters,
Mediterranean Expeditionary Force,
20th May, 1915.

My Lord,

I have the honour to submit my report on the operations in the Gallipoli Peninsula up to and including the 5th May.

In accordance with Your Lordship's instructions I left London on 13th March with my General Staff by special train to Marseilles, and thence in H.M.S. *Phaeton* to the scene of the naval operations in the Eastern Mediterranean, reaching Tenedos on the 17th March shortly after noon.

Immediately on arrival I conferred with Vice-Admiral de Robeck, Commanding the Eastern Mediterranean Fleet, General d'Amade, Commanding the French Corps Expéditionnaire; and Contre Amiral Guepratte, in command of the French Squadron. At this conference past difficulties were explained to me, and the intention to make a fresh attack on the morrow was announced. The amphibious battle between warships and land fortresses took place next day, the 18th of March.

I witnessed these stupendous events, and thereupon cabled Your Lordship my reluctant deduction that the co-operation of the whole of the force under my command would be required to enable the Fleet effectively to force the Dardanelles.

The Gallipoli Peninsula.

By that time, I had already carried out a preliminary reconnaissance of the north-western shore of the Gallipoli Peninsula, from its isthmus, where it is spanned by the Bulair fortified lines, to Cape Helles, at its extremest point. From Bulair this singular feature runs in a south-westerly direction for 52 miles, attaining near its centre a breadth of 12 miles. The northern coast of the northern half of the promontory slopes downwards steeply to the Gulf of Xeros, in a chain of hills, which extend as far as Cape Sulva. The precipitous fall of these hills precludes landing, except at a few narrow gullies, far too restricted for any serious military movements. The southern half of the peninsula is shaped like a badly worn boot. The ankle lies between Gaba Tepe and Kalkmaz Dagh; beneath the heel lie the cluster of forts at Kilid Bahr; whilst the toe is that promontory five miles in width, stretching from Tekke Burnu to Sedd-el-Bahr.

The three dominating features in this southern section seemed to me to be:—

(1) Saribair Mountain, running up in a succession of almost perpendicular escarpments to 970 feet. The whole mountain seemed to be a network of ravines and covered with thick jungle.
(2) Kilid Bahr plateau, which rises, a natural fortification artificially fortified, to a height of 700 feet to cover the forts of the Narrows from an attack from the Aegean.
(3) Achi Babi, a hill 600 feet in height, dominating at long field gun range what I have described as being the toe of the peninsula.

A peculiarity to be noted as regards this last southern sector is that from Achi Babi to Cape Helles the ground is hollowed out like a spoon, presenting only its outer edges to direct fire from the sea. The inside of the spoon appears to be open and undulating, but actually it is full of spurs, *nullahs*, and confused under-features.

The Landing-Places.

Generally speaking, the coast is precipitous, and good landing-places are few. Just south of Tekke Burnu is a small sandy bay (W), and half a mile north of it is another small break in the cliffs (X). Two miles farther up the coast the mouth of a stream indents these same cliffs (Y 2), and yet another mile and a half up a scrub-covered gully looked as if active infantry might be able to scramble up it on to heights not altogether dissimilar to those of Abraham, by Quebec (Y). Inside Sedd-el-Bahr is a sandy beach (V), about 300 yards across, facing a semi-circle of steeply-rising ground, as the flat bottom of a half-saucer faces the rim, a rim flanked on one side by an old castle, on the other by a modern fort. By Eski Hissarlik, on the east of Morto Bay (S), was another small beach, which was, however, dominated by the big guns from Asia. Turning northwards again, there are two good landing-places on either side of Gaba Tepe.

Farther to the north of that promontory the beach was supposed to be dangerous and difficult. In most of these landing-places the trenches and lines of wire entanglements were plainly visible from on board ship. What seemed to be gun emplacements and infantry redoubts could also be made out through a telescope, but of the full extent of these defences and of the forces available to man them there was no possibility of judging except by practical test.

Altogether the result of this and subsequent reconnaissances was to convince me that nothing but a thorough and systematic scheme for flinging the whole of the troops under my command very rapidly ashore could be expected to meet with success; whereas, on the other hand, a tentative or piecemeal programme was bound to lead to disaster. The landing of an army upon the theatre of operations I have described—a theatre strongly garrisoned throughout, and prepared for any such attempt—involved difficulties for which no precedent was forthcoming in military history except possibly in the sinister legends of Xerxes.

The beaches were either so well defended by works and guns or else so restricted by nature that it did not seem possible, even by two or three simultaneous landings, to pass the troops ashore quickly enough to enable them to maintain themselves against the rapid concentration and counterattack which the enemy was bound in such case to attempt. It became necessary, therefore, not only to land simultaneously at as many points as possible, but to threaten to land at other points as well. The first of these necessities involved another unavoidable if awkward contingency, the separation by considerable intervals of the force.

The weather was also bound to play a vital part in my landing. Had it been British weather there would have been no alternative but instantly to give up the adventure. To land two or three thousand men, and then to have to break off and leave them exposed for a week

New Zealanders at Gaba Tepe

to the attacks of 34,000 regular troops, with a hundred guns at their back was not an eventuality to be lightly envisaged. Whatever happened the weather must always remain an incalculable factor, but at least by delay till the end of April we had a fair chance of several days of consecutive calm.

The Sailing of the Transports.

Before doing anything else I had to redistribute the troops on the transports to suit the order of their disembarkation. The bulk of the forces at my disposal had, perforce, been embarked without its having been possible to pay due attention to the operation upon which I now proposed that they should be launched.

Owing to lack of facilities at Mudros redistribution in that harbour was out of the question. With Your Lordship's approval, therefore, I ordered all the transports, except those of the Australian Infantry Brigade and the details encamped at Lemnos Island, to the Egyptian ports. On the 24th March I myself, together with the general staff, proceeded to Alexandria, where I remained until 7th April, working out the allocation of troops to transports in minutest detail as a prelude to the forthcoming disembarkation. General d'Amade did likewise.

On the 1st April the remainder of the General Headquarters, which had not been mobilised when I left England, arrived at Alexandria.

Apart from the rearrangements of the troops, my visit to Egypt was not without profit, since it afforded me opportunities of conferring with the G.O.C. Egypt and of making myself acquainted with the troops, drawn from all parts of the French Republic and of the British Empire, which it was to be my privilege to command.

By the 7th April my preparations were sufficiently advanced to enable me to return with my General Staff to Lemnos, so as to put the finishing touches to my plan in close co-ordination with the Vice-Admiral Commanding the Eastern Mediterranean Fleet.

The covering force of the 29th Division left Mudros Harbour on the evening of 23rd April for the five beaches, S, V, W, X, and Y. Of these, V, W, and X were to be main landings, the landings at S and Y being made mainly to protect the flanks, to disseminate the forces of the enemy, and to interrupt the arrival of his reinforcements. The landings at S and Y were to take place at dawn, whilst it was planned that the first troops for V, W, and X beaches should reach the shore simultaneously at 5.30 a.m. after half an hour's bombardment from the Fleet.

The transports conveying the covering force arrived off Tenedos on the morning of the 24th, and during the afternoon the troops were transferred to the warships and fleet-sweepers in which they were to approach the shore. About midnight these ships, each towing a number of cutters and other small boats, silently slipped their cables and, escorted by the 3rd Squadron of the Fleet, steamed slowly towards their final rendezvous at Cape Helles. The rendezvous was reached just before dawn on the 25th.

The morning was absolutely still; there was no sign of life on the shore; a thin veil of mist hung motionless over the promontory; the surface of the sea was as smooth as glass. The four battleships and four cruisers which formed the 3rd Squadron at once took up the positions that had been allotted to them, and at 5 a.m., it being then light enough to fire, a violent bombardment of the enemy's defences was begun. Meanwhile the troops were being rapidly transferred to the small boats in which they were to be towed ashore. Not a move on the part of the enemy; except for shells thrown from the Asiatic side of the Straits the guns of the Fleet remained unanswered.

The Landing at Beaches S, Y, and X.

The detachment detailed for S beach (Eski Hissarlik Point) consisted of the 2nd South Wales Borderers (less one company) under Lieut.-Colonel Casson. Their landing was delayed by the current, but by 7.30 a.m. it had been successfully effected at the cost of some 50 casualties, and Lieut. Colonel Casson was able to establish his small force on the high ground near De Totts Battery. Here he maintained himself until the general advance on the 27th brought him into touch with the main body.

The landing on Y beach was entrusted to the King's Own Scottish Borderers and the Plymouth (Marine) Battalion, Royal Naval Division, specially attached to the 29th Division for this task, the whole under the command of Lieut.-Colonel Koe. The beach at this point consisted merely of a narrow strip of sand at the foot of a crumbling scrub-covered cliff some 200 feet high immediately to the west of Krithia.

A number of small gullies running down the face of the cliff facilitated the climb to the summit, and so impracticable had these precipices appeared to the Turks that no steps had been taken to defend them. Very different would it have been had we, as was at one time intended, taken Y 2 for this landing. There a large force of infantry, entrenched up to their necks, and supported by machine and Hotchkiss

The Manchesters at Krithia

guns, were awaiting an attempt which could hardly have made good its footing. But at Y both battalions were able in the first instance to establish themselves on the heights, reserves of food, water, and ammunition were hauled up to the top of the cliff, and, in accordance with the plan of operations, an endeavour was immediately made to gain touch with the troops landing at X beach. Unfortunately, the enemy's strong detachment from Y 2 interposed, our troops landing at X were fully occupied in attacking the Turks immediately to their front, and the attempt to join hands was not persevered with.

Later in the day a large force of Turks were seen to be advancing upon the cliffs above Y beach from the direction of Krithia, and Colonel Koe was obliged to entrench. From this time onward his small force was subjected to strong and repeated attacks, supported by field artillery, and owing to the configuration of the ground, which here drops inland from the edge of the cliff, the guns of the supporting ships could render him little assistance. Throughout the afternoon and all through the night the Turks made assault after assault upon the British line. They threw bombs into the trenches, and, favoured by darkness, actually led a pony with a machine-gun on its back over the defences and were proceeding to come into action in the middle of our position when they were bayoneted.

The British repeatedly counter-charged with the bayonet, and always drove off the enemy for the moment, but the Turks were in a vast superiority and fresh troops took the place of those who temporarily fell back. Colonel Koe (since died of wounds) had become a casualty early in the day, and the number of officers and men killed and wounded during the incessant fighting was very heavy. By 7 a.m. on the 26th only about half of the King's Own Scottish Borderers remained to man the entrenchment made for four times their number. These brave fellows were absolutely worn out with continuous fighting; it was doubtful if reinforcements could reach them in time, and orders were issued for them to be re-embarked.

Thanks to H.M.S. *Goliath, Dublin, Amethyst,* and *Sapphire,* thanks also to the devotion of a small rearguard of the King's Own Scottish Borderers, which kept off the enemy from lining the cliff, the re-embarkation of the whole of the troops, together with the wounded, stores, and ammunition, was safely accomplished, and both battalions were brought round the southern end of the peninsula. Deplorable as the heavy losses had been, and unfortunate as was the tactical failure to make good so much ground at the outset, yet, taking the operation as it stood, there can be no doubt it has contributed greatly to the success of the main attack, seeing that the plucky stand made at Y beach had detained heavy columns of the enemy from arriving at the southern end of the peninsula during what it will be seen was a very touch-and-go struggle.

WORK OF "IMPLACABLE'S" GUNS.

The landing-place known as X beach consists of a strip of sand some 200 yards long by 8 yards wide at the foot of a low cliff. The troops to be landed here were the 1st Royal Fusiliers, who were to be towed ashore from H.M.S. *Implacable* in two parties, half a battalion at a time, together with a beach working party found by the Anson Battalion, Royal Naval Division. About 6 a.m. H.M.S. *Implacable*, with a boldness much admired by the army, stood quite close in to the beach, firing very rapidly with every gun she could bring to bear. Thus seconded, the Royal Fusiliers made good their landing with but little loss.

The battalion then advanced to attack the Turkish trenches on the Hill 114, situated between V and W beaches, but were heavily counterattacked and forced to give ground. Two more battalions of the 87th Brigade soon followed them, and by evening the troops had established themselves in an entrenched position extending from half a mile round the landing-place and as far south as Hill 114. Here they were in touch with the Lancashire Fusiliers, who had landed on W beach. Brigadier-General Marshall, commanding the 87th Brigade, had been wounded during the day's fighting, but continued in command of the brigade.

THE LANDING AT BEACH V.

The landing on V beach was planned to take place on the following lines:—

As soon as the enemy's defences had been heavily bombarded by the Fleet, three companies of the Dublin Fusiliers were to be towed ashore. They were to be closely followed by the collier *River Clyde* (Commander Unwin, R.N.), carrying between decks the balance of the Dublin Fusiliers, the Munster Fusiliers, half a battalion of the Hampshire Regiment, the West Riding Field Company, and other details.

The *River Clyde* had been specially prepared for the rapid disembarkation of her complement, and large openings for the exit of the troops had been cut in her sides, giving on to a wide gang-plank by which the men could pass rapidly into lighters which she had in tow. As soon as the first tows had reached land the *River Clyde* was to be run straight ashore. Her lighters were to be placed in position to form a gangway between the ship and the beach, and by this means it was hoped that 2,000 men could be thrown ashore with the utmost rapidity. Further, to assist in covering the landing, a battery of machine-guns, protected by sandbags, had been mounted in her bows.

The remainder of the covering force detailed for this beach was then to follow in tows from the attendant battleships.

V beach is situated immediately to the west of Sedd-el-Bahr. Between the bluff on which stands Sedd-el-Bahr village and that which is crowned by No. 1 Fort the ground forms a very regular amphitheatre of three or four hundred yards radius. The slopes down to the beach are slightly concave, so that the whole area contained within the limits of this natural amphitheatre, whose grassy terraces rise gently to a height of a hundred feet above the shore, can be swept by the fire of a defender. The beach itself is a sandy strip some 10 yards wide and 350 yards long, backed along almost the whole of its extent by a low sandy escarpment about 4 feet high, where the ground falls nearly sheer down to the beach. The slight shelter afforded by this escarpment played no small part in the operations of the succeeding thirty-two hours.

At the south-eastern extremity of the beach, between the shore and the village, stands the old fort of Sedd-el-Bahr, a battered ruin with wide breaches in its walls and mounds of fallen masonry within and around it. On the ridge to the north, overlooking the amphitheatre, stands a ruined barrack. Both of these buildings, as well as No. 1 Fort, had been long bombarded by the Fleet, and the guns of the forts had been put out of action; but their crumbled walls and the ruined outskirts of the village afforded cover for riflemen, while from the terraced slopes already described the defenders were able to command the open beach, as a stage is overlooked from the balconies of a theatre.

On the very margin of the beach a strong barbed-wire entanglement, made of heavier metal and longer barbs than I have ever seen elsewhere, ran right across from the old fort of Sedd-el-Bahr to the foot of the north-western headland. Two-thirds of the way up the ridge a second and even stronger entanglement crossed the amphitheatre, passing in front of the old barrack and ending in the outskirts of the village. A third transverse entanglement, joining these two, ran up the hill near the eastern end of the beach, and almost at right angles to it. Above the upper entanglement the ground was scored with the enemy's trenches, in one of which four pom-poms were emplaced; in others were dummy pom-poms to draw fire, while the debris of the shattered buildings on either flank afforded cover and concealment for a number of machine-guns, which brought a cross-fire to bear on the ground already swept by rifle fire from the ridge.

Needless to say, the difficulties in the way of previous reconnaissance had rendered it impossible to obtain detailed information with regard either to the locality or to the enemy's preparations.

As often happens in war, the actual course of events did not quite correspond with the intentions of the Commander. The *River Clyde* came into position off Sedd-el-Bahr in advance of the tows, and, just as the latter reached the shore, Commander Unwin beached his ship also. Whilst the boats and the collier were approaching the landing-place the Turks made no sign. Up to the very last moment it appeared as if the landing was to be unopposed. But the moment the first boat touched bottom the storm broke. A tornado of fire swept over the beach, the incoming boats, and the collier.

The Dublin Fusiliers and the naval boats' crews suffered exceedingly heavy losses while still in the boats. Those who succeeded in landing and in crossing the strip of sand managed to gain some cover when they reached the low escarpment on the farther side. None of the boats, however, were able to get off again, and they and their crews were destroyed upon the beach.

Now came the moment for the *River Clyde* to pour forth her living freight; but grievous delay was caused here by the difficulty of placing the lighters in position between the ship and the shore. A strong current hindered the work and the enemy's fire was so intense that almost every man engaged upon it was immediately shot. Owing, however, to the splendid gallantry of the naval working party, the lighters were eventually placed in position, and then the disembarkation began.

A company of the Munster Fusiliers led the way; but, short as was the distance, few of the men ever reached the farther side of the beach through the hail of bullets which poured down upon them from both flanks and the front. As the second company followed, the extemporized pier of lighters gave way in the current. The end nearest to the shore drifted into deep water, and many men who had escaped being shot were drowned by the weight of their equipment in trying to swim from the lighter to the beach. Undaunted workers were still forthcoming, the lighters were again brought into position, and the third company of the Munster Fusiliers rushed ashore, suffering heaviest loss this time from shrapnel as well as from rifle, pom-pom, and machine-gun fire.

For a space the attempt to land was discontinued. When it was resumed the lighters again drifted into deep water, with Brigadier-General Napier, Captain Costeker, his Brigade-Major, and a number of men of the Hampshire Regiment on board. There was nothing for them all but to lie down on the lighters, and it was here that General Napier and Captain Costeker were killed. At this time, between 10 and 11 a.m., about 1,000 men had left the collier, and of these nearly half had been killed or wounded before they could reach the little cover afforded by the steep, sandy bank at the top of the beach. Further attempts to disembark were now given up. Had the troops all been in open boats but few of them would have lived to tell the tale. But, most fortunately, the collier was so constructed as to afford fairly efficient protection to the men who were still on board, and, so long as they made no attempt to land, they suffered comparatively little loss.

Throughout the remainder of the day there was practically no change in the position of affairs. The situation was probably saved by the machine-guns on the *River Clyde*, which did valuable service in keeping down the enemy's fire and in preventing any attempt on their part to launch a counterattack. One half-company of the Dublin Fusiliers, which had been landed at a camber just east of Sedd-el-Bahr village, was unable to work its way across to V beach, and by mid-day had only twenty-five men left. It was proposed to divert to Y beach that part of the main body which had been intended to land on V beach; but this would have involved considerable delay owing to the distance, and the main body was diverted to W beach, where the Lancashire Fusiliers had already effected a landing.

Late in the afternoon part of the Worcestershire Regiment and the Lancashire Fusiliers worked across the high ground from W beach, and seemed likely to relieve the situation by taking the defenders of V beach in flank. The pressure on their own front, however, and the numerous barbed-wire entanglements which intervened, checked this advance, and at nightfall the Turkish garrison still held their ground. Just before dark some small parties of our men made their way along the shore to the outer walls of the Old Fort, and when night had fallen the remainder of the infantry from the collier were landed. A good force was now available for attack, but our troops were at such a cruel disadvantage as to position, and the fire of the enemy was still so accurate in the bright moonlight, that all attempts to clear the fort and the outskirts of the village during the night failed one after the other. The wounded who were able to do so without support returned to the collier under cover of darkness; but otherwise the situation at daybreak on the 26th was the same as it had been on the previous day, except that the troops first landed were becoming very exhausted.

Twenty-four hours after the disembarkation began there were ashore on V beach the survivors of the Dublin and Munster Fusiliers and of two companies of the Hampshire Regiment. The brigadier and his brigade-major had been killed; Lieutenant-Colonel Carrington Smith, commanding the Hampshire Regiment, had been killed and the adjutant had been wounded. The Adjutant of the Munster Fusiliers was wounded, and the great majority of the senior officers were either wounded or killed. The remnant of the landing-party still crouched on the beach beneath the shelter of the sandy escarpment which had saved so many lives. With them were two officers of my general staff—Lieutenant-Colonel Doughty-Wylie and Lieutenant-Colonel Williams. These two officers, who had landed from the *River Clyde*, had been striving, with conspicuous contempt for danger, to keep all their comrades in good heart during this day and night of ceaseless imminent peril.

Now that it was daylight once more, Lieutenant-Colonels Doughty-Wylie and Williams set to work to organise an attack on the hill above the beach. Any soldier who has endeavoured to pull scattered units together after they have been dominated for many consecutive hours by close and continuous fire will be able to take the measure of their difficulties. Fortunately, General Hunter-Weston had arranged with Rear-Admiral Wemyss about this same time for a heavy bombardment to be opened by the ships upon the Old Fort, Sedd-el-Bahr Village, the Old Castle north of the village, and on the ground leading up from the beach.

Under cover of this bombardment, and led by Lieutenant-Colonel Doughty-Wylie, and Captain Walford, Brigade-Major R.A., the troops gained a footing in the village by 10 a.m. They encountered a most stubborn opposition and suffered heavy losses from the fire of well-concealed riflemen and machine-guns. Undeterred by the resistance, and supported by the naval gunfire, they pushed forward, and soon after midday they penetrated to the northern edge of the village, whence they were in a position to attack the Old Castle and Hill 141.

During this advance Captain Walford was killed. Lieutenant-Colonel Doughty-Wylie had most gallantly led the attack all the way up from the beach through the west side of the village, under a galling fire. And now, when, owing so largely to his own inspiring example and intrepid courage, the position had almost been gained, he was killed while leading the last assault. But the attack was pushed forward without wavering, and, fighting their way across the open with great dash, the troops gained the summit and occupied the Old Castle and Hill 141 before 2 p.m.

The Landing at Beach W.

W beach consists of a strip of deep, powdery sand some 350 yards long and from 15 to 40 yards wide, situated immediately south of Tekke Burnu, where a small gully running down to the sea opens out a break in the cliffs. On either flank of the beach the ground rises precipitously, but, in the centre, a number of sand dunes afford a more gradual access to the ridge overlooking the sea. Much time and ingenuity had been employed by the Turks in turning this landing-place into a death trap. Close to the water's edge a broad wire entanglement extended the whole length of the shore and a supplementary barbed network lay concealed under the surface of the sea in the shallows. Land mines and sea mines had been laid.

The high ground overlooking the beach was strongly fortified with trenches to which the gully afforded a natural covered approach. A number of machine-guns also were cunningly tucked away into holes in the cliff so as to be immune from a naval bombardment whilst they were converging their fire on the wire entanglements. The crest of the hill overlooking the beach was in its turn commanded by high ground to the north-west and south-east, and especially by two strong infantry redoubts near point 138. Both these redoubts were protected by wire entanglements about 20 feet broad, and could be approached only by a bare glacis-like slope leading up from the high ground above W beach or from the Cape Helles lighthouse. In addition, another separate entanglement ran down from these two redoubts to the edge of the cliff near the lighthouse, making intercommunication between V and W beaches impossible until these redoubts had been captured.

So strong, in fact, were the defences of W beach that the Turks may well have considered them impregnable, and it is my firm conviction that no finer feat of arms has ever been achieved by the British soldier or any other soldier than the storming of these trenches from open

60-POUNDER, CAPE HELLES, JUNE 1915

boats on the morning of 25th April.

The landing at W had been entrusted to the 1st Battalion Lancashire Fusiliers (Major Bishop), and it was to the complete lack of the senses of danger or of fear of this daring battalion that we owed our astonishing success. As in the case of the landing at X, the disembarkation had been delayed for half an hour, but at 6 a.m. the whole battalion approached the shore together, towed by eight picket boats in line abreast, each picket boat pulling four ship's cutters. As soon as shallow water was reached, the tows were cast off and the boats were at once rowed to the shore. Three companies headed for the beach and a company on the left of the line made for a small ledge of rock immediately under the cliff at Tekke Burnu. Brigadier-General Hare, commanding the 88th Brigade, accompanied this latter party, which escaped the cross fire brought to bear upon the beach, and was also in a better position than the rest of the battalion to turn the wire entanglements.

While the troops were approaching the shore, no shot had been fired from the enemy's trenches, but as soon as the first boat touched the ground a hurricane of lead swept over the battalion. Gallantly led by their officers, the fusiliers literally hurled themselves ashore, and, fired at from right, left, and centre, commenced hacking their way through the wire. A long line of men was at once mown down as by a scythe, but the remainder were not to be denied. Covered by the fire of the warships, which had now closed right in to the shore, and helped by the flanking fire of the company on the extreme left, they broke through the entanglements and collected under the cliffs on either side of the beach. Here the companies were rapidly reformed, and set forth to storm the enemy's entrenchments wherever they could find them.

In making these attacks the bulk of the battalion moved up towards Hill 114 whilst a small party worked down towards the trenches on the Cape Helles side of the landing-place.

Several landmines were exploded by the Turks during the advance, but the determination of the troops was in no way affected. By 10 a.m. three lines of hostile trenches were in our hands, and our hold on the beach was assured.

About 9.30 a.m. more infantry had begun to disembark, and two hours later a junction was effected on Hill 114 with the troops who had landed on X beach.

On the right, owing to the strength of the redoubt on Hill 138, little progress could be made. The small party of Lancashire Fusiliers which had advanced in this direction succeeded in reaching the edge of the wire entanglements, but were not strong enough to do more, and it was here that Major Frankland, Brigade-Major of the 86th Infantry Brigade, who had gone forward to make a personal reconnaissance, was unfortunately killed. Brigadier-General Hare had been wounded earlier in the day, and Colonel Woolly-Dod, General Staff 29th Division, was now sent ashore to take command at W beach and organise a further advance.

At 2 p.m., after the ground near Hill 138 had been subjected to a heavy bombardment, the Worcester Regiment advanced to the assault. Several men of this battalion rushed forward with great spirit to cut passages through the entanglement; some were killed, others persevered, and by 4 p.m. the hill and redoubt were captured.

An attempt was now made to join hands with the troops on V beach, who could make no headway at all against the dominating defences of the enemy. To help them out the 86th Brigade pushed forward in an easterly direction along the cliff. There is a limit, however, to the storming of barbed-wire entanglements. More of these barred the way. Again, the heroic wire-cutters came out. Through glasses they could be seen quietly snipping away under a hellish fire as if they were pruning a vineyard. Again, some of them fell. The fire pouring out of No. 1 fort grew hotter and hotter, until the troops, now thoroughly exhausted by a sleepless night and by the long day's fighting under a hot sun, had to rest on their laurels for a while.

When night fell, the British position in front of W beach extended from just east of Cape Helles lighthouse, through Hill 138, to Hill 114. Practically every man had to be thrown into the trenches to hold this line, and the only available reserves on this part of our front were the 2nd London Field Company R.E. and a platoon of the Anson Battalion, which had been landed as a beach working party.

During the night several strong and determined counterattacks were made, all successfully repulsed without loss of ground. Meanwhile the disembarkation of the remainder of the division was proceeding on W and X beaches.

The Landing at Gaba Tepe.

The Australian and New Zealand Army Corps sailed out of Mudros Bay on the afternoon of 24th April, escorted by the 2nd Squadron of the Fleet, under Rear-Admiral Thursby. The rendezvous was reached just after half-past one in the morning of the 25th, and there the

1,500 men who had been placed on board H.M. ships before leaving Mudros were transferred to their boats. This operation was carried out with remarkable expedition, and in absolute silence. Simultaneously the remaining 2,500 men of the covering force were transferred from their transports to six destroyers. At 2.30 a.m. H.M. ships, together with the tows and the destroyers, proceeded to within some four miles of the coast, H.M.S. *Queen* (flying Rear-Admiral Thursby's flag) directing on a point about a mile north of Gaba Tepe. At 3.30 a.m. orders to go ahead and land were given to the tows and at 4.10 a.m. the destroyers were ordered to follow.

All these arrangements worked without a hitch, and were carried out in complete orderliness and silence. No breath of wind ruffled the surface of the sea, and every condition was favourable save for the moon, which, sinking behind the ships, may have silhouetted them against its orb, betraying them thus to watchers on the shore.

A rugged and difficult part of the coast had been selected for the landing, so difficult and rugged that I considered the Turks were not at all likely to anticipate such a descent. Indeed, owing to the tows having failed to maintain their exact direction the actual point of disembarkation was rather more than a mile north of that which I had selected, and was more closely overhung by steeper cliffs. Although this accident increased the initial difficulty of driving the enemy off the heights inland, it has since proved itself to have been a blessing in disguise, inasmuch as the actual base of the force of occupation has been much better defiladed from shell fire.

The beach on which the landing was actually effected is a very narrow strip of sand, about 1,000 yards in length, bounded on the north and the south by two small promontories. At its southern extremity a deep ravine, with exceedingly steep, scrub-clad sides, runs inland in a north-easterly direction. Near the northern end of the beach a small but steep gully runs up into the hills at right angles to the shore. Between the ravine and the gully the whole of the beach is backed by the seaward face of the spur which forms the north-western side of the ravine. From the top of the spur the ground falls almost sheer except near the southern limit of the beach, where gentler slopes give access to the mouth of the ravine behind.

Farther inland lie in a tangled knot the under-features of Saribair, separated by deep ravines, which take a most confusing diversity of direction. Sharp spurs, covered with dense scrub, and falling away in many places in precipitous sandy cliffs, radiate from the principal mass of the mountain, from which they run north-west, west, south-west, and south to the coast.

The boats approached the land in the silence and the darkness, and they were close to the shore before the enemy stirred. Then about one battalion of Turks was seen running along the beach to intercept the lines of boats. At this so critical a moment the conduct of all ranks was most praiseworthy. Not a word was spoken—everyone remained perfectly orderly and quiet awaiting the enemy's fire, which sure enough opened, causing many casualties. The moment the boats touched land the Australians' turn had come. Like lightning they leapt ashore, and each man as he did so went straight as his bayonet at the enemy. So vigorous was the onslaught that the Turks made no attempt to withstand it and fled from ridge to ridge pursued by the Australian infantry.

This attack was carried out by the 3rd Australian Brigade, under Major (temporary Colonel) Sinclair Maclagan, D.S.O. The 1st and 2nd Brigades followed promptly, and were all disembarked by 2 p.m., by which time 12,000 men and two batteries of Indian Mountain Artillery had been landed. The disembarkation of further artillery was delayed owing to the fact that the enemy's heavy guns opened on the anchorage and forced the transports, which had been subjected to continuous shelling from his field guns, to stand farther out to sea.

The broken ground, the thick scrub, the necessity for sending any formed detachments post haste as they landed to the critical point of the moment, the headlong valour of scattered groups of the men who had pressed far farther into the peninsula than had been intended all these led to confusion and mixing up of units. Eventually the mixed crowd of fighting men, some advancing from the beach, others falling back before the oncoming Turkish supports, solidified into a semicircular position with its right about a mile north of Gaba Tepe and its left on the high ground over Fisherman's Hut. During this period parties of the 9th and 10th Battalions charged and put out of action three of the enemy's Krupp guns. During this period also the disembarkation of the Australian Division was being followed by that of the New Zealand and Australian Division (two brigades only).

From 11 a.m. to 3 p.m. the enemy, now reinforced to a strength of 20,000 men, attacked the whole line, making a specially strong effort against the 3rd Brigade and the left of the 2nd Brigade. This counterattack was, however, handsomely repulsed with the help of the guns of H.M. ships. Between 5 and 6.30 p.m. a third most determined counter-attack was made against the 3rd Brigade, who held their ground with more than equivalent stubbornness. During the night again the Turks made constant attacks, and the 8th Battalion repelled a bayonet charge; but in spite of all the line held firm.

The troops had had practically no rest on the night of the 24th-25th; they had been fighting hard all day over most difficult country, and they had been subjected to heavy shrapnel fire in the open. Their casualties had been deplorably heavy. But, despite their losses and in spite of their fatigue, the morning of the 26th found them still in good heart and as full of fight as ever.

It is a consolation to know that the Turks suffered still more seriously. Several times our machine-guns got on to them in close formation, and the whole surrounding country is still strewn with their dead of this date.

The reorganisation of units and formations was impossible during the 26th and 27th owing to persistent attacks. An advance was impossible until a reorganisation could be effected, and it only remained to entrench the position gained and to perfect the arrangements for bringing up ammunition, water, and supplies to the ridges in itself a most difficult undertaking. Four battalions of the Royal Naval Division were sent up to reinforce the Army Corps on the 28th and 29th April.

On the night of 2nd May a bold effort was made to seize a commanding knoll in front of the centre of the line. The enemy's enfilading machine-guns were too scientifically posted, and 800 men were lost without advantage beyond the infliction of a corresponding loss to the enemy. On 4th May an attempt to seize Gaba Tepe was also unsuccessful, the barbed-wire here being something beyond belief. But a number of minor operations have been carried out, such as the taking of a Turkish observing station; the strengthening of entrenchments; the reorganisation of units, and the perfecting of communication with the landing-place.

Also, a constant strain has been placed upon some of the best troops of the enemy, who, to the number of 24,000, are constantly kept fighting and being killed and wounded freely, as the Turkish sniper is no match for the Kangaroo shooter, even at his own game.

The assistance of the Royal Navy, here as elsewhere, has been invaluable. The whole of the arrangements have been in Admiral Thursby's hands, and I trust I may be permitted to say what a trusty and powerful friend he has proved himself to be to the Australian and New Zealand Army Corps.

The French at Kum Kale.

Concurrently with the British landings a regiment of the French Corps was successfully disembarked at Kum Kale under the guns of the French Fleet, and remained ashore till the morning of the 26th, when they were re-embarked. 500 prisoners were captured by the French on this day.

This operation drew the fire of the Asiatic guns from Morto Bay and V beach on to Kum Kale, and contributed largely to the success of the British landings.

On the evening of the 20th the main disembarkation of the French Corps was begun, V beach being allotted to our Allies for this purpose, and it was arranged that the French should hold the portion of the front between the telegraph wire and the sea.

The following day I ordered a general advance to a line stretching from Hill 236 near Eski Hissarlik Point to the mouth of the stream two miles north of Tekke Burnu. This advance, which was commenced at midday, was completed without opposition, and the troops at once consolidated their new line. The forward movement relieved the growing congestion on the beaches, and by giving us possession of several new wells afforded a temporary solution to the water problem, which had hitherto been causing me much anxiety.

By the evening of the 27th the Allied forces had established themselves on a line some three miles long, which stretched from the mouth of the *nullah*, 3,200 yards north-east of Tekke Burnu, to Eski Hissarlik Point, the three brigades of the 29th Division less two battalions on the left and in the centre, with four French battalions on the right, and beyond them again the South Wales Borderers on the extreme right.

The General Advance Begun.

Owing to casualties this line was somewhat thinly held. Still, it was so vital to make what headway we could before the enemy recovered himself and received fresh reinforcements that it was decided to push on as quickly as possible. Orders were therefore issued for a general advance to commence at 8 a.m. next day.

The 29th Division were to march on Krithia, with their left brigade leading, the French were directed to extend their left in conformity with the British movements and to retain their right on the coastline south of the Kereves Dere.

The advance commenced at 8 a.m. on the 28th, and was carried out with commendable vigour, despite the fact that from the moment of landing the troops had been unable to obtain any proper rest.

The 87th Brigade, with which had been incorporated the Drake Battalion, Royal Naval Division, in the place of the King's Own Scottish Borderers and South Wales Borderers, pushed on rapidly, and by 10 a.m. had advanced some two miles. Here the further progress of the Border Regiment was barred by a strong work on the left flank. They halted to concentrate and make dispositions to attack it, and at that moment had to withstand a determined counterattack by the Turks. Aided by heavy gun fire from H.M.S. *Queen Elizabeth*, they succeeded in beating off the attack, but they made no further progress that day. and when night fell entrenched themselves on the ground they had gained in the morning.

The Inniskilling Fusiliers, who advanced with their right on the Krithia ravine, reached a point about three-quarters of a mile southwest of Krithia. This was, however, the farthest limit attained, and later on in the day they fell back into line with other corps.

The 88th Brigade on the right of the 87th progressed steadily until about 11.30 a.m., when the stubbornness of the opposition, coupled with a dearth of ammunition, brought their advance to a standstill. The 86th Brigade, under Lieutenant-Colonel Casson, which had been held in reserve, were thereupon ordered to push forward through the 88th Brigade in the direction of Krithia.

The movement commenced at about 1 p.m., but though small reconnoitring parties got to within a few hundred yards of Krithia, the main body of the brigade did not get beyond the line held by the 88th Brigade. Meanwhile, the French had also pushed on in the face of strong opposition along the spurs on the western bank of the Kereves Dere, and had got to within a mile of Krithia with their right thrown back and their left in touch with the 88th Brigade. Here they were unable to make further progress; gradually the strength of the resistance made itself felt, and our Allies were forced during the afternoon to give ground.

Ammunition Running Short.

By 2 p.m. the whole of the troops with the exception of the Drake Battalion had been absorbed into the firing line. The men were exhausted, and the few guns landed at the time were unable to afford them adequate artillery support. The small amount of transport available did not suffice to maintain the supply of munitions, and cartridges were running short despite all efforts to push them up from the landing-places.

Hopes of getting a footing on Achi Babi had now perforce to be abandoned at least for this occasion. The best that could be expected was that we should be able to maintain what we had won, and when at 3 p.m. the Turks made a determined counterattack with the bayonet against the centre and right of our line, even this seemed exceedingly doubtful. Actually, a partial retirement did take place. The French were also forced back, and at 6 p.m. orders were issued for our troops to entrench themselves as best they could in the positions they then held, with their right flank thrown back so as to maintain connection with our Allies. In this retirement the right flank of the 88th Brigade was temporarily uncovered, and the Worcester Regiment suffered severely.

Had it been possible to push in reinforcements in men, artillery, and munitions during the day, Krithia should have fallen, and much subsequent fighting for its capture would have been avoided.

Two days later this would have been feasible, but I had to reckon with the certainty that the enemy would, in that same time, have received proportionately greater support. I was faced by the usual choice of evils, and although the result was not what I had hoped, I have no reason to believe that hesitation and delay would better have answered my purpose.

For, after all, we had pushed forward quite appreciably on the whole. The line eventually held by our troops on the night of the 28th ran from a point on the coast three miles north-east of Tekke Burnu to a point one mile north of Eski Hissarlik, whence it was continued by the French southeast to the coast.

Much inevitable mixing of units of the 86th and 88th Brigades had occurred during the day's fighting, and there was a dangerous re-entrant in the line at the junction of the 87th and 88th Brigades near the Krithia *nullah*. The French had lost heavily, especially in officers, and required time to reorganise.

The 29th April was consequently spent in straightening the line, and in consolidating and strengthening the positions gained. There was a certain amount of artillery and musketry fire, but nothing serious.

Similarly, on the 30th, no advance was made, nor was any attack delivered by the enemy. The landing of the bulk of the artillery was completed, and a readjustment of the line took place, the portion held by the French being somewhat increased.

Two more battalions of the Royal Naval Division had been disembarked, and these, together with three battalions of the 88th Brigade withdrawn from the line, were formed into a reserve.

The Turkish Counterattack.

This reserve was increased on the 1st May by the addition of the 29th Indian Infantry Brigade, which released the three battalions of the 88th Brigade to return to the trenches. The Corps Expéitionnaire d'Orient had disembarked the whole of their infantry and all but two of their batteries by the same evening.

At 10 p.m. the Turks opened a hot shell fire upon our position, and half an hour later, just before the rise of the moon, they delivered a series of desperate attacks. Their formation was in three solid lines, the men in the front rank being deprived of ammunition to make them rely only upon the bayonet. The officers were served out with coloured Bengal lights to fire from their pistols, red indicating to the Turkish guns that they were to lengthen their range; white that our front trenches had been stormed; green that our main position had been carried. The Turkish attack was to crawl on hands and knees until the time came for the final rush to be made. An eloquent hortative was signed by Von Zowenstern and addressed to the Turkish rank and file, who were called upon, by one mighty effort, to fling us all back into the sea.

> Attack the enemy with the bayonet and utterly destroy him!
> We shall not retire one step; for, if we do, our religion, our country, and our nation will perish!
> Soldiers! The world is looking at you! Your only hope of salvation is to bring this battle to a successful issue or gloriously to give up your life in the attempt!

The first momentum of this ponderous onslaught fell upon the right of the 86th Brigade, an unlucky spot, seeing all the officers thereabouts had already been killed or wounded. So, when the Turks came right on without firing and charged into the trenches with the bayonet, they made an ugly gap in the line. This gap was instantly filled by the 5th Royal Scots (Territorials), who faced to their flank and executed a brilliant bayonet charge against the enemy, and by the Essex Regiment detached for the purpose by the Officer Commanding 88th Brigade. The rest of the British line held its own with comparative ease, and it was not found necessary to employ any portion of the reserve. The storm next broke in fullest violence against the French left, which was held by the Senegalese. Behind them were two British

Field Artillery Brigades and a Howitzer Battery. After several charges and counter-charges the Senegalese began to give ground, and a company of the Worcester Regiment and some gunners were sent forward to hold the gap. Later, a second company of the Worcester Regiment was also sent up, and the position was then maintained for the remainder of the night, although about 2 a.m. it was found necessary to dispatch one battalion Royal Naval Division to strengthen the extreme right of the French.

About 5 a.m. a counter-offensive was ordered and the whole line began to advance. By 7.30 a.m. the British left had gained some 500 yards, and the centre had pushed the enemy back and inflicted heavy losses. The right also had gained some ground in conjunction with the French left, but the remainder of the French line was unable to progress.

As the British centre and left were now subjected to heavy cross fire from concealed machine-guns, it was found impossible to maintain the ground gained, and therefore, about 11 a.m., the whole line withdrew to its former trenches.

The net result of the operations was the repulse of the Turks and the infliction upon them of very heavy losses. At first, we had them fairly on the run, and had it not been for those inventions of the devil machine-guns and barbed wire which suit the Turkish character and tactics to perfection, we should not have stopped short of the crest of Achi Babi. As it was, all brigades reported great numbers of dead Turks in front of their lines, and 350 prisoners were left in our hands.

On the 2nd, during the day, the enemy remained quiet, burying his dead under a red crescent flag, a work with which we did not interfere. Shortly after 9 p.m., however, they made another attack against the whole Allied line, their chief effort being made against the French front, where the ground favoured their approach. The attack was repulsed with loss.

During the night 3rd-4th the French front was again subjected to a heavy attack, which they were able to repulse without assistance from my general reserve.

The day of the 4th was spent in reorganisation, and a portion of the line held by the French, who had lost heavily during the previous night's fighting, was taken over by the 2nd Naval Brigade. The night passed quietly.

During the 5th the Lancashire Fusilier Brigade of the East Lancashire Division was disembarked and placed in reserve behind the

British left.

Orders were issued for an advance to be carried out next day, and these and the three days' battle which ensued will be dealt with in my next dispatch.

Our Losses.

The losses, exclusive of the French, during the period covered by this dispatch, were, I regret to say, very severe, numbering:—

177 Officers and 1,990 other ranks killed.
412 Officers and 7,807 other ranks wounded.
13 Officers and 3,580 other ranks missing.

From a technical point of view, it is interesting to note that my administrative staff had not reached Mudros by the time when the landings were finally arranged. All the highly elaborate work involved by these landings was put through by my general staff working in collaboration with Commodore Roger Keyes, C.B., M.V.O., and the naval transport officers allotted for the purpose by Vice-Admiral de Robeck. Navy and army carried out these combined duties with that perfect harmony which was indeed absolutely essential to success.

Work of the Navy.

Throughout the events I have chronicled the Royal Navy has been father and mother to the army. Not one of us but realises how much he owes to Vice-Admiral de Robeck; to the warships, French and British; to the destroyers, mine sweepers, picket boats, and to all their dauntless crews, who took no thought of themselves, but risked everything to give their soldier comrades a fair run in at the enemy.

Throughout these preparations and operations Monsieur le General d'Amade has given me the benefit of his wide experiences of war, and has afforded me, always, the most loyal and energetic support. The landing of Kum Kale planned by me as a mere diversion to distract the attention of the enemy was transformed by the Commander of the Corps Expéditionnaire de l'Orient into a brilliant operation, which secured some substantial results. During the fighting which followed the landing of the French Division at Sedd-el-Bahr no troops could have acquitted themselves more creditably under very trying circumstances, and under very heavy losses, than those working under the orders of Monsieur le General d'Amade.

Lieutenant-General Sir W. R. Birdwood, K.C.S.I., C.B., C.I.E.,

D.S.O., was in command of the detached landing of the Australian and New Zealand Army Corps above Gaba Tepe, as well as during the subsequent fighting. The fact of his having been responsible for the execution of these difficult and hazardous operations—operations which were crowned with a very remarkable success speaks, I think, for itself.

Major-General A. G. Hunter-Weston, C.B., D.S.O., was tried very highly, not only during the landings, but more especially in the day and night attacks and counterattacks which ensued. Untiring, resourceful, and ever more cheerful as the outlook (on occasion) grew darker, he possesses, in my opinion, very special qualifications as a commander of troops in the field.

Major-General W. P. Braithwaite, C.B., is the best Chief of the General Staff it has ever been my fortune to encounter in war. I will not pile epithets upon him. I can say no more than what I have said, and I can certainly say no less.

I have many other names to bring to notice for the period under review, and these will form the subject of a separate report at an early date.

   I have the honour to be,
     Your Lordship's most obedient Servant,
      Ian Hamilton,
      General,
      Commanding Mediterranean Expeditionary Force.

CHAPTER 8

The Deadlock at Gallipoli

We had chosen to attack the Turks in one of the strongest natural fortresses in the world. The convex arc of the Achi Baba heights might have been created for a modern defence. Not a yard of it was dead ground. Every foot was exposed to bombardment from the well-placed guns and the concentric trench lines. With a base a few miles square, we attempted by frontal fighting to win a step forward now and then.

It is true that the Australasian Corps had secured a position on the enemy's right rear; but that, too, was a step of a staircase, and our overseas troops clung precariously to the edge of the cliffs. Every inch of our position was under fire, and there was no safe hinterland for wounded and reserves except that gained by an embarkation and a voyage. The wounded had to go to Alexandria and Malta, and munitions, food, and water had to travel many leagues of sea. The position is best described in Sir Ian Hamilton's words:—

> The country is broken, mountainous, arid, and void of supplies; the water found in the areas occupied by our forces is quite inadequate for their needs; the only practicable beaches are small, cramped breaks in impracticable lines of cliffs; with the wind in certain quarters no sort of landing is possible; the wastage, by bombardment and wreckage, of lighters and small craft has led to crisis after crisis in our carrying capacity; whilst over every single beach plays fitfully throughout each day a devastating shell-fire at medium ranges.

Such a position would have been grave against a feeble opponent. But the Turk was no despicable foe. He had long before at Plevna proved himself a great master of defensive war. He was aided by the best German military skill and the latest German science. He was holding the gate of his sacred capital against the *infidel*—a gate, like the bridge of Horatius, where a thousand might be stopped by three; but his numbers were greater than ours. He was like a posse of mailed men on the summit of a narrow stairway, with every advantage of ground, weapon, and forewarning.

In June, 1915, the political and strategic importance of the Dardanelles expedition had been amply proved. What had not been dreamed of in April had come to pass. The determined attack upon Russia could not yet be balanced by a counter-offensive in the West, and the Dardanelles was the only *terrain* where the Allies could directly aid the hard-pressed armies of the *Tsar*.

The Allies could not win the war within reasonable time without the help of the Russian Armies, and anything which conduced to their aid was a contribution to the whole Allied cause. Provided that someday the enemy's field forces were destroyed, it mattered little in what part of Europe that destruction took place. Besides, Germany had given the East a special significance. It was clear that, as a great land power, she was turning her eyes more and more to those vast continental tracts of Eastern Europe and Western Asia where sea-power was meaningless. Whatever happened in the West, her victory there might threaten India and Egypt, points as vital for the British Empire as Verdun and Belfort were vital for France. Only in the Aegean and the Marmara could we use our fleets to strike at this aggression.

But if by midsummer the political and strategical value of the Dardanelles expedition was beyond criticism, the passing of the weeks raised the gravest doubts as to the wisdom of the actual plan adopted. We had chosen to attack the Turks in their central fortress, where they had all the advantages. It is easy to imagine the kind of argument which led us to the attempt. Our business was to secure as quickly as possible a passage for our fleet, and for this purpose to destroy the Narrows forts by taking them in the rear. To land in Gallipoli seemed the shortest way of accomplishing our desires. But it could only seem the shortest way to those who were ignorant of the nature of the ground and the quality of the Turkish defence.

Had we had the chance of making a surprise attack it would have been different, but for weeks and months we had advertised our intentions to the world. There was no lack of people to give us accurate information. Englishmen had been employed in the Turkish service; Englishmen had helped to fortify the Bulair line; and there were scores of our countrymen who could have explained the precise difficulties of Gallipoli. There is reason, too, to believe that we had the benefit of the advice of the Greek general staff.

For Greece the Dardanelles was one of the chief problems, and for years she had carefully studied it. Her opinion was undoubtedly adverse to a landing in Gallipoli, and the guess may be hazarded that the absence of Greek co-operation in April was not wholly due to her political difficulties. She may well have declined the honour of being massacred in our company in an adventure which she believed foredoomed to failure.

Gallipoli was not the only avenue to Constantinople. Troops might have been landed at the head of the Gulf of Saros to move through Thrace, or on the coast of the Trojan plain to advance along the southern shores of the Marmara. There were difficulties in both cases, but none comparable to those encountered in Gallipoli. In those areas the Allied forces would have been able to move on a broad front, and to fight a campaign of manoeuvre battles. Success in either would in time have led to the fall of Gallipoli, since the supplies of that fortress would have been cut. Why neither alternative was adopted is not yet clear, but a possible explanation may be found in the fact that the whole affair in its inception was an Admiralty enterprise.

The fleet was the main thing, the landing force was a mere adjunct to assist the passage of the ships, and success was looked for from a combination of naval fire and infantry attacks. In these circumstances an elaborate land campaign which would take the troops far inland seemed out of the question. That is the difficulty of all amphibious warfare. The special interests of each service may be sacrificed in attempting a compromise. There can be little doubt but that, if the Allies had landed in April in Asia Minor or Thrace, the situation by midsummer would have been greatly in their favour. The world would have lacked the tale of a heroic feat of arms, but Constantinople would have been gravely menaced. As it was, in June the menace had scarcely begun. We were locked up in a neck of land where there was no room for strategy, and where at the most, by great expenditure of life, we could steal at intervals a few hundred yards of trenches from the enemy.

The Mediterranean Expeditionary Force, according to its first conception, was now complete. The British troops had been organised into the Eighth Corps, under Lieutenant-General Hunter-Weston. The constituents were the regular 29th Division of glorious memory, in the command of which General Hunter-Weston had been succeeded by General De Lisle, formerly commanding the 1st Cavalry Division on the Western Front; the 42nd Territorial Division (East Lancashire), under Major-General Douglas; the Naval Division, under Major-General Paris; the 29th Indian Infantry Brigade, under Major-General H. B. Cox; and the Scottish Lowland Territorial Division, under MajorGeneral Egerton.

The Australian and New Zealand Corps at Gaba Tepe, under Lieutenant-General Sir W. R. Birdwood, embraced the Australian Division, under Major-General H. B, Walker, who had succeeded to the command after the death of General Bridges on 15th May, and the New Zealand and Australian Division, under Major-General Sir A. J. Godley. The French Corps Expéditionnaire had been completed in the second week of May by the arrival of its 2nd Division. Its troops—*Zouaves*, Senegalese, Colonial Infantry, and the Foreign Legion—were under General Gouraud, who succeeded General d'Amade on 14th May. General Gouraud, the youngest and the most brilliant of French corps commanders, had earned the name of the "Lion of the Argonne" from his winter's work in that forest campaign with a corps of Sarrail's 3rd Army.

In Sir Ian Hamilton's phrase, "a happy mixture of daring in danger and of calm in crisis" made him an ideal leader for the French Colonials. No one who ever met General Gouraud was likely to forget him. His grave and splendid presence, the fire in his dark eyes, the lofty resolution in every line and gesture, gave him the air of some great *paladin* of France who had held the marches with Roland and Oliver.

Our narrative of the campaign broke off after the battle of 4th June. On that day we had advanced in the centre from 200 to 400 yards on a front of three miles. Our left wing had moved only a little way forward, and the French on the extreme right were still held up by the ravine of the Kereves Dere. Our front was now in the form of a semicircle, with the horns flung well back, and our next business was to straighten our line. The time for bold and sweeping efforts had gone by. There had been a moment on 28th April when Krithia and the Achi Baba heights had been almost at our mercy; but, as the Turkish defence consolidated itself, all that remained for us was a slow war of "nibbling" and attrition. Surprise was out of the question. In Sir Ian Hamilton's words:—

> The enemy was as much in possession of my numbers and dispositions as I was in possession of their first line of defence; the

opposing fortified fronts stretched parallel from sea to straits; there was little space left now, either at Achi Baba or at Gaba Tepe, for tactics which would fling flesh and blood battalions against lines of unbroken barbed wire. Advance must more and more tend to take the shape of concentrated attacks on small sections of the enemy's line after full artillery preparation. Siege warfare was soon bound to supersede manoeuvre battles in the open. Consolidation and fortification of our front, improvement of approaches, selection of machine-gun emplacements, and scientific grouping of our artillery under a centralised control must erelong form the tactical basis of our plans.

These words were written of the situation after 11th May, but they applied with equal force to the position on 5th June.

During the first fortnight of June there were frequent Turkish attacks, directed to regain the trenches lost on the 4th. The French on the south side of the Kereves Dere were slowly working from point to point among the entrenched gullies and redoubts, and many fine deeds of small volunteer parties were recorded. On 5th June Second-Lieutenant Dallas Moor, of the 3rd Hampshires, won the Victoria Cross for his gallant rallying of a detachment which broke for a moment under a Turkish assault.

On the night of the 11th, on our left centre, a local advance was made by the 1st Border Regiment and the 2nd South Wales Borderers from the 29th Division, and two trenches were won. On the 16th the Turks attacked the section held by the 88th Brigade, and that night the trenches gained on the 11th were so heavily bombed that we were forced to fall back thirty yards and dig ourselves in. The Turkish position, however, was a salient which we could enfilade, and at dawn the 1st Dublin Fusiliers won back the trenches with the bayonet and filled them with the enemy's dead.

Our centre, especially on its left, formed an awkward salient, and till the wings could be brought forward, this was a point of danger. On the 18th the Turks made a resolute attempt to drive us back. They began with a heavy bombardment after the approved pattern, and thereafter massed their infantry as if for an attack. Something restrained them; but on the evening of the following day they carried the point of the salient, and we were hard put to recover it. The 5th Royal Scots—Territorials from the Lothians—under Lieutenant-Colonel Wilson, assisted by a company of the 4th Worcesters, managed by a brilliant charge to drive out the Turks and clear the ground. The Scots Territorials had already distinguished themselves in the action of 1st May, and formed not the least doughty battalion of the immortal 29th Division.

On 21st June a beginning was made with the straightening of the Allied front. The most critical position was that of the French corps on the right, which was still held up south of the Kereves Dere. At 1.30 in the morning a great bombardment began. All the south-eastern shoulder of Achi Baba was plastered with heavy shells, and the 75-mm. field guns played incessantly on the slopes of the ravine. Then came the infantry rush. The 2nd French Division on the left, under General Bailloud, made good progress. By midday it had captured the first two lines of the Turkish position, and taken the much-contested Haricot Redoubt, with its tangle of wire and deep-cut trenches and machine-gun *fortins*.

They were across the ravine, when they found that their right flank was in the air. For General Simonin's 1st Division, between them and the Straits, though it had kept line in its first onslaught, had been driven back by counterattacks. Twice the division advanced, and twice it was compelled to retire. At a quarter to three in the afternoon there was some risk that all the gains of the 2nd Division would be lost. General Gouraud accordingly issued the order that in the five hours of daylight that remained the right of the advance must at all costs succeed. British artillery was brought up, and every gun that could be massed poured shells on the Turkish lines, while the *St. Louis* in the Straits kept the Asiatic batteries quiet.

At six o'clock the last assault was delivered, and the position carried. Turkish reinforcements coming up were spotted by an aeroplane, caught by the 75's in the open, and destroyed. By nightfall the French had won 600 yards of Turkish trenches, and the whole Allied right wing was well beyond the Kereves ravine. The French losses were 2,500; those of the Turks at least 7,000, including fifty prisoners. Sir Ian Hamilton reported that the striplings of the latest French drafts had especially distinguished themselves by their dash and contempt of danger. The enemy fought with superb courage and resolution, and French officers who had campaigned in the West declared that as a fighting man the Turk was worth two Germans.

A distinguished writer, (Mr. Compton Mackenzie), who was present at the action, has given us a vivid picture of that great bombardment:—

The dawn had been clear, but soon a curtain of silver, through which gleamed, the ghost of the rising sun, hung over the Kereves Dere. This was the smoke of bursting shells. Slowly as the sun climbed up, the curtain became more substantial. Then it seemed to droop and sweep along the hollows like a vanishing mist of dawn, and during a respite the thin blue smoke of the bivouac fires came tranquilly up into the still air. The respite was very brief, and the bombardment began again with greater fierceness than before.

The 75's drummed unceasingly. The reverberation of the 125's and of the howitzers shook the observation post. Over the Kereves Dere, and beyond up the sloping shoulders of Achi Baba, the curtain became a pall. The sun climbed higher and higher. All that first mirage of beauty had disappeared, and there was nothing but the monstrous shapes of bursting shells, giants of smoke that appeared one after another along the Turkish lines. ... The smoke of the shells, which at dawn had been ethereal, almost translucent, was now, in the sunset, turbid and sinister; yet the sunset was very splendid, flaming in crimson streamers over Imbros, tinting the East with rosy reflections, and turning the peaks of Asia to sapphires.

It had a peculiar significance on this longest day of the year, crowning as it did those five precious hours of daylight that, for the French, had been fraught with such achievement. Slowly the colour faded out, and now, minute by minute, the flashes of the guns became more distinct, the smoke was merged in the gathering dusk, and away over the more distant Turkish lines the bursts of shrapnel came out like stars against the brief twilight. One knew the anxiety there would be in the darkness that now was falling upon this 21st of June, but in the morning, we heard gladly that the enemy's counterattacks had failed, and that our Allies were indeed firmly established.

The right wing having advanced, it remained to bring on the left. That left ran from the Krithia road, crossed the ravine called the Saghir Dere, about half-way between its head and its mouth, and rested on the high ground above the Gulf of Saros. The Saghir Dere was one of those desolate and arid water-courses common in Gallipoli and on the Anatolian coast. At the sea end its sides were 200 feet high, clothed for the most part with a light scrub, but with open patches of yellow

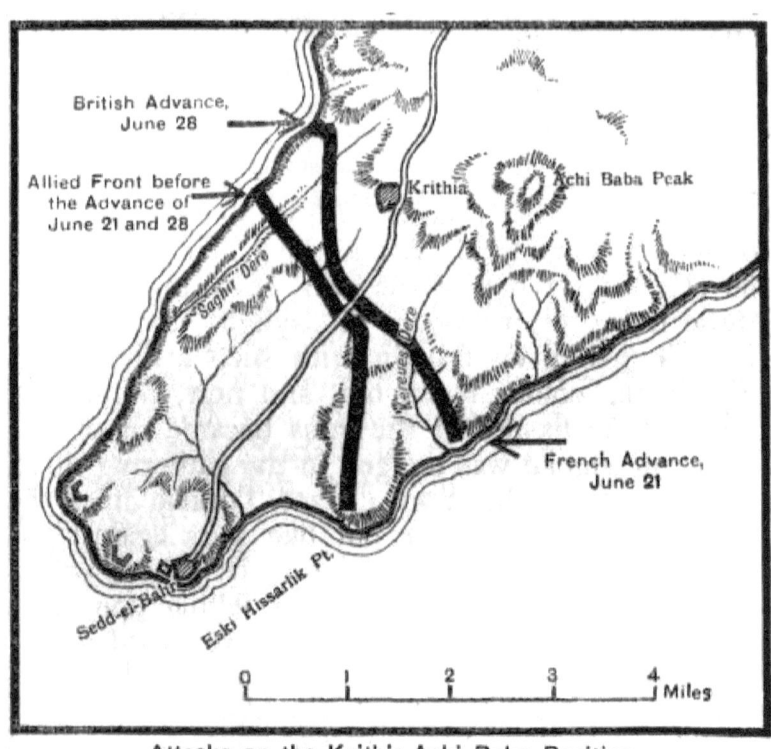

Attacks on the Krithia-Achi Baba Position,
June 21 and 28.

clay. A small stream, generally dry, trickled down it, and there were a few springs. Towards its head it grew shallower, and finally died away in the Krithia plateau. The north end was held strongly by the Turks, who had entrenched themselves on the top of the banks on both sides, and had fortified a small redoubt, which we called the Boomerang Fort, in front of their position.

The Allied plan was to pivot upon a point in our front about a mile from the sea, and to swing forward our left wing until its outer rim had advanced 1,000 yards. This meant that the distance to be covered decreased as the pivoting point was neared. The extreme left had to carry five Turkish trenches, the left centre no more than two. The forces to whom the task was entrusted were, from right to left, the 156th Brigade of the Scottish Lowland Territorial Division, the 29th Division, and the 29th Indian Brigade. The movement was in the charge of General Hunter-Weston.

On the morning of 28th June, the wind blew steadily from the west. At 9 a.m. the bombardment began with high explosive shells, and columns of dust hid Achi Baba. The French lent some of their big trench mortars, and the cruiser *Talbot* and the destroyers *Wolverine* and *Scorpion* from the sea enfiladed the trenches of the Turkish right. Our field guns, firing shrapnel, succeeded effectually in cutting the enemy's wire. At 10.20 the bombardment increased, every Allied piece firing in conjunction. At 10.45 our infantry leaped from the trenches. The 1st Border Regiment from the 87th Brigade carried the Boomerang works on the east side of the ravine with little opposition. The place was full of dead, and the survivors were dazed and blinded by our artillery.

At 11 a.m. the gunners lengthened the range, and the rest of the 87th Brigade, under Major-General Marshall—the 1st K.O.S.B., 1st Royal Inniskilling Fusiliers, and 2nd South Wales Borderers—captured three lines of trenches between the ravine and the sea. East of the gully the left of the 156th Brigade—the 4th and 7th Royal Scots—made good progress, and took the two trench lines allotted to them. But their right nearer the pivoting point met with heavy opposition, and could make little ground.

At 11.30 the second attack was launched. The 86th Brigade, led by the and Royal Fusiliers, passed through the 87th Brigade, and carried two farther lines of trenches, making up the required total of five. A correspondent wrote:—

This advance was a magnificent sight, the men never wavering or losing their formations under a heavy artillery and rifle fire.

On the extreme left the Gurkhas from the 29th Indian Brigade, moving just above the shore, carried a green spur called the Knoll, which joined up the line from the farthest captured Turkish trench to the sea, while some companies of the 1st Lancashire Fusiliers completed the connection with the 86th Brigade. In an hour and a half, we had done all we aimed at, except for a small section of trench near the pivoting point. That section was attacked again at 5.30 in the afternoon, but it proved impregnable. The British losses were moderate, some 1,750 in all, and most were incurred in the difficult point on the right of the 156th Brigade.

We captured large quantities of rifles and many thousand rounds of ammunition—booty scarcely less valuable than prisoners. The action was admirably planned and conducted. Our artillery work had been perfect, and the path of the infantry was made plain.

The whole Saghir Dere was now in our hands, and our left wing, instead of facing north-east, now faced due east, and was less than a mile west of Krithia. The captured upper section of the ravine was a horrible place, half graveyard, half rubbish-heap, for the Turks had no gift of cleanliness. A correspondent wrote:—

> All the way up, there is a litter of debris of the camp and the great fight—scattered bodies half-protruding from the ground, hastily-dug graves, hundreds of rifles and bayonets, some broken but the majority intact, thousands upon thousands of rounds of ammunition . . entrenching tools, loaves of bread, soldiers' packs, Turkish letters, a Mullah's prayer stool (a souvenir eagerly sought after), greatcoats and kits, blankets and old socks, cooking utensils and firewood, left just where the enemy abandoned them, when our gallant infantry broke through at the bayonet's point. Great fires are burning at intervals. They are avoided by all, and give forth a horrid, sickly stench. On these the Turkish dead, who have been hastily collected, are being burnt, for it is all important to get the dead out of the way as quickly as possible in this hot climate.
>
> Add to this a baking sun, air shimmering with heat, some stagnant pools of green water, an indescribable smell of decaying refuse, and everywhere swarms of flies, and the picture is complete.

The Turkish counterattacks of the afternoon were repulsed, and the night of the 28th was fairly quiet. On the afternoon of the 29th we observed a moving of troops on the Turkish right, and during the evening there were mines exploded against our right centre, a good deal of firing, and an abortive bayonet attack on our left. At the same time there was much activity at Gaba Tepe. About midnight heavy rifle fire broke out, to which the Australian Corps replied with cheers. At 1.30 on the morning of the 30th a Turkish column advanced with bayonets and bombs against General Godley's division.

It never came to the shock, for it was completely broken by the musketry and machine-gun fire of the 7th and 8th Light Horse. By two o'clock the enemy were routed, and many fell in the withdrawal. On the Australian left they had come up against a well-concealed sap ahead of our main line, and the dead lay in swathes before it. At 3 a.m. they tried again. A small party came over the parapets in front of Quinn's Post, and died to a man. The main threat against the left and left centre was similarly broken up by our rifle and gunfire.

There was fighting all round the peninsula on that last day of June. About two in the morning the searchlights of the *Scorpion* discovered the enemy advancing near the sea north-west of Krithia, and the ship drove them back by her fire. At the same time the Knoll due west of Krithia was attacked, the point which we had captured on the 28th. The Turks got within forty yards of the parapet, and then melted away under our guns. Several times during the night the enemy won a few yards of trenches by bomb attack, but these were regained by us with the bayonet in the morning. At 5.30 a.m. on 1st July, 2,000 Turks attempted to get from Krithia into the Saghir Dere, but were driven off by machine-guns. At ten o'clock in the evening another bomb attack was delivered against the most northerly of the trenches which we had captured on the 28th. Of the results let Sir Ian Hamilton tell:—

> An officer of the Gurkhas being wounded—not dangerously, as it turned out—the men became infuriated, flung all their bombs at the enemy, and then, charging down out of the trench, used their *kukris* for the first time, and with excellent effect. About dawn the Turks once more attempted an attack on the open, but nearly the whole of their attacking forces, about half a battalion, were shot down; and a final bomb attack, though commenced, failed utterly.

On the Allied right there was heavy fighting. On the night of the 29th the Turks attempted a surprise attack along the shore of the straits, but the movement was discovered by the searchlights of the

AUSTRALIAN GIVING WATER TO A WOUNDED TURK

Wolverine and brought to a standstill. The van of the attack was not stopped till it was some forty yards from our trenches. At 6.30 on the morning of the 30th the French moved forward, and in less than an hour had carried the fortified network known as the Quadrilateral, east of the head of the Kereves Dere. The Infanterie Coloniale carried seven lines of trenches, and their leading companies for a moment were in danger of being cut off. They held, however, to the ground they had won, and by the afternoon had beaten off all counterattacks and consolidated their position. This advance, taken in conjunction with the advance of the Allied left on the 38th, straightened out the dangerous bulge in our front.

One serious loss marred the success of the day. General Gouraud was struck by shell splinters while visiting an ambulance on his return from congratulating his troops on their victory. The wound, which later involved the amputation of his right arm, compelled him to return home and relinquish the command of the French Corps to General Bailloud.

These violent Turkish counterattacks resulted in nothing but the needless loss of many brave men. General Liman von Sanders had instructed his troops to act strictly on the defensive, and not to attempt to recover lost ground. But Enver, arriving during the fight on the 28th, reversed the policy, and ordered counterattacks along the whole front. He is believed to have used considerable reinforcements for the purpose, which disappeared under our fire. Sir Ian Hamilton estimated the Turkish losses during the five days following upon 28th June at 5,150 killed and 15,000 wounded, and these casualties produced no single gain. A captured order, issued by the commander of the 11th Division, showed the disquiet felt by the Turkish Staff at the Allied gains, and their fear of demoralisation among their men.

> There is nothing that causes us more sorrow, increases the courage of the enemy, and encourages him to advance more freely, causing us great losses, than the losing of these trenches. Henceforth commanders who surrender trenches, from whatever side the attack may come, before the last man is killed, will be punished in the same way as if they had run away. Especially will the commanders of units told off to guard a certain point be punished if, instead of thinking about their work, supporting their units, and giving information to the Higher Command, they only take action after a regrettable incident has taken place.

I hope that this will not occur again. I give notice that if it does, I shall carry out the punishment. I do not desire to see a blot made on the courage of our men by those who escape from the trenches to avoid the rifle and machine-gun fire of the enemy. Henceforth I shall hold responsible all officers who do not shoot with their revolvers all the privates who try to escape from the trenches on any pretext.

The July fighting was of the same nature as that of June, save that it did not reveal any large Allied movement, but was composed mainly of sporadic Turkish counterattacks. What ground we won was on a level with the French gains in the Artois during June, when, after a heavy bombardment, a small advance would be made and consolidated at a great expense of life. We were now close up against the main strength of the Achi Baba fortress.

On 2nd July, after bombarding our advanced position on the left with high explosives and shrapnel, the enemy attempted an advance, but was repulsed by our musketry and the guns of the *Scorpion*. At seven in the evening the Turkish artillery began again, and two battalions emerged from the *nullah* beyond Krithia, and charged in two lines across the open. Our field batteries played havoc with them, and the arrival of Gurkha supports dispersed the attack with heavy losses. Next day it was obvious that the enemy were receiving reinforcements, which some put as high as 10,000 men.

On the morning of 4th July, a general attack on our whole position was undertaken. About 3 a.m. all the Allied front and hinterland was bombarded, a Turkish battleship moored between Maidos and Chanak assaulted the Australian lines at Gaba Tepe, and aeroplanes made an attempt to drop bombs at several points in our trenches. The cannonade did little harm, and died away about 6 a.m. The infantry attack came at 7.30, and was directed chiefly against our right centre, where the British Naval Division joined with the French. At the start the Turks gained a footing in our first trenches, but we drove them out by a counterattack. Their advance on the right of the 29th Division was checked by our rifles and machine-gun fire, and that against our extreme left fared no better. Before noon the action had died away.

From the French report it would appear that the affair was no better than a costly fiasco:—

> Notwithstanding an ostentatious display of all sorts of reserves, of which the Turks had never yet given us an exhibition, their

infantry attacks were lifeless, spasmodic, and ineffective. In front of the French left, and at very many points in front of the British line, the Ottoman infantry left their trenches and advanced, but nowhere with the valour and the ardour which they had manifested in previous engagements. The Allies awaited their assailants calmly, allowed them to approach, and then almost at point-blank range opened a murderous fire from rifles and machine-guns. Very few survivors indeed were fortunate enough to return to their lines; the majority remained on the ground in front of our trenches. The hesitating attempts of the Turks had never for a single moment threatened any of our positions, and had resulted only in hecatombs in their ranks. Our losses were slight.

On 12th July the Allies made a resolute attempt to advance their front and take the Krithia position. The first attack was made by the Allied right and right centre, the French Corps, and the Scottish Lowland Division. Our bombardment began at dawn, and thereafter our infantry carried the first two lines of Turkish trenches. The Scots Territorials reached a third line; but they could not hold it, for they lost touch with the French on their right. The bombardment continued all day, and at 4 p.m. a special cannonade was delivered on the enemy positions in the upper ravines of the Kereves Dere, where they run into the face of Achi Baba.

On the right, overlooking a ravine, the Turks had a great rectangular redoubt, bristling with machine-guns. At five our guns lengthened and attacked the ground where the Turkish reserves might be looked for, while a warship bombarded the observation station on the top of Achi Baba with 12-inch shells. Then the Scots surged forward against the redoubt. An observer wrote:—

> The ground resembled a gigantic steaming cauldron, into whose thick vapours the gallant brigade poured without once hesitating or looking back.

The redoubt, owing to the preliminary bombardment, was carried easily with the bayonet. The second line was taken, after some confused fighting, and by nightfall 400 yards of ground had been gained.

The night was thick with counterattacks. The Turks came on repeatedly with bombs, and the British right centre, which had advanced too far, was forced to evacuate two lines of trenches. At dawn the two wearied Scots brigades were withdrawn, and their place taken by the Naval Division. All day our artillery fire played on the battered trenches, and at 4.30 in the afternoon, our right centre succeeded in retaking the two trenches lost on the previous night.

There we stuck fast; but our left, which now came into action, had an easier road, and advanced our front considerably. The French on the extreme right had strengthened the line by extending their positions to the mouth of the Kereves Dere. During the night of the 13th there were severe counterattacks, in the face of which the Allies succeeded in maintaining the ground they had won. It was a considerable advance, which brought us very near to Krithia. But the heights of Achi Baba were as far off as ever.

The rest of the month saw the inevitable Turkish counterattacks, and small local improvements of the Allied line. Both the British and French sections were raided on the 18th. On the 21st a small Turkish redoubt was captured. On the 23rd there was an attack on our left which was repulsed after a twenty minutes' struggle. On the 28th there was a slight advance by the French right. The day of concerted frontal attacks was over, and the mind of the High Command was busied with a new plan.

While we were battling against the outer walls of the Turkish fortifications, we did not neglect the duty of striking at the routes of supply. The work of our submarines in the Marmara continued, and there is no question but that we hampered and occasionally held up both munitions and reinforcements. At the same time the complete closing of the Marmara, even had we accomplished it, would not have cut Turkish communications, as was too readily assumed in some quarters at the time. A brief examination of Turkey's transport problem is necessary for a proper understanding of the situation.

Turkey had three possible passages to her Gallipoli position. She could send troops and supplies by sea all the way from Constantinople to the ports of Maidos and Gallipoli. She could send them by rail through Thrace to Uzun Keupru, whence a fair military road would carry them to the peninsula by way of Bulair. For troops the distance from railhead was perhaps forty-eight hours' march; for heavy transport, by means of oxen and buffalo carts, it would mean a journey of some five days. At Bulair, it is true, the road was open to our naval guns; but in dry weather the wagons could leave the path and find a more sheltered cross-country route.

Finally, troops and supplies could travel by the Anatolian and Ottoman railways *via* Smyrna and Soma to the port of Panderma, in the southwestern half of the Marmara. Most of the reinforcements came from Syria and Anatolia; and they naturally used the Panderma line, embarking at that port for the short sea journey to Gallipoli in the Bosphorus passenger steamers which were used as transports. Heavy material, such as shells and guns, either used the through sea route from Constantinople or were railed down to Smyrna and back to Panderma.

Our submarines made the Marmara road nearly impossible. They also interfered gravely with the short sea voyage from Panderma to the peninsula. Turkey was accordingly flung back more and more upon her land routes—by rail to Uzun Keupru and thence to Bulair, and by rail to Panderma and thence by road to the port of Lapsaki, on the Dardanelles, opposite Galata. This was a real inconvenience, but it was by no means an insuperable difficulty. Since most of the fresh troops came from Asia, Panderma was the natural point of arrival, and the farther road to Lapsaki was easy. Nor was the route so bad for shells and heavy material which came from Constantinople, for a good railway system took them to Smyrna, and the railway journey from Smyrna to Panderma occupied no more than nine hours, while there was the Uzun Keupru-Bulair road as an alternative. Our submarine warfare, brilliant as it was, hampered and delayed, but it did not cut, or perhaps seriously cripple, the communications of the Turkish fortress.

How audacious and devoted the warfare was may be gathered from the exploit of Lieutenant Guy D'Oyly-Hughes, R.N., who on 21st August made a single-handed attempt to cut the first section of the Anatolian railway which runs along the northern shore of the Gulf of Ismed, at the eastern end of the Marmara. He swam ashore from a submarine, pushing a raft carrying his clothes and explosives. Finding the cliffs unclimbable, he had to prospect along the coast till he found a point which could be scaled. He then moved towards the railway line, but discovered that it was strongly guarded. At first his idea was to destroy the viaduct; but finding this impossible, he resolved to blow up a low brickwork support over a small hollow. The sound of the fuse pistol brought up the guards, and Lieutenant D'Oyly-Hughes had to retire, fighting a running fight for about a mile. From this point we may quote the official account

> He plunged into the water about three-quarters of a mile to the eastward of the small bay in which the boat was lying. The charge exploded as he entered the water, fragments falling into the sea near the boat, although the distance between the boat

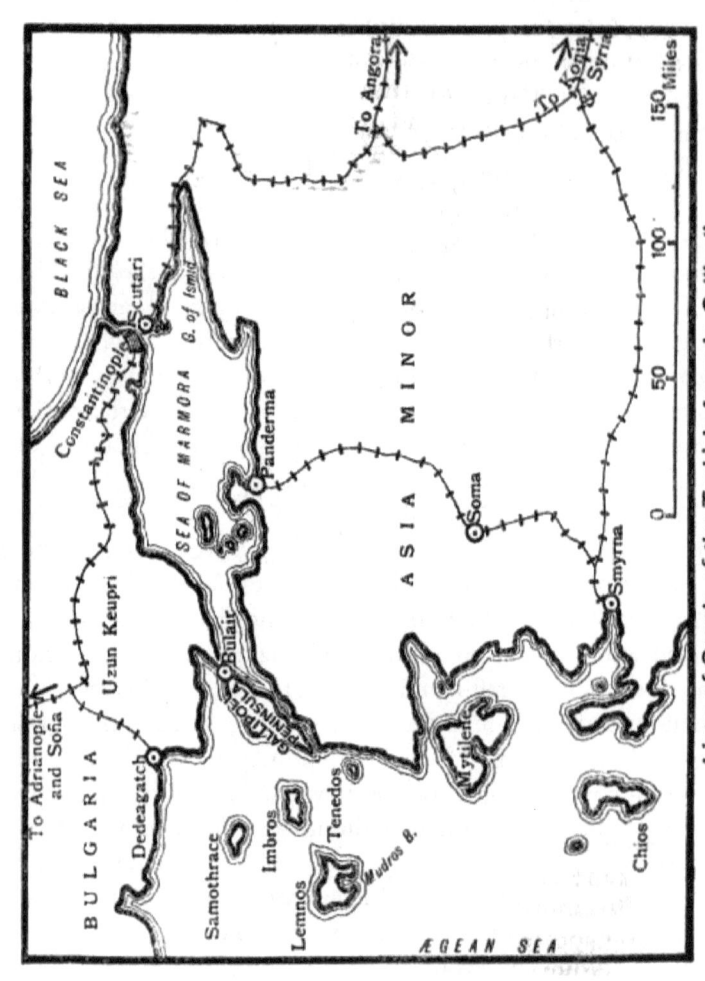

Lines of Supply of the Turkish Army in Gallipoli.

and the charge was between a quarter and half a mile. After swimming for four or five hundred yards straight out to sea, he blew a long blast on his whistle; but the boat, being in a small bay behind the cliffs, did not hear it.

Day was breaking very rapidly, so after swimming back to the shore, and resting for a short time on the rocks, he commenced swimming towards the bay in which the boat was lying. At this point he discarded his pistol, bayonet, and electric torch, their weight making his progress very slow. It was not until he had rounded the last point that the whistle was heard, and at the same time he heard shots from the cliffs overhead, and rifle fire was opened on the boat.

As the boat came astern out of the bay the early morning mist made her appear to him to be three rowing boats—the bow, the gun, and the conning tower being the three objects actually seen. He swam ashore, and tried to hide under the cliffs; but on climbing a few feet out of the water he realised his mistake, and shouted again before entering the water. We picked him up in an extremely exhausted condition about forty yards from the rocks, after he had swum the best part of a mile in his clothes. (Lieutenant D'Oyly-Hughes received the Distinguished Service Order.)

The work of the navy was not confined to below the water. In Sir Ian Hamilton's phrase, the fleet was father and mother to the army on land. The appearance of German submarines in the middle of May compelled us to keep our large transports at Mudros. From Lemnos to the peninsula was forty miles, and all troops and stores had to be brought in fleet sweepers, trawlers, drifters, and other small craft which were least vulnerable to submarine attack. Apart from the good work done by the naval guns in the land battle, the mere transport services of the ships could not be overstated. Take the work of the picket boats, the steam pinnaces which towed the laden lighters to the beaches. Their crews were often at work for sixteen hours out of the twenty-four, and were constantly under fire. Mr. Ashmead-Bartlett has drawn an interesting picture of this strenuous and well-ordered activity:—

> The line of demarcation between the authority of the army and of the navy is strictly drawn. As long as a soldier, a horse, a gun, or a biscuit is in a ship or in a lighter on its way to the shore, all are under the control of our beach parties. Standing on one

of the piers in the sweltering heat of the last few days, with the beach behind him crammed with men, stores, and animals, a young officer, with a megaphone in his hand, shouts orders to a dozen different lighters, each towed by a steam pinnace, in the offing. One contains mules, another guns, a third biscuits, a fourth tinned meat, a fifth ammunition, a sixth troops, a seventh generals and staff officers.

Everyone is directed to its right destination as if by some enchanter's wand, and no one dares to step ashore until he has received his orders. At the end of the pier the naval authority ceases and that of the army begins. Here are Army Service Corps officers, who are waiting to seize what the navy has brought them. The thousand miscellaneous articles, which look as if they never could be sorted out, are speedily divided, checked, and sent on their way down the lines of communication to the troops in the front trenches. The whole is a marvel of organisation.

The Allied airmen, who fulfilled the duties of long-range artillery. Turkish camps far back on the peninsula, or on the southern shore of the Marmara, were bombarded from the heavens. The Narrows and both sides of the Straits were always under their surveillance. They regulated the range of our guns, and they detected the movements of the enemy's transports and battleships.

The discomforts of the life in the peninsula grew as the summer advanced and the heat waxed greater. The whole of our position was honeycombed with trenches and dug-outs like a colony of sand-martins in the bank of a river. There was no shade from nature, for the copses were only scrub. The sun beat down pitilessly on the acres of rock and gravel, and was reflected from the blue waters around. Our men were very close together, and the whole earth soon became tainted in spite of all our care. Sunstroke cases were few, for the sun of Gallipoli is not the sun of India; but fevers and dysentery began to take their toll.

The scarcity of water, the difficult journeys for the sick down communication trenches and cliff roads, and the long voyage before hospital was reached, intensified our discomfort. And everywhere fell a plague of flies. Men who had fought in South Africa remembered the curse of the fly on the veld, but the South African scourge was feeble compared to the clouds which hung over the baked peninsula.

Remember there was no movement or chance of movement. The troops had to sit still in their stifling trenches, and every acre of that butt-end of Gallipoli was searched by the enemy's fire.

Under such conditions—no movement, grave losses, grave discomforts—it was a marvel that we maintained so high a spirit and so steady a cheerfulness. Men returned to the habits of their first parents. Khaki "shorts," a shirt, and a sun-helmet formed the only wear of even exalted generals. The Australians and New Zealanders especially, perched in their eyrie at Gaba Tepe, showed a noble disregard of apparel. These troops, embracing in their ranks every class and condition, had shown themselves superb fighting men. There was a perpetual competition for the posts of danger, and money was offered freely for the right to a place in some hot corner. Their easy discipline knew none of the usual military conventions; but it was real enough, and got through the work required. There were endless tales of their keenness:—

> The other day a group of four millionaires were working at a mine-shaft. The task was not done when another regiment came to relieve the one to which they belonged. These four men refused to go with their battalion till they had finished the job, as they wished it to be known as their job and no one else's.

They probably represented the finest average of physique in any of the belligerent armies—those lean, great-limbed men, without an ounce of soft flesh on their bodies. In the midsummer heats they were burned to a dull brick-red, for they fought almost naked. Coats, shirts, boots, and *putties* disappeared in succession, their trousers shrank into "shorts," as they toiled in the dust of the trenches till the hour of relief came, and they could wash in the shrapnel-dotted Aegean.

Humour never fails the British soldier. He showed it in the fantastic names he gave to the various points within his survey, and in the noticeboards in the trenches, like that which read:—

> Casualty Corner. Do not pass this Board, but if you have to, for God's sake hustle.

There were trench newspapers, which contained as much authentic news as the journals at home. And in those days of heart-searching they found out the officers who were leaders of men, and gave them their undivided trust. General Birdwood, of the Anzac Corps, to take one conspicuous case, was a commander after the heart of his soldiers.

The three summer months had been among the most costly in our

New Zealanders on the March

military history. Out of some six British divisions we had lost by the end of May over 38,000. By the end of June, the total was over 42,000; by the end of July it was nearly 50,000, of whom 8,000 were killed, 30,000 wounded, and 11,000 missing. The French losses were on a similar scale, and the naval losses must be added to the total casualties of the expedition. All our divisions had suffered, and, to the people of the Scottish Lowlands especially, the word Dardanelles came to bear the fateful meaning which Flodden bore for their ancestors. The results gained were not proportionate to this huge wastage.

★★★★★★

In addition to the instances mentioned in the text, the Victoria Cross was conferred on Captain Gerald O'Sullivan, of the 1st Inniskilling Fusiliers, for his gallantry in retaking lost trenches on the nights of 18th June and 1st July; on Second-Lieutenant Herbert James, of the 4th Worcesters, for rallying an attack on 28th June, and for holding a trench with bombs single-handed on 3rd July; and to Sergeant James Somers, of the 1st Inniskilling Fusiliers, for a similar performance on the night of 1st July.

★★★★★★

No kind of warfare involves a sterner trial for the human spirit than the slow sapping towards a fortress, when there is no obvious advance, no chance of the swift excitement of a manoeuvre battle. We may take the 29th Division as a type of the others. Sir Ian Hamilton's words of praise, addressed to it after the battle of 28th June, were applicable to the whole British Army:—

> The general officer commanding feels sure that he voices the sentiments of every soldier serving with this army when he congratulates the incomparable 29th Division upon yesterday's splendid attack, carried out, as it was, in a manner more than upholding the best traditions of the distinguished regiments of which it is composed.
> The 29th suffered cruel losses at the first landing. Since then they have never been made up to strength, and they have remained under fire every hour of the night and day for two months on end. Opposed to them were fresh troops, holding line upon line of entrenchments, flanked by redoubts and machine-guns.
> But when, yesterday, the 29th Division were called upon to advance, they dashed forward as eagerly as if this were only

their baptism of fire. Through the entanglements they swept northwards, clearing our left of the enemy for a full thousand yards. Heavily counterattacked at night, they killed or captured every Turk who had penetrated their incomplete defences, and today stand possessed of every yard they had so hardly gained. Therefore it is that Sir Ian Hamilton is confident he carries with him all ranks of his force when he congratulates Generals Hunter-Weston and De Lisle, the Staff, and each officer, N.C.O., and man in this division, whose sustained efforts have added fresh lustre to British arms all the world over.

By the end of July, the complete stalemate had compelled the High Command to revise its strategy. A certain daring Englishman, who knew Turkey well, contrived to be taken blindfold one night into the enemy's trenches, and for several hours talked to the Turkish officers. He was told on parting:—

Someday you may take Constantinople, but Achi Baba—never.

This was rapidly becoming the view of those responsible for the expedition. Large reinforcements had been asked for, and during July were arriving at Egypt and Lemnos. To fling these into the congested butt of the peninsula was clearly folly. A new strategical plan was being devised, which should utilize them against a fresh objective. As we shall see later, the peninsula still dominated the minds of those responsible for our policy. That is the worst of a false step. It is hard to retrace, and, though the road may be shifted a point or two, it still tends to bear in the same direction.

Appendix to Chapter 8

The Campaign in Gallipoli

Sir Ian Hamilton's Second Dispatch.
From the General Commanding, Mediterranean Expeditionary Force,
To the Secretary of State for War, War Office, London, S.W.

General Headquarters,
Mediterranean Expeditionary Force,
26th August, 1915.

My Lord,

At the close of the ten days and ten nights described in my first dispatch our troops had forced their way forward for some 5,000 yards from the landing places at the point of the peninsula. Opposite them lay the Turks, who since their last repulse had fallen back about half a mile upon previously prepared redoubts and entrenchments. Both sides had drawn heavily upon their stock of energy and munitions, but it seemed clear that whichever could first summon up spirit to make another push must secure at least several hundreds of yards of the debatable ground between the two fronts.

And several hundred yards, whatever it might mean to the enemy, was a matter of life or death to a force crowded together under gun fire on so narrow a tongue of land. Such was the situation on the 5th of May, the date last mentioned in my dispatch of the 20th of that month.

On that day I determined to continue my advance, feeling certain that even if my tired troops could not carry the formidable opposing lines, they would at least secure the use of the intervening ground. Orders were forthwith issued for an attack.

Dispositions on 5th May.

The many urgent calls for reinforcements made during the previous critical fighting had forced me to disorganise and mix together several of the formations in the southern group, to the extent even of the French on our right having a British battalion holding their own extremest right. For the purposes of the impending fight it became therefore necessary to create temporarily a Composite Division, consisting of the 2nd Australian and New Zealand Infantry Brigades (withdrawn for the purpose from the northern section), together with a Naval Brigade formed of the Plymouth and Drake Battalions. The 29th Division was reconstituted into four brigades—*i.e.*, the 88th and 87th Brigades, the Lancashire Fusilier Brigade (T.F.), and the 29th Indian Infantry Brigade. The French Corps Expéditionnaire was reinforced by the 2nd Naval Brigade, and the new Composite Division formed my General Reserve.

The 29th Division, whose left rested on the coast about three miles north-east of Cape Tekke, was ordered to direct, its right moving on the south-east edge of Krithia, while the Corps Expéditionnaire with the 2nd Naval Brigade had assigned to them for their first point of attack the commanding ridge running from north to south above the Kereves Dere. A foothold upon this ridge was essential, as its capture would ensure a safe pivot on which the 29th Division could swing in making any further advance. Communication between these two sections of the attack was to be maintained by the Plymouth and Drake battalions.

The Attack Begins.

During the three days (6th-8th May) our troops were destined to be very severely tried. They were about to attack a series of positions scientifically selected in advance which although not yet joined up into one line of entrenchment, were already strengthened by works on their more important tactical features.

The 29th Division led off at 11 a.m., the French Corps followed suit at 11.30 a.m. Every yard was stubbornly contested; some brigades were able to advance, others could do no more than maintain themselves. Positions were carried and held, other positions were carried and lost; but, broadly, our gunners kept lengthening the fuses of their shrapnel, and by 1.30 p.m. the line had been pushed forward two to three hundred yards. Here and there this advance included a Turkish trench, but generally speaking the main enemy position still lay some distance ahead of our leading companies.

By 4.30 p.m. it became clear that we should make no more progress that day. The French Corps were held up by a strong field work. They had made good a point upon the crest line of the lower slope of the Kereves Dere ridge, but there they had come under a fire so galling that they were unable, as it turned out, to entrench until nightfall. The 88th Brigade could not carry a clump of fir trees to their front: company after company made the perilous essay, but the wood, swept by hidden machine-guns, proved a veritable death-trap. The Lancashire Fusiliers Brigade also were only just barely holding on, and were suffering heavy losses from those same concealed machine-guns. The troops were ordered to entrench themselves in line and link up their flanks on either side.

At night, save for rifle fire, there was quiet along the whole British line. On the right a determined bayonet charge was made upon the French, who gave ground for the moment, but recovered it again.

The Movement on the Left.

Next morning (the 7th May) we opened with shrapnel upon the enemy's trenches opposite our extreme left, and at 10 a.m. the Lancashire Fusiliers Brigade began the attack. But our artillery had not been able to locate the cleverly sited German machine-gun batteries, whose fire rendered it physically impossible to cross that smooth glacis. Next to the right the 88th Brigade swept forward, and the 1/5th Royal Scots, well supported by artillery fire, carried the fir trees with a rush. This time it was discovered that not only the enfilading machine-guns had made the wood so difficult to hold.

Amongst the branches of the trees Turkish snipers were perched, sometimes upon small wooden platforms. When these were brought down the surroundings became much healthier. The Royal Inniskilling Fusiliers, of the 87th Brigade, were pushed up to support the left of the 88th, and all seemed well, when, at 1.20 p.m., a strong Turkish counterattack drove us back out of the fir clump. As an offset to this check the Royal Inniskilling Fusiliers captured three Turkish trenches, and a second battalion of the 87th Brigade, the King's Own Scottish Borderers, was sent forward on the left to make these good.

At 3 p.m. the Lancashire Fusiliers Brigade again reported they were definitely held up by the accurate cross-fire of batteries of machine-guns concealed in the scrub on the ridge between the ravine and the sea—batteries which also enfiladed the left flank of the 88th Brigade as it endeavoured to advance in the centre. Unless we were to acquiesce in a stalemate the moment for our effort had arrived, and a general attack was ordered for 4.45 p.m., the whole of the 87th Brigade to reinforce the 88th Brigade, and the New Zealand Brigade to support it.

The General Attack.

Despite their exhaustion and their losses, the men responded with a will. The whole force, French and British, rose simultaneously and made a rush forward. All along the front we made good a certain amount of ground, excepting only on our extreme left. For the third time British bayonets carried the fir clump in our centre, and when darkness fell the whole line (excepting always the left) had gained from 200 to 300 yards, and had occupied or passed over the first line of Turkish trenches.

The troops were now worn out; the new lines needed consolidating, and it was certain that fresh reinforcements were reaching the Turks. Balancing the actual state of my own troops against the probable condition of the Turks, I decided to call upon the men to make one more push before the new enemy forces could get into touch with their surroundings.

Orders were therefore issued to dig in at sundown on the line gained, to maintain that line against counterattack, and to prepare to advance again next morning. The Lancashire Fusiliers Brigade was withdrawn into reserve, and its place on the left was taken by the brigade of New Zealanders.

General Headquarters were shifted to an entrenchment on a hill in rear of the left of our line. Under my plan for the fresh attack the New Zealand Brigade was to advance through the line held during the night by the 88th Brigade and press on towards Krithia. Simultaneously, the 87th Brigade was to threaten the works on the west of the ravine, whilst endeavouring, by means of parties of scouts and volunteers, to steal patches of ground from the areas dominated by the German machine-guns.

The Battle of 8th May.

At 10.15 a.m. heavy fire from ships and batteries was opened on the whole front, and at 10.30 a.m. the New Zealand Brigade began to move, meeting with strenuous opposition from the enemy, who had received his reinforcements. Supported by the fire of the batteries and the machine-guns of the 88th Brigade, they pushed forward on the right and advanced their centre beyond the fir trees, but could make little further progress. By 1.30 p.m. about 200 yards had been gained beyond the previously most advanced trenches of the 88th Brigade.

At this hour the French Corps reported they could not advance up the crest of the spur west of Kereves Dere till further progress was made by the British.

At 4 p.m. I gave orders that the whole line, reinforced by the 2nd Australian Brigade, would fix bayonets, slope arms, and move on Krithia precisely at 5.30 p.m.

At 5.15 p.m. the ships' guns and our heavy artillery bombarded the enemy's position for a quarter of an hour, and at 5.30 p.m. the field guns opened a hot shrapnel fire to cover the infantry advance.

The co-operation of artillery and infantry in this attack was perfect, the timing of the movement being carried out with great precision. Some of the companies of the New Zealand regiments did not get their orders in time, but acting on their own initiative they pushed on as soon as the heavy howitzers ceased firing, thus making the whole advance simultaneous.

Steady British Advance.

The steady advance of the British could be followed by the sparkle of their bayonets until the long lines entered the smoke clouds. The French at first made no move, then, their drums beating and bugles sounding the charge, they suddenly darted forward in a swarm of skirmishers, which seemed in one moment to cover the whole southern face of the ridge of the Kereves Dere. Against these the Turkish gunners now turned their heaviest pieces, and as the leading groups stormed the first Turkish redoubt the ink-black bursts of high explosive shells blotted out both assailants and assailed.

The trial was too severe for the Senegalese *tirailleurs*. They recoiled. They were rallied. Another rush forward, another repulse, and then a small supporting column of French soldiers was seen silhouetted against the sky as they charged upwards along the crest of the ridge of the Kereves Dere, whilst elsewhere it grew so dark that the whole of the battlefield became a blank.

Not until next morning did any reliable detail come to hand of what had happened. The New Zealanders' firing line had marched over the cunningly concealed enemy's machine-guns without seeing them, and these, reopening on our supports as they came up, caused them heavy losses. But the first line pressed on and arrived within a few yards of the Turkish trenches which had been holding up our advances beyond the fir wood. There they dug themselves in.

The Australian Brigade had advanced through the Composite Brigade, and, in spite of heavy losses from shrapnel, machine-gun, and rifle fire, had progressed from 300 to 400 yards.

The determined valour shown by these two brigades, the New Zealand Brigade, under Brigadier-General F. E. Johnston, and the 2nd Australian Infantry Brigade, under Brigadier-General the Hon. J. W. McCay, is worthy of particular praise. Their losses were correspondingly heavy, but in spite of fierce counterattacks by numerous fresh troops they stuck to what they had won with admirable tenacity.

On the extreme left the 87th Brigade, under Major-General W. R. Marshall, made a final and especially gallant effort to advance across the smooth, bullet-swept area between the ravine and the sea; but once more the enemy machine-guns thinned the ranks of the leading companies of the South Wales Borderers, and again there was nothing for it but to give ground. But when night closed in the men of the 87th Brigade of their own accord asked to be led forward, and achieved progress to the extent of just about 200 yards. During the darkness the British troops everywhere entrenched themselves on the line gained.

On the right the French column, last seen as it grew dark, had stormed and still held the redoubt round which the fighting had centred until then. Both General d'Amade and General Simonin had been present in person with this detachment, and had rallied the Senegalese and encouraged the white troops in their exploit. With their bayonets these brave fellows of the 8th Colonials had inflicted exceedingly heavy losses upon the enemy.

The French troops whose actions have hitherto been followed belonged, all of them, to the 2nd Division. But beyond the crest of the ridge the valley of the Kereves Dere lies dead to any one occupying my post of command. And in this area the newly-arrived Brigade of the French 1st Division had been also fighting hard. Here they had advanced simultaneously with the 2nd Division and achieved a fine success in their first rush, which was jeopardised when a battalion of Zouaves was forced to give way under a heavy bombardment. But, as in the case of the 2nd Division, the other battalions of the 1st Regiment de Marche d'Afrique, under Lieutenant-Colonel Nieger, restored the situation, and in the end the division carried and held two complete lines of Turkish redoubts and trenches.

The Result of the Three Days' Battle.

The net result of the three days' fighting has been a gain of 600 yards on the right of the British line and 400 yards on the left and centre. The French had captured all the ground in front of the Farm Zjimmerman, as well as a redoubt, for the possession of which there had been obstinate fighting during the whole of the past three days.

This may not seem very much, but actually more had been won than at first meets the eye. The German leaders of the Turks were quick to realise the fact. From nightfall till dawn on the 9th-10th efforts were made everywhere to push us back. A specially heavy attack was made upon the French, supported by a hot cannonade and culminating in a violent hand-to-hand conflict in front of the Brigade Simonin. Everywhere the assailants were repulsed, and now for the first time I felt that we had planted a fairly firm foothold upon the point of the Gallipoli Peninsula.

Meanwhile in the Northern Zone also the Australian and New Zealand Army Corps had strengthened their grip on Turkish soil. Whilst in the south we had been attacking and advancing, they had been defending and digging themselves more and more firmly into those cliffs on which it had seemed at first that their foothold was so precarious.

On the 11th May, the first time for eighteen days and nights, it was found possible to withdraw the 29th Division from the actual firing line and to replace it by the 29th Indian Infantry Brigade and by the 42nd Division, which had completed its disembarkation two days previously. The withdrawal gave no respite from shells, but at least the men were, most nights, enabled to sleep.

The Beginning of Siege Warfare.

The moment lent itself to reflection, and during this breathing space I was able to realise we had now nearly reached the limit of what could be attained by mingling initiative with surprise. The enemy was as much in possession of my numbers and dispositions as I was in possession of their first line of defence; the opposing fortified fronts stretched parallel from sea to straits; there was little scope left now, either at Achi Baba or at Kaba Tepe, for tactics which would fling flesh-and-blood battalions against lines of unbroken barbed wire. Advances must more and more tend to take the shape of concentrated attacks on small sections of the enemy's line after full artillery preparation. Siege warfare was soon bound to supersede manoeuvre battles in the open. Consolidation and fortification of our front, improvement of approaches, selection of machine-gun emplacements and scientific grouping of our artillery under a centralized control must ere long form the tactical basis of our plans.

So soon, then, as the troops had enjoyed a day or two of comparative rest, I divided my front into four sections. On the left was the 29th Division, to which the 29th Indian Infantry Brigade was attached. In the left centre came the 42nd (East Lancashire) Division, on the right centre stood the Royal Naval Division, and at my right was the Corps Expéditionnaire. Thus, I secured organisation in depth as well as front, enabling each division to arrange for its own reliefs, supports, and reserves, and giving strength for defence as well as attack. Hitherto the piecemeal arrival of reinforcements had forced a hand-to-mouth procedure upon headquarters; now the control became more decentralised.

A Gurkha Performance.

Already, before the new system of local efforts had come into working order, the 29th Indian Brigade had led the way towards it by a brilliant little affair on the night of the 10th-11th May. The Turkish right rested upon the steep cliff north-east of "Y" beach, where the King's Own Scottish Borderers and the Plymouth Battalion, Royal Naval Division, had made their first landing. Since those days the enemy had converted the bluff into a powerful bastion, from which the fire of machine-guns had held up the left of our attacks. Two gallant attempts by the Royal Munster Fusiliers and the Royal Dublin Fusiliers to establish a footing on this cliff on the 8th and 9th May had both of them failed.

During the night of the 10th-11th May the 6th Gurkhas started off to seize this bluff. Their scouts descended to the sea, worked their way for some distance through the broken ground along the shore, and crawled hands and knees up the precipitous face of the cliff. On reaching the top they were heavily fired on. As a surprise the enterprise had failed, but as a reconnaissance it proved very useful. On the following day Major-General H. B. Cox, commanding 29th Indian Infantry Brigade, submitted proposals for a concerted attack on this bluff (now called Gurkha Bluff), and arrangements were made with the navy for co-operation.

These arrangements were completed on 12th May; they included a demonstration by the Manchester Brigade of the 42nd Division, and by our artillery and the support of the attack from the sea by the guns of H.M.S. *Dublin* and H.M.S. *Talbot*. At 6.30 p.m. on the 12th May the Manchester Brigade and the 29th Divisional artillery opened fire on the Turkish trenches, and under cover of this fire a double company of the 1/6th Gurkhas once more crept along the shore and assembled below the bluff. Then, the attention of the Turks being taken up with the bombardment, they swiftly scaled the cliffs and carried the work with a rush. The machine-gun section of the Gurkhas was hurried forward, and at 4.30 a.m. a second double company was pushed up to join the first.

An hour later these two double companies extended and began to entrench to join up their new advanced left diagonally with the right of the trenches previously held by their battalion.

At 6 a.m. a third double company advanced across the open from their former front line of trenches under a heavy rifle and machine-gun fire, and established themselves on this diagonal line between the main ravine on their right and the newly captured redoubt. The 4th double company moved up as a support, and held the former firing line.

Our left flank, which had been firmly held up against all attempts on the 6th-8th, was now, by stratagem, advanced nearly 500 yards. Purchased as it was with comparatively slight losses (21 killed, 92 wounded), this success was due to careful preparation and organisation by Major-General H.V. Cox, commanding 29th Indian Infantry Brigade, Lieutenant-Colonel Hon. C. G. Bruce, commanding 1/6th Gurkhas, and Major (temporary Lieutenant-Colonel) F. A. Wynter, R.G.A., commanding the Artillery Group supporting the attack. The co-operation of the two cruisers was excellent, and affords another instance of the admirable support by the navy to our troops.

Arrival of General Gouraud.

On May 14th General Gouraud arrived and took over from General d'Amade the command of the Corps Expéditionnaire. As General d'Amade quitted the shores of the peninsula he received a spontaneous ovation from the British soldiers at work upon the beaches.

The second division of the Corps Expéditionnaire, commanded by General Bailloud, had now completed disembarkation.

From the time of the small local push forward made by the 6th Gurkhas on the night of the 10th-11th May until the 4th of June the troops under my command pressed against the enemy continuously by sapping, reconnaissance, and local advances; whilst, to do them justice, they (the enemy) did what they could to repay us in like coin. I have given the escalade of Gurkha Bluff as a sample; no forty-eight hours passed without something of the sort being attempted or achieved either by the French or ourselves.

The Anzac Corps.

Turning now to where the Australian and New Zealand Army Corps were perched upon the cliffs of Sari Bair, I must begin by explaining that their role at this stage of the operations was—first, to keep open a door leading to the vitals of the Turkish position; secondly, to hold up as large a body as possible of the enemy in front of them, so as to lessen the strain at Cape Helles. Anzac, in fact, was cast to play second fiddle to Cape Helles—a part out of harmony with the daredevil spirit animating those warriors from the South; and so it has come about that, as Your Lordship will now see, the defensive of the Australians and New Zealanders has always tended to take on the character of an attack.

The line held during the period under review by the Australian and New Zealand Army Corps formed a rough semicircle inland from the beach of Anzac Cove, with a diameter of about 1,100 yards. The firing line is everywhere close to the enemy's trenches, and in all sections of the position sapping, counter-sapping, and bomb attacks have been incessant. The shelling both of the trenches and beaches has been impartial and liberal. As many as 1,400 shells have fallen on Anzac within the hour, and these of all calibres, from 11 inches to field shrapnel. Around Quinn's Post, both above and below ground, the contest has been particularly severe. This section of the line is situated on the circumference of the Anzac semicircle at the farthest point from its diameter. Here our fire trenches are mere ledges on the brink of a sheer precipice falling 200 feet into the valley below. The enemy's trenches are only a few feet distant.

On 9th May a night assault, supported by enfilade fire, was delivered on the enemy's trenches in front of Quinn's Post. The trenches were carried at the point of the bayonet, troops established in them, and reinforcements sent up.

At dawn on the 10th May a strong counterattack forced our troops to evacuate the trenches and fall back on Quinn's Post. In opposing this counterattack our guns did great execution, as we discovered later from a Turkish officer's diary that two Turkish regiments on this date lost 600 killed and 2,000 wounded.

On the night of 14th-15th May a sortie was made from Quinn's Post with the object of filling in Turkish trenches in which bomb-throwers were active. The sortie, which cost us some 70 casualties, was not successful.

On 14th May Lieutenant-General Sir W. B. Birdwood was slightly wounded, but I am glad to say he was not obliged to relinquish the command of his corps.

Death of General Bridges.

On 15th May, I deeply regret to say, Major-General W. T. Bridges, commanding the Australian Division, received a severe wound, which proved fatal a few days later. Sincere and single-minded in his devotion to Australia and to duty, his loss still stands out even amidst the hundreds of other brave officers who have gone.

On 18th May Anzac was subjected to a heavy bombardment from large-calibre guns and howitzers. At midnight of the 18th-19th the most violent rifle and machine-gun fire yet experienced broke out along the front. Slackening from 3 a.m. to 4 a.m. it then broke out again, and a heavy Turkish column assaulted the left of No. 2 section. This assault was beaten off with loss. Another attack was delivered before daylight on the centre of this section; it was repeated four times and repulsed each time with very serious losses to the enemy. Simultaneously a heavy attack was delivered on the north-east salient of No. 4 section, which was repulsed and followed up, but the pressing of the counterattack was prevented by shrapnel.

Attacks were also delivered on Quinn's Post, Courtney's Post, and along the front of our right section. At about 5 a.m. the battle was fairly joined, and a furious cannonade was begun by a large number of enemy guns, including 12-inch and 9.2-inch, and other artillery that had not till then opened. By 9.30 a.m. the Turks were pressing hard against the left of Courtney's and the right of Quinn's Post. At 10 a.m. this attack, unable to face fire from the right, swung round to the left, where it was severely handled by our guns and the machine-guns of our left section. By 11 a.m. the enemy, who were crowded together in the trenches beyond Quinn's Post, were giving way under their heavy losses.

According to prisoners' reports, 30,000 troops, including five fresh regiments, were used against us. General Liman von Sanders was himself in command.

The enemy's casualties were heavy, as may be judged from the fact that over 3,000 dead were lying in the open in view of our trenches. A large proportion of these losses was due to our artillery fire. Our casualties amounted to about 100 killed and 500 wounded, including nine officers wounded.

A Suspension of Arms.

The next four days were chiefly remarkable for the carrying through of the negotiations for the suspension of arms, which actually took place on 24th May. About 5 p.m. on 20th May white flags and Red Crescents began to appear all along the line. In No. 2 section a Turkish staff officer, two medical officers, and a company commander came out, and were met by Major-General H. B. Walker, commanding the Australian Division, half-way between the trenches. The staff officer explained that he was instructed to arrange a suspension of arms for the removal of dead and wounded. He had no written credentials, and he was informed that neither he nor the General Officer Commanding Australian Division had the power to arrange such a suspension of arms, but that at 8 p.m. an opportunity would be given of exchanging letters on the subject, and that meanwhile hostilities would recommence after 10 minutes' grace.

At this time some stretcher parties on both sides were collecting wounded, and the Turkish trenches opposite ours were packed with men standing shoulder to shoulder two deep. Matters were less regular in front of other sections, where men with white flags came out to collect wounded. Meanwhile it was observed that columns were on the march in the valley up which the Turks were accustomed to bring up their reinforcements.

On hearing the report of these movements. General Sir W. R. Birdwood, commanding Australian and New Zealand Army Corps, ordered his trenches to be manned against a possible attack. As the evening drew in the enemy's concentration continued, and everything pointed to their intention of making use of the last of the daylight to get their troops into position without being shelled by our artillery. A message was therefore sent across to say that no clearing of dead or wounded could be allowed during the night, and that any negotiations for such a purpose should be opened through the proper channel and initiated before noon on the following day.

Stretcher and other parties fell back, and immediately fire broke out. In front of our right section masses of men advanced behind lines of unarmed men holding up their hands. Firing became general all along the line, accompanied by a heavy bombardment of the whole position, so that evidently this attack must have been prearranged. Musketry and machine-gun fire continued without interruption till after dark, and from then up to about 4 a.m. next day.

Except for a half-hearted attack in front of Courtney's Post, no assault was made till 1.20 a.m., when the enemy left their trenches and advanced on Quinn's Post. Our guns drove the Turks back to their trenches, and beat back all other attempts to assault. By 4.30 a.m. on 21st May musketry fire had died down to normal dimensions.

As the Turks seemed anxious to bury their dead, and as human sentiment and medical science were both of one accord in favour of such a course, I sent Major-General W. P. Braithwaite, my Chief of the General Staff, on 22nd May, to assist Lieutenant-General Sir W. R. Birdwood, commanding the Army Corps, in coming to some suitable arrangements with the representatives sent by Essad Pasha. The negotiations resulted in a suspension of arms from 7.30 a.m. to 4.30 p.m. on 24th May. The procedure laid down for this suspension of arms was, I am glad to inform Your Lordship, correctly observed on both sides.

The burial of the dead was finished about 3 p.m. Some 3,000 Turkish dead were removed or buried in the area between the opposing lines. The whole of these were killed on or since the 18th of May. Many bodies of men killed earlier were also buried.

On the 25th May, with the assistance of two destroyers of the Royal Navy, a raid was carried out on Nibrunesi Point. A fresh telephone line was destroyed and an observing station demolished.

MAJOR QUINN KILLED.

On 28th May, at 9 p.m., a raid was made on a Turkish post overlooking the beach 1,200 yards north of Kaba Tepe, H.M.S. *Rattlesnake* co-operating. A party of 50 rifles rushed the post, killing or capturing the occupants. A similar raid was made against an enemy trench to the left of our line which cost the Turks 200 casualties, as was afterwards ascertained.

From 28th May till 5th June the fighting seemed to concentrate itself around Quinn's Post. Three enemy galleries had been detected there, and work on them stopped by counter-mines, which killed 20 Turks and injured 30. One gallery had, however, been overlooked, and at 3.30 a.m. on 29th May a mine was sprung in or near the centre of Quinn's Post. The explosion was followed by a very heavy bomb attack, before which our left centre subsection fell back, letting in a storming party of Turks. This isolated one subsection on the left from the two other subsections on the right.

At 5.30 a.m. our counterattack was launched, and by 6 a.m. the position had been retaken with the bayonet by the 15th Australian Infantry Battalion, led by Major Quinn, who was unfortunately killed. All the enemy in the trench were killed or captured, and the work of restoration was begun.

At 6.30 a.m. the Turks again attacked, supported by artillery, rifle, and machine-gun fire and by showers of bombs from the trenches. The fine shooting of our guns and the steadiness of the infantry enabled us to inflict upon the enemy a bloody repulse, demoralizing them to such an extent that the bomb-throwers of their second line flung the missiles into the middle of their own first line.

At 8.15 a.m. the attack slackened, and by 8.45 a.m. the enemy's attacks had practically ceased.

Our casualties in this affair amounted to 2 officers, 31 other ranks killed, 12 officers and 176 other ranks wounded. The enemy's losses must have been serious, and were probably equal to those sustained on 9th-10th May. Except for the first withdrawal in the confusion of the mine explosion, all ranks fought with the greatest tenacity and courage.

On 30th May preparations were made in Quinn's Post to attack and destroy two enemy saps, the heads of which had reached within 5 yards of our fire trench. Two storming parties of 35 men went forward at 1 p.m., cleared the sap heads and penetrated into the trenches beyond; but they were gradually driven back by Turkish counterattacks, in spite of our heavy supporting fire, our casualties being chiefly caused by bombs, of which the enemy seem to have an unlimited supply.

During 31st May close fighting continued in front of Quinn's Post.

On 1st June, an hour after dark, two sappers of the New Zealand Engineers courageously crept out and laid a charge of gun-cotton against a timber and sandbag bomb-proof. The structure was completely demolished.

The Anzac Movements.

After sunset on the 4th of June three separate enterprises were carried out by the Australian and New Zealand Army Corps. These were undertaken in compliance with an order which I had issued that the enemy's attention should be distracted during an attack I was about to deliver in the southern zone.

(1) A demonstration in the direction of Kaba Tepe, the navy co-operating by bombarding the Turkish trenches.

(2) A sortie at 11 p.m. towards a trench 200 yards from Quinn's Post. This failed, but a second sortie by 100 men took place at 2.55 a.m. on 5th June and penetrated to the Turkish trench, demolished a machine-gun emplacement which enfiladed Quinn's Post, and withdrew in good order.

(3) At Quinn's Post an assault was delivered at 11 p.m. A party of 60 men, accompanied by a bomb-throwing party on either flank, stormed the enemy's trench. In the assault many Turks were bayoneted and 28 captured. A working party followed up the attack and at once set to work. Meanwhile the Turkish trenches on the left of the post were heavily assailed with machine-gun fire and grenades, which drew from them a very heavy fire. After daybreak a strong bomb attack developed on the captured trench, the enemy using a heavier type of bomb than hitherto.

At 6.30 a.m. the trench had to be abandoned, and it was found necessary to retire to the original fire trench of the post and the bomb-proof in front of its left. Our casualties were 80; those of the enemy considerably greater.

On 5th June a sortie was made from Quinn's Post by 2 officers and 100 men of the 1st Australian Infantry, the objective being the destruction of a machine-gun in a trench known as German Officer's Trench. A special party of 10 men with the officer commanding the party (Lieutenant E. E. L. Lloyd, 1st Battalion (New South Wales) Australian Imperial Force) made a dash for the machine-gun; one of the 10 men managed to fire three rounds into the gun at a range of five feet and another three at the same range through a loophole. The darkness of the trench and its overhead cover prevented the use of the bayonet, but some damage was done by shooting down over the parapet.

As much of the trench as possible was dismantled. The party suffered some casualties from bombs, and was enfiladed all the time by machine-guns from either flank. The aim of this gallant assault being attained, the party withdrew in good order with their wounded. Casualties in all were 36.

The Battle of 4th June.

I now return to the Southern Zone and to the battle of the 4th of June.

From 25th May onwards the troops had been trying to work up within rushing distance of the enemy's front trenches. On the 25th May the Royal Naval and 42nd Divisions crept 100 yards nearer to the Turks, and on the night of 28th-29th May the whole of the British line made a further small advance. On that same night the French Corps Expéditionnaire was successful in capturing a small redoubt on the extreme Turkish left west of the Kereves Dere.

All Turkish counterattacks during 29th May were repulsed. On the night of 30th May two of their many assaults effected temporary lodgement. But on both occasions, they were driven out again with the bayonet.

On every subsequent night up to that of the 3rd-4th June assaults were made upon the redoubt and upon our line, but at the end of that period our position remained intact.

This brings the narrative up to the day of the general attack upon the enemy's front line of trenches which ran from the west of the Kereves Dere in a northerly direction to the sea.

Taking our line of battle from right to left, the troops were deployed in the following order:—The Corps Expéditionnaire, the Royal Naval Division, the 42nd (East Lancs) Division, and the 29th Division.

The length of the front, so far as the British troops were concerned, was rather over 4,000 yards, and the total infantry available amounted to 24,000 men, which permitted the General Officer Commanding 8th Army Corps to form a corps reserve of 7,000 men.

My General Headquarters for the day were at the command post on the peninsula.

At 8 a.m. on 4th June our heavy artillery opened with a deliberate bombardment, which continued till 10.30 a.m. At 11 a.m. the bombardment recommenced, and continued till 11.20 a.m., when a feint attack was made which successfully drew heavy fire from the enemy's guns and rifles. At 11.30 a.m. all our guns opened fire, and continued with increasing intensity till noon.

On the stroke of noon, the artillery increased their range, and along the whole line the infantry fixed bayonets and advanced.

The assault was immediately successful. On the extreme right the French 1st Division carried a line of trench, whilst the French 2nd Division, with the greatest dash and gallantry, captured a strong redoubt called the "Haricot," for which they had already had three desperate contests. Only the extreme left of the French was unable to gain any ground—a feature destined to have an unfortunate effect upon the final issue.

The 2nd Naval Brigade of the Royal Naval Division rushed forward with great dash; the *Anson* Battalion captured the southern face of a Turkish redoubt which formed a salient in the enemy's line, the *Howe* and *Hood* Battalions captured trenches fronting them, and by 12.15 p.m. the whole Turkish line forming their first objective was in their hands. Their consolidating party went forward at 12.25 p.m.

The Manchester Brigade of the 42nd Division advanced magnificently. In five minutes the first line of Turkish trenches was captured, and by 12.30 p.m. the brigade had carried with a rush the line forming their second objective, having made an advance of 600 yards in all. The working parties got to work without incident, and the position here could not possibly have been better.

On the left the 29th Division met with more difficulty. All along the section of the 88th Brigade the troops jumped out of their trenches at noon and charged across the open at the nearest Turkish trench. In most places the enemy crossed bayonets with our men and inflicted severe loss upon us. But the 88th Brigade was not to be denied. The Worcester Regiment was the first to capture trenches, and the remainder of the 88th Brigade, though at first held up by flanking as well as fronting fire, also pushed on doggedly until they had fairly made good the whole of the Turkish first line.

The Check on the Left.

Only on the extreme left did we sustain a check. Here the Turkish front trench was so sited as to have escaped damage from our artillery bombardment, and the barbed wire obstacle was intact. The result was that, though the 14th Sikhs on the right flank pushed on despite losses amounting to three-fourths of their effectives, the centre of the Brigade could make no headway. A company of the 6th Gurkhas on the left, skilfully led along the cliffs by its commander, actually forced its way into a Turkish work; but the failure of the rest of the Brigade threatened isolation, and it was as skilfully withdrawn under fire. Reinforcements were therefore sent to the left, so that, if possible, a fresh attack might be organised.

Meanwhile, on the right of the line, the gains of the morning were being compromised. A very heavy counterattack had developed against the "Haricot." The Turks poured in masses of men through prepared communication trenches, and, under cover of accurate shell fire, were able to recapture that redoubt. The French, forced to fall back, uncovered in doing so the right flank of the Royal Naval Division. Shortly before 1 p.m. the right of the 2nd Naval Brigade had to retire with very heavy loss from the redoubt they had captured, thus exposing in their turn the *Howe* and *Hood* Battalions to enfilade, so that they, too, had nothing for it but to retreat across the open under exceedingly heavy machine-gun and musketry fire.

By 1.30 p.m. the whole of the captured trenches in this section had been lost again, and the brigade was back in its original position—the *Collingwood* Battalion, which had gone forward in support, having been practically destroyed.

The question was now whether this rolling up of the newly captured line from the right would continue until the whole of our gains were wiped out. It looked very like it, for now the enfilade fire of the Turks began to fall upon the Manchester Brigade of the 42nd Division, which was firmly consolidating the furthest distant line of trenches it had so brilliantly won. After 1.30 p.m. it became increasingly difficult for this gallant brigade to hold its ground. Heavy casualties occurred; the brigadier and many other officers were wounded or killed; yet it continued to hold out with the greatest tenacity and grit.

Every effort was made to sustain the brigade in its position. Its right flank was thrown back to make face against the enfilade fire, and reinforcements were sent to try to fill the diagonal gap between it and the Royal Naval Division. But ere long it became clear that unless the right of our line could advance again it would be impossible for the Manchesters to maintain the very pronounced salient in which they now found themselves.

The Final Attack.

Orders were issued, therefore, that the Royal Naval Division should co-operate with the French Corps in a fresh attack, and reinforcements were dispatched to this end. The attack, timed for 3 p.m., was twice postponed at the request of General Gouraud, who finally reported that he would be unable to advance again that day with any prospect of success. By 6.30 p.m., therefore, the 42nd Division had to be extricated with loss from the second line Turkish trenches, and had to content themselves with consolidating on the first line, which they had captured within five minutes of commencing the attack. Such was the spirit displayed by this brigade that there was great difficulty in persuading the men to fall back. Had their flanks been covered nothing would have made them loosen their grip.

No further progress had been found possible in front of the 88th Brigade and Indian Brigade. Attempts were made by their reserve battalions to advance on the right and left flanks respectively, but in both cases heavy fire drove them back.

At 4 p.m., under support of our artillery, the Royal Fusiliers were able to advance beyond the first line of captured trenches, but the fact that the left flank was held back made the attempt to hold any isolated position in advance inadvisable.

As the reserves had been largely depleted by the dispatch of reinforcements to various parts of the line, and information was to hand of the approach of strong reinforcements of fresh troops to the enemy, orders were issued for the consolidation of the line then held.

Although we had been forced to abandon so much of the ground gained in the first rush, the net result of the day's operations was considerable—namely, an advance of 200 to 400 yards along the whole of our centre, a front of nearly 3 miles. That the enemy suffered severely was indicated, not only by subsequent information, but by the fact of his attempting no counterattack during the night, except upon the trench captured by the French 1st Division on the extreme right. Here two counterattacks were repulsed with loss.

The prisoners taken during the day amounted to 400, including 11 officers: amongst these were 5 Germans, the remains of a volunteer machine-gun detachment from the *Goeben*. Their commanding officer was killed and the machine-gun destroyed. The majority of these captures were made by the 42nd Division under Major-General W. Douglas.

The Battle of 21st June.

From the date of this battle to the end of the month of June the incessant attacks and counterattacks which have so grievously swelled our lists of casualties have been caused by the determination of the Turks to regain ground they had lost—a determination clashing against our firm resolve to continue to increase our holding. Several of these daily encounters would have been the subject of a separate dispatch in the campaigns of my youth and middle age, but, with due regard to proportion, they cannot even be so much as mentioned here. Only one example each from the French, British, and Australian and

New Zealand spheres of action will be most briefly set down, so that Your Lordship may understand the nature of the demands made upon the energies and fortitude of the troops.

1. At 4.30 a.m. on June the 21st the French Corps Expéditionnaire attacked the formidable works that flank the Kereves Dere. By noon their 2nd Division had stormed all the Turkish first and second line trenches to their front, and had captured the Haricot redoubt. On their right the 1st Division took the first line of trenches, but were counterattacked and driven out. Fresh troops were brought up and launched upon another assault; but the Turks were just as obstinate, and drove out the second party before they had time to consolidate. At 2.45 p.m. General Gouraud issued an order that full use must be made of the remaining five hours of daylight, and that, before dark, these trenches must be taken and held, otherwise the gains of the 2nd Division would be sacrificed.

At 6 p.m. the third assault succeeded; 600 yards of trenches remained in our hands, despite all the heavy counterattacks made through the night by the enemy. In this attack the striplings belonging to the latest French drafts specially distinguished themselves by their forwardness and contempt of danger. Fifty prisoners were taken, and the enemy's casualties (mostly incurred during counterattacks) were estimated at 7,000. The losses of the Corps Expéditionnaire were 2,500.

The Battle of 28th June.

2. The Turkish right had hitherto rooted itself with special tenacity into the coast. In the scheme of attack submitted by Lieutenant-General A. G. Hunter Weston, commanding VIIIth Army Corps, our left, pivoting upon a point in our line about one mile from the sea, was to push forward until its outer flank advanced about 1,000 yards. If the operation was successful, then, at its close, we should have driven the enemy back for a thousand yards along the coast, and the trenches of this left section of our line would be facing east instead of, as previously, north-east. Obviously, the ground to be gained lessened as our line drew back from the sea towards its fixed or pivoted right. Five Turkish trenches must be carried in the section nearest the sea: only two Turkish trenches in the section farthest from the sea.

At 10.20 a.m. on the 28th June our bombardment began. At 10.43 a.m. a small redoubt known as the Boomerang was rushed by the Border Regiment. At 11 a.m. the 87th Brigade, under Major-General W. R. Marshall, captured three lines of Turkish trenches. On their right the 4th and 7th Royal Scots captured the two Turkish trenches allotted to them, but further to the east; near the pivotal point the remainder of the 156th Brigade were unable to get on. Precisely at 11.30 a.m. the second attack took place. The 86th Brigade, led by the 2nd Royal Fusiliers, dashed over the trenches already captured by their comrades of the 87th Brigade, and, pushing on with great steadiness, took two more lines of trenches, thus achieving the five successive lines along the coast.

This success was further improved upon by the Indian Brigade, who managed to secure, and to place into a state of defence, a spur running from the west of the furthest captured Turkish trench to the sea. Our casualties were small—1,750 in all. The enemy suffered heavily, especially in the repeated counterattacks, which for many days and nights afterwards they launched against the trenches they had lost.

Enver Pasha's Order.

3. On the night of the 29th-30th June the Turks, acting, as we afterwards ascertained, under the direct personal order of Enver Pasha, to drive us all into the sea, made a big attack on the Australian and New Zealand Army Corps, principally on that portion of the line which was under the command of Major-General Sir A. J. Godley. From midnight till 1.30 a.m. a fire of musketry and guns of greatest intensity was poured upon our trenches. A heavy column then advanced to the assault, and was completely crumpled up by the musketry and machine-guns of the 7th and 8th Light Horse. An hour later another grand attack took place against our left and left centre, and was equally cut to pieces by our artillery and rifle fire. The enemy's casualties may be judged by the fact that in areas directly exposed to view between 400 and 500 were actually seen to fall.

On the evening of this day, the 30th of June, the Mediterranean Expeditionary Force suffered grievous loss owing to the wounding of General Gouraud by a shell. This calamity—for I count it nothing less—brings us down to the beginning of the month of July.

The command of the Corps Expéditionnaire Français d'Orient was then taken over by General Bailloud, at which point I shall close my dispatch.

The Problem of Transport.

During the whole period under review the efforts and expedients whereby a great army has had its wants supplied upon a wilderness have, I believe, been breaking world records.

The country is broken, mountainous, arid, and void of supplies; the water found in the areas occupied by our forces is quite inadequate for their needs; the only practicable beaches are small, cramped breaks in impracticable lines of cliffs; with the wind in certain quarters no sort of landing is possible; the wastage, by bombardment and wreckage, of lighters and small craft has led to crisis after crisis in our carrying capacity, whilst over every single beach plays fitfully throughout each day a devastating shell fire at medium ranges.

Upon such a situation appeared quite suddenly the enemy submarines. On 22nd May all transports had to be dispatched to Mudros for safety. Thenceforth men, stores, guns, horses, etc., etc., had to be brought from Mudros—a distance of 40 miles—in fleet sweepers and other small and shallow craft less vulnerable to submarine attack. Every danger and every difficulty was doubled.

But the navy and the Royal Engineers were not to be thwarted in their landing operations either by nature or by the enemy, whilst the Army Service Corps, under Brigadier-General F. W. B. Koe, and the Army Ordnance Corps, under Brigadier-General R. W. M. Jackson, have made it a point of honour to feed men, animals, guns, and rifles in the fighting line as regularly as if they were only out for manoeuvres on Salisbury Plain.

I desire, therefore, to record my admiration for the cool courage and unfailing efficiency with which the Royal Navy, the beach personnel, the engineers, and the administrative services have carried out these arduous duties.

A Corporal's Apology.

In addition to its normal duties the Signal Service, under the direction of Lieutenant-Colonel M. G. E. Bowman-Manifold, Director of Army Signals, has provided the connecting link between the Royal Navy and the Army in their combined operations, and has rapidly readjusted itself to amphibious methods. All demands made on it by sudden expansion of the fighting forces or by the movements of General Headquarters have been rapidly and effectively met. The working of the telegraphs, telephones, and repair of lines, often under heavy fire, has been beyond praise.

Casualties have been unusually high, but the best traditions of the Corps of Royal Engineers have inspired the whole of their work. As an instance, the central telegraph office at Cape Helles (a dug-out) was recently struck by a high explosive shell. The officer on duty and twelve other ranks were killed or wounded and the office entirely demolished. But No. 72003 Corporal G. A. Walker, Royal Engineers, although much shaken, repaired the damage, collected men, and within 39 minutes reopened communication by apologising for the incident and by saying he required no assistance.

The Royal Army Medical Service have had to face unusual and very trying conditions. There are no roads, and the wounded who are unable to walk must be carried from the firing line to the shore. They and their attendants may be shelled on their way to the beaches, at the beaches, on the jetties, and again, though I believe by inadvertence, on their way out in lighters to the hospital ships. Under shell fire it is not as easy as some of the critically disposed seem to imagine to keep all arrangements in apple-pie order. Here I can only express my own opinion that efficiency, method, and even a certain quiet heroism have characterised the evacuations of the many thousands of our wounded.

Commands and Staff.

In my three commanders of corps I have indeed been thrice fortunate.

General Gouraud brought a great reputation to our help from the battlefields of the Argonne, and in so doing he has added to its lustre. A happy mixture of daring in danger and of calm in crisis, full of energy and resource, he has worked hand in glove with his British comrades in arms, and has earned their affection and respect.

Lieutenant-General Sir W. R. Birdwood has been the soul of Anzac. Not for one single day has he ever quitted his post. Cheery and full of human sympathy, he has spent many hours of each twenty-four inspiring the defenders of the front trenches; and if he does not know every soldier in his force, at least every soldier in the force believes he is known to his chief.

Lieutenant-General A. G. Hunter Weston possesses a genius for war. I know no more resolute commander. Calls for reinforcements, appeals based on exhaustion or upon imminent counterattack are powerless to divert him from his aim. And this aim, in so far as he may be responsible for it, is worked out with insight, accuracy, and that wisdom which comes from close study in peace combined with long experience in the field.

In my first dispatch I tried to express my indebtedness to Major-General W. P. Braithwaite, and I must now again, however inadequately, place on record the untiring, loyal assistance he has continued to render me ever since.

The thanks of everyone serving in the peninsula are due to Lieutenant-General Sir John Maxwell. All the resources of Egypt and all of his own remarkable administrative abilities have been ungrudgingly placed at our disposal.

Finally, if my dispatch is in any way to reflect the feelings of the force, I must refer to the shadow cast over the whole of our adventure by the loss of so many of our gallant and true-hearted comrades. Some of them we shall never see again; some have had the mark of the Dardanelles set upon them for life; but others, and, thank God, by far the greater proportion, will be back in due course at the front.

    I have the honour to be

        Your Lordship's most obedient Servant,

        Ian Hamilton,

        General,

        Commanding Mediterranean Expeditionary Force.

CHAPTER 9

The War in Mesopotamia

The campaign between the Euphrates and Tigris was, of all the movements of the war, the least known to Western observers. Its terrain was far away, and to most people no more than a geographical term. Our opponents there were not Germans, but an outlying force of Turks. It had no striking objective, such as the possession of a great capital like Constantinople or the conquest of a province like South-West Africa. It was an enterprise of the Indian Government, and in India alone were published the details. But this modest campaign had a strategical importance of the first order. Its purpose was no less than the defence of India, and therefore of the Empire.

Germany's ambition, cut off from the sea, burned the more intensely on land. Like Napoleon, she thought India and the East to be the Achilles-heel of the British power, for she realised that Britain's main interest was her empire, and she believed that a blow struck at some of the far-flung links of the Imperial chain would do much to paralyze our efforts in Europe. For years before the war she had striven to drive a wedge of German influence towards the north-west frontier of India. The Baghdad railway, trading schemes on the littoral of the Persian Gulf, much secret diplomacy in Persia, *coquetting* with disaffected *sheikhs* and brigand tribes, gun-running for the benefit of Indian borderers, and stately overtures to the Amir of Afghanistan were part of the machinery employed.

Mesopotamia for its own sake was her first object, for she coveted that ruin of one of the great granaries of the world. But she had always an eye on India. The methods which at one time we were inclined to ascribe to wandering Russian agents from beyond the Pamirs were diligently practised by Berlin. Its agents were in every little town of Southern Persia and in every caravanserai of Baghdad.

The march into Mesopotamia, artist's impression

The outbreak of the war between the Allies and Turkey seemed to give the long-sought opportunity. The millions of Indian Moslems, Germany argued, must view with suspicion an attack upon the political capital of their faith. In this she miscalculated, for east of the Euphrates the Sultan of Roum was no name to conjure with universally. His title to the *caliphate* was too recent and too precarious, and the endless divisions of Islam tended to particularism in tradition and devotion. The Young Turks, always singularly inept in their calculations on matters of religion, built much on an Indian revolution, assisted by border raids from the north. The sustained loyalty of India left them aghast, and Enver lost his temper. He sent to the Amir of Afghanistan a present of women's bangles—the greatest insult which an Oriental can contrive.

The result was to infuriate that ruler, and confirm him, if confirmation were needed, in his support of the British alliance. In a world war, of course, the echoes carry far, and they roused some of the more turbulent hill tribes to descend from their fastnesses. During the first half of 1915 we had various troubles on the north-west frontier of India, troubles of the kind with which we were familiar, but directly inspired in this case by the unrest which had moved like a dry wind across the world. For this we were prepared.

★★★★★★

It should be noted that the loyalty of many of the Border peoples was beyond praise. The Frontier militias volunteered their services, the Khyber tribes asked permission to furnish an armed contingent, and the Wazirs of Bannu subscribed their allowance for one month to the Indian Relief Fund.

★★★★★★

None the less that open back-door of India, to which Germany had access, remained an eternal possibility of trouble. The East is incalculable. Waves of emotion rise like dust-devils in the desert without apparent cause. Germany's patient subterranean diplomacy might yet effect something which would cripple our efforts in the West. A small detachment of Border tribesmen deserted to the German lines in Flanders during the winter—the one case of the kind in the war. The deserters were sent across Europe and Asia Minor, and their course was traced into Persia on their way by Seistan to the Indian frontier to further the cause of their new friends. It was a trivial incident, but it showed the way the wind might blow. With Turkey on Germany's side, and with Persia in confusion, there was too clear a road to that

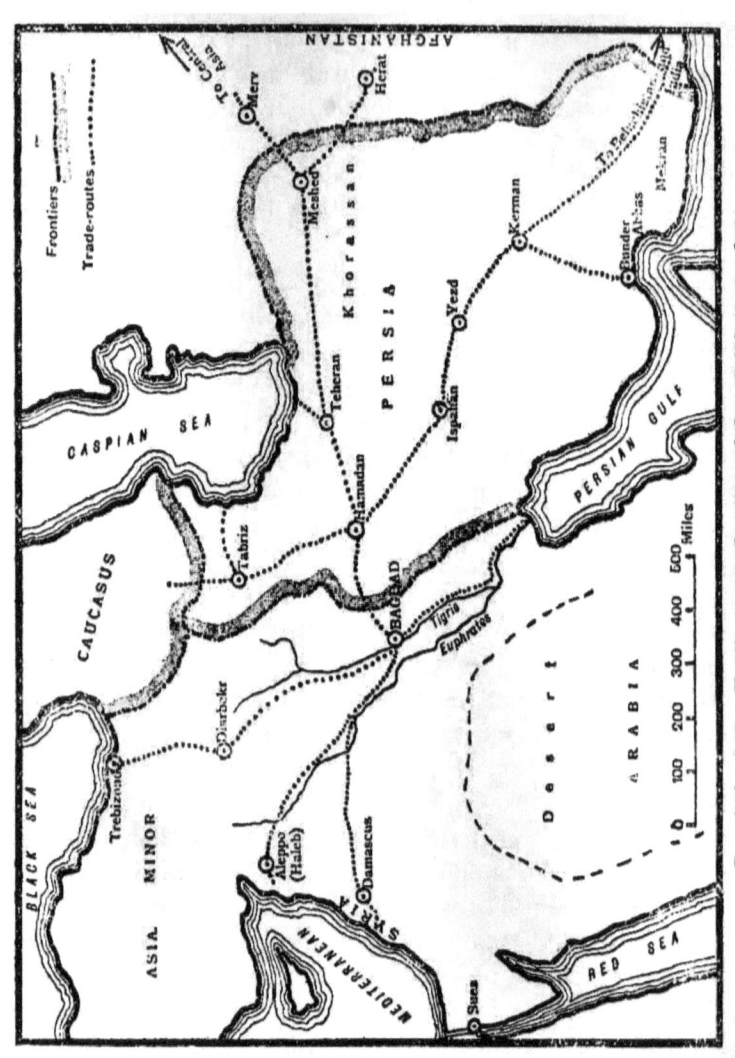

Bagdad as the Trade-route Centre of South-Western Asia.

old battlefield of races, the gates of the Hindu Kush. The Government of India could not afford to be supine in its wardenship of the northern marches.

The Mesopotamia Expedition was undertaken primarily to keep the enemy from the shores of the Gulf, in case he should establish himself on the flank of our highway to India. As we have seen in an earlier chapter, Basra, the port of Baghdad, fell to us on November 23, 1914, and Kurna on 9th December. Thereafter we entrenched ourselves astride the Tigris, apparently with the object of holding the road to the sea and doing nothing more. But the Turkish counteroffensive compelled us to revise our plan. The defeat of the enemy's assaults during April at Kurna, Ahwaz, and most notably at Shaiba, and the pursuit which our success involved, drew us farther and farther into the hinterland. The whole history bears a curious resemblance to the tale of the reconquest of the Sudan. There was the same advance simultaneously by land and water, the same strip of green between deserts on either side, the same desire to put a limit to the advance, the same eternal shifting of the limit a little farther on.

The Sudan wars did not stop till Khartoum fell, and it looked as if the Mesopotamia campaign must lead sooner or later to an assault on Baghdad. For through that city ran the channel of German communication with the Indian frontier. Its possession, too, by the Turks meant that the ancient capital and one of the most sacred cities of Islam was under Germany's influence. More than Constantinople it cast its spell over the Moslem world. The golden minarets of the great Shiah tombs, which catch from far off on the plain the traveller's eye, had a compelling sanctity greater than St. Sophia. Moreover, of all the Turkish possessions it was knit least closely to the centre on the Bosphorus. Till the coming of Midhat Pasha the Baghdad *vilayet* had been almost independent. For the orthodox Turk, whether soldier or civilian, to be sent to Baghdad was to be sent into exile. Of all Turkey's provinces it seemed that Mesopotamia was the most easily detachable.

Germany, having foreseen this, had sent her officers to stiffen the 13th Baghdad Corps and instruct them in her latest military methods. More especially she trained them in trench-making and in the various branches of modern defensive warfare. It does not appear that she sent with them any special artillery or any stock of munitions. The Baghdad Corps was, indeed, in some difficulties about its supply of material, beyond the stocks which had been accumulated in the depots. There was no sea route, and no easy land route, Damascus

British troops in trenches, Mesopotamia

being separated from it by great deserts, and the Anatolian centres of Erzhingian and Erzerum having their hands full with munitioning the army in the Caucasus. The corps, too, was depleted in men, one Arab division having been lent to Transcaucasia.

The campaign in Mesopotamia was of the old-fashioned type which we had almost ceased to look for in Europe. There was no fixed line of trenches buttressed by impregnable flanks. The Turks were skilful at taking up positions and digging themselves in, but once their front was broken there was a rout and a chance for the effective use of cavalry. But the land was not without its strategic difficulties. The floods, which began in February, created huge lagoons on both sides of the river, and as these shrank there remained isolated meres and large areas of swamp. Old irrigation canals, often deep and wide, ran out from the river, and complicated the problem of transport.

The power of the sun in the summer months was not the least of our trials. At dawn it might be 110° F., and in the afternoon well over 120°, and the baked sands retained the heat so that night brought little coolness. Shade there was none. A blinding glare was reflected from yellow earth and blue water, and many a British soldier yearned for the trenches in the deep meadowlands of Flanders. Happily, we used for the operations men who had served an apprenticeship to the Indian heats. With less seasoned troops the summer's campaign must have come to a standstill.

Sir Mark Sykes, than whom there could be no better authority, has described the conditions of the campaign:—

> A winding river which is restless in its bed, capricious in its fall, uncertain in its rise, and sown with shifting shoals and sands is the sole means of communication between Baghdad and the sea; it is the inevitable line of supply, advance, or retreat for Turks and British. On either hand stretches limitless plain, showing a horizon as level as the sea save for here and there a mound of ancient ruin, a rare ridge or faint undulation. This unending plain, however, must not be imagined to be of completely easy passage, for its faint depressions are swamps of unknown shape with bays and inlets, while at right angles to the river banks run dried canals and cuttings with hard ridges on either hand.
>
> As for the population, it is base, semi-nomadic Arab, cruel, treacherous, and rascally as the town influence can make it, yet predatory with primitive Bedawi instinct. To these people,

Turkish corruption, smugglers, and a year's war have brought a wealth of arms and munitions; without any cohesion or policy they are neither for British nor Turk; on the day of battle they haunt the outskirts of the fight, plunder the wounded and stragglers impartially, harass the retreat of the defeated side, hoist white flags over their tents, and make professions of unswerving fidelity to whosoever seems to be in the ascendant.

Thus, in the present stage, there are three natural factors—the river, the land, and the people. The river may block your advance by a new and unexpected mud bank; the land may thwart your plans by an unmapped swamp; the people will not delay or impede you, but will accentuate every mishap that may befall, plunder your convoys, threaten your hospitals, cut your telegraph wires, and supply you and your opponents with unreliable information.

On the last day of May, it will be remembered that, hearing of a Turkish concentration north of Kurna, we resolved to disperse it, and, taking the enemy by surprise, drove him to precipitate retreat. On the first day of June we had advanced north of Ezra's Tomb, and on the 3rd, we took Amara, seventy-five miles from Kurna, made large captures, and scattered the rest of the garrison into the adjacent marshes. Amara was an important point, for from it runs a desert road, a hundred miles long, to Ahwaz, on the Karun River. By the possession of it we prevented trouble in the Ahwaz district, through which passed the pipe line of the Anglo-Persian Oil Company. The remains of the Turkish forces under Nur-ed-Din Pasha withdrew 150 miles up the Tigris to Kut-el-Amara.

This place must be noted, for it was the strategic key of the next movement. From the Tigris at that point runs one of those mysterious river channels of Mesopotamia, the Shatt-al-Hai, which joins the Euphrates at Nasiriyeh, about a hundred miles north-west of Basra. From Kut-el-Amara the Turks could use this channel as a route by which to make an assault upon the British left rear. Until Nasiriyeh was held and the line of the Euphrates between it and Basra, an advance from Amara was attended with grave danger. Even if Kut was reached and taken, it might only be to find that the enemy had got round our flank.

Early in July an expedition under Major-General G. F. Gorringe started from Kurna against Nasiriyeh. All the country between the two rivers was flood and marsh, through which ran many old channels. The expedition, consisting of infantry and a naval contingent, forced its way to the Euphrates by way of the Hamar Lake. That amphibious journey, now wading, now embarked in boats, now making portages—through a maze of creeks and lagoons and thick date groves under a pitiless sky and amid swarms of flies—must rank as one of the most uncomfortable ever undertaken by British troops. We found the entrance to the main stream of the Euphrates mined and barricaded, but we succeeded in dislodging the enemy from the river bank and forcing him back upon Nasiriyeh.

On 24th July we drove in the main Turkish position in front of that town. The Turks were astride the river, and had prepared strong entrenchments defended with barbed wire. By eleven o'clock they were broken, and our gunboats pushed on and shelled Nasiriyeh, while the main enemy force retreated twenty-five miles in the direction of Kut-el-Amara. Next morning, we occupied the town, which as the old capital of the Mustafik tribe of Arabs had a political importance in addition to its strategical situation. The victory was very complete, for the Turkish casualties were 2,500, including over 700 prisoners; we captured practically all their guns and huge stores of ammunition; and our losses were under 600. The vital junction of the Shatt-al-Hai and the Euphrates was in our hands.

Kut-el-Amara remained, from which a flanking movement might start. With it under our control, quite apart from greater objectives, we believed that Basra would be safe. Accordingly, early in August Sir John Nixon gave orders for an advance by General Townshend's Division up the Tigris. Along that river of endless twists and turnings the progress of troops must be slow. Riverine marshes had to be crossed or circumvented, and canals had to be bridged. The enemy offered no serious opposition. He was content to wait for us some seven miles downstream from Kut-el-Amara, on a front extending on both sides of the Tigris for a distance of about six miles. His troops were nearly 10,000 men, regulars of the Baghdad Corps, and he had the usual motley following of mounted Arab tribesmen, whose future conduct depended upon which way the battle went.

On the 25th of September we came in touch with him. The Turkish position, which had been occupied for three months, was curious and elaborate. On the right bank was the Turkish right wing, with its front to a canal embankment twenty feet high, on which watchtowers had been built. On the left bank were the Turkish centre and left. The trenches extended for two miles, from the river bank to a marsh two

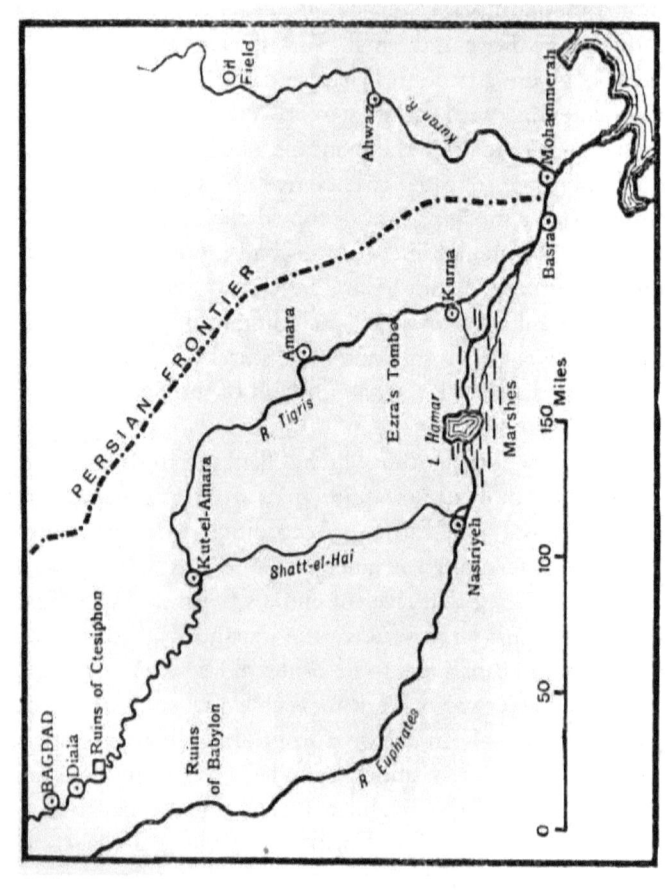

The Mesopotamian Campaign.

miles wide, and beyond that for two and a half miles to another marsh which protected the left flank. The river had been strongly boomed.

General Fry's Belgaum Brigade entrenched itself about two miles in front of the Turkish left centre. General Delamain began by feinting against the Turkish right. Then, under cover of dusk on the 27th, he took his own Poona Brigade, as well as General Hoghton's, across to the left bank of the Tigris by a pontoon bridge which we had constructed. Our heavy guns were behind Fry's Brigade. There had been a good deal of shelling during the day, and a reconnaissance by the 7th Lancers in which thirty-six prisoners were taken. The Turkish position was strongly entrenched, and was clearly beyond our power to carry by a frontal assault. General Delamain's plan was to get round the enemy's flank. He was to attack between the two marshes, while General Hoghton circumvented the marsh on the extreme Turkish left.

The action began at dawn on the 28th. Delamain succeeded in driving in the Turkish flank by ten o'clock in the morning, while Fry's Brigade, 450 yards in front of the enemy, pinned to its position the left centre. In this action the 2nd Dorsets and 117th Mahrattas distinguished themselves. Meantime General Hoghton had performed his part, and was well to the west of the extreme marsh. By two in the afternoon the whole of the enemy's left was rolled up, in spite of a gallant resistance which necessitated the clearing of trench after trench. We took several hundred prisoners, some field guns, and great quantities of rifles and ammunition.

Delamain then swung southwards towards the river, partly for the sake of water—for his troops were suffering severely from thirst, and the marsh water was undrinkable—and partly to assist Fry's attack on the Turkish centre. He now came under heavy artillery fire from the right bank of the river, and resolved to change his course and attack the Turkish centre in rear. Suddenly he discovered strong Turkish reinforcements—seven regiments with guns—marching parallel to him.

He promptly fell upon them about half-past five, and after a sharp attack put them to flight, capturing four of their guns. It was a severe test for troops which had been fighting and marching for thirty hours, much of it in blinding heat and under a scorching desert wind. Meanwhile all the day of the battle the British right had been guarded by our armed motorcars and our cavalry, which prevented any succour being sent to the hard-pressed Turkish left. H.M.S. *Comet* and the armed launches had been busy during the action, and the senior naval officer, Lieutenant-Commander Cookson, lost his life in a gallant effort to break down one of the river booms.

At dawn on the 29th the sun rising through the haze of the riverside revealed an empty battlefield. The enemy had retired by road and river towards Baghdad. Our cavalry was loosed, and entered Kut-el-Amara, a native town of some 6,000 inhabitants, with a large trade in grain and liquorice. They pushed on up the solid plain, for between Kut and Baghdad the marshes cease, while our gunboats led the pursuit upstream, followed by General Townshend with an infantry brigade in steamers. One of our aeroplanes succeeded in dropping bombs on the rearguard of the Turkish flotilla. The result of the day was very large captures of prisoners, two thousand and more, representing nearly a quarter of the Turkish command.

An inspection of the battlefield showed the strength of the enemy's position. The German teachers had found apt pupils. Communication trenches extended for miles, and the firing trenches, as at Gallipoli, were eight or ten feet deep, with loopholes and head-cover. Ranges were marked by flags. Good arrangements had been made for covering the retirement of troops and their embarkation.

There was an elaborate system of observation posts and of contact mines, most of which were exploded by our engineers without accident. The field of fire was everywhere absolutely open and flat. To have carried so strong a place, with casualties which were under five hundred, and many of them slight, after weeks of arduous marching under a torrid sun through difficult country, was no slight achievement. General Delamain, who had been fighting in Mesopotamia from the start of the campaign, had proved himself an admirable leader of troops, and General Townshend had shown both judgment and boldness in his final tactics.

By the end of September his force was distant some two hundred miles by river and one hundred by land from Baghdad, with an easy open country before them, and no place of importance short of the capital to serve as a rallying-point for the enemy. The winter, too, was approaching, and with it a pleasant climate for campaigning. The war of the arduous summer months had been amply successful. The British Prime Minister on 2nd November said:—

> I do not think that in the whole course of the war there has been a series of operations more carefully contrived, more brilliantly conducted, and with a better prospect of final success.

One other incident must be recorded. In Persia itself the tribes-

British column marching towards Kut

men, always inclined to turbulence, were stirred by German intrigue and the general unrest of the world to various sinister activities. On 12th July a commando appeared in the neighbourhood of Bushire, the chief Persian port, 180 miles from the Euphrates' mouth. Two British officers, Major Oliphant and Captain Ranking, went out to reconnoitre with a mixed patrol, and lost their lives in an ambush. Following this outrage, we occupied Bushire, and on 8th and 9th September had to fight an action to defend the place.

The enemy were prevented from crossing the gap which separates the island from the mainland, and were beaten off with heavy losses. The great prominence given to this fight in the Berlin reports suggested that the whole affair had been sedulously stage-managed by Germany. (The British occupation of Bushire terminated on 29th October, the trouble being over. There were other outrages or attempted outrages during these months at Ispahan, Shiraz, and Kermanshah).

By the end of September, the Mesopotamia campaign, which for months had been almost forgotten in Europe, assumed a very real importance in the eyes of the Allied statesmen. Our sporadic efforts there and in the Dardanelles were suddenly linked up by the German menace to the Balkans, and the revelation of a strategy which threatened India and the whole Near and Middle East. The Gallipoli offensive, so light-heartedly undertaken, was no nearer its goal. In the early days of August, we had flung into the struggle there the new forces which Sir Ian Hamilton had demanded, and, daring greatly, had greatly failed.

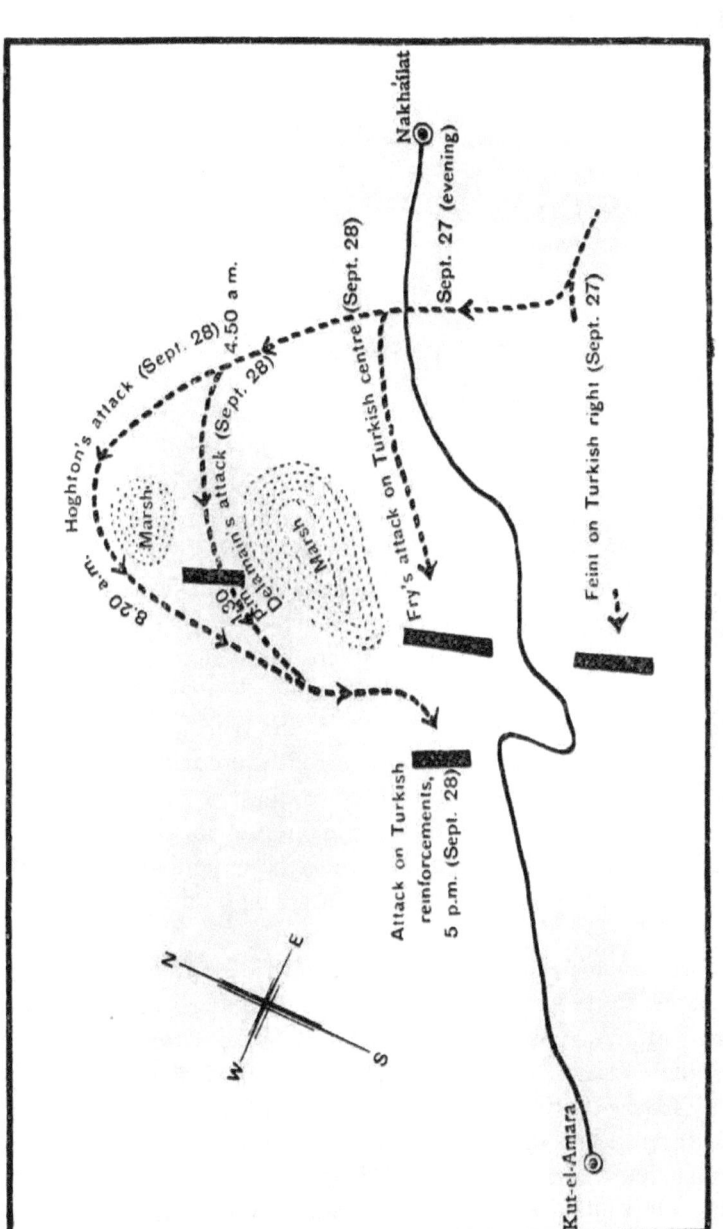

The Battle of Kut-ei-Amara (Sept. 28).

CHAPTER 10

The New Landing at Gallipoli

By the end of July, 1915, preparations had been made for a final effort against the Gallipoli defences. Three divisions of the New Army and two Territorial Divisions had arrived in the Eastern Mediterranean, and a Mounted Division had been for some months in Egypt. The submarine menace had sent the monsters of the British Fleet back to home waters or to the shelter of protected harbours, and during the summer only the destroyers, a few light cruisers, and an occasional battleship were seen off the shores of the peninsula. But in July new craft arrived, specially constructed to meet the case.

A strange type of monitor, with a freeboard almost flush with the water, and looking, as one observer reported, more like a Chinese *pagoda* than a ship, suddenly appeared in the Northern Aegean. They were of different sizes, the smaller being little more than floating gun-platforms; but they were admirably suited for their purpose. Even the little ones, with a crew of seventy, could fling 100 lbs. of high explosive twelve miles, and they feared submarines no more than a gull fears a swordfish. The preliminaries of the new assault on the naval side were prepared.

The plan which the High Command had evolved was bold and ingenious. To understand it we must note the features of the peninsula north of the Anzac position. The Australians held, as we have seen, the edge of the plateau at the top of the long ravines which run to the coast. Eastwards the land rises in the uplands of Sari Bair, till about a mile and a half north-east of the position the culminating point of the system is reached in the peak marked 971, and called by the Turks Koja Chemen. (This is the hill referred to in Sir Ian Hamilton's dispatch as Hill 305.) On all sides the ground slopes away from the crest, which is distant some four miles as the crow flies from the waters of the Straits. North and west a jumble of ridges falls towards the Gulf of Saros—ridges wildly broken and confused, sometimes bare scree and clay, sometimes matted with scrub and separated by dry and tortuous *nullahs*.

From a point on the shore of the Gulf of Saros south of the Fisherman's Hut a fairly well-marked ridge, called Walker's Ridge in the lower part, runs up to the Koja Chemen summit. On this there are various points which were to become only too famous, notably Chunuk Bair, nearly 900 feet high, and Q, or Nameless Peak, between it and Hill 971. North of this spur is a water-course called the Sazli Beit Dere, and a little farther north the Chailak Dere. Separating the two is a long spur which leaves the parent *massif* just west of Chunuk Bair. Its upper part was called by our men Rhododendron Ridge, (the scrub covering it was not rhododendron but daphne), and the under features nearer the coast were known as Big and Little Table Tops. North of Chailak Dere is another ridge, with the feature known as Bauchop's Hill.

Still farther north is a wide water-course, the Aghyl Dere, which near its head splits into two forks, both descending from Hill 971. From the Fisherman's Hut the flat ground between the hills and the sea widens northwards, as the coast sweeps towards the cape called Niebruniessi. Beyond is the halfmoon of Suvla or Anafarta Bay, two miles wide, enclosed between Niebruniessi and the cape of Suvla Burnu, the north-western extremity of the Gallipoli Peninsula.

The hinterland of Suvla Bay is curious. It consists of a rectangle of hills lying north of the Azmak Dere water-course, and connected towards the east with the outflankers of the Koja Chemen system. The north side, lining the coast, is the ridge of Karakol Dagh, over 400 feet high. The south side, lining the Azmak Dere, and breaking down into flats, two miles from the coast, is a blunt range, rising as high as 500 feet, of which the westerly part is called Yilghin Burnu, and was to become noted later as Chocolate Hill. The eastern side of the rectangle is a rocky crest, rising in one part to nearly 900 feet, and falling shorewards in two well-marked terraces. Between the three sides of hill, from the eastern terraces to the sea, the ground is nearly flat.

Along the edge of Suvla Bay runs a narrow causeway of sand, and immediately behind it lies a large salt lake, in summer partly dried up, but always liable to be converted by rain into an impassable swamp. Eastwards of it the hills and flats are patched with farms and scrub, mostly dwarf oaks, and on the edge of the terraces the scrub grows into something like woodland. Everywhere the plain is cracked with futile watercourses. Two villages are points in the hinterland—Kuchuk

Australians attacking Gallipoli

(or Little) Anafarta on the slopes at the south-eastern angle of the enclosing hills, and Biyuk (or Big) Anafarta two miles south across the water-course of the Azmak Dere, and just under the northern spurs of Koja Chemen. The road connecting the two runs southwards to Boghali Kalessi on the Straits.

In the beginning of August, the Fast of Ramadan was drawing to its close, and for a little there had been something like stagnation in the opposing lines. We were aware that the Turks were massing forces for a new attack, and were resolved to anticipate them. The plan we adopted involved four separate actions. In the first place, a feint was to be made at the head of the Gulf of Saros, as if to take in flank and rear the Bulair lines. Next a strong offensive would be assumed by the troops in the Cape Helles region against their old objective, Achi Baba. These two movements would be read by the Turks as the main British offensive and its covering feint, and it was hoped would lead them to send their reserves to Krithia.

But in the meantime, the Anzac Corps were to advance with its left, and attempt to gain the heights of Koja Chemen and the seaward ridges. Simultaneously, a great new landing would be made at Suvla Bay, where it was believed the Turks would be wholly unprepared. Suvla Bay had the advantage that it was well sheltered from the prevailing winds, and afforded a submarine-proof base. If the Anafarta hills could be taken, and the right of the new landing force linked up with the left of the Australasians, the British would hold the central crest of the spine of upland which runs through the western end of the peninsula.

Such gains would enable them to cut the communications of the Turks in the butt-end, Achi Baba must fall, and in time the frowning tableland of the Pasha Dagh. The one land route to Maidos would be commanded, and the way would be prepared for an action in open country, where the grim Turkish fortifications would be taken in flank and in reverse. If the undertaking attained the most reasonable success, the western end of the peninsula would be ours, and the European defences of the Narrows would be won.

The plan was bold, but entirely legitimate, and its details were worked out with great care by Sir Ian Hamilton's Headquarters' Staff. The element of surprise could be rightly counted upon. Some of the operations would be difficult, but no one was beyond the capacity of seasoned troops. We had the necessary force to make the attempt, and ample reserves behind our first attack. The danger lay in the fact that all the movements were so closely interdependent. Exact timing was imperative, and for this we needed not only a good Headquarters' plan, but the most assiduous staff supervision from hour to hour. Moreover, the troops employed must be of uniform capacity, for the failure of any unit would jeopardise the success of the whole. A defect in divisional leading or in the stamina of one brigade would nullify the most splendid victories of other parts of the line. Some risk of this sort is inevitable in any elaborate movement, but in this case, it was accentuated by the fact that a considerable portion of the attacking force was wholly untried. The three new divisions destined for the attempt had never before been in action.

Let us consider first the preliminaries to the main assault. On the afternoon of Friday, 6th August, the Allied forces at Cape Helles made a general attack upon the Turkish position at Achi Baba. The brunt of the fighting fell to the 29th Division, holding the left of the line, and the East Lancashire Territorials of the 42nd Division on their right. In the early afternoon the 88th Brigade, after an artillery preparation, attacked across open ground against a section of the enemy's front which had defied all our previous assaults. The attack was boldly delivered, but failed to win its objective, and there were many losses among the 2nd Hampshires and the 4th Worcesters, who were the leading battalions. The 1st Essex managed to carry the trenches opposite them, but were forced out by bombs and flanking rifle fire. The Lancashire Territorials were also heavily engaged east of the Krithia road, and advanced the line at one point 200 yards.

The Turkish line had been reinforced by two fresh divisions, and we had only anticipated their offensive by an hour or two. Consequently, next morning we had to face a counterattack, which we repelled, and which was followed by an advance of the 125th and 129th Brigades. For the next two days the struggle raged, principally in the centre round the Vineyard west of the Krithia road. Here it was that Lieutenant W. T. Forshaw, of the 1/9 Manchesters, won the Victoria Cross for an act of conspicuous gallantry and endurance. On the second night of the fighting, while holding the Vineyard with a half-company, he was attacked by the enemy advancing from three converging trenches. The official account ran:—

> He held his own, not only directing his men and encouraging them by exposing himself with the utmost disregard of danger, but personally throwing bombs continuously for forty-one

hours. When his detachment was relieved, after twenty-four hours, he volunteered to continue the direction of operations. Three times during the night of August 8-9 he was again heavily attacked, and once the Turks got over the barricade; but, after shooting three with his revolver, he led his men forward and recaptured it. When he rejoined his battalion he was choked and sickened by bomb fumes, badly bruised by a fragment of shrapnel, and could barely lift his arm from continuous bomb throwing.

This engagement was intended as a holding battle, and as such it must be regarded as successful. It distracted the attention of the Turks for the moment from the main theatre farther north, and induced them to send the bulk of their new reserves to Achi Baba.

We pass to the desperate struggle in the area of the Anzac Corps, the most desperate in many ways and the most brilliant which Gallipoli had yet seen. The operation was arranged in two parts. An attack was first to be made by troops of the Australian Division on the right against the Lone Pine Plateau, a position which commanded one of the main sources of the Turkish water supply. It was in essence a feint to cover the movements of General Godley's New Zealand and Australian division on the left, which was to move up the coast and deliver a converging assault with two columns against the heights of Koja Chemen.

The Australians began the attack at five in the afternoon of the 6th, when the action at Cape Helles had well started, and the troops employed were the 1st Infantry Brigade, the men of New South Wales, under Brigadier-General Smyth. (The attack was initiated by the 2nd, 3rd, and 4th battalions, with the 1st in reserve.) The Turkish trenches at the Lone Pine were enormously strong, and had been roofed in with great logs as a cover against shrapnel. After half an hour's bombardment by the artillery and the ships' guns, the Australians—every man with a white band on his sleeve—raced across the open, and in a few minutes were upon the enemy's position. Then began a deadly struggle for the roofed trenches, while the Turkish artillery and machine-guns played upon the exposed attack. No cover was to be had, for the shell of the position had to be broken before the men could get into the entrenchments. An observer has described that strange contest.

Some fired down into the loopholes; some, who happened to find small gaps in the line of head-cover in front of them, jumped down there and began to work into the dark shelters under the head-cover where the Turks were; others went on over the first trench, and even over the second trench, and into communication trenches which had no head-cover over them, and through which the Turks were fleeing. Others noticed that in the solid roof in front of them, near the edge where the loopholes were, there were manholes left at intervals, apparently to allow the listening patrols to creep through at night. They were just large enough to allow a man to wriggle through, and that was enough for the 1st Brigade. They wriggled down into them, feet foremost, as a burglar might into a skylight.

In a quarter of an hour the first Turkish line had been carried, and before the summer night fell the Lone Pine position had been won. The victors had to maintain their ground for the next few days, until 12th August, against violent counterattacks, and this they achieved with a stubbornness as conspicuous as the fury of their assault. The Turkish losses in this action alone were estimated at 5,000. The action was highly fruitful, for it drew all the local Turkish reserves to meet it. As a feat of arms, it cannot be overpraised. In Sir Ian Hamilton's words:—

> One weak Australian Brigade, numbering at the outset but 2,000 rifles, and supported only by two weak battalions, carried the work under the eyes of a whole enemy division, and maintained their grip upon it like a vice during six days' successive counterattacks.

The conspicuous gallantry of the performance may be realised from the fact that of the nine Victoria Crosses awarded for the August battles at Gallipoli, seven went to the conquerors of Lone Pine.

******

They were given to Captain Alfred John Short, Private John Hamilton, and Private Leonard Keyser of the 1st Battalion; and Lieutenant W. J. Symons, Lieutenant F. H. Tubb, Corporal A. S. Burton, and Corporal William Dunstan of the 7th Battalion.

******

Meantime the Anzac left wing had begun to move in the first darkness of that night of the 6th. General Godley's force consisted of the New Zealand and Australian Division, less the 1st and 3rd Light Horse Brigades, the 13th Division of the New Army, less five battalions, and General Cox's 29th Indian Infantry Brigade. The 29th Brigade of the new 10th Division and the 38th Brigade of the 13th

Carrying a wounded mate, Anzac, Gallipoli

Division were held in reserve. The plan was to divide the force into right and left covering columns and right and left columns of assault. The right covering column, under Brigadier-General Russell, was to seize the Table Tops, and the position between the Sazli Beit Dere and the Chailak Dere ravines. The left covering column, under Brigadier-General Travers, was directed to occupy the hill called Damakjelik Bair, north of the Aghyl Dere *nullah*. The right column of assault, under Brigadier-General Johnston, was to move up the ravines against the Chunuk Bair ridge, and the left column, under Brigadier-General Cox, to work up the Aghyl Dere against the summit peak, Hill 971.

At 9.30 p.m. General Russell's column, including the New Zealand Mounted Rifle Brigade, the Otago Mounted Rifles, and the Maori contingent, moved along the coast as pioneers to clear the foothills. A destroyer bombarded as usual the Turkish trenches, and the occupants took cover; but to their amazement, when the firing ceased, they found the New Zealand bayonets upon them. The Auckland and Wellington Mounted Rifles on the right cleared the Little and Big Table Tops, which are the lowest points on the ridge between the Sazli Beit Dere and the Chailak Dere, while the Otago and Canterbury Regiments swung farther north to occupy the ridge named Bauchop's Hill, after the Otago colonel.

The work was done in silence, and as in all night attacks there was some confusion. Men lost their way in the darkness, for the foothills were a maze of broken ridges and indeterminate gullies. Soon the Turks were alive to the movement, and their fire sputtered over the whole hillside. By dawn much had been won, including the two Table Tops and part of Bauchop's Hill, where the officer who gave the place his name had fallen.

Meanwhile General Travers's column, which included part of the 40th Brigade of the 13th Division, the 4th South Wales Borderers, and the 5th Wiltshires, pushed up the coast and attacked Damakjelik Bair. By 1.30 in the morning the whole place was carried, a fine piece of work for the New Army, which was largely due to the brilliant leading of Lieutenant-Colonel Gillespie of the South Wales Borderers. The way was now prepared for the columns of assault.

On Saturday, the 7th, at dawn, the main operation began. Before we consider the attack of the left wing on Koja Chemen, we must glance at the supporting movement in the centre, designed to engage part of the enemy's strength. Very early in the morning part of the 3rd Australian Light Horse Brigade advanced from their trenches on

Walker's Ridge, while part of the 1st Light Horse Brigade attacked on the right from Quinn's Post at the head of Shrapnel Valley, where they were supported by a detachment of the Welsh Fusiliers. The attack of those magnificent troopers, unequalled both in physique and in courage, had never a chance of succeeding. Line after line left the parapets, to be met with a storm of fire in which no mortal could live.

For a moment, but only for a moment, the flag of the Light Horse fluttered from a corner of the Turkish position, where a few desperate adventurers had carried it, but presently it had gone. The affair was over in a quarter of an hour, and must stand as one of the most heroic and forlorn of the episodes of the campaign. Of the 450 men who attacked from Walker's Ridge less than 100 came back, and of the 300 at Quinn's Post no more than 13.

We must now follow the fortunes of General Godley's two columns of assault. General Johnston's column, on the right, consisting of the New Zealand Infantry Brigade, was ordered to advance up the gullies on each side of the Table Tops ridge against the summit of Chunuk Bair. On the left. General Cox's column, made up of the 4th Australian Brigade and the 29th Indian Infantry Brigade, was to make a circuit to the north, and move up the Aghyl Dere against the northern flanks of Koja Chemen.

It was a day of blistering heat, one of the hottest yet experienced in that torrid summer. All night the troops had been on the road, and the force on the left of the attack had to fetch a long and weary circuit. The New Zealanders on the right at first made good progress. Advancing up the Chailak Dere and the Sazli Beit Dere, they carried the hogs-back called Rhododendron Ridge, which joins the main massif just west of Chunuk Bair. That was at ten o'clock in the morning, when the Australians and Indians on the left should have been well up the Aghyl Dere ready to take the defences of Chunuk Bair in flank. But there was at first no sign of the left wing.

It had been held up by the difficult country in the lower reaches of the Aghyl Dere, and where the ravine forks had split into two, the Australians going up the left-hand gully and the Indians the right. The 10th Gurkhas on the extreme right managed to get into touch with General Johnston's forces, but by this time the men of both columns were exhausted, and were forced to call a halt. Later in the day the New Zealanders reconnoitred the main ridge, and prepared for the great offensive on the morrow.

Before 6th August reinforcements had arrived in the Anzac zone.

The "Anzac" Front.
The water-courses shown on the map are mostly dry in summer.

These were the 13th Division of the New Army, under Major-General Shaw, troops which had previously been given a short spell of service at Cape Helles, and were now destined to be flung into one of the severest actions of the campaign.

✶✶✶✶✶✶

The division was comprised chiefly of men from the west and north-west of England, and was made up of the 38th Brigade (Brigadier-General Baldwin), the 39th Brigade (Brigadier-General Cayley), and the 40th Brigade (Brigadier-General Travers).

✶✶✶✶✶✶

On the night of 7th August two of its battalions—the 7th Gloucesters and the 8th Welsh (Pioneers)—reinforced the New Zealanders on Rhododendron Ridge. At dawn on the 8th the Zealanders, to whom the Maori contingent and the Auckland Mounted Rifles had now been added, attacked, and after a hard struggle carried the crest of Chunuk Bair, from which, through a gap in the hills, a glimpse could be got of the waters of the Dardanelles. The losses were heavy, as may be judged from the case of the Wellington Battalion, which had been 700 strong on the 6th and was now reduced to 53. The 7th Gloucesters also suffered terribly, losing their gallant commander, Lieutenant-Colonel Malone. In Sir Ian Hamilton's words:—

> Every single officer, company sergeant-major, or company quartermaster-sergeant, was either killed or wounded, and the battalion by midday consisted of small groups of men commanded by junior non-commissioned officers or privates. Chapter and verse may be quoted for the view that the rank and file of an army cannot long endure the strain of close hand-to-hand fighting unless they are given confidence by the example of good officers. Yet here is at least one instance where a battalion of the New Army fought right on, from midday till sunset, without any officers.

That day the left wing again made little progress. It was now formed in two columns. On the right the 39th Brigade of the 13th Division and the 29th Indian Brigade moved against the farm on the slopes of Chunuk Bair, and on the left the 4th Australian Brigade attempted a northern spur of Koja Chemen. The Australians lost over 1,000, and were compelled to fall back to their original position, where they stood at bay.

In the great heat, and through a country so arduous, no movement could be long sustained. It must resolve itself into a series of dashes, with intervals for rest and reorganisation. There was no water in those parched *nullahs*, and every drop had to be brought up the ridges from the beaches. The fighting died away on the afternoon of the 8th. The great effort was fixed for the following morning, when the Australians and the Indians on the left should attack Koja Chemen from the head of the Aghyl Dere, and the New Zealanders push in the same direction from their position on Chunuk Bair. Five battalions—two each from the 29th and 38th Brigades, and one from the 40th—were put under the command of General Baldwin, and sent up to form a third column on the right centre of the movement.

The 9th of August dawned with the same airless and pitiless heat. From the first dawn the artillery and the guns of the warships had been in action against the upper slopes of Koja Chemen. Then they ceased, and the British attack advanced in three columns. On the left the Indians moved straight up hill against the summit called Q, or Nameless Peak, the chief feature of the ridge between Chunuk Bair and Hill 971. The New Zealanders on the right held their position on Chunuk Bair, and between the two, General Baldwin's force moved in the confusion of broken downs and gullies north of Rhododendron Ridge. The last force was tired from the night march, and since no proper reconnaissance had been possible, they lost their way.

Baldwin, finding that he could not reach the summit ridge in time to take part in the main attack, deployed at the farm to the left of the New Zealand trenches on Rhododendron Spur. The New Zealanders, being the pivot of the movement, were not required to advance, and were able to maintain themselves safely. The Indians made the farthest progress, for, led by the 6th Gurkhas, and assisted by some of the 6th South Lancashires, they scaled the summit of Hill Q, and for half an hour looked down on the great white road to the east which threaded the peninsula, and which now was crowded with Turkish convoys, and beyond it to the blue waters of the Straits.

It was a sight that no British soldier had seen since that day in April, the first of the landing, when the Australian vanguard had gazed on the Dardanelles. But the ground could not be maintained. A shower of high explosive shell descended on the trenches on the summit. It was followed by a rush of Turkish supports, and before our line could be consolidated, we had been driven back from the crest. Our position that evening was a line from the northern slopes of Hill Q to the New Zealand position on Chunuk Bair, where about 200 yards were occupied by some 800 men. Our total casualties were nearly 8,500.

Had the Suvla Expedition succeeded, and the Anafarta hills been by this time won, the left flank of the Anzacs would have been safe, and we should have been astride the central ridge of the peninsula. During the violent fighting of the past two days the New Zealanders on the ridge had seen clearly the details of the landing. They saw the shell and shrapnel of the Turks sweep the beaches, and the covering fire of our naval guns. But their left, hard pressed on the Aghyl Dere, saw nothing of the right of the Suvla advance, which by this time should have made contact with them. Nor did the Turkish strength on Koja Chemen seem in any way to diminish, as would have been the case if they had been in difficulties with General Stopford's men at Anafarta. Rather it seemed to grow, and an ugly suspicion filled the troops on the ridge that the new effort, which had been planned as the culminating blow, had failed. Next day the doubt became a certainty.

For on Tuesday morning came a desperate Turkish counterattack on Chunuk Bair. The New Zealanders, who had been engaged in since Friday night, had been relieved by two battalions—the 6th Loyal North Lancashires and the 5th Wiltshires—of the 13th Division. At 4.30 a.m. the Yemen Division, supported by an extra regiment of three battalions, was launched against the British front. They came on in close formation, line after line, with the wild valour of fanatics. Our battalions were driven back from Chunuk Bair, and the Turks poured down the slopes to where Rhododendron Ridge juts from the parent massif. Their object was to gain the Sazli Beit Dere, and so cut off the British left from the rest of the Anzac forces. General Baldwin fell at this stage of the action.

The Indians on the slopes of Hill Q were also driven back, and for a moment it looked as if the attack would succeed. But the enemy, pouring solidly down the slopes, offered a superb target for our gunners. A stream of high explosives and shrapnel burst from our land batteries and the ships' guns. In the Indian section ten machine-guns caught them in flank at short range. The attack could not retire, for fresh men kept sweeping over the crest and driving the wedge forward to its destruction. Soon it slackened, then broke, and with fierce hand-to-hand fighting among the scrub we began to win back the lost ground. By midday the danger was over. It had been grave indeed, for the last two battalions of the Anzac general reserve had been sent up in support. Of one party of 5,000 Turks who had swarmed over the crest but 500 returned. That afternoon the fighting ceased from the sheer exhaustion of both sides. We had leisure to reconstruct our line, which now ran from the top of Rhododendron Ridge north-east to a position among the spurs of the Aghyl Dere. (One Victoria Cross was awarded for the Chunuk Bair fighting—to Corporal Cyril Bassett, of the New Zealand Divisional Signal Corps.)

Two days later, on 12th August, General Godley at last obtained touch with the right wing of the Suvla Bay force at a place called Susuk Kuyu, on the Azmak Dere, a little west of its junction with the Asma Dere. It had been a most glorious but a most costly enterprise. By the evening of 10th August, the casualties had reached 12,000, including a very large proportion of officers. Let General Godley speak for the quality of the men:—

> I cannot close my report without placing on record my unbounded admiration of the work performed, and the gallantry displayed, by the troops and their leaders during the severe fighting involved in these operations. Though the Australian, New Zealand, and Indian units had been confined to trench duty in a cramped space for some four months, and though the troops of the New Armies had only just landed from a sea voyage, and many of them had not been previously under fire, I do not believe that any troops in the world could have accomplished more.

We must turn now to the fortunes of the Suvla landing.

The force destined for Suvla Bay under Lieutenant-General Sir F. W. Stopford was for the most part the new Ninth Corps. It consisted of two divisions of the New Army—the 10th (Irish), under Major-General Sir Bryan Mahon, less one brigade; the 11th (Northern), under Major-General Hammersley; and two Territorial Divisions, the 53rd and 54th. All day of the 6th the 11th Division was busy embarking at Kephalos Bay, in Imbros, each man being given rations and water for two days. When the transports set sail after dusk it was to a destination unknown to all save the staff. About 9.30 p.m. the ships, showing no light, entered the little Bay of Suvla, four miles north of the main Anzac position. The night was dark, for the moon did not rise till two o'clock.

The enemy had no inkling of our plan. That day we had made a pretence of landing at Karachali, at the head of the Gulf of Saros, on the coast road from Enos to Bulair. That day, too, the attack at Cape Helles and Lone Pine had begun, and the enemy's attention was diverted to the extreme ends of his front. We are justified therefore in claiming the Suvla Expedition as a successful surprise. As the transports crept northwards the New Zealanders, on the dark shore to starboard, were already moving along their saps, and before the landing was well begun, the firing had started where the Mounted Brigades were clearing the foothills. But at Suvla there was no sign of life, till searchlights from the Anafarta slopes, in their periodic sweeping of the horizon, discovered the strange flotilla, and an intermittent rifle fire broke out upon the beach.

Three landing places had been selected—A, north of the Salt Lake, and B and C, south-west of it. All night long the work of disembarkation went on. The 32nd and 33rd Brigades landed at B and C, and the 34th at A. Opposite B and C was a little hill called Lala Baba, held by the enemy. It was readily carried with the bayonet by the 9th West Yorks and 6th Yorkshires, and for the rest of the night our only trouble was from scattered snipers in the scrub. The 34th Brigade had some difficulties at A with a Turkish outpost on Hill 10, but with the assistance of the 32nd Brigade they pushed northward and carried the ridge of the Karakol Dagh. At dawn on the 7th the 11th Division was ashore, and held both sides of the bay and the neck of land between them.

At daybreak six battalions of the 10th Division arrived in the bay from Mitylene. It was General Stopford's intention to use the 10th Division on his left, but for some reason not yet clear the troops could not be landed at A beach, but were landed at C, and marched slowly northwards along the coast. Presently the remaining three battalions of the division arrived from Mudros along with General Sir Bryan Mahon.

It was now necessary to deploy into the plain and take up a broad front east of the Salt Lake. The earliest light brought the Turkish artillery into action. At first, we heard only the guns of the New Zealanders, now far up on the slopes of Chunuk Bair. Then suddenly a storm of shrapnel broke on the beaches, which burst too high to do much damage, while the ordinary shells buried themselves in the sand. The 10th Division, in perfect order, moved along the causeway to the north end of the lake, while a field battery which we had established on Lala Baba provided a useful support.

At the same time the cruisers, monitors, and destroyers in the bay made good practice against the Turkish batteries on the heights. By two o'clock, with few casualties, the two divisions—the 10th on the left—held a line east of the lake running from the Karakol Dagh to near the butt-end of the ridge called Yilghin Burnu. So far, the operation had been conducted with perfect precision and success.

It was imperative to push on if we were to get the benefit of surprise. But as the afternoon advanced, we seemed to come to a standstill. It was very hot, and the troops were very weary and tormented with an unbearable thirst, most of the men having emptied their water-bottles by eight o'clock that morning. At 4 p.m. there came a thunderstorm and a heavy shower of rain, which cleared the air, and at five we managed to advance our front a little, under a violent shelling from the guns on Anafarta Ridge. Late that night our right won a real success, for two battalions of the 11th Division succeeded in carrying the position of Yilghin Burnu—which we called Chocolate Hill after its scrub had caught fire and been reduced to a barren desolation. This, and the parallel position of Karakol Dagh in the north, where Sir Bryan Mahon made a spirited attack, safeguarded our flanks; and, in the event of our advance on the morrow succeeding, would allow us to link up with the left of the Anzac Corps on the Azmak Dere.

Next day, Sunday, the 8th, the day on which the New Zealanders won Chunuk Bair, was the critical stage at Suvla. We had a strength of some 25,000 men. The Turks on the Anafarta heights were weak in numbers—our intelligence reports put them at no more than 4,000—and an attack resolutely pushed forward must have carried the position. East of Salt Lake there is a wide stretch of flat, sandy plain. Beyond this is a strip 2,000 yards deep of tillage, scrub, and woodland, and little farms stretching to the edge of the slopes.

To the south-east there is a gap in the hills, where stands the village of Kuchuk Anafarta in a dark clump of cypresses. The plan of the Turkish commander was to hold his trenches on the heights very thinly, while he pushed forward a screen of riflemen into the cover of the patches of scrub. This screen was brilliantly handled, and from its mobility and invisibility seems to have given our men the impression that they were facing a huge enemy force. Meanwhile the Turkish guns in the rear bombarded our lines and supports, and searched every road leading from the beaches.

All through that unlucky day we made sporadic attempts to advance, losing heavily in the process and gaining little ground. A whole British corps were held up by a screen of sharpshooters, well backed by artillery. The full story of the failure will probably never be known, and criticism is idle. The troops were new, and lacked that self-reliance and individual initiative which is necessary in open-order fighting in a difficult country, while there was undoubtedly a lack of purpose and

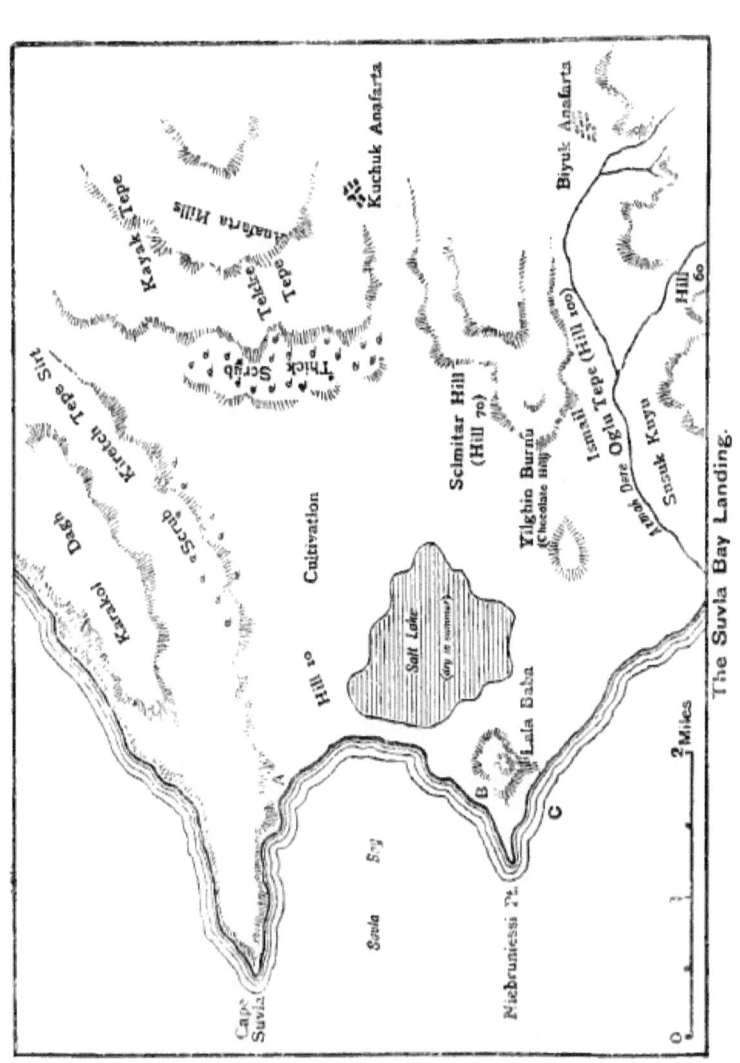

The Suvla Bay Landing.

resolution in their leadership. General Stopford was not satisfied with his artillery support, and the water arrangements were imperfect. But he did not sufficiently recognize the vital importance of an infantry advance at all costs when it is a question of making good a landing in hostile territory. In Sir Ian Hamilton's words:—

> The very existence of the force, its water supply, its facilities for munitions and supplies, its power to reinforce, must absolutely depend on the infantry being able instantly to make good sufficient ground without the aid of the artillery other than can be supplied for the purpose by *floating* batteries. . . . Driving power was required, and even a certain ruthlessness, to brush aside pleas for a respite for tired troops. The one fatal error was inertia. And inertia prevailed.

A fair summary of the situation may be quoted from the letter of an officer engaged in the movement:—

> Our sufferings were by no means caused entirely by the action of the foe. Hundreds and hundreds of men, fighting under a tropical heat, dropped out of the ranks after atrocious suffering caused by the lack of water. Apart from any question of the command, two causes contributed mainly to the lack of success which attended the expedition. The scene of combat presented extraordinary difficulties to the attacking force. On the other hand, a body of perfectly green troops, who had never been in action before, was called upon to undertake a task under the most nerve-trying conditions, which only could have been successfully achieved by men inured to the conditions existing in connection with the most recent and bloodiest of wars.

On Monday, the 9th, our chance had almost vanished. The heart had gone out of the attack, and we were settling down to a war of positions. Sir Ian Hamilton had arrived the night before from Imbros, and had striven to inspire the corps and divisional commanders with the spirit of the offensive. In his report, the fullest, most candid, and most luminous account which we possess of any of the operations of the war, he has described the situation. The general commanding the 11th Division declared himself unable to make a night attack. Another commander-in-chief might have insisted; Sir Ian was content to try to persuade, and failed. Early on the morning of the 9th an attack was indeed attempted by the 32nd Brigade.

THE SUVLA BAY LANDINGS, AUGUST

It was a gallant endeavour to carry the main Anafarta ridge, and one company of the 6th East Yorks (Pioneers) actually won the crest. But the effort had been made too late, for the Turkish defence was already thickening. Our difficulties were increased by an event which happened at midday. A strong wind was blowing from the north, and either by shell-fire or by Turkish design the scrub on Hill 70 was set ablaze. From that place, henceforth christened Burnt Hill, the tongues of flame leaping with the wind swept across our front, and drove us back.

An observer has described the scene:—

It was a weird sight, for in all directions you saw Turkish snipers and British infantry crawling out from amongst the scrub and trees and hedges, where they had been lying invisible, and, turning their backs on one another, crawling or running to get out of the track of the flames and dense black clouds of suffocating smoke.

The incident suspended all serious operations for the day. Next day, the 10th, the opportunity had gone for good. The Turks had received reinforcements—part of the Yemen Division which was on that day charging our position on Chunuk Bair. The 33rd Brigade attacked at dawn on Hill 100, which the Turks called Ismail Oglu Tepe. Some of the men reached the summit, but could not hold it. The 53rd Territorial Division, under General Lindley, had now arrived, and the 54th followed next day. On the 10th the 53rd attacked the main Anafarta Ridge, but failed to reach it.

For the next few days, we laboured to consolidate our front, which now ran from the Azmak Dere across Chocolate Hill to the 10th Division on the left. In the latter area we pushed forward a little on the Karakol Dagh, and presently had a continuous trench-line across the plain. On the 12th the 163rd Brigade on our left centre won some ground, and there the 1/5 Norfolks, under Colonel Sir H. Beauchamp, charged so vigorously that their colonel with 16 officers and 250 men disappeared for good in the forest. On that day, as we have seen, our right obtained touch with the men of Anzac on the Azmak Dere. On the 15th General Stopford relinquished the command of the 9th Corps. (He was succeeded by Lieutenant-General the Hon. Julian Byng, who had commanded the Cavalry Corps in France.)

For the next ten days the Suvla operations languished. Meantime we were preparing for a second effort, and for that purpose brought fresh troops to the scene of action. The new striking force was no less than the famous 29th Division, temporarily commanded by General Marshall, which was brought up from Cape Helles in trawlers and landed before the Turks were aware of its presence. To it was added the 2nd Mounted Division of Yeomanry, under Major-General Paton, and the whole force was put under the direction of General De Lisle. The objective was the encircling hills behind the Suvla plain, extending from Hill 70, now in the possession of the Turks, to Hill 100. (This feature is given in some maps as Hill 112.) By this time all the advantage of surprise had gone, and the Turkish position was held in equal or superior force. The only tactics left to us were those of a frontal assault.

The attack of the 29th Division was entrusted to the 86th and 87th Brigades; the 88th Brigade, which had been seriously depleted by the Cape Helles fighting of 6th August, being held in reserve. At three o'clock in the afternoon of the 21st a great bombardment was opened on the ridges. The enemy's guns replied, and soon the remainder of the scrub on Chocolate Hill was blazing, and our right was enveloped in a fog of smoke. Unfortunately, there was also a natural mist which discomfited our gunners. We had reckoned on the Turks being blinded by the setting sun, which should at the same time show up their positions; whereas the opposite was the case.

At 3.30 the 87th Brigade advanced against Hill 70 or Scimitar Hill, and the 86th against Hill 100; while on their right the 11th Division moved against the trenches in front of it, with orders, if successful, to swing northwards and assault Hill 100 from the south. The 87th Brigade at first made good progress. The 1st Inniskilling Fusiliers attacked the west face, and the 1st Border Regiment moved against the south slope. Both battalions almost won the crest, but the shell fire from behind Hill 100 was too strong, and the Turkish machine-guns held them back in the last hundred yards. The 2nd South Wales Borderers, the reserve battalion, attacked late in the afternoon on the south side; but they, too, failed, and were compelled to dig themselves in below the crest.

Meanwhile the 86th Brigade made repeated and most gallant attacks on Hill 100, but their efforts were fruitless. The New Army division on the right was held fast in the flats, and could do nothing in the way of a flanking attack.

About five o'clock the Mounted Division was ordered into action. They had been held in reserve below the knoll of Lala Baba, and now advanced across the open in perfect order under a devastating rain of Turkish shrapnel. For two miles they moved forward, as if on parade, and formed up below the 87th Brigade between Hill 70 and Hill 100. Sir Ian Hamilton has described the scene:—

> Such superb martial spectacles are rare in modern war.... Here, for a mile and a half, there was nothing to conceal a mouse, much less some of the most stalwart soldiers England has ever sent from her shores. Despite the critical events in other parts of the field, I could hardly take my glasses from the Yeomen. Here and there a shell would take toll of a cluster; there they lay; there was no straggling; the others moved steadily on; not a man was there who hung back or hurried.

As the darkness was falling, the Yeomanry rose from their cover and charged the hill. Lord Longford's 2nd (South Midland) Brigade, consisting of the Bucks, Berks, and Dorset regiments, led the assault; and the watchers in the plains saw the troopers near the crest, reach it, and then disappear as the first ranks leaped into the Turkish trenches. It was a splendid feat of arms, and a great shout went up that Hill 100 was won. In the gathering dark, made thicker by the smoke from the burning scrub, it was difficult to tell the result; but the perpetual patter of rifles and machine-gun fire showed that the conquest would be hard to maintain.

As it happened, the Yeomen had only won an under-feature; the Turks still held the crest, whence their machine-guns enfiladed the troops below. During the night it became clear that we could not hold the position, and by daylight we had fallen back upon our old lines. The final effort against Anafarta had failed. (Captain P. H. Hansen of the 6th Lincolns and Private Potts of the Berkshire Yeomanry received the Victoria Cross for the Suvla Bay actions.)

The one gleam of success that day was on the Azmak Dere, where the left of the Anzac Corps effected a lodgement on Hill 60, and enabled our front to be fully consolidated. On the 27th, after a brilliant attack by the 5th Connaught Rangers and the New Zealand Mounted Rifles, Hill 60 was finally won.

It is not easy to see how the second Suvla attack could have succeeded. It was another of those desperate frontal assaults of which, in the Cape Helles region, we had already learned the futility. The Turk entrenched on his hills was not to be driven out by the finest infantry in the world. But no failure can detract from the merits of the performance of the 29th and the Mounted Divisions. The Yeomanry suffered terribly. Two brigadiers fell—General Lord Longford, and, a little later, General Kenna, V.C.; so, did the gallant commander of the Sherwood Rangers, Sir John Milbanke, V.C, and some regiments, like the Bucks, were almost destroyed. Once again, as on 13th May at Ypres, the English Yeoman had shown "the mettle of the pasture." Had the troops used on the 21st been used on 7th August, the Anafarta heights might have been won.

The August fighting was the most costly part of the Dardanelles campaign. For the first three weeks of the month our casualties were close on 40,000, of which at least 30,000 were incurred between 6th August and 10th August. It was an intensity of loss greater than the First and Second Battles of Ypres, and, considering the numbers engaged, greater than the advance at Loos in the following month. It was, moreover, a fruitless sacrifice, for nothing material was gained. We had extended the length of our battle front by six miles, and we had advanced it on the left of the Anzac Corps by winning a mile or so of the Koja Chemen ridges. But we were no nearer to a decision. Our new line commanded no part of the enemy's communications, and it was in no way easier to hold. We had secured a little more room to move in in the Anzac zone, and that may be taken as the sum of our achievement.

The enterprise was an example of a bold and practicable scheme which miscarried owing to mistakes in detail. There was no fault to find with the general plan. Whether its success would have given us an immediate decision may be doubted, but it would have struck a deadly blow at the Turkish land communications, and prepared the way for a converging attack upon the central Turkish fortress of the Pasha Dagh. (The enemy on Pasha Dagh and Achi Baba could still have drawn supports across the Narrows from the Asiatic side, till such time as we took Maidos.) But it was of necessity a complex plan, demanding a simultaneous success at more than one point. There was no real lack of men, for the reserves both at Anzac and Suvla were sufficient, and there seems to have been no shortage of shell. We failed, partly because we used for a vital movement troops not yet inured to this kind of war, and partly because in the handling of these troops there was a conspicuous lack of skill and resolution.

The heroic performance of the New Zealanders and the Indians on the ridges of Koja Chemen was nullified by the bareness of their left flank, which prevented the proper use of the Anzac reserves, and

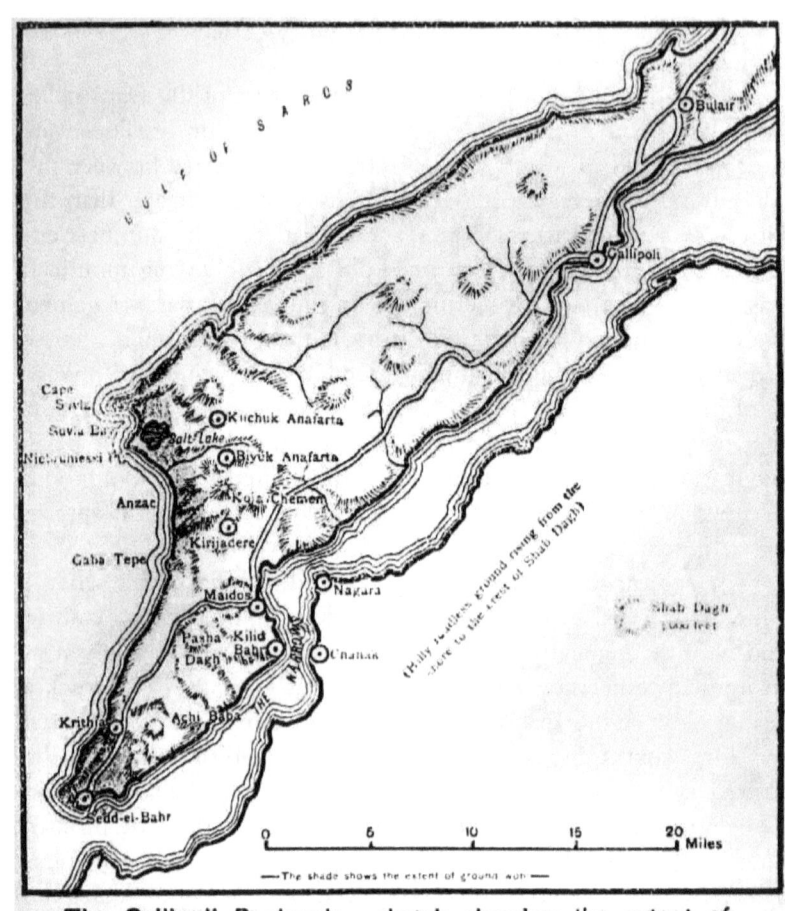

The Gallipoli Peninsula — sketch showing the extent of ground occupied at the close of the attack in August.

by the fact that they were face to face with an enemy in no way weakened by the attack to the north. The check to General Stopford's corps on that torrid Saturday in the Suvla flats was the undoing of the whole enterprise.

Appendix to Chapter 10

ANZAC AND SUVLA

Sir Ian Hamilton's Third Dispatch.

War Office.
6th January, 1916.

The following dispatch has been received by the Secretary of State for War from General Sir Ian Hamilton. G.C.B.:—

1 Hyde Park Gardens, London, W.,
11th December, 1915.

My Lord,

For the understanding of the operations about to be described I must first set forth the situation as it appeared to me early in July.

The three days' battle of the 6th-8th May had shown that neither of my forces, northern or southern, were strong enough to fight their way to the Narrows. On the 10th of May I had cabled asking that two fresh divisions might be sent me to enable me to press on and so prevent my attack degenerating into trench warfare. On the 17th of May I again cabled, saying that if we were going to be left to face Turkey on our own resources, we should require two army corps additional to my existing forces at the Dardanelles.

The 52nd (Lowland) Division had been sent me, but between their dates of dispatch and arrival Russia had given up the idea of co-operating from the coast of the Black Sea. Thereby several Turkish divisions were set free for the Dardanelles, and the battle of the 4th June, locally successful as it was, found us just as weak, relatively, as we had been a month earlier.

During June Your Lordship became persuaded of the bearing of these facts, and I was promised three regular divisions, plus the infantry of two Territorial divisions. The advance guard of these troops was due to reach Mudros by the 10th of July; by the 10th of August their concentration was to be complete.

Alternative Plans.

Eliminating the impracticable, I had already narrowed down the methods of employing these fresh forces to one of the following four:—

(*a*) Every man to be thrown on to the southern sector of the peninsula to force a way forward to the Narrows.

(*b*) Disembarkation on the Asiatic side of the Straits, followed by a march on Chanak.

(*c*) A landing at Enos or Ibrije for the purpose of seizing the neck of the isthmus at Bulair.

(*d*) Reinforcement of the Australian and New Zealand Army Corps, combined with a landing in Suvla Bay. Then with one strong push to capture Hill 305, and, working from that dominating point, to grip the waist of the peninsula.

As to (*a*) I rejected that course—

(1) Because there were limits to the numbers which could be landed and deployed in one confined area.

(2) Because the capture of Krithia could no longer be counted upon to give us Achi Baba, an entirely new system of works having lately appeared upon the slopes of that mountain—works so planned that even if the enemy's western flank was turned and driven back from the coast the central and eastern portions of the mountain could still be maintained as a bastion to Kilid Bahr.

(3) Because if I tried to disengage myself both from Krithia and Achi Baba by landing due west of Kilid Bahr my troops would be exposed to artillery fire from Achi Baba, the Olive Grove, and Kilid Bahr itself; the enemy's large reserves were too handy; there were not fair chances of success.

As to (*b*), although much of the Asiatic coast had now been wired and entrenched, the project was still attractive. Thereby the Turkish forces on the peninsula would be weakened; our beaches at Cape Helles would be freed from Asiatic shells; the threat to the enemy's sea communications was obvious. But when I descended into detail, I found that the expected reinforcements would not run to a double operation. I mean that, unless I could make a thorough, whole-hearted attack on the enemy in the peninsula I should reap no advantage in that theatre from the transference of the Turkish peninsular troops to reinforce Asia, whereas, if the British forces landed in Asia were not strong enough in themselves seriously to threaten Chanak, the Turks for their part would not seriously relax their grip upon the peninsula.

To cut the land communications of the whole of the Turkish peninsular army, as in (*c*), was a better scheme on paper than on the spot. The naval objections appeared to my coadjutor, Vice-Admiral de Robeck, well-nigh insurmountable. Already, owing to submarine dangers, all reinforcements, ammunition, and supplies had to be brought up from Mudros to Helles or Anzac by night in fleet-sweepers and trawlers. A new landing near Bulair would have added another 50 miles to the course such small craft must cover, thus placing too severe a strain upon the capacities of the flotilla.

The landing promised special hazards owing to the difficulty of securing the transports and covering ships from submarine attack. Ibrije has a bad beach, and the distance to Enos, the only point suitable to a disembarkation on a large scale, was so great that the enemy would have had time to organise a formidable opposition from his garrisons in Thrace. Four divisions at least would be required to overcome such opposition. These might now be found; but, even so, and presupposing every other obstacle overcome, it was by no manner of means certain that the Turkish Army on the peninsula would thereby be brought to sue for terms, or that the Narrows would thereby be opened to the Fleet. The enemy would still be able to work supplies across the Straits from Chanak. The swiftness of the current, the shallow draft of the Turkish lighters, the guns of the forts, made it too difficult even for our dauntless submarine commanders to paralyse movement across these land-locked waters. To achieve that purpose, I must bring my artillery fire to bear both on the land and water communications of the enemy.

The Possibilities of Anzac and Suvla.

This brings me to (*d*), the storming of that dominating height, Hill 305, with the capture of Maidos and Gaba Tepe as its sequel.

From the very first I had hoped that by landing a force under the heights of Sari Bair we should be able to strangle the Turkish communications to the southwards, whether by land or sea, and so clear the Narrows for the Fleet. Owing to the enemy's superiority, both in numbers and in position; owing to underestimates of the strength of the original entrenchments prepared and sited under German direction; owing to the constant dwindling of the units of my force through wastage; owing also to the intricacy and difficulty of the terrain, these hopes had not hitherto borne fruit. But they were well founded. So much at least had clearly enough been demonstrated by the desperate and costly nature of the Turkish attacks. The Australians and New Zealanders had rooted themselves in very near to the vitals of the enemy. By their tenacity and courage, they still held open the doorway from which one strong thrust forward might give us command of the Narrows.

From the naval point of view the auspices were also favourable. Suvla Bay was but one mile further from Mudros than Anzac, and its possession would ensure us a submarine-proof base and a harbour good against gales, excepting those from the south-west. There were, as might be expected, some special difficulties to be overcome. The broken, intricate country—the lack of water—the consequent anxious supply questions. Of these it can only be said that a bad country is better than an entrenched country, and that supply and water problems may be countered by careful preparation.

Before a man of the reinforcements had arrived my mind was made up as to their employment, and by means of a vigorous offensive from Anzac, combined with a surprise landing to the north of it, I meant to try and win through to Maidos, leaving behind me a well-protected line of communications starting from the bay of Suvla.

Another point which had to be fixed in advance was the date. The new troops would gain in fighting value if they could first be given a turn in the trenches. So much was clear. But the relief of the troops already holding those trenches would have been a long and difficult task for the navy, and time was everything, seeing that everywhere the enemy was digging in as fast as he possibly could dig. Also, where large numbers of troops were to be smuggled into Anzac and another large force was to land by surprise at Suvla, it was essential to eliminate the moon. Unless the plunge could be taken by the second week in August the whole venture must be postponed for a month. The dangers of such delay were clear. To realise them I had only to consider how notably my prospects would have been bettered had these same reinforcements arrived in time to enable me to anticipate the moon of July.

PRELIMINARY FIGHTING.

Place and date having shaped themselves, the intervening period had to be filled in with as much fighting as possible. First, to gain ground; secondly, to maintain the moral ascendancy which my troops had by this time established; thirdly, to keep the enemy's eyes fixed rather upon Helles than Anzac.

Working out my ammunition allowance, I found I could accumulate just enough high explosive shell to enable me to deliver one serious attack per each period of three weeks. I was thus limited to a single effort on the large scale, plus a prescribed unceasing offensive routine, with bombing, sniping, and mining as its methods.

The action of the 12th and 13th of July was meant to be a sequel to the action of the 28th June. That advance had driven back the Turkish right on to their second main system of defence just south of Krithia. But, on my centre and right, the enemy still held their forward system of trenches, and it was my intention on the 12th July to seize the remaining trenches of this foremost system from the sea at the mouth of the Kereves Dere to the main Sedd-el-Bahr—Krithia road, along a front of some 2,000 yards.

On our right the attack was to be entrusted to the French Corps; on the right centre to the 52nd (Lowland) Division. On the 52nd Division's front the operation was planned to take place in two phases: our right was to attack in the morning, our left in the afternoon. Diversions by the 29th Division on the left of the southern section and at Anzac were to take place on the same day, so as to prevent the enemy's reserves from reinforcing the real point of attack.

At 7.35 a.m., after a heavy bombardment, the troops, French and Scottish, dashed out of their trenches and at once captured two lines of enemy trenches. Pushing forward with fine *élan* the 1st Division of the French Corps completed the task assigned to it by carrying the whole of the Turkish forward system of works, namely, the line of trenches skirting the lower part of the Kereves Dere. Further to the left the 2nd French Division and our 155th Brigade maintained the two lines of trenches they had gained. But on the left of the 155th Brigade the 4th Battalion King's Own Scottish Borderers pressed on too eagerly. They not only carried the third line of trenches, but charged on up the hill and beyond the third line, then advanced indeed until they came under the "*feu de barrage*" of the French artillery. Nothing could live under so cruel a cross fire from friend and foe, so the King's Own Scottish Borderers were forced to fall back with heavy losses to the second line of enemy trenches which they had captured in their first rush.

During this fighting telephone wires from forward positions were cut by enemy's shell fire, and here and there in the elaborate network of trenches numbers of Turks were desperately resisting to the last. Thus, though the second line of captured trenches continued to be held as a whole, much confused fighting ensued; there were retirements in part of the line, reserves were rapidly being used up, and generally the situation was anxious and uncertain. But the best way of clearing it up seemed to be to deliver the second phase of the attack by the 157th Brigade just as it had originally been arranged. Accordingly, after a preliminary bombardment, the 157th Brigade rushed forward under heavy machine-gun and rifle fire, and splendidly carried the whole of the enemy trenches allotted as their objective. Here, then, our line had advanced some 400 yards, while the 155th Brigade and the 2nd French Division had advanced between 200 and 300 yards. At 6 p.m. the 52nd Division was ordered to make the line good; it seemed to be fairly in our grasp.

All night long determined counterattacks, one after another, were repulsed by the French and the 155th Brigade, but about 7.30 a.m. the right of the 157th Brigade gave way before a party of bombers, and our grip upon the enemy began to weaken.

I therefore decided that three battalions of the Royal Naval Division should reinforce a fresh attack to be made that afternoon, 13th July, on such portions of our original objectives as remained in the enemy's hands. This second attack was a success. The 1st French Division pushed their right down to the mouth of the Kereves Dere; the 2nd French Division attacked the trenches they had failed to take on the preceding day; the Nelson Battalion, on the left of the Royal Naval Division attack, valiantly advanced and made good, well supported by the artillery of the French. The Portsmouth Battalion, pressing on too far, fell into precisely the same error at precisely the same spot as did the 4th King's Own Scottish Borderers on the 12th, an over-impetuosity which cost them heavy losses.

The 1/5th Royal Scots Fusiliers, commanded by Lieutenant-Colonel J. B. Pollok-McCall; the 1/7th Royal Scots, commanded by Lieutenant-Colonel W. C. Peebles; the 1/5th King's Own Scottish Borderers, commanded by Lieutenant-Colonel W. J. Millar; and the 1/6th Highland Light Infantry, commanded by Major J. Anderson, are mentioned as having specially distinguished themselves in this engagement.

Generally, the upshot of the attack was this. On our right and on the French left two lines had been captured, but in neither case was the third, or last, line of the system in their hands. Elsewhere a fine feat of arms had been accomplished, and a solid and enduring advance had been achieved, giving us far the best sited line for defence with much the best field for machine-gun and rifle fire we had hitherto obtained upon the peninsula.

A machine-gun and 200 prisoners were captured by the French; the British took a machine-gun and 329 prisoners. The casualties in the French Corps were not heavy, though it is with sorrow that I have to report the mortal wound of General Masnou, commanding the 1st Division. Our own casualties were a little over 3,000; those of the enemy about 5,000.

Reinforcements and New Commands.

On 17th July Lieutenant-General Hunter Weston, commanding the 8th Corps, left the peninsula for a few days' rest, and, to my very deep regret, was subsequently invalided home. I have already drawn attention to his invincible self-confidence, untiring energy and trained ability.

As I was anxious to give the commander of the new troops all the local experience possible, I appointed Lieutenant General Hon. Sir Frederick Stopford, whose own corps were now assembling at Mudros, temporarily to succeed Lieutenant-General Hunter Weston, but on 24th July, when General Stopford had to set to work with his own corps, Major-General W. Douglas, General Officer Commanding 42nd Division, took over temporary command of the 8th Corps; while MajorGeneral W. R. Marshall, General Officer Commanding 87th Brigade, assumed temporary command of the 42nd Division.

Only one other action need be mentioned before coming to the big operations of August. On the extreme right of Anzac, the flank of a work called Tasmania Post was threatened by the extension of a Turkish trench. The task of capturing this trench was entrusted to the 3rd Australian Brigade. After an artillery bombardment, mines were to be fired, whereupon four columns of 50 men each were to assault and occupy specified lengths of the trench. The regiment supplying the assaulting columns was the 11th Australian Infantry Battalion.

At 10.15 p.m. on 31st July the bombardment was opened. Ten minutes later and the mines were duly fired. The four assaulting parties dashed forward at once, crossed our own barbed wire on planks, and were into the craters before the whole of the debris had fallen. Total casualties: 11 killed and 74 wounded; Turkish killed, 100.

By the time this action was fought a large proportion of my reinforcements had arrived, and, on the same principle which induced me to put General Stopford in temporary command at Helles, I relieved the war-worn 29th Division at the same place by the 13th Division under Major-General Shaw. The experiences here gained, in looking after themselves, in forgetting the thousand and one details of peace soldiering and in grasping the two or three elementary rules of conduct in war soldiering, were, it turned out, to be of priceless advantage to the 13th Division throughout the heavy fighting of the following month.

1

The Preliminaries.

And now it was time to determine a date for the great venture. The moon would rise on the morning of the 7th at about 2 a.m. A day or two previously the last reinforcements, the 53rd and 54th Divisions, were due to arrive. The first day of the attack was fixed for the 6th of August.

Various Ruses.

Once the date was decided a certain amount of ingenuity had to be called into play so as to divert the attention of the enemy from my main strategical conception. This—I repeat for the sake of clearness—was:—

(1) To break out with a rush from Anzac and cut off the bulk of the Turkish Army from land communication with Constantinople.

(2) To gain such a command for my artillery as to cut off the bulk of the Turkish Army from sea traffic whether with Constantinople or with Asia.

(3) Incidentally, to secure Suvla Bay as a winter base for Anzac and all the troops operating in the northern theatre.

My schemes for hoodwinking the Turks fell under two heads: First, strategical diversions, meant to draw away enemy reserves not yet committed to the peninsula. Secondly, tactical diversions meant to hold up enemy reserves already on the peninsula. Under the first heading came a surprise landing by a force of 300 men on the northern shore of the Gulf of Saros; demonstrations by French ships opposite Mitylene along the Syrian coast; concentration at Mitylene; inspections at Mitylene by the admiral and myself; making to order of a whole set of maps of Asia in Egypt, as well as secret service work, most of which bore fruit.

Amongst the tactical diversions were a big containing attack at

Helles. Soundings, registration of guns, etc., by monitors between Gaba Tepe and Kum Tepe. An attack to be carried out by Anzac on Lone Pine trenches, which lay in front of their right wing and as far distant as the local terrain would admit from the scene of the real battle. Thanks entirely to the reality and vigour which the navy and the troops threw into them, each one of these ruses was, it so turned out, entirely successful, with the result that the Turks, despite their excellent spy system, were caught completely off their guard at dawn on the 7th of August.

COMPLEXITIES OF THE STAFF PROBLEM.

Having settled upon the manner and time of the diversions, orders had to be issued for the main operation. And here I must pause a moment to draw Your Lordship's attention to the extraordinary complexity of the staff work caused by the unique distribution of my forces. Within the narrow confines of the positions I held on the peninsula it was impossible to concentrate even as much as one-third of the fresh troops about to be launched to the attack. Nor could Mudros and Imbros combined absorb the whole of the remainder. The strategic concentration which precedes a normal battle had in my case to be a very wide dispersion. Thus, of the forces destined for my offensive, on the day before the battle, part were at Anzac, part at Imbros, part at Mudros, and part at Mitylene. These last three detachments were separated respectively by 14, 60, and 120 miles of sea from the arena into which they were simultaneously to appear.

To ensure the punctual arrival of all these masses of inexperienced troops at the right moment and spot, together with their material, munitions, stores, supplies, water, animals, and vehicles, was a prodigious undertaking demanding not only competence, but self-confidence; and I will say for my General Staff that I believe the clearness and completeness of their orders for this concentration and landing will hereafter be studied as models in military academies. The need for economy in sea transport, the awkwardness and restriction of open beaches, the impossibility of landing guns, animals, or vehicles rapidly—all these made it essential to create a special, separate organisation for every single unit taking part in the adventure. A pack mule corps to supply 80,000 men had also to be organised for that specific purpose until such time as other transport could be landed.

As to water, that element of itself was responsible for a whole chapter of preparations. An enormous quantity had to be collected secretly, and as secretly stowed away at Anzac, where a high-level reservoir had to be built, having a holding capacity of 30,000 gallons, and fitted out with a regular system of pipes and distribution tanks. A stationary engine was brought over from Egypt to fill that reservoir. Petroleum tins, with a carrying capacity of 80,000 gallons, were got together, and fixed up with handles, etc., but the collision of the *Moorgate* with another vessel delayed the arrival of large numbers of these just as a breakdown in the stationary engine upset for a while the well-laid plan of the high-level reservoir.

But Anzac was ever resourceful in face of misadventures, and when the inevitable accidents arose it was not with folded hands that they were met.

Turning to Suvla Bay, it was believed that good wells and springs existed both in the Biyuk, Anafarta valley, and in Suvla plain. But nothing so vital could possibly be left to hearsay, and although, as it turned out, our information was perfectly correct, yet the War Office were asked to dispatch with each reinforcing division water receptacles for pack transport at the rate of half a gallon per man.

The Work of the Navy.

The sheet anchor on which hung the whole of these elaborate schemes was the navy. One tiny flaw in the perfect mutual trust and confidence animating the two services would have wrecked the whole enterprise. Experts at a distance may have guessed as much; it was self-evident to the rawest private on the spot. But with men like Vice-Admiral de Robeck. Commodore Roger Keyes, Rear-Admiral Christian, and Captain F. H, Mitchell at our backs, we soldiers were secured against any such risk, and it will be seen how perfect was the precision the sailors put into their job.

The hour was now approaching, and I waited for it with as much confidence as is possible when to the inevitable uncertainties of war are to be added those of the weather. Apart from feints, the first blow was to be dealt in the southern zone.

In that theatre I had my own *Poste de Commandement*. But upon the 6th of August attacks in the south were only to form a subsidiary part of one great concerted attack. Anzac was to deliver the knockdown blow; Helles and Suvla were complementary operations. Were I to commit myself at the outset to any one of these three theatres I must lose my sense of proportion. Worse, there being no lateral communication between them, as soon as I landed at one, I was cut off from present touch with both of the others. At Imbros I was 45 minutes from Helles, 40 minutes from Anzac, and 50 minutes from Suvla. Imbros was the centre of the cable system, and thence I could follow each phase of the triple attack and be ready with my two divisions of reserve to throw in reinforcements where they seemed most to be required. Therefore, I decided to follow the opening moves from General Headquarters.

2
The Feint at Helles.

At Helles the attack of the 6th was directed against 1,200 yards of the Turkish front opposite our own right and right centre, and was to be carried out by the 88th Brigade of the 29th Division. Two small Turkish trenches enfilading the main advance had, if possible, to be captured simultaneously, an affair which was entrusted to the 42nd Division.

After bombardment the infantry assaulted at 3.50 p.m. On the left large sections of the enemy's line were carried, but on our centre and right the Turks were encountered in masses, and the attack, pluckily and perseveringly as it was pressed, never had any real success. The 1st Battalion, Essex Regiment, in particular forced their way into the crowded enemy trench opposite them, despite the most determined resistance, but, once in, were subjected to the heaviest musketry fire from both flanks, as well as in reverse, and were shattered by showers of bombs. Two separate resolute attacks were made by the 42nd Division, but both of them recoiled in face of the unexpected volume of fire developed by the Turks.

After dark officer's patrols were sent up to ascertain the exact position of affairs. Heavy Turkish counterattacks were being pressed against such portions of the line we still retained. Many of our men fought it out where they stood to the last, but by nightfall none of the enemy's line remained in our possession.

Our set back was in no wise the fault of the troops. That ardour which only dashed itself to pieces against the enemy's strong entrenchments and numerous stubborn defenders on the 6th of August would, a month earlier, have achieved notable success. Such was the opinion of all. But the moral, as well as the strength of the Turks, had had time to rise to great heights since our last serious encounters with them on the 21st and 28th of June and on the 12th of July. On those dates all ranks had felt, as an army feels, instinctively, yet with certitude, that they had fairly got the upper hand of the enemy, and that, given the wherewithal, they could have gone on steadily advancing. Now that self-same, half-beaten enemy were again making as stout a resistance as they had offered us at our original landing.

For this recovery of the Turks there were three reasons: one moral, one material, and one fortuitous.

(1) The news of the enemy's advance on the Eastern Front had come to hand and had been advertised to us on posters from the Turkish trenches before we heard about it from home.

(2) Two new divisions had come down south to Helles to replace those we had most severely handled.

(3) The enemy trenches selected for our attack were found to be packed with troops and so were their communication trenches, the reason being, as explained to us by prisoners, that the Turkish commander had meant to launch from them an attack upon us. We had in fact, by a coincidence, as strange as it was unlucky, anticipated a Turkish offensive by an hour or two at most!

Sure enough, next morning, the enemy in their turn attacked the left of the line from which our own troops had advanced to the assault. A few of them gained a footing in our trenches and were all killed or captured. The remainder were driven back by fire.

As the aim of my action in this southern zone was to advance if I could, but in any case, to contain the enemy, and prevent him reinforcing to the northwards, I persevered on the 7th with my plans, notwithstanding the counterattack of the Turks which was actually in progress.

My objective this time was a double line of Turkish trenches on a front of about 800 yards between the Mai Tepe Dere and the west branch of the Kanli Dere. After a preliminary bombardment the troops of the 125th Brigade on the right and the 129th on the left made the assault at 9.40 a.m. From the outset it was evident that the enemy were full of fight and in great force, and that success would only be gained after a severe struggle.

On the right and on the centre the first enemy line was captured, and small parties pushed on to the second line, where they were unable to maintain themselves for long. On the left but little ground was gained, and by 11 a.m. what little had been taken had been relinquished.

The Battle of a Vineyard.

But in the centre a stiff battle raged all day up and down a vineyard some 200 yards long by 100 yards broad on the west of the Krithia road. A large portion of the vineyard had been captured in the first dash, and the East Lancashire men in this part of the field gallantly stood their ground here against a succession of vigorous counterattacks. The enemy suffered very severely in these counterattacks, which were launched in strength and at short intervals. Both our brigades had also lost heavily during the advance and in repelling the fierce onslaughts of the enemy, but, owing to the fine endurance of the 6th and 7th Battalions of the Lancashire Fusiliers, it was found possible to hold the vineyard through the night, and a massive column of the enemy which strove to overwhelm their thinned ranks was shattered to pieces in the attempt.

On 8th August Lieutenant-General Sir F. J. Davies took over command of the 8th Army Corps, and Major-General W. Douglas reverted to the command of the 42nd Division. For two more days his troops were called upon to show their qualities of vigilance and power of determined resistance, for the enemy had by no means yet lost hope of wresting from us the ground we had won in the vineyard. This unceasing struggle was a supreme test for battalions already exhausted by 48 hours' desperate fighting and weakened by the loss of so many good leaders and men; but the peculiar grit of the Lancastrians was equal to the strain, and they did not fail. Two specially furious counterattacks were delivered by the Turks on the 8th August, one at 4.40 a.m. and another at 8.30 p.m., where again our bayonets were too much for them. Throughout the night they made continuous bomb attacks, but the 6th Lancashire Fusiliers and the 4th East Lancashire Regiment stuck gamely to their task at the eastern corner of the vineyard.

There was desperate fighting also at the northern corner, where the personal bravery of Lieutenant W. T. Forshaw, 1/9th Manchester Regiment, who stuck to his post after his detachment had been relieved (an act for which he has since been awarded the V.C.), was largely instrumental in the repulse of three very determined onslaughts.

By the morning of the 9th August things were quieter, and the sorely tried troops were relieved. On the night of the 12th-13th the enemy made one more sudden, desperate dash for their vineyard—and got it! But, on the 13th, our bombers took the matter in hand. The Turks were finally driven out; the new fire trenches were wired and loopholed, and have since become part of our line.

These two attacks had served their main purpose. If the local successes were not all that had been hoped for, yet a useful advance had been achieved, and not only had they given a fresh, hard fighting enemy more than he had bargained for, but they had actually drawn down Turkish reinforcements to their area. And how can a commander say enough for the troops who, aware that their task was only a subsidiary one, fought with just as much vim and resolution as if they were storming the battlements of Constantinople!

THE ANZAC PLAN.

I will now proceed to tell of the assault on Chunuk Bair by the forces under General Birdwood, and of the landing of the 9th Corps in the neighbourhood of Suvla Bay. The entire details of the operations allotted to the troops to be employed in the Anzac area were formulated by Lieutenant-General Birdwood, subject only to my final approval. So excellently was this vital business worked out on the lines of the instructions issued that I had no modifications to suggest, and all these local preparations were completed by 6th August in a way which reflects the greatest credit, not only on the corps commander and his staff, but also upon the troops themselves, who had to toil like slaves to accumulate food, drink, and munitions of war.

Alone the accommodation for the extra troops to be landed necessitated an immense amount of work in preparing new concealed bivouacs, in making interior communications, and in storing water and supplies, for I was determined to put on shore as many fighting men as our modest holding at Anzac could possibly accommodate or provision. All the work was done by Australian and New Zealand soldiers almost entirely by night, and the uncomplaining efforts of these much-tried troops in preparation are in a sense as much to their credit as their heroism in the battles that followed. Above all, the water problem caused anxiety to the admiral, to Lieutenant-General Birdwood, and to myself.

The troops to advance from Suvla Bay across the Anafarta valley might reckon on finding some wells—it was certain, at least, that no water was waiting for us on the crests of the ridges of Sari Bair! Therefore, first, several days' supply had to be stocked into tanks along the beach and thence pumped up into other tanks half-way up the mountains; secondly, a system of mule transport had to be worked out, so that in so far as was humanly possible, thirst should not be allowed to overcome the troops after they had overcome the difficulties of the country and the resistance of the enemy.

3

THE ANZAC BATTLES.

On the nights of the 4th, 5th, and 6th August the reinforcing troops were shipped into Anzac very silently at the darkest hours. Then, still silently, they were tucked away from enemy aeroplanes or observatories in their prepared hiding places. The whole sea route lay open to the view of the Turks upon Achi Baba's summit and Battleship Hill. Aeroplanes could count every tent and every ship at Mudros or at Imbros. Within rifle fire of Anzac's open beach hostile riflemen were looking out across the Aegean no more than 20 feet from our opposing lines. Every modern appliance of telescope, telegraph, wireless was at the disposal of the enemy. Yet the Instructions worked out at General Headquarters in the minutest detail (the result of conferences with the Royal Navy, which were attended by Brigadier-General Skeen, of General Birdwood's Staff) were such that the scheme was carried through without a hitch.

The preparation of the ambush was treated as a simple matter by the services therein engaged, and yet I much doubt whether any more pregnant enterprise than this of landing so large a force under the very eyes of the enemy, and of keeping them concealed there three days, is recorded in the annals of war.

The troops now at the disposal of General Birdwood amounted in round numbers to 37,000 rifles and 72 guns, with naval support from two cruisers, four monitors, and two destroyers. Under the scheme these troops were to be divided into two main portions. The task of holding the existing Anzac position, and of making frontal assaults therefrom, was assigned to the Australian Division (plus the 1st and 3rd Light Horse Brigades and two battalions of the 40th Brigade); that of assaulting the Chunuk Bair ridge was entrusted to the New Zealand and Australian Division (less the 1st and 3rd Light Horse Brigades), to the 13th Division (less five battalions), and to the 29th Indian Infantry Brigade, and to the Indian Mountain Artillery Brigade. The 29th Brigade of the 10th Division (less one battalion) and the 38th Brigade were held in reserve.

THE ATTACK ON THE LONE PINE TRENCHES.

The most simple method of developing this complicated series of operations will be first to take the frontal attacks from the existing

Anzac position, and afterwards to go on to the assault on the more distant ridges. During the 4th, 5th, and 6th of August the works on the enemy's left and centre were subjected to a slow bombardment, and on the afternoon of the 6th August an assault was made upon the formidable Lone Pine entrenchment. Although, in its essence, a diversion to draw the enemy's attention and reserves from the grand attack impending upon his right, yet, in itself, Lone Pine was a distinct step on the way across to Maidos. It commanded one of the main sources of the Turkish water supply, and was a work, or, rather, a series of works, for the safety of which the enemy had always evinced a certain nervousness. The attack was designed to heighten this impression.

The work consisted of a strong *point d'appui* on the southwestern end of a plateau, where it confronted, at distances varying from 60 to 120 yards, the salient in the line of our trenches named by us the Pimple. The entrenchment was evidently very strong; it was entangled with wire, and provided with overhead cover, and it was connected by numerous communication trenches with another *point d'appui* known as Johnston's Jolly on the north, as well as with two other works on the east and south. The frontage for attack amounted at most to some 220 yards, and the approaches lay open to heavy enfilade fire, both from the north and from the south.

The detailed scheme of attack was worked out with care and forethought by Major-General H. B. Walker, commanding 1st Australian Division, and his thoroughness contributed, I consider, largely to the success of the enterprise.

The action commenced at 4.30 p.m. with a continuous and heavy bombardment of the Lone Pine and adjacent trenches, H.M.S. *Bacchante* assisting by searching the valleys to the north-east and east, and the monitors by shelling the enemy's batteries south of Gaba Tepe. The assault had been entrusted to the 1st Australian Brigade (Brigadier-General N. M. Smyth), and punctually at 5.30 p.m. it was carried out by the 2nd, 3rd, and 4th Australian Battalions, the 1st Battalion forming the brigade reserve.

Two lines left their trenches simultaneously, and were closely followed up by a third. The rush across the open was a regular race against death, which came in the shape of a hail of shell and rifle bullets from front and from either flank. But the Australians had firmly resolved to reach the enemy's trenches, and in this determination, they became for the moment invincible. The barbed wire entanglement was reached and was surmounted. Then came a terrible moment, when it seemed as though it would be physically impossible to penetrate into the trenches. The overhead cover of stout pine beams resisted all individual efforts to move it, and the loopholes continued to spit fire.

Groups of our men then bodily lifted up the beams and individual soldiers leaped down into the semi-darkened galleries amongst the Turks. By 5.47 p.m. the 3rd and 4th Battalions were well into the enemy's vitals, and a few minutes later the reserves of the 2nd Battalion advanced over their *parados*, and driving out, killing, or capturing the occupants, made good the whole of the trenches. The reserve companies of the 3rd and 4th Battalions followed, and at 6.20 p.m. the 1st Battalion (in reserve) was launched to consolidate the position.

At once the Turks made it plain, as they have never ceased to do since, that they had no intention of acquiescing in the capture of this capital work. At 7.0 p.m. a determined and violent counterattack began, both from the north and from the south. Wave upon wave the enemy swept forward with the bayonet. Here and there a well-directed salvo of bombs emptied a section of a trench, but whenever this occurred the gap was quickly filled by the initiative of the officers and the gallantry of the men.

The Counterattacks.

The enemy allowed small respite. At 1.30 that night the battle broke out afresh. Strong parties of Turks swarmed out of the communication trenches, preceded by showers of bombs. For seven hours these counterattacks continued. All this time consolidation was being attempted, although the presence of so many Turkish prisoners hampered movement and constituted an actual danger. In beating off these desperate counterattacks very heavy casualties were suffered by the Australians. Part of the 12th Battalion, the reserve of the 3rd Brigade, had therefore to be thrown into the *mêlée*.

Twelve hours later, at 1.30 p.m. on the 7th, another effort was made by the enemy, lasting uninterruptedly at closest quarters till 5 p.m., then being resumed at midnight and proceeding intermittently till dawn. At an early period of this last counterattack the 4th Battalion were forced by bombs to relinquish portion of a trench, but later on, led by their commanding officer, Lieutenant-Colonel McNaghten, they killed every Turk who had got in.

During the 8th of August advantage was taken of every cessation in the enemy's bombing to consolidate. The 2nd Battalion, which had lost its commanding officer and suffered especially severely, was withdrawn and replaced by the 7th Battalion, the reserve to the 2nd Infantry Brigade.

At 5 a.m. on 9th August the enemy made a sudden attempt to storm from the east and south-east after a feint of fire attack from the north. The 7th Battalion bore the brunt of the shock, and handled the attack so vigorously that by 7.45 a.m. there were clear signs of demoralisation in the enemy's ranks. But, although this marked the end of counterattacks on the large scale, the bombing and sniping continued, though in less volume, throughout this day and night, and lasted till 12th August, when it at last became manifest that we had gained complete ascendancy. During the final grand assault our losses from artillery fire were large, and ever since the work has passed into our hands it has been a favourite daily and nightly mark for heavy shells and bombs.

The Australian Achievement.

Thus, was Lone Pine taken and held. The Turks were in great force and very full of fight, yet one weak Australian Brigade, numbering at the outset but 2,000 rifles, and supported only by two weak battalions, carried the work under the eyes of a whole enemy division, and maintained their grip upon it like a vice during six days' successive counterattacks. High praise is due to Brigadier-General N. M. Smyth and to his battalion commanders. The irresistible dash and daring of officers and men in the initial charge were a glory to Australia. The stout-heartedness with which they clung to the captured ground in spite of fatigue, severe losses, and the continual strain of shell fire and bomb attacks may seem less striking to the civilian; it is even more admirable to the soldier.

From start to finish the artillery support was untiring and vigilant. Owing to the rapid, accurate fire of the 2nd New Zealand Battery, under Major Sykes, several of the Turkish onslaughts were altogether defeated in their attempts to get to grips with the Australians. Not a chance was lost by these gunners, although time and again the enemy's artillery made direct hits on their shields. The hand-to-hand fighting in the semi-obscurity of the trenches was prolonged and very bitterly contested.

In one corner eight Turks and six Australians were found lying as they had bayoneted one another. To make room for the fighting men the dead were ranged in rows on either side of the gangway. After the first violence of the counterattacks had abated, 1,000 corpses—our own and Turkish—were dragged out from the trenches.

For the severity of our own casualties some partial consolation may be found in the facts, first, that those of the enemy were much heavier, our guns and machine-guns having taken toll of them as they advanced in mass formation along the reverse slopes; secondly, that the Lone Pine attack drew all the local enemy reserves towards it, and may be held, more than any other cause, to have been the reason that the Suvla Bay landing was so lightly opposed, and that comparatively few of the enemy were available at first to reinforce against our attack on Sari Bair. Our captures in this feat of arms amounted to 134 prisoners, seven machine-guns, and a large quantity of ammunition and equipment.

The Frontal Attacks from Anzac.

Other frontal attacks from the existing Anzac positions were not so fortunate. They fulfilled their object in so far as they prevented the enemy from reinforcing against the attack upon the high ridges, but they failed to make good any ground. Taken in sequence of time, they included an attack upon the work known as German Officer's Trench, on the extreme right of our line, at midnight on August 6-7, also assaults on the Nek and Baby 700 trenches opposite the centre of our line, delivered at 4.30 a.m. on the 7th. The 2nd Australian Brigade did all that men could do; the 8th Light Horse only accepted their repulse after losing three-fourths of that devoted band who so bravely sallied forth from Russell's Top. Some of the works were carried, but in these cases the enemy's concealed machine-guns made it impossible to hold on. But all that day, as the result of these most gallant attacks, Turkish reserves on Battleship Hill were being held back to meet any dangerous development along the front of the old Anzac line, and so were not available to meet our main enterprise, which I will now endeavour to describe.

The first step in the real push—the step which above all others was to count—was the night attack on the summits of the Sari Bair ridge. The crest line of this lofty mountain range runs parallel to the sea, dominating the under-features contained within the Anzac position, although these fortunately defilade the actual landing-place. From the main ridge a series of spurs run down towards the level beach, and are separated from one another by deep, jagged gullies choked up with dense jungle. Two of these leading up to Chunuk Bair are called Chailak Dere and Sazli Beit Dere; another deep ravine runs up to

Koja Chemen Tepe (Hill 305), the topmost peak of the whole ridge, and is called the Aghyl Dere.

The Plan of the Great Movement.

It was our object to effect a lodgement along the crest of the high main ridge with two columns of troops, but, seeing the nature of the ground and the dispositions of the enemy, the effort had to be made by stages. We were bound, in fact, to undertake a double subsidiary operation before we could hope to launch these attacks with any real prospect of success.

(1) The right covering force was to seize Table Top, as well as all other enemy positions commanding the foothills between the Chailak Dere and the Sazli Beit Dere ravines. If this enterprise succeeded it would open up the ravines for the assaulting columns, whilst at the same time interposing between the right flank of the left covering force and the enemy holding the Sari Bair main ridge.

(2) The left covering force was to march northwards along the beach to seize a hill called Damakjelik Bair, some 1,400 yards north of Table Top. If successful it would be able to hold out a hand to the 9th Corps as it landed south of Nibrunesi Point, whilst at the same time protecting the left flank of the left assaulting column against enemy troops from the Anafarta valley during its climb up the Aghyl Dere ravine.

(3) The right assaulting column was to move up the Chailak Dere and Sazli Beit Dere ravines to the storm of the ridge of Chunuk Bair.

(4) The left assaulting column was to work up the Aghyl Dere and prolong the line of the right assaulting column by storming Hill 305 (Koja Chemen Tepe), the summit of the whole range of hills.

To recapitulate, the two assaulting columns, which were to work up three ravines to the storm of the high ridge, were to be preceded by two covering columns. One of these was to capture the enemy's positions commanding the foothills, first to open the mouths of the ravines, secondly to cover the right flank of another covering force whilst it marched along the beach. The other covering column was to strike far out to the north until, from a hill called Damakjelik Bair, it could at the same time facilitate the landing of the 9th Corps at

Nibrunesi Point, and guard the left flank of the column assaulting Sari Bair from any forces of the enemy which might be assembled in the Anafarta valley.

General Godley's Command.

The whole of this big attack was placed under the command of Major-General Sir A. J. Godley, General Officer Commanding New Zealand and Australian Division. The two covering and the two assaulting columns were organised as follows:—

Right Covering Column, under Brigadier-General A. H. Russell.—New Zealand Mounted Rifles Brigade, the Otago Mounted Rifles Regiment, the Maori Contingent and New Zealand Field Troop.

Right Assaulting Column, under Brigadier-General F. E. Johnston.—New Zealand Infantry Brigade, Indian Mountain Battery (less one section), one Company New Zealand Engineers.

Left Covering Column, under Brigadier-General J. H. Travers.—Headquarters 40th Brigade, half the 72nd Field Company, 4th Battalion, South Wales Borderers, and 5th Battalion, Wiltshire Regiment.

Left Assaulting Column, under Brigadier-General (now Major-General) H.V. Cox.—29th Indian Infantry Brigade, 4th Australian Infantry Brigade, Indian Mountain Battery (less one section), one company New Zealand Engineers.

Divisional Reserve.—6th Battalion, South Lancashire Regiment, and 8th Battalion, Welsh Regiment (Pioneers) at Chailak Dere, and the 39th Infantry Brigade and half 72nd Field Company at Aghyl Dere.

The right covering column, it will be remembered, had to gain command of the Sazli Beit Dere and the Aghyl Dere ravines, so as to let the assaulting column arrive intact within striking distance of the Chunuk Bair ridge. To achieve this object, it had to clear the Turks off from their right flank positions upon Old No. 3 Post and Table Top.

Old No. 3 Post, connected with Table Top by a razor back, formed the apex of a triangular piece of hill sloping gradually down to our No. 2 and No. 3 outposts. Since its recapture from us by the Turks on 30th May working parties had done their best with unstinted material to convert this commanding point into an impregnable redoubt. Two lines of fire trench, very heavily entangled, protected its southern face—the only one accessible to us—and, with its head cover of solid timber baulks and its strongly revetted outworks, it dominated the approaches of both the Chailak Dere and the Sazli Beit Dere.

STRATAGEMS.

Table Top is a steep-sided, flat-topped hill, close on 400 feet above sea level. The sides of the hill are mostly sheer and quite impracticable, but here and there a ravine, choked with scrub, and under fire of enemy trenches, gives precarious foothold up the precipitous cliffs. The small plateau on the summit was honeycombed with trenches, which were connected by a communication alley with that under-feature of Sari Bair known as Rhododendron Spur.

Amongst other stratagems the Anzac troops, assisted by H.M.S. *Colne*, had long and carefully been educating the Turks how they should lose Old No. 3 Post, which could hardly have been rushed by simple force of arms. Every night, exactly at 9 p.m., H.M.S. *Colne* threw the beams of her searchlight on to the redoubt, and opened fire upon it for exactly 10 minutes. Then, after a 10 minutes' interval, came a second illumination and bombardment, commencing always at 9.20 and ending precisely at 9.30 p.m.

The idea was that, after successive nights of such practice, the enemy would get into the habit of taking the searchlight as a hint to clear out until the shelling was at an end. But on the eventful night of the 6th, the sound of their footsteps drowned by the loud cannonade, unseen as they crept along in that darkest shadow which fringes a searchlight's beam—came the right covering column. At 9.30 the light switched off, and instantly our men poured out of the scrub jungle and into the empty redoubt. By 11 p.m. the whole series of surrounding entrenchments were ours!

Once the capture of Old No. 3 Post was fairly under way, the remainder of the right covering column carried on with their attack upon Bauchop's Hill and the Chailak Dere. By 10 p.m. the northernmost point, with its machine-gun, was captured, and by 1 o'clock in the morning the whole of Bauchop's Hill, a maze of ridge and ravine, everywhere entrenched, was fairly in our hands.

The attack along the Chailak Dere was not so cleanly carried out—made, indeed, just about as ugly a start as any enemy could wish. Pressing eagerly forward through the night, the little column of stormers found themselves held up by a barbed-wire erection of unexampled height, depth, and solidity, which completely closed the river bed—that is to say, the only practicable entrance to the ravine. The entanglement was flanked by a strongly-held enemy trench running right across the opening of the Chailak Dere. Here that splendid body of men, the Otago Mounted Rifles, lost some of their bravest and their best, but in the end, when things were beginning to seem desperate, a passage was forced through the stubborn obstacle with most conspicuous and cool courage by Captain Shera and a party of New Zealand Engineers, supported by the Maoris, who showed themselves worthy descendants of the warriors of the Gate Pah. Thus, was the mouth of the Chailak Dere opened in time to admit of the unopposed entry of the right assaulting column.

Capture of Table Top.

Simultaneously the attack on Table Top had been launched under cover of a heavy bombardment from H.M.S. *Colne*. No general on peace manoeuvres would ask troops to attempt so break-neck an enterprise. The flanks of Table Top are so steep that the height gives an impression of a mushroom shape—of the summit bulging out over its stem. But just as faith moves mountains, so valour can carry them. The Turks fought bravely. The angle of Table Top's ascent is recognised in our regulations as "impracticable for infantry." But neither Turks nor angles of ascent were destined to stop Russell or his New Zealanders that night. There are moments during battle when life becomes intensified, when men become supermen, when the impossible becomes simple—and this was one of those moments.

The scarped heights were scaled, the plateau was carried by midnight. With this brilliant feat the task of the right covering force was at an end. Its attacks had been made with the bayonet and bomb only; magazines were empty by order; hardly a rifle shot had been fired. Some 150 prisoners were captured as well as many rifles and much equipment, ammunition, and stores. No words can do justice to the achievement of Brigadier-General Russell and his men. There are exploits which must be seen to be realised.

The right assaulting column had entered the two southerly ravines—Sazli Beit Dere and Chailak Dere—by midnight. At 1.30 a.m. began a hotly-contested fight for the trenches on the lower part of Rhododendron Spur, whilst the Chailak Dere column pressed steadily up the valley against the enemy.

The left covering column, under Brigadier-General Travers, after marching along the beach to No. 3 outpost, resumed its northerly advance as soon as the attack on Bauchop's Hill had developed. Once the Chailak Dere was cleared the column moved by the mouth of the

Aghyl Dere, disregarding the enfilade fire from sections of Bauchop's Hill still uncaptured. The rapid success of this movement was largely due to Lieutenant-Colonel Gillespie, a very fine man, who commanded the advance guard consisting of his own regiment, the 4th South Wales Borderers, a corps worthy of such a leader. Every trench encountered was instantly rushed by the Borderers, until having reached the predetermined spot, the whole column was unhesitatingly launched at Damakjelik Bair. Several Turkish trenches were captured at the bayonet's point, and by 1.30 a.m. the whole of the hill was occupied, thus safeguarding the left rear of the whole of the Anzac attack.

Here was an encouraging sample of what the New Army, under good auspices, could accomplish. Nothing more trying to Inexperienced troops can be imagined than a long night march exposed to flanking fire, through a strange country, winding up at the end with a bayonet charge against a height, formless and still in the starlight, garrisoned by those spectres of imagination, worst enemies of the soldier.

Beginning of the Grand Attack.

The left assaulting column crossed the Chailak Dere at 12.30 a.m., and entered the Aghyl Dere at the heels of the left covering column. The surprise, on this side, was complete. Two Turkish officers were caught in their pyjamas; enemy arms and ammunition were scattered in every direction.

The grand attack was now in full swing, but the country gave new sensations in cliff climbing even to officers and men who had graduated over the goat tracks of Anzac. The darkness of the night, the density of the scrub, hands and knees progress up the spurs, sheer physical fatigue, exhaustion of the spirit caused by repeated hairbreadth escapes from the hail of random bullets—all these combined to take the edge off the energies of our troops. At last, after advancing some distance up the Aghyl Dere, the column split up into two parts. The 4th Australian Brigade struggled, fighting hard as they went, up to the north of the northern fork of the Aghyl Dere, making for Hill 305 (Koja Chemen Tepe). The 29th Indian Infantry Brigade scrambled up the southern fork of the Aghyl Dere and the spurs north of it to the attack of a portion of the Sari Bair ridge known as Hill Q.

Capture of Rhododendron Spur.

Dawn broke and the crest line was not yet in our hands, although, considering all things, the left assaulting column had made a marvellous advance. The 4th Australian Infantry Brigade was on the line of the Asma Dere (the next ravine north of the Aghyl Dere) and the 29th Indian Infantry Brigade held the ridge west of the farm below Chunuk Bair and along the spurs to the north-cast. The enemy had been flung back from ridge to ridge; an excellent line for the renewal of the attack had been secured, and (except for the exhaustion of the troops) the auspices were propitious.

Turning to the right assaulting column, one battalion, the Canterbury Infantry Battalion, clambered slowly up the Sazli Beit Dere. The remainder of the force, led by the Otago Battalion, wound their way amongst the pitfalls and forced their passage through the scrub of the Chailak Dere, where fierce opposition forced them ere long to deploy. Here, too, the hopeless country was the main hindrance, and it was not until 5.45 a.m. that the bulk of the column joined the Canterbury Battalion on the lower slopes of Rhododendron Spur. The whole force then moved up the spur, gaining touch with the left assaulting column by means of the 10th Gurkhas, in face of very heavy fire and frequent bayonet charges. Eventually they entrenched on the top of Rhododendron Spur, a quarter of a mile short of Chunuk Bair—i.e., of victory.

At 7 a.m. the 5th and 6th Gurkhas, belonging to the left assaulting column, had approached the main ridge northeast of Chunuk Bair, whilst, on their left, the 14th Sikhs had got into touch with the 4th Australian Brigade on the southern watershed of the Asma Dere. The 4th Australian Brigade now received orders to leave half a battalion to hold the spur, and, with the rest of its strength, plus the 14th Sikhs, to assault Hill 305 (Koja Chemen Tepe). But by this time the enemy's opposition had hardened, and his reserves were moving up from the direction of Battleship Hill. Artillery support was asked for and given, yet by 9 a.m. the attack of the right assaulting column on Chunuk Bair was checked, and any idea of a further advance on Koja Chemen Tepe had to be, for the moment, suspended. The most that could be done was to hold fast to the Asma Dere watershed whilst attacking the ridge north-east of Chunuk Bair, an attack to be supported by a fresh assault launched against Chunuk Bair itself.

At 9.30 a.m. the two assaulting columns pressed forward whilst our guns pounded the enemy moving along the Battleship Hill spurs. But in spite of all their efforts their increasing exhaustion as opposed to the gathering strength of the enemy's fresh troops began to tell—they had shot their bolt. So, all day they clung to what they had captured and strove to make ready for the night. At 11 a.m. three battalions of the 39th Infantry Brigade were sent up from the general reserve to be at hand when needed, and, at the same hour, one more battalion of the reserve was dispatched to the 1st Australian Division to meet the drain caused by all the desperate Lone Pine fighting.

By the afternoon the position of the two assaulting columns was unchanged. The right covering force were in occupation of Table Top, Old No. 3 Post, and Bauchop Hill, which General Russell had been ordered to maintain with two regiments of Mounted Rifles, so that he might have two other regiments and the Maori Contingent available to move as required. The left covering force held Damakjelik Bair. The forces which had attacked along the front of the original Anzac line were back again in their own trenches. The Lone Pine work was being furiously disputed. All had suffered heavily and all were very tired.

So ended the first phase of the fighting for the Chunuk Bair ridge. Our aims had not fully been attained, and the help we had hoped for from Suvla had not been forthcoming. Yet I fully endorse the words of General Birdwood when he says:—

The troops had performed a feat which is without parallel.

Great *kudos* is due to Major-General Godley and Shaw for their arrangements; to Generals Russell, Johnston, Cox, and Travers for their leading; but most of all, as every one of these officers will gladly admit, to the rank and file for their fighting. Nor may I omit to add that the true destroyer spirit with which H.M.S. *Colne* (Commander Claude Seymour, R.N.) and H.M.S. *Chelmer* (Commander Hugh T. England, R.N.) backed us up will live in the grateful memories of the army.

THE FIGHT OF 8TH AUGUST.

In the course of this afternoon (7th August) reconnaissances of Sari Bair were carried out and the troops were got into shape for a fresh advance in three columns, to take place in the early morning.

The columns were composed as follows:—

Right Column, Brigadier-General F. E. Johnston.—26th Indian Mountain Battery (less one section), Auckland Mounted Rifles, New Zealand Infantry Brigade, two battalions 13th Division, and the Maori Contingent.

Centre and Left Columns, Major-General H.V. Cox.—21st Indian Mountain Battery (less one section), 4th Australian Brigade, 39th Infantry Brigade (less one battalion), with 6th Battalion South Lancashire Regiment attached, and the 29th Indian Infantry Brigade.

The right column was to climb up the Chunuk Bair ridge; the left column was to make for the prolongation of the ridge north-east to Koja Chemen Tepe, the topmost peak of the range.

The attack was timed for 4.15 a.m. At the first faint glimmer of dawn observers saw figures moving against the sky-line of Chunuk Bair. Were they our own men, or were they the Turks? Telescopes were anxiously adjusted; the light grew stronger; men were seen climbing up from our side of the ridge; they *were* our own fellows—the topmost summit was ours!

On the right General Johnston's column, headed by the Wellington Battalion and supported by the 7th Battalion, Gloucestershire Regiment, the Auckland Mounted Rifles Regiment, the 8th Welsh Pioneers, and the Maori Contingent, the whole most gallantly led by Lieutenant-Colonel W. G. Malone, had raced one another up the steep. Nothing could check them. On they went, until, with a last determined rush, they fixed themselves firmly on the south-western slopes and crest of the main knoll known as the height of Chunuk Bair. With deep regret I have to add that the brave Lieutenant-Colonel Malone fell mortally wounded as he was marking out the line to be held. The 7th Gloucesters suffered terrible losses here.

THE 7TH GLOUCESTERS.

The fire was so hot that they never got a chance to dig their trenches deeper than some six inches, and there they had to withstand attack after attack. In the course of these fights every single officer, company sergeant-major, or company quartermaster-sergeant was either killed or wounded, and the battalion by midday consisted of small groups of men commanded by junior non-commissioned officers or privates. Chapter and verse may be quoted for the view that the rank-and-file of an army cannot long endure the strain of close hand-to-hand fighting unless they are given confidence by the example of good officers. Yet here is at least one instance where a battalion of the New Army fought right on, from midday till sunset, without any officers.

In the centre the 39th Infantry Brigade and the 29th Indian Brigade moved along the gullies leading up to the Sari Bair ridge—the right moving south of the farm on Chunuk Bair, the left up the spurs to the north-east of the farm against a portion of the main ridge north-east of Chunuk Bair, and the col to the north of it. So murderous was the enemy's fire that little progress could be made, though some ground was gained on the spurs to the north-east of the farm. On the left the 4th Australian Brigade advanced from the Asma Dere against the lower slopes of Abdul Rahman Bair (a spur running due north from Koja Chemen Tepe) with the intention of wheeling to its right and advancing up the spur. Cunningly placed Turkish machine-guns and a strong entrenched body of infantry were ready for this move, and the brigade were unable to get on. At last, on the approach of heavy columns of the enemy, the Australians, virtually surrounded, and having already suffered losses of over 1,000, were withdrawn to their original position. Here they stood at bay, and though the men were by now half dead with thirst and with fatigue, they bloodily repulsed attack after attack delivered by heavy columns of Turks.

CAPTURE OF CHUNUK BAIR.

So stood matters at noon. Enough had been done for honour and much ground had everywhere been gained. The expected support from Suvla hung fire, but the capture of Chunuk Bair was a presage of victory; even the troops who had been repulsed were quite undefeated—quite full of fight—and so it was decided to hold hard as we were till nightfall, and then to essay one more grand attack, wherein the footing gained on Chunuk Bair would this time be used as a pivot.

In the afternoon the battle slackened, excepting always at Lone Pine, where the enemy were still coming on in mass, and being mown down by our fire. Elsewhere the troops were busy digging and getting up water and food, no child's play, with their wretched lines of communication running within musketry range of the enemy.

That evening the New Zealand Brigade, with two regiments of the New Zealand Mounted Rifles, and the Maoris. held Rhododendron Spur and the south-western slopes of the main knoll of Chunuk Bair. The front line was prolonged by the columns of General Cox and General Monash (with the 4th Australian Brigade). Behind the New Zealanders were the 38th Brigade in reserve, and in rear of General Monash two battalions of the 40th Brigade. The inner line was held as before, and the 29th Brigade (less two battalions) had been sent up from the general reserve, and remained still further in rear.

The columns for the renewed attack were composed as follows:—

No. 1 Column, Brigadier-General F. E. Johnston.—26th Indian Mountain Battery (less one section), the Auckland and Wellington Mounted Rifles Regiments, the New Zealand Infantry Brigade, and two battalions of the 13th Division.

No. 2 Column, Major-General H.V. Cox.—21st Indian Mountain Battery (less one section), 4th Australian Brigade, 39th Brigade (less the 7th Gloucesters, relieved), with the 6th Battalion South Lancashire Regiment attached, and the Indian Infantry Brigade.

No. 3 Column, Brigadier-General A. H. Baldwin, Commanding 38th Infantry Brigade.—Two battalions each from the 38th and 29th Brigades and one from the 40th Brigade.

No. 1 Column was to hold and consolidate the ground gained on the 6th, and, in co-operation with the other columns, to gain the whole of Chunuk Bair, and extend to the southeast. No. 2 Column was to attack Hill Q on the Chunuk Bair ridge, and No. 3 Column was to move from the Chailak Dere, also on Hill Q. This last column was to make the main attack, and the others were to co-operate with it.

The Attack of 9th August.

At 4.30 a.m. on August 9th the Chunuk Bair ridge and Hill Q were heavily shelled. The naval guns, all the guns on the left flank, and as many as possible from the right flank (whence the enemy's advance could be enfiladed), took part in this cannonade, which rose to its climax at 5.15 a.m., when the whole ridge seemed a mass of flame and smoke, whence huge clouds of dust drifted slowly upwards in strange patterns on to the sky. At 5.16 a.m. this tremendous bombardment was to be switched off on to the flanks and reverse slopes of the heights.

General Baldwin's column had assembled in the Chailak Dere, and was moving up towards General Johnston's headquarters. Our plan contemplated the massing of this column immediately behind the trenches held by the New Zealand Infantry Brigade. Thence it was intended to launch the battalions in successive lines, keeping them as much as possible on the high ground. Infinite trouble had been taken to ensure that the narrow track should be kept clear, guides also were provided; but in spite of all precautions the darkness, the rough scrub-covered country, its sheer steepness, so delayed the column that they were unable to take full advantage of the configuration of the ground, and, inclining to the left, did not reach the line of the farm—Chunuk Bair till 5.15 a.m. In plain English, Baldwin, owing to the darkness and the awful country, lost his way—through no fault of his own. The mischance was due to the fact that time did not admit of the detailed careful reconnaissance of routes which is so essential where operations are to be carried out by night.

The Gurkhas Reach the Summit Ridge.

And now, under that fine leader, Major C. G. L. Allanson, the 6th Gurkhas of the 29th Indian Infantry Brigade pressed up the slopes of Sari Bair, crowned the heights of the col between Chunuk Bair and Hill Q, viewed far beneath them the waters of the Hellespont, viewed the Asiatic shores along which motor transport was bringing supplies to the lighters. Not only did this battalion, as well as some of the 6th South Lancashire Regiment, reach the crest, but they began to attack down the far side of it, firing as they went at the fast retreating enemy. But the fortune of war was against as. At this supreme moment Baldwin's column was still a long way from our trenches on the crest of Chunuk Bair, whence they should even now have been sweeping out towards Q along the whole ridge of the mountain. And instead of Baldwin's support came suddenly a salvo of heavy shell.

These falling so unexpectedly among the stormers threw them into terrible confusion. The Turkish commander saw his chance; instantly his troops were rallied and brought back in a counter-charge, and the South Lancashires and Gurkhas, who had seen the promised land and had seemed for a moment to have held victory in their grasp, were forced backwards over the crest and on to the lower slopes whence they had first started.

But where was the main attack—where was Baldwin? When that bold but unlucky commander found he could not possibly reach our trenches on the top of Chunuk Bair in time to take effective part in the fight, he deployed for attack where he stood—*i.e.* at the farm to the left of the New Zealand Brigade's trenches on Rhododendron Spur. Now his men were coming on, in fine style and, just as the Turks topped the ridge with shouts of elation, two companies of the 6th East Lancashire Regiment, together with the 10th Hampshire Regiment, charged up our side of the slope with the bayonet. They had gained the high ground immediately below the commanding knoll on Chunuk Bair, and a few minutes earlier would have joined hands with the Gurkhas and South Lancashires and, combined with them, would have carried all before them. But the Turks by this time were lining the whole of the high crest in overwhelming numbers.

The New Army troops attacked with a fine audacity, but they were flung back from the height and then pressed still further down the slope, until General Baldwin had to withdraw his command to the vicinity of the farm, whilst the enemy, much encouraged, turned their attention to the New Zealand troops and the two New Army battalions of No.1 Column still holding the south-west half of the main knoll of Chunuk Bair. Constant attacks, urged with fanatical persistence, were met here with a sterner resolution, and although, at the end of the day, our troops were greatly exhausted, they still kept their footing on the summit.

And if that summit meant much to us, it meant even more to the Turks. For the ridge covered our landing-places, it is true, but it covered not only the Turkish beaches at Kilia Leman and Maidos, but also the Narrows themselves and the roads leading northward to Bulair and Constantinople.

That evening our line ran along Rhododendron Spur up to the crest of Chunuk Bair, where about 200 yards were occupied and held by some 800 men. Slight trenches had hastily been dug, but the fatigue of the New Zealanders and the fire of the enemy had prevented solid work being done. The trenches in many places were not more than a few inches deep. They were not protected by wire. Also, many officers are of opinion that they had not been well sited in the first instance. On the South African system, the main line was withdrawn some twenty-five yards from the crest instead of being actually on the crest-line itself, and there were not even look-out posts along the summit. Boer skirmishers would thus have had to show themselves against the skyline before they could annoy. But here we were faced by regulars taught to attack in mass with bayonet or bomb. And the power of collecting overwhelming numbers at very close quarters rested with whichever side held the true skyline in force.

From Chunuk Bair the line ran down to the farm and almost due north to the Asma Dere southern watershed, whence it continued westward to the sea near Asmak Kuyu. On the right the Australian division was still holding its line and Lone Pine was still being furiously attacked. The 1st Australian Brigade was now reduced from 2,900 to 1,000, and the total casualties up to 8 p.m. on the 9th amounted to about 8,500. But the troops were still in extraordinarily good heart, and nothing could damp their keenness. The only discontent shown was by men who were kept in reserve.

THE TURKISH COUNTERATTACK.

During the night of the 9th-10th the New Zealand and New Army troops on Chunuk Bair were relieved. For three days and three nights they had been ceaselessly fighting. They were half dead with fatigue. Their lines of communication, started from sea level, ran across trackless ridges and ravines to an altitude of 800 feet, and were exposed all the way to snipers' fire and artillery bombardment. It had become imperative, therefore, to get them enough food, water, and rest; and for this purpose, it was imperative also to withdraw them. Chunuk Bair, which they had so magnificently held, was now handed over to two battalions of the 13th Division, which were connected by the 10th Hampshire Regiment with the troops at the farm. General Sir William Birdwood is emphatic on the point that the nature of the ground is such that there was no room on the crest for more than this body of 800 to 1,000 rifles.

The two battalions of the New Army chosen to hold Chunuk Bair were the 6th Loyal North Lancashire Regiment and the 5th Wiltshire Regiment. The first of these arrived in good time and occupied the trenches. Even in the darkness their commanding officer, Lieutenant-Colonel Levinge, recognised how dangerously these trenches were sited, and he began at once to dig observation posts on the actual crest and to strengthen the defences where he could. But he had not time given him to do much. The second battalion, the Wiltshires, were delayed by the intricate country. They did not reach the edge of the entrenchment until 4 a.m., and were then told to lie down in what was believed, erroneously, to be a covered position.

At daybreak on Tuesday, 10th August, the Turks delivered a grand attack from the line Chunuk Bair—Hill Q against these two battalions, already weakened in numbers, though not in spirit, by previous fighting. First our men were shelled by every enemy gun, and then at 5.30 a.m. were assaulted by a huge column, consisting of no less than a full division plus a regiment of three battalions. The North Lancashire men were simply overwhelmed in their shallow trenches by sheer weight of numbers, whilst the Wilts, who were caught out in the open, were literally almost annihilated. The ponderous mass of the enemy swept over the crest, turned the right flank of our line below, swarmed round the Hampshires and General Baldwin's column, which had to give ground, and were only extricated with great difficulty and very heavy losses.

The Counterattack Checked.

Now it was our turn. The warships and the New Zealand and Australian Artillery, the Indian Mounted Artillery Brigade, and the 69th Brigade Royal Field Artillery were getting the chance of a lifetime. As the successive solid lines of Turks topped the crest of the ridge gaps were torn through their formation and an iron rain fell on them as they tried to re-form in the gullies.

Not here only did the Turks pay dearly for their recapture of the vital crest. Enemy reinforcements continual to move up Battleship Hill under heavy and accurate fire from our guns, and still they kept topping the ridges and pouring down the western slopes of the Chunuk Bair as if determined to regain everything they had lost. But once they were over the crest, they became exposed not only to the full blast of the guns, naval and military, but also to a battery of ten machine-guns belonging to the New Zealand Infantry Brigade, which played upon their serried ranks at close range until the barrels were red-hot. Enormous losses were inflicted, especially by these ten machine-guns; and of the swarms which had once fairly crossed the crest line only the merest handful ever straggled back to their own side of Chunuk Bair.

At this same time strong forces of the enemy (forces which I had reckoned would have been held back to meet our advance from Suvla Bay) were hurled against the farm and the spurs to the north-east, where there arose a conflict so deadly that it may be considered as the climax of the four days' fighting for the ridge. Portions of our line were pierced and the troops driven clean down the hill. At the foot of the hill the men were rallied by Staff Captain Street, who was there supervising the transport of food and water.

Without a word, unhesitatingly, they followed him back to the farm, where they plunged again into the midst of that series of struggles in which generals fought in the ranks and men dropped their scientific weapons and caught one another by the throat. So desperate a battle cannot be described.

The Turks came on again and again, fighting magnificently, calling upon the name of God. Our men stood to it, and maintained, by many a deed of daring, the old traditions of their race. There was no flinching. They died in the ranks where they stood.

Here Generals Cayley, Baldwin, and Cooper and all their gallant men achieved great glory. On this bloody field fell Brigadier-General Baldwin, who earned his first laurels on Caesar's Camp at Ladysmith. There, too, fell Brigadier-General Cooper, badly wounded; and there, too, fell Lieutenant-Colonel M. H. Nunn, commanding the 9th Worcestershire Regiment; Lieutenant-Colonel H. G. Levinge, commanding the 6th Loyal North Lancashire Regiment; and Lieutenant-Colonel J. Carden, commanding the 5th Wiltshire Regiment.

Casualties.

Towards this supreme struggle the absolute last two battalions from the General Reserve were now hurried, but by 10 a.m. the effort of the enemy was spent. Soon their shattered remnants began to trickle back, leaving a track of corpses behind them, and by night, except prisoners or wounded, no live Turk was left upon our side of the slope.

That same day, 10th August, two attacks, one in the looming and the other in the afternoon, were delivered on our positions along the Asmak Dere and Damakjelik Bair. Both were repulsed with heavy loss by the 4th Australian Brigade and the 4th South Wales Borderers, the men of the New Army showing all the steadiness of veterans. Sad to say, the Borderers lost their intrepid leader, Lieutenant-Colonel Gillespie, in the course of this affair.

By evening the total casualties of General Birdwood's force had reached 12,000, and included a very large proportion of officers. The 13th Division of the New Army, under Major-General Shaw, had alone lost 6,000 out of a grand total of 10,500. Baldwin was gone, and all his staff. Ten commanding officers out of thirteen had disappeared from the fighting effectives. The Warwicks and the Worcesters had lost literally every single officer. The old German notion that no unit would stand a loss of more than 25 *per cent,* had been completely falsified.

The 13th Division and the 29th Brigade of the 10th (Irish) Division had lost more than twice that proportion, and, in spirit, were game for as much more fighting as might be required. But physically, though Birdwood's forces were prepared to hold all they had got, they were now too exhausted to attack—at least until they had rested and reorganised. So *far*, they had held on to all they had gained, excepting only the footholds on the ridge between Chunuk Bair and Hill Q, momentarily carried by the Gurkhas, and the salient of Chunuk Bair itself, which they had retained for forty-eight hours. Unfortunately, these two pieces of ground, small and worthless as they seemed, were worth, according to the ethics of war, 10,000 lives, for by their loss or retention they just marked the difference between an important success and a signal victory.

At times I had thought of throwing my reserves into this stubborn central battle, where probably they would have turned the scale. But each time the water troubles made me give up the idea, all ranks at Anzac being reduced to one pint a day. True thirst is a sensation unknown to the dwellers in cool, well-watered England. But at Anzac, when mules with water *"pakhals"* arrived at the front, the men would rush up to them in swarms, just to lick the moisture that had exuded through the canvas bags. It will be understood, then, that until wells had been discovered under the freshly-won hills, the reinforcing of Anzac by even so much as a brigade was unthinkable.

HEROISM OF THE TROOPS.

The grand *coup* had not come off. The Narrows were still out of sight and beyond field-gun range. But this was not the fault of Lieutenant-General Birdwood or any of the officers and men under his command. No mortal can command success; Lieutenant-General Birdwood had done all that mortal man can do to deserve it. The way in which he worked out his instructions into practical arrangements and dispositions upon the terrain reflect high credit upon his military capacity. I also wish to bring to Your Lordship's notice the valuable services of Major-General Godley, commanding the New Zealand and Australian Division. He had under him at one time a force amounting to two divisions, which he handled with conspicuous ability. Major-General F C. Shaw, commanding 13th Division, also rose superior to all the trials and tests of these trying days. His calm and sound judgment proved to be of the greatest value throughout the arduous fighting I have recorded.

As for the troops, the joyous alacrity with which they faced danger, wounds, and death, as if they were some new form of exciting recreation, has astonished me—old campaigner as I am. I will say no more, leaving Major-General Godley to speak for what happened under his eyes, he says:—

> I cannot close my report, without placing on record my unbounded admiration of the work performed, and the gallantry displayed, by the troops and their leaders during the severe fighting involved in these operations. Though the Australian, New Zealand, and Indian units had been confined to trench duty in a cramped space for some four months, and though the troops of the New Armies had only just landed from a sea voyage, and many of them had not been previously under fire, I do not believe that any troops in the world could have accomplished more. All ranks vied with one another in the performance of gallant deeds, and more than worthily upheld the best traditions of the British Army.
>
> Although the Sari Bair ridge was the key to the whole of my tacti-

cal conception, and although the temptation to view this vital Anzac battle at closer quarters was very hard to resist, there was nothing in its course or conduct to call for my personal intervention.

4

THE LANDING AT SUVLA.

The conduct of the operations which were to be based upon Suvla Bay was entrusted to Lieutenant-General the Hon. Sir F. Stopford. At his disposal was placed the 9th Army Corps, less the 13th Division and the 29th Brigade of the 10th Division.

We believed that the Turks were still unsuspicious about Suvla and that their only defences near that part of the coast were a girdle of trenches round Lala Baba and a few unconnected lengths of fire trench on Hill 10 and on the hills forming the northern arm of the bay. There was no wire. Inland a small work had been constructed on Yilghin Burnu (locally known as Chocolate Hills), and a few guns had been placed upon these hills, as well as upon Ismail Oglu Tepe, whence they could be brought into action either against the beaches of Suvla Bay or against any attempt from Anzac to break out northwards and attack Chunuk Bair.

The numbers of the enemy allotted for the defence of the Suvla and Ejelmer areas (including the troops in the Anafarta villages, but exclusive of the general reserves in rear of the Sari Bair) were supposed to be under 4,000. Until the Turkish version of these events is in our hands it is not possible to be certain of the accuracy of this estimate. All that can be said at present is that my Intelligence Department were wonderfully exact in their figures as a rule, and that, in the case in question, events, the reports made by prisoners, etc., etc., seem to show that the forecast was correct.

Arrangements for the landing of the 9th Corps at Suvla were worked out in minute detail by my General Headquarters Staff in collaboration with the staff of Vice-Admiral de Robeck, and every precaution was taken to ensure that the destination of the troops was kept secret up to the last moment.

Whilst concentrated at the island of Imbros the spirit and physique of the 11th Division had impressed me very favourably. They were to lead off the landing. From Imbros they were to be ferried over to the peninsula in destroyers and motor-lighters. Disembarkation was to begin at 10.30 p.m., half an hour later than the attack on the Turkish outposts on the northern flank of Anzac, and I was sanguine enough to hope that the elaborate plan we had worked out would enable three complete brigades of infantry to be set ashore by daylight. Originally it had been intended that all three brigades should land on the beach immediately south of Nibrunesi Point, but in deference to the representations of the corps commander I agreed, unfortunately, as it turned out, to one brigade being landed inside the bay.

The first task of the 9th Corps was to seize and hold the Chocolate and Ismail Oglu Hills, together with the high ground on the north and east of Suvla Bay. If the landing went off smoothly, and if my information regarding the strength of the enemy were correct, I hoped that these hills, with their guns, might be well in our possession before daybreak. In that case I hoped, further, that the first division which landed would be strong enough to picket and hold all the important heights within artillery range of the bay, when General Stopford would be able to direct the remainder of his force, as it became available, through the Anafartas to the east of the Sari Bair, where it should soon smash the mainspring of the Turkish opposition to Anzacs.

Arrangements for the Landing.

On the 22nd July I issued secret instructions and tables showing the number of craft available for the 9th Corps Commander, their capacity, and the points whereat the troops could be disembarked; also, what numbers of troops, animals, vehicles, and stores could be landed simultaneously. The allocation of troops to the ships and boats was left to General Stopford's own discretion, subject only to naval exigencies, otherwise the order of the disembarkation might not have tallied with the order of his operations.

The factors governing the hour of landing were: First, that no craft could quit Kephalos Bay before dark (about 9 p.m.); secondly, that nothing could be done which would attract the attention of the enemy before 10 p.m., the moment when the outposts on the left flank of the Anzac position were to be rushed.

General Stopford next framed his orders on these secret instructions, and after they had received my complete approval he proceeded to expound them to the general officer commanding 11th Division and general officer commanding 10th Division, who came over from Mudros for the purpose.

As in the original landing, the luck of calm weather favoured us, and all the embarkation arrangements at Kephalos were carried out by the Royal Navy in their usual shipshape style. The 11th Division were to be landed at three places, designated and shown on the map as A, B, and C. Destroyers were told off for these landing-places, each destroyer towing a steam-lighter and picket-boat. Every light was to be dowsed, and as they neared the shore the destroyers were to slip their motor-lighters and picket-boats, which would then take the beach and discharge direct on to it. The motor-lighters were new acquisitions since the first landing, and were to prove the greatest possible assistance. They moved five knots an hour under their own engines, and carried 500 men, as well as stores of ammunition and water.

After landing their passengers they were to return to the destroyers, and in one trip would empty them also. Ketches with service launches and transport lifeboats were to follow the destroyers and anchor at the entrance of the bay, so that in case of accidents or delays to any one of the motor-lighters a picket-boat could be sent at once to a ketch to pick up a tow of lifeboats and take the place of a disabled motor-lighter. These ketches and tows were afterwards to be used for evacuating the wounded.

THE TRANSPORTS.

H.M.S. *Endymion* and H.M.S. *Theseus*, each carrying a thousand men, were also to sail from Imbros, after the destroyers, and, lying off the beach, were to discharge their troops directly the motor-lighters—three to each ship—were ready to convey the men to the shore, *i.e.*, after they had finished disembarking their own loads and those of the destroyers. When this was done—*i.e.*, after three trips—the motor-lighters would be free to go on transporting guns, stores, mules, etc.

The following crafts brought up the rear:—

(1) Two ketches, each towing four horse-boats, carrying four 18-pounder guns and twenty-four horses.
(2) One ketch, towing horse-boats with forty horses.
(3) The sloop *Aster*, with 500 men, towing a lighter containing eight mountain guns.
(4) Three ketches, towing horse-boats containing eight 18-pounder guns and seventy-six horses.

Water-lighters, towed by a tank steamer, were also timed to arrive at A beach at daylight. When they had been emptied, they were to return at once to Kephalos to refill from the parent water-ship.

A specially fitted-out steamer, the *Prah*, with stores (shown by our experience of 25th April to be most necessary)—*i.e.*, water-pumps, hose, tanks, troughs, entrenching tools and all ordnance stores requisite for the prompt development of wells or springs—was also sent to Suvla.

So much detail I have felt bound, for the sake of clearness, to give in the body of my dispatch.

WATER.

When originally, I conceived the idea of these operations, one of the first points to be weighed was that of the water supply in the Biyuk Anafarta valley and the Suvla plain. Experience at Anzac had shown quite clearly that the whole plan must be given up unless a certain amount of water could be counted upon, and, fortunately, the information I received was reassuring. But, in case of accidents, and to be on the safe side, so long ago as June had I begun to take steps to counter the chance that we might, from one cause or another, find difficulty in developing the wells. Having got from the War Office all that they could give me, I addressed myself to India and Egypt, and eventually from these three sources I managed to secure portable receptacles for 100,000 gallons, including petrol tins, milk cans, camel tanks, water bags, and *pakhals*.

Supplementing these were lighters and water ships, all under naval control. Indeed, by arrangement with the admiral, the responsibility of the army was confined to the emptying of the lighters and the distribution of the water to the troops, the navy undertaking to bring the full lighters to the shore to replace the empty ones, thus providing a continuous supply.

Finally, 3,700 mules, together with 1,750 water carts, were provided for Anzac and Suvla—this in addition to 950 mules already at Anzac. Representatives of the Director of Supplies and Transport at Suvla and Anzac were sent to allot the transport which was to be used for carrying up whatever was most needed by units ashore, whether water, food, or ammunition. This statement, though necessarily brief, will, I hope, suffice to throw some light upon the complexity of the arrangements thought out beforehand in order, so far as was humanly possible, to combat the disorganisation, the hunger and the thirst which lie in wait for troops landing on a hostile beach.

On the evening of 6th August the 11th Division sailed on its short journey from Imbros (Kephalos) to Suvla Bay and, meeting with no mischance, the landing took place, the brigades of the 11th Division getting ashore practically simultaneously; the 32nd and 33rd Brigades at B and C beaches, the 34th at A beach.

Surprise of the Turks.

The surprise of the Turks was complete. At B and C, the beaches were found to be admirably suited to their purpose, and there was no opposition. The landing at A was more difficult, both because of the shoal water and because there the Turkish pickets and sentries—the normal guardians of the coast—were on the alert and active. Some of the lighters grounded a good way from the shore, and men had to struggle towards the beach in as much as four feet six inches of water. Ropes in several instances were carried from the lighters to the shore to help to sustain the heavily accoutred infantry. To add to the difficulties of the 34th Brigade the lighters came under flanking rifle fire from the Turkish outposts at Lala Baba and Ghazi Baba. The enemy even, knowing every inch of the ground, crept down in the very dark night on to the beach itself, mingling with our troops and getting between our firing line and its supports.

Fortunately, the number of these enterprising foes was but few, and an end was soon put to their activity on the actual beaches by the sudden storming of Lala Baba from the south. This attack was carried out by the 9th West Yorkshire Regiment and the 6th Yorkshire Regiment, both of the 32nd Brigade, which had landed at B beach and marched up along the coast. The assaults succeeded at once and without much loss, but both battalions deserve great credit for the way it was delivered in the inky darkness of the night.

The 32nd Brigade was now pushed on to the support of the 34th Brigade, which was held up by another outpost of the enemy on Hill 10 (117 R. and S.), and it is feared that some of the losses occurred here were due to misdirected fire. While this fighting was still in progress the 11th Battalion Manchester Regiment, of the 34th Brigade, was advancing northwards in very fine style, driving the enemy opposed to them back along the ridge of the Karakol Dagh towards the Kiretch Tepe Sirt. Beyond doubt these Lancashire men earned much distinction, fighting with great pluck and grit against an enemy not very numerous perhaps, but having an immense advantage in knowledge of the ground.

The Landings.

As they got level with Hill 10 it grew light enough to see, and the enemy began to shell. No one seems to have been present who could take hold of the two brigades, the 32nd and 34th, and launch them in a concerted and cohesive attack. Consequently, there was confusion and hesitation, increased by gorse fires lit by hostile shell, but redeemed, I am proud to report, by the conspicuously fine soldierly conduct of several individual battalions. The whole of the Turks locally available were by now in the field, and they were encouraged to counterattack by the signs of hesitation, but the 9th Lancashire Fusiliers and the 11th Manchester Regiment took them on with the bayonet, and fairly drove them back in disorder over the flaming Hill 10.

As the infantry were thus making good, the two Highland Mountain batteries and one battery, 59th Brigade, Royal Field Artillery, were landed at B beach. Day was now breaking, and with the dawn sailed into the bay six battalions of the 10th Division, under Brigadier-General Hill, from Mitylene.

Here perhaps I may be allowed to express my gratitude to the Royal Navy for their share in this remarkable achievement, as well as a very natural pride at staff arrangements, which resulted in the infantry of a whole division and three batteries being landed during a single night on a hostile shore, whilst the arrival of the first troops of the supporting division, from another base distant 120 miles, took place at the very psychological moment when support was most needed, namely, at break of dawn.

The intention of the corps commander was to keep the 10th Division on the left, and with it to push on as far forward as possible along the Kiretch Tepe Sirt towards the heights above Ejelmer Bay. He wished, therefore, to land these six battalions of the 10th Division at A beach and, seeing Brigadier-General Hill, he told him that as the left of the 34th Brigade was being hard pressed he should get into touch with General Officer Commanding 11th Division, and work in support of his left until the arrival of his own Divisional General. But the naval authorities, so General Stopford reports, were unwilling, for some reason not specified, to land these troops at A beach, so that they had to be sent in lighters to C beach, whence they marched by Lala Baba to Hill 10 under fire. Hence were caused loss, delay, and fatigue. Also, the angle of direction from which these fresh troops entered the fight was not nearly so effective.

The Fighting of 7th August.

The remainder of the 10th Division, three battalions (from Mudros), and with them the G.O.C. Lieutenant-General Sir B. Mahon, began to arrive, and the naval authorities having discovered a suitable landing-place near Ghazi Baba, these battalions were landed there together with one battalion of the 31st Brigade, which had not yet been sent round to C beach. By this means it was hoped that both the brigades of the 10th Division would be able to rendezvous about half a mile to the north-west of Hill 10.

After the defeat of the enemy round and about Hill 10, they retreated in an easterly direction towards Sulajik and Kuchuk Anafarta Ova, followed by the 34th and 32nd Brigades of the 11th Division and by the 31st Brigade of the 10th Division, which had entered into the fight, not, as the corps commander had intended, on the left of the 11th Division, but between Hill 10 and the Salt Lake. I have failed in my endeavours to get some live human detail about the fighting which followed, but I understand from the corps commander that the brunt of it fell upon the 31st Brigade of the 10th (Irish) Division, which consisted of the 6th Royal Inniskilling Fusiliers, the 6th Royal Irish Fusiliers, and the 6th Royal Dublin Fusiliers, the last-named battalion being attached to the 31st Brigade.

By the evening General Hammersley had seized Yilghin Burnu (Chocolate Hills) after a fight for which he specially commends the 6th Lincoln Regiment and the 6th Border Regiment. At the same time, he reported that he was unable to make any further progress towards the vital point, Ismail Oglu Tepe. At nightfall his brigade and the 31st Brigade were extended from about Hetman Chair through Chocolate Hills, Sulajik, to near Kuchuk Anafarta Ova.

This same day Sir B. Mahon delivered a spirited attack along the Kiretch Tepe Sirt ridge, in support of the 11th Battalion Manchester Regiment, and, taking some small trenches *en route*, secured and established himself on a position extending from the sea about 135 p., through the high ground about the p. of Kiretch Tepe Sirt, to about 135 Z. 8. In front of him, on the ridge, he reported the enemy to be strongly entrenched. The 6th Royal Munster Fusiliers have been named as winning special distinction here. The whole advance was well carried out by the Irishmen over difficult ground against an enemy—500 to 700 *gendarmerie*—favoured by the lie of the land.

Sufferings from Want of Water.

The weather was very hot, and the new troops suffered much from want of water. Except at the southernmost extremity of the Kiretch Tepe Sirt ridge there was no water in that part of the field, and although it existed in some abundance throughout the area over which the 11th Division was operating, the corps commander reports that there was no time to develop its resources. Partly this seems to have been owing to the enemy's fire; partly to a want of that nous which stands by as second nature to the old campaigner; partly it was inevitable. Anyway, for as long as such a state of things lasted, the troops became dependent on the lighters and upon the water brought to the beaches in tins, *pakhals*, etc.

Undoubtedly the distribution of this water to the advancing troops was a matter of great difficulty, and one which required not only well-worked-out schemes from corps and divisional staffs, but also energy and experience on the part of those who had to put them into practice. As it turned out, and judging merely by results, I regret to say that the measures actually taken in regard to the distribution proved to be inadequate, and that suffering and disorganisation ensued. The disembarkation of artillery horses was therefore at once, and rightly, postponed by the corps commander, in order that mules might be landed to carry up water.

Reasons for Failure.

And now General Stopford, recollecting the vast issues which hung upon his success in forestalling the enemy, urged his divisional commanders to push on. Otherwise, as he saw, all the advantages of the surprise landing must be nullified. But the divisional commanders believed themselves, it seems, to be unable to move. Their men, they said, were exhausted by their efforts of the night of the 6th-7th and by the action of the 7th. The want of water had told on the new troops. The distribution from the beaches had not worked smoothly.

In some cases, the hose had been pierced by individuals wishing to fill their own bottles; in others lighters had grounded so far from the beach that men swam out to fill batches of water-bottles. All this had added to the disorganisation inevitable after a night landing, followed by fights here and there with an enemy scattered over a country to us unknown. These pleas for delay were perfectly well founded. But it seems to have been overlooked that the half-defeated Turks in front of us were equally exhausted and disorganised, and that an advance was the simplest and swiftest method of solving the water trouble and every other sort of trouble.

Be this as it may, the objections overbore the corps commander's resolution. He had now got ashore three batteries (two of them mountain batteries), and the great guns of the ships were ready to speak at his request. But it was lack of artillery support which finally decided him to acquiesce in a policy of going slow which, by the time it reached the troops, became translated into a period of inaction. The divisional generals were, in fact, informed that, "in view of the inadequate artillery support," General Stopford did not wish them to make frontal attacks on entrenched positions, but desired them, so far as was possible, to try and turn any trenches which were met with. Within the terms of this instruction lies the root of our failure to make use of the priceless daylight hours of the 8th of August.

Normally, it may be correct to say that in modern warfare infantry cannot be expected to advance without artillery preparation. But in a landing on a hostile shore the order has to be inverted. The infantry must advance and seize a suitable position to cover the landing and to provide artillery positions for the main thrust. The very existence of the force, its water supply, its facilities for munitions and supplies, its power to reinforce, must absolutely depend on the infantry being able instantly to make good sufficient ground without the aid of the artillery other than can be supplied for the purpose by *floating* batteries.

This is not a condition that should take the commander of a covering force by surprise. It is one already foreseen. Driving power was required, and even a certain ruthlessness, to brush aside pleas for a respite for tired troops. The one fatal error was inertia. And inertia prevailed.

Sir Ian Hamilton Goes to Suvla.

Late in the evening of the 7th the enemy had withdrawn the few guns which had been in action during the day. Beyond half a dozen shells dropped from very long range into the bay in the early morning of the 8th, no enemy artillery fired that day in the Suvla area. The guns had evidently been moved back, lest they should be captured when we pushed forward. As for the entrenched positions, these, in the ordinary acceptance of the term, were non-existent. The General Staff Officer whom I had sent on to Suvla early in the morning of the 8th reported by telegraph the absence of hostile gun-fire, the small amount of rifle fire, and the enemy's apparent weakness. He also drew attention to the inaction of our own troops, and to the fact that golden opportunities were being missed.

Before this message arrived at general headquarters, I had made up my mind, from the corps commander's own reports, that all was not well at Suvla. There was risk in cutting myself adrift, even temporarily, from touch with the operations at Anzac and Helles; but I did my best to provide against any sudden call by leaving Major-General W. P. Braithwaite, my Chief of the General Staff, in charge, with instructions to keep me closely informed of events at the other two fronts; and, having done this, I took ship and set out for Suvla.

On arrival at about 5 p.m. I boarded H.M.S. *Jonquil*, where I found corps headquarters, and where General Stopford informed me that the general officer commanding 11th Division was confident of success in an attack he was to make at dawn next morning (the 9th). I felt no such confidence. Beyond a small advance by a part of the 11th Division between the Chocolate Hills and Ismail Oglu Tepe, and some further progress along the Kiretch Tepe Sirt ridge by the 10th Division, the day of the 8th had been lost.

The commander of the 11th Division had, it seems, ordered strong patrols to be pushed forward so as to make good all the strong positions in advance which could be occupied without serious fighting; but, as he afterwards reported, "little was done in this respect." Thus, a priceless twelve hours had already gone to help the chances of the Turkish reinforcements which were, I knew, both from naval and aerial sources, actually on the march for Suvla. But when I urged that even now, at the eleventh hour, the 11th Division should make a concerted attack upon the hills, I was met by a *non possumus*. The objections of the morning were no longer valid; the men were now well rested, watered, and fed. But the divisional commanders disliked the idea of an advance by night, and General Stopford did not care, it seemed, to force their hands.

So, it came about that I was driven to see whether I could not, myself, put concentration of effort and purpose into the direction of the large number of men ashore. The corps commander made no objection. He declared himself to be as eager as I could be to advance. The representations made by the divisional commanders had seemed to him insuperable. If I could see my way to get over them no one would be more pleased than himself.

Accompanied by Commodore Roger Keyes and Lieutenant-Colonel Aspinall, of the Headquarters General Staff, I landed on the beach, where all seemed quiet and peaceful, and saw the commander of the 11th Division, Major-General Hammersley. I warned him the sands were running out fast, and that by dawn the high ground to his front might very likely be occupied in force by the enemy.

He saw the danger, but declared that it was a physical impossibility, at so late an hour (6 p.m.), to get out orders for a night attack, the troops being very much scattered. There was no other difficulty now, but this was insuperable; he could not recast his orders or get them round to his troops in time. But one brigade, the 32nd, was, so General Hammersley admitted, more or less concentrated and ready to move. The general staff officer of the division, Colonel Neil Malcolm, a soldier of experience, on whose opinion I set much value, was consulted. He agreed that the 32nd Brigade was now in a position to act. I therefore issued a direct order that, even if it were only with this 32nd Brigade, the advance should begin at the earliest possible moment, so that a portion at least of the 11th Division should anticipate the Turkish reinforcements on the heights and dig themselves in there upon some good tactical point.

In taking upon myself the serious responsibility of thus dealing with a detail of divisional tactics I was careful to limit the scope of the interference. Beyond directing that the one brigade which was reported ready to move at once should try and make good the heights before the enemy got on to them, I did nothing, and said not a word calculated to modify or in any way affect the attack already planned for the morning. Out of the thirteen battalions which were to have advanced against the heights at dawn four were now to anticipate that movement by trying to make good the key of the enemy's position at once and under cover of darkness,

I have not been able to get a clear and coherent account of the doings of the 32nd Brigade; but I have established the fact that it did not actually commence its advance till 4 a.m. on the 9th of August. The reason given is that the units of the brigade were scattered. In General Stopford's despatch he says that:—

> One company of the 6th East Yorks Pioneer Battalion succeeded in getting to the top of the hill north of Anafarta Sagir, but the rest of the battalion and the 32nd Brigade were attacked from both flanks during their advance, and fell back to a line north and south of Sulajik. Very few of the leading company of the Royal Engineers who accompanied it got back, and that evening the strength of the battalion was nine officers and 380 men.

The Attack of 9th August.

After their retirement from the hill north of Anafarta Sagir (which commanded the whole battlefield) this 32nd Brigade then still marked the high-water level of the advance made at dawn by the rest of the division. When their first retirement was completed, they had to fall back further, so as to come into line with the most forward of their comrades. The inference seems clear. Just as the 32nd Brigade in their advance met with markedly less opposition than the troops who attacked an hour and a half later, so, had they themselves started earlier, they would probably have experienced less opposition. Further, it seems reasonable to suppose that had the complete division started at 4 a.m. on the 9th, or, better still, at 10 p.m. on the 8th, they would have made good the whole of the heights in front of them.

That night I stayed at Suvla, preferring to drop direct cable contact with my operations as a whole to losing touch with a corps battle which seemed to be going wrong.

At dawn on the 9th I watched General Hammersley's attack, and very soon realised, by the well-sustained artillery fire of the enemy (so silent the previous day) and by the volume of the musketry, that Turkish reinforcements had arrived; that with the renewed confidence caused by our long delay the guns had been brought back; and that, after all, we were forestalled. This was a bad moment. Our attack failed; our losses were very serious. The enemy's enfilading shrapnel fire seemed to be especially destructive and demoralising, the shell bursting low and all along our line. Time after time it threw back our attack just as it seemed upon the point of making good. The 33rd Brigade at first made most hopeful progress in its attempt to seize Ismail Oglu Tepe. Some of the leading troops gained the summit, and were able to look over on to the other side. Many Turks were killed here. Then the centre seemed to give way.

Whether this was the result of the shrapnel fire or whether, as some say, an order to retire came up from the rear, the result was equally fatal to success. As the centre fell back the steady, gallant behaviour of the 6th Battalion, Border Regiment, and the 6th Battalion, Lincoln Regiment, on either flank was especially noteworthy. Scrub fires on Hill 70 did much to harass and hamper our troops. When the 32nd Brigade fell back before attacks from the slopes of the hill north of Anafarta Sagir and from the direction of Abrijka they took up the line north and south through Sulajik.

Here their left was protected by two battalions of the 34th Brigade, which came up to their support. The line was later on prolonged by the remainder of the 34th Brigade and two battalions of the 159th Brigade of the 53rd Division. Their right was connected with the Chocolate Hills by the 33rd Brigade on the position to which they had returned after their repulse from the upper slopes of Ismail Oglu Tepe.

Some of the units which took part in this engagement acquitted themselves very bravely. I regret I have not had sufficient detail given me to enable me to mention them by name. The divisional commander speaks with appreciation of one freshly-landed battalion of the 53rd Division, a Hereford battalion, presumably the 1/1st Herefordshire, which attacked with impetuosity and courage between Hetman Chair and Kaslar Chair, about Azmak Dere, on the extreme right of his line.

During the night of the 8th-9th and early morning of the 9th the whole of the 53rd (Territorial) Division (my general reserve) had arrived and disembarked. I had ordered it up to Suvla, hoping that by adding its strength to the 9th Corps General Stopford might still be enabled to secure the commanding ground round the bay. The infantry brigades of the 53rd Division (no artillery had accompanied it from England) reinforced the 11th Division.

The Attack of 10th August.

On August 10th the corps commander decided to make another attempt to take the Anafarta ridge. The 11th Division were not sufficiently rested to play a prominent part in the operation, but the 53rd Division, under General Lindley, was to attack, supported by General Hammersley. On the 10th there were one brigade of Royal Field Artillery ashore, with two mountain batteries, and all the ships' guns were available to co-operate. But the attack failed, though the corps commander considers that seasoned troops would have succeeded, especially as the enemy were showing signs of being shaken by our artillery fire. General Stopford points out, however, and rightly so, that the attack was delivered over very difficult country, and that it was a high trial for troops who had never been in action before, and with no regulars to set a standard.

Many of the battalions fought with great gallantry, and were led forward with much devotion by their officers. At a moment when things were looking dangerous two battalions of the 11th Division (not specified by the corps commander) rendered very good service on the left of the Territorials. At the end of the day our troops occupied the line Hill east of Chocolate Hill—Sulajik, whilst the enemy—who had been ably commanded throughout—were still receiving reinforcements, and, apart from their artillery, were three times as strong as they had been on the 7th August.

Orders were issued to the General Officer Commanding 9th Corps to take up and entrench a line across the whole front from near the Azmak Dere, through the knoll east of the Chocolate Hill, to the ground held by the 10th Division about Kiretch Tepe Sirt. General Stopford took advantage of this opportunity to reorganise the divisions, and, as there was a gap in the line between the left of the 53rd Division and the right of the 10th Division, gave orders for the preparation of certain strong points to enable it to be held.

The Chance Vanishes.

The 54th Division (infantry only) arrived, and were disembarked on August 11th and placed in reserve. On the following day—August 12th—I proposed that the 54th Division should make a night march in order to attack, at dawn on the 13th, the heights Kavak Tepe—Teke Tepe. The corps commander having reason to believe that the enclosed country about Kuchuk Anafarta Ova and the north of it was held by the enemy, ordered one brigade to move forward in advance, and make good Kuchuk Anafarta Ova, so as to ensure an unopposed march for the remainder of the division as far as that place. So that afternoon the 163rd Brigade moved off, and, in spite of serious opposition, established itself about the A of Anafarta (118m. 4 and 7), in difficult and enclosed country.

In the course of the fight, creditable in all respects to the 163rd Brigade, there happened a very mysterious thing. The 1/5th Norfolks were on the right of the line, and found themselves for a moment less strongly opposed than the rest of the brigade. Against the yielding forces of the enemy Colonel Sir H. Beauchamp, a bold, self-confident officer, eagerly pressed forward, followed by the best part of the battalion. The fighting grew hotter, and the ground became more wooded and broken. At this stage many men were wounded or grew exhausted with thirst. These found their way back to camp during the night. But the colonel, with 16 officers and 250 men, still kept pushing on, driving the enemy before him. Amongst these ardent souls was part of a fine company enlisted from the King's Sandringham estates. Nothing more was ever seen or heard of any of them. They charged into the forest, and were lost to sight or sound. Not one of them ever came back.

The night march and projected attack were now abandoned, owing to the corps commander's representations as to the difficulties of keeping the division supplied with food, water, etc., even should they gain the height. General Birdwood had hoped he would soon be able to make a fresh attack on Sari Bair, provided that he might reckon on a corresponding vigorous advance to be made by the 11th and 54th Divisions on Ismail Oglu Tepe. On August 13th I so informed General Stopford. But when it came to business. General Birdwood found he could not yet carry out his new attack on Sari Bair—and, indeed, could only help the 9th Corps with one brigade from Damakjelik Bair. I was obliged, therefore, to abandon this project for the nonce, and directed General Stopford to confine his attention to strengthening his line across his present front. To straighten out the left of this line General Stopford ordered the General Officer Commanding the 10th Division to advance on the following day (15th August), so as to gain possession of the crest of the Kiretch Tepe Sirt, the 54th Division to co-operate.

The 30th and 31st Infantry Brigades of the 10th Irish Division were to attack frontally along the high ridge. The 162nd Infantry Brigade of the 54th Division were to support on the right. The infantry were to be seconded by a machine-gun detachment of the Royal Naval Air Service, by the guns of H.M.S. *Grampus*, and H.M.S. *Foxhound* from the Gulf of Saros, by the Argyll Mountain Battery, the 15th Heavy Battery, and the 58th Field Battery. After several hours of indecisive artillery and musketry fighting, the 6th Royal Dublin Fusiliers charged forward with loud cheers, and captured the whole ridge, together with eighteen prisoners. The vigorous support rendered by the naval guns was a feature of this operation. Unfortunately, the point of the ridge was hard to hold, and means for maintaining the forward trenches had not been well thought out. Casualties became very heavy, the 5th Royal Irish Fusiliers having only one officer left, and the 5th Inniskilling Fusiliers also losing heavily in officers.

Reinforcements were promised, but before they could arrive the officer left in command decided to evacuate the front trenches. The strength of the Turks opposed to us was steadily rising, and had now reached 20,000.

New Commander at Suvla Bay.

On the evening of the 15th August General Stopford handed over command of the 9th Corps.

The units of the 10th and 11th Divisions had shown their mettle when they leaped into the water to get more quickly to close quarters, or when they stormed Lala Baba in the darkness. They had shown their resolution later when they tackled the Chocolate Hills and drove the enemy from Hill 10 right back out of rifle range from the beaches.

Then had come hesitation. The advantage had not been pressed. The senior commanders at Suvla had had no personal experience of the new trench warfare; of the Turkish methods; of the paramount importance of time. Strong, clear leadership had not been promptly enough applied. These were the reasons which induced me, with Your Lordship's approval, to appoint Major-General H. de B. De Lisle to take over temporary command.

I had already seen General De Lisle on his way from Cape Helles, and my formal instructions were handed to him by my Chief of the General Staff. Under these he was to make it his most pressing business to get the corps into fighting trim again, so that as big a proportion of it as possible might be told off for a fresh attack upon Ismail Oglu Tepe and the Anafarta spur. At his disposal were placed the 10th Division (less one brigade), the 11th Division, the 53rd and 54th Divisions—a force imposing enough on paper, but totalling, owing to casualties, under 30,000 rifles.

The fighting strength of ourselves and of our adversaries stood at this time at about the following figures:—Lieutenant-General Birdwood commanded 25,000 rifles, at Anzac; Lieutenant-General Davies, in the southern zone, commanded 23,000 rifles; whilst the French Corps alongside of him consisted of some 17,000 rifles. The Turks had been very active in the south, doubtless to prevent us reinforcing Anzac or Suvla; but it is doubtful If there were more than 35,000 of them in that region. The bulk of the enemy were engaged against Anzac or were in reserve in the valleys east and north of Sari Bair. Their strength was estimated at 75,000 rifles.

AN APPEAL FOR REINFORCEMENTS.

The Turks then, I reckoned, had 110,000 rifles to our 95,000, and held all the vantages of ground; they had plenty of ammunition, also drafts wherewith to refill ranks depleted in action within two or three days. My hopes that these drafts would be of poor quality had been every time disappointed. After weighing all these points, I sent Your Lordship a long cable. In it I urged that if the campaign was to be brought to a quick, victorious decision, large reinforcements must at once be sent out. Autumn, I pointed out, was already upon us, and there was not a moment to be lost. At that time (16th August) my British divisions alone were 45,000 under establishment, and some of my fine battalions had dwindled down so far that I had to withdraw them from the fighting line. Our most vital need was the replenishment of these sadly depleted ranks. When that was done, I wanted 50,000 fresh rifles. From what I knew of the Turkish situation, both in its local and general aspects, it seemed humanly speaking a certainty that if this help could be sent to me *at once* we could still clear a passage for our fleet to Constantinople.

It may be judged, then, how deep was my disappointment when I learnt that the essential drafts, reinforcements, and munitions could not be sent to me, the reason given being one which prevented me from any further insistence. So, I resolved to do my very best with the means at my disposal, and forthwith reinforced the northern wing with the 2nd Mounted Division (organised as dismounted troops) from Egypt and the 29th Division from the southern area. These movements, and the work of getting the 9th Corps and attached divisions into battle array took time, and it was not until the 21st that I was ready to renew the attack—an attack to be carried out under very different conditions from those of the 7th and 8th August.

The enemy's positions were now being rapidly entrenched, and, as I could not depend on receiving reinforcing drafts, I was faced with the danger that if I could not drive the Turks back I might lose so many men that I would find myself unable to hold the very extensive new area of ground which had been gained. I therefore decided to mass every available man against Ismail Oglu Tepe, a *sine qua non* to my plans whether as a first step towards clearing the valley, or, if this proved impossible, towards securing Suvla Bay and Anzac Cove from shell fire.

The Attack of 21st August.

The scheme for this attack was well planned by General De Lisle. The 53rd and 54th Divisions were to hold the enemy from Sulajik to Kiretch Tepe Sirt while the 29th Division and 11th Division stormed Ismail Oglu Tepe. Two brigades, 10th Division, and the 2nd Mounted Division were retained in Corps Reserve. I arranged that General Birdwood should co-operate by swinging forward his left flank to Susuk Kuyu and Kaiajik Aghala. Naturally I should have liked still further to extend the scope of my attack by ordering an advance of the 9th Corps all along their line, but many of the battalions had been too highly tried, and I felt it was unwise to call upon them for another effort so soon. The attack would only be partial, but it was an essential attack if any real progress was to be made. Also, once the Anafarta Ridge was in my hands the enemy would be unable to reinforce through the gap between the two Anafartas, and then, so I believed, my left would find no difficulty in getting on.

My special objective was the hill which forms the southwest corner of the Anafarta Sagir spur. Ismail Oglu Tepe, as it is called, forms a strong natural barrier against an invader from the Aegean who might wish to march direct against the Anafartas, The hill rises 350 feet from the plain, with steep spurs jutting out to the west and south-west, the whole of it covered with dense holly oak scrub, so nearly impenetrable that it breaks up an attack and forces troops to move in single file along goat tracks between the bushes.

The comparatively small number of guns landed up to date was a weakness, seeing we had now to storm trenches, but the battleships were there to back us, and as the bombardment was limited to a narrow front of a mile it was hoped the troops would find themselves able to carry the trenches and that the impetus of the charge would carry them up to the top of the crest.

Our chief difficulty lay in the open nature and shallow depth of the ground available for the concentration for attack. The only cover we possessed was the hill Lala Baba, 200 yards from the sea, and Yilghin Burnu, half a mile from the Turkish front, the ground between these two being an exposed plain.

The 29th Division, which was to make the attack on the left, occupied the front trenches during the preceding night; the 11th Division, which was to attack on the right, occupied the front trenches on the right of Yilghin Burnu.

By some freak of nature Suvla Bay and plain were wrapped in a strange mist on the afternoon of the 21st of August. This was sheer bad luck, as we had reckoned on the enemy's gunners being blinded by the declining sun and upon the Turkish trenches being shown up by the evening light with singular clearness, as would have been the case on ninety-nine days out of a hundred. Actually, we could hardly see the enemy lines this afternoon, whereas out to the westward targets stood out in strong relief against the luminous mist. I wished to postpone the attack, but for various reasons this was not possible, and so from 2.30 p.m. to 3 p.m. a heavy but none too accurate artillery bombardment from land and sea was directed against the Turkish first line of trenches, whilst 24 machine-guns in position on Yilghin Burnu did what they could to lend a hand.

At 3 p.m. an advance was begun by the infantry on the right of the line. The 34th Brigade of the 11th Division rushed the Turkish trenches between Hetman Chair and Aire Kavak, practically without loss, but the 32nd Brigade, directed against Hetman Chair and the communication trench connecting that point with the south-west corner of the Ismail Oglu Tepe spur, failed to make good its point.

The brigade had lost direction in the first instance, moving north-east instead of east, and though it attempted to carry the communication trench from the north-east with great bravery and great disregard of life, it never succeeded in rectifying the original mistake. The 33rd Brigade, sent up in haste with orders to capture this communication trench at all costs, fell into precisely the same error, part of it marching northeast and part south-east to Susuk Kuyu.

Meanwhile the 29th Division, whose attack had been planned for 3.30 p.m., had attacked Scimitar Hill (Hill 70) with great dash. The 87th Brigade, on the left, carried the trenches on Scimitar Hill, but the 86th Brigade were checked and upset by a raging forest fire across their front. Eventually pressing on, they found themselves unable to advance up the valley between the two spurs owing to the failure of the 32nd Brigade of the 11th Division on their right.

The brigade then tried to attack eastwards, but were decimated by a cross fire of shell and musketry from the north and south-east. The leading troops were simply swept off the top of the spur, and had to fall back to a ledge south-west of Scimitar Hill, where they found a little cover. Whilst this fighting was in progress the 2nd Mounted Division moved out from Lala Baba in open formation to take up a position of readiness behind Yilghin Burnu. During this march they came under a remarkably steady and accurate artillery fire.

THE CHARGE OF THE YEOMEN.

The advance of these English Yeomen was a sight calculated to send a thrill of pride through anyone with a drop of English blood running in their veins. Such superb martial spectacles are rare in modern war. Ordinarily it should always be possible to bring up reserves under some sort of cover from shrapnel fire. Here, for a mile and a half, there was nothing to conceal a mouse, much less some of the most stalwart soldiers England has ever sent from her shores. Despite the critical events in other parts of the field. I could hardly take my glasses from the Yeomen; they moved like men marching on parade. Here and there a shell would take toll of a cluster; there they lay; there was no straggling; the others moved steadily on; not a man was there who hung back or hurried. But such an ordeal must consume some of the battlewinning fighting energy of those subjected to it, and it is lucky indeed for the Turks that the terrain, as well as the lack of trenches, forbade us from letting the 2nd Mounted Division loose at close quarters to the enemy without undergoing this previous too heavy baptism of fire.

Now that the 11th Division had made their effort, and failed, the 2nd South Midland Brigade (commanded by Brigadier-General Earl of Longford) was sent forward from its position of readiness behind Yilghin Burnu, in the hope that they might yet restore the fortunes of the day. This brigade, in action for the first time, encountered both bush fires and musketry without flinching, but the advance had in places to be almost by inches, and the actual close attack by the Yeomen did not take place until night was fast falling.

On the left they reached the foremost line of the 29th Division, and on the right also they got as far as the leading battalions. But, as soon as it was dark, one regiment pushed up the valley between Scimitar Hill and Hill 100 (or Ismail Oglu Tepe), and carried the trenches on a small knoll near the centre of this horseshoe. The regiment imagined it had captured Hill 100, which would have been a very notable success, enabling as it would the whole of our line to hang on and dig in.

But when the report came in some doubt was felt as to its accuracy, and a reconnaissance by staff officers showed that the knoll was a good way from Hill 100, and that a strongly held semicircle of Turkish trenches (the enemy having been heavily reinforced) still denied us access to the top of the hill. As the men were too done, and had lost too heavily to admit of a second immediate assault, and as the knoll actually held would have been swept by fire at daybreak, there was nothing for it but to fall back under cover of darkness to our original line. The losses in this attack fell most heavily on the 29th Division. They were just under 5,000.

I am sorry not to be able to give more detail as to the conduct of individuals and units during this battle. But the 2nd South Midland Brigade has been brought to my notice, and it consisted of the Bucks Yeomanry, the Berks Yeomanry, and the Dorset Yeomanry. The Yeomanry fought very bravely, and on personal, as well as public grounds, I specially deplore the loss of Brigadier-General Earl of Longford, K.P., M.V.O., and Brigadier-General P. A. Kenna, V.C, D.S.O., A.D.C.

The same day, as pre-arranged with General Birdwood, a force consisting of two battalions of New Zealand Mounted Rifles, two Battalions of the 29th Irish Brigade, the 4th South Wales Borderers, and 29th Indian Infantry Brigade, the whole under the command of Major-General H.V. Cox, was working independently to support the main attack.

Movements on Anzac Left.

General Cox divided his force into three sections: the left section to press forward and establish a permanent hold on the existing lightly-held outpost line covering the junction of the 11th Division with the Anzac front; the centre section to seize the well at Kabak Kuyu, an asset of utmost value, whether to ourselves or the enemy; the right section to attack and capture the Turkish trenches on the north-east side of the Kaiajik Aghala.

The advance of the left section was a success; after a brisk engagement the well at Kabak Kuyu was seized by the Indian Brigade, and, by 4.30, the right column, under Brigadier General Russell, under heavy fire, effected a lodgement on the Kaiajik Aghala, where our men entrenched, and began to dig communications across the Kaiajik Dere towards the lines of the 4th Australian Brigade south of the Dere.

A pretty stiff bomb fight ensued, in which General Russell's troops held their own through the night against superior force. At 6 a.m. on the morning of the 22nd August, General Russell, reinforced by the newly-arrived 18th Australian Battalion, attacked the summit of the Kaiajik Aghala. The Australians carried 150 yards of the trenches, losing heavily in so doing, and were then forced to fall back again owing to enfilade fire, though in the meantime the New Zealand Mounted Rifles managed, in spite of constant counterattacks, to make good another 80 yards.

A counterattack in strength launched by the Turks at 10 a.m., was repulsed; the new line from the Kaiajik Aghala to Susuk Kuyu was gradually strengthened, and eventually joined on to the right of the 9th Army Corps, thereby materially improving the whole situation. During this action the 4th Australian Brigade, which remained facing the Turks on the upper part of the Kaiajik Aghala, was able to inflict several hundred casualties on the enemy as they retreated or endeavoured to reinforce.

On the 21st of August we had carried the Turkish entrenchments at several points, but had been unable to hold what we had gained except along the section where Major-General Cox had made a good advance with Anzac and Indian troops. To be repulsed is not to be defeated, as long as the commander and his troops are game to renew the attack. All were eager for such a renewal of the offensive; but clearly, we would have for some time to possess our souls in patience, seeing that reinforcements and munitions were short, that we were already outnumbered by the enemy, and that a serious outbreak of sickness showed how it had become imperative to give a spell of rest to the men who had been fighting so magnificently and so continuously.

To calculate on rest, it may be suggested, was to calculate without the enemy. Such an idea has no true bearing on the feelings of the garrison of the peninsula. That the Turks should attack had always been the earnest prayer of all of us, just as much after the 21st August as before it. And now that we had to suspend progress for a bit, work was put in hand upon the line from Suvla to Anzac, a minor offensive routine of sniping and bombing was organised, and, in a word, trench warfare set in on both sides.

On 24th August Lieutenant-General the Hon. J. H. G. Byng, K.C.M.G., C.B., M.V.O., assumed command of the 9th Army Corps.

The last days of the month were illumined by a brilliant affair carried through by the troops under General Birdwood's command. Our object was to complete the capture of Hill 60 north of the Kaiajik Aghala, commenced by Major-General Cox on the 21st August. Hill 60 overlooked the Biyuk Anafarta valley, and was therefore tactically a very important feature.

The conduct of the attack was again entrusted to MajorGeneral Cox, at whose disposal were placed detachments from the 4th and 5th Australian Brigades, the New Zealand Mounted Rifles Brigade, and the 5th Connaught Rangers. The advance was timed to take place at 5 p.m. on the 27th of August, after the heaviest artillery bombardment we could afford.

This bombardment seemed effective; but the moment the assailants broke cover they were greeted by an exceeding hot fire from the enemy field guns, rifles, and machine-guns, followed after a brief interval by a shower of heavy shell, some of which, most happily, pitched into the trenches of the Turks. On the right the detachment from the 4th and 5th Australian Brigades could make no headway against a battery of machine-guns which confronted them. In the centre the New Zealanders made a most determined onslaught, and carried one side of the topmost knoll. Hand-to-hand fighting continued here till 9.30 p.m., when it was reported that nine-tenths of the summit had been gained.

Capture of Hill 60.

On the left the 250 men of the 5th Connaught Rangers excited the admiration of all beholders by the swiftness and cohesion of their charge. In five minutes, they had carried their objective, the northern

Turkish communications, when they at once set to and began a lively bomb-fight along the trenches against strong parties which came hurrying up from the enemy supports and afterwards from their reserves. At midnight fresh troops were to have strengthened our grip upon the hill, but before that hour the Irishmen had been out-bombed, and the 9th Australian Light Horse, who had made a most plucky attempt to recapture the lost communication trench, had been repulsed.

Luckily, the New Zealand Mounted Rifles refused to recognize that they were worsted. Nothing would shift them. All that night and all next day, through bombing, bayonet charges, musketry, shrapnel, and heavy shell, they hung on to their 150 yards of trench. At 1 a.m. on August 29th the 10th Light Horse made another attack on the lost communication trenches to the left, carried them, and finally held them. This gave us complete command of the under-feature, an outlook over the Anafarta Sagir valley, and safer lateral communications between Anzac and Suvla Bay.

Our casualties in this hotly contested affair amounted to 1,000. The Turks lost out of all proportion more. Their line of retreat was commanded from our Kaiajik Dere trenches, whence our observers were able to direct artillery fire equally upon their fugitives and their reinforcements. The same observers estimated the Turkish casualties as no less than 5,000. Three Turkish machine-guns and forty-six prisoners were taken, as well as three trench mortars, 300 Turkish rifles, 60,000 rounds of ammunition, and 500 bombs. Four hundred acres were added to the territories of Anzac. Major-General Cox showed his usual forethought and wisdom. Brigadier-General Russell fought his men splendidly.

My narrative of battle incidents must end here. From this date onwards up to the date of my departure on October 17th the flow of munitions and drafts fell away. Sickness, the legacy of a desperately trying summer, took heavy toll of the survivors of so many arduous conflicts. No longer was there any question of operations on the grand scale, but with such troops it was difficult to be downhearted. All ranks were cheerful; all remained confident that, so long as they stuck to their guns, their country would stick to them, and see them victoriously through the last and greatest of the crusades.

The Question of Evacuation.

On the 11th October Your Lordship cabled asking me for an estimate of the losses which would be involved in an evacuation of the peninsula. On the 12th October I replied in terms showing that such a step was to me unthinkable. On the 16th October I received a cable recalling me to London for the reason, as I was informed by Your Lordship on my arrival, that His Majesty's Government desired a fresh, unbiased opinion, from a responsible Commander, upon the question of early evacuation.

In bringing this dispatch to a close I wish to refer gratefully to the services rendered by certain formations, whose work has so far only been recognized by a sprinkling of individual rewards.

Praise for Various Services.

Much might be written on the exploits of the Royal Naval Air Service, but these bold flyers are laconic, and their feats will mostly pass unrecorded. Yet let me here thank them, with their Commander, Colonel F. H. Sykes, of the Royal Marines, for the nonchalance with which they appear to affront danger and death, when and where they can. So doing, they quicken the hearts of their friends on land and sea—an asset of greater military value even than their bombs or aerial reconnaissances, admirable in all respects as these were.

With them I also couple the Service de l'Aviation of the Corps Expéditionnaire d'Orient, who daily wing their way in and out of the shrapnel under the distinguished leadership of M. le Capitaine Césari.

The Armoured Car Division (Royal Naval Air Service) have never failed to respond to any call which might be made upon them. Their organisation was broken up; their work had to be carried out under strange conditions—from the bows of the *River Clyde*, as independent batteries attached to infantry divisions, etc.—and yet they were always cheerful, always ready to lend a hand in any sort of fighting that might give them a chance of settling old scores with the enemy.

Next, I come to the Royal Artillery. By their constant vigilance, by their quick grasp of the key to every emergency, by their thundering good shooting, by hundreds of deeds of daring, they have earned the unstinted admiration of all their comrade services. Where all fought so remarkably, the junior officers deserve a little niche of their own in the Dardanelles record of fame. Their audacity in reconnaissance, their insouciance under the hottest of fires, stand as a fine example not only to the army, but to the nation at large.

A feature of every report, narrative, or diary I have read has been a tribute to the stretcher-bearers. All ranks, from generals in command to wounded men in hospitals, are unanimous in their praise. I have watched a party from the moment when the telephone summoned them from their dug-out to the time when they returned with their wounded. To see them run light-heartedly across fire-swept slopes is to be privileged to witness a superb example of the hero in man. No braver corps exists, and I believe the reason to be that all thought of self is instinctively flung aside when the saving of others is the motive.

The services rendered by Major-General (temporary Lieutenant-General) E. A. Altham, C.B., C.M.G., Inspector-General of Communications, and all the Departments and Services of the Lines of Communications assured us a lifegiving flow of drafts, munitions, and supplies. The work was carried out under unprecedented conditions, and is deserving, I submit, of handsome recognition.

With General Altham were associated Brigadier-General (temporary Major-General) C. R. R. McGrigor, C.B., at first Commandant of the Base at Alexandria and later Deputy Inspector-General of Communications, and Colonel T. E. O'Leary, Deputy Adjutant-General, 3rd Echelon. Both of these officers carried out their difficult duties to my entire satisfaction.

My Military Secretary, Lieutenant-Colonel S. H. Pollen, has displayed first-class ability in the conduct of his delicate and responsible duties.

Also, I take the opportunity of my last dispatch to mention two of my *aides-de-camp*—Major F. L. Makgill-Crichton-Maitland, Gordon Highlanders, Lieutenant Hon. G. St. J. Brodrick, Surrey Yeomanry.

A Farewell Tribute.

I have many other names to bring to notice for distinguished and gallant service during the operations under review, and these will form the subject of a separate communication.

And now, before affixing to this dispatch my final signature as Commander-in-Chief of the Mediterranean Expeditionary Force, let me first pay tribute to the everlasting memory of my dear comrades who will return no more. Next, let me thank each and all, generals, staff, regimental leaders, and rank and file, for their wonderful loyalty, patience, and self-sacrifice. Our progress was constant, and if it was painfully slow—they know the truth.

So I bid them all farewell with a special God-speed to the campaigners who have served with me right through from the terrible yet most glorious earlier days—the incomparable 29th Division; the young veterans of the Naval Division; the ever-victorious Australians

and New Zealanders; the stout East Lancs, and my own brave fellow-countrymen of the Lowland Division of Scotland,
 I have the honour to be.
   Your Lordship's most obedient servant,
    Ian Hamilton,
   General, Commander-in-Chief
   Mediterranean Expeditionary Force.

CHAPTER 11

The New Situation in the Near East

By the beginning of October, 1915, it was clear to observers in the West that our position in the Eastern Mediterranean, never strategically good, was about to be complicated by that very event which we had hoped to frustrate. The Turks, depleted in men, and with their stock of munitions running low, were about to receive dangerous reinforcements.

After the second failure at Suvla on 21st August there could be no question of a renewed offensive. Sir Ian Hamilton on 16th August had asked for large reinforcements from home, and they had been refused him. For some weeks the peninsula saw the ordinary routine of trench warfare like the preceding winter in the West. Local attacks and counterattacks kept the fronts from stagnation, but there was no plan of advance on either side. By the third week of September the new menace in the Balkans was apparent, and the Gallipoli campaign became only a part of the highly complex strategical situation. It was clear that we should presently be compelled to operate on another part of the Aegean littoral, and it was not clear where the troops were to come from.

About this time, we may date the complete surrender of the original Gallipoli plan. The Allied scheme was in the melting-pot, and we were back in the position of the end of March, but faced with the results of failure and a far more intricate military problem. The time has not yet come for a final judgment on the adventure, but our knowledge is sufficient to see the main reasons for our lack of success. The original idea of landing on the peninsula was, as we have argued elsewhere, open to serious criticism. It proposed to gain ends clearly desirable by means which at the best must be costly and slow.

But, admitting that the plan was feasible, the troops allotted to it were manifestly insufficient. It is almost certain that Krithia would have been won if sufficient men had been forthcoming by the end of April. But as time went on the Turkish defence developed. Soon Krithia did not involve Achi Baba, nor Achi Baba the Pasha Dagh. What had been the key-points of the citadel soon became no more than outworks. It may be questioned whether even a complete success at Suvla and Anzac in August would have really given us what we desired. The failure there was not to be blamed upon the general strategy; it was a disaster which must occur now and then to a nation which has to improvise armies, and has no great area of choice among its commanders.

But the root of error was in the original plan, and the blame for it must be laid upon the government which, without due consideration, embarked upon so hazardous an enterprise, and allotted for it such an inadequate fighting strength. Nor can Sir Ian Hamilton be relieved of responsibility for consenting to carry out a plan, of the imperfection of which any trained soldier must have been convinced. It is the business of a general to resign rather than be a party to the waste of gallant men. On this point Napoleon's example is worthy of imitation. In 1796 he tendered his resignation when the Directory wished him to execute a futile scheme, and conversely in 1800 he cancelled his orders to Moreau when he was unable to make him understand their advantages.

When a plan has failed and a campaign is brought to a stalemate in one *terrain* it is common sense to try to break it off and employ the troops more fruitfully elsewhere. But it is not always easy to retrace one's steps. We had landed great forces in Gallipoli at a heavy cost. The question was—Could they be withdrawn without a far greater cost? This was obviously a matter for experts, and the experts differed. There were those—and among them Sir Ian Hamilton may be reckoned—who believed that to move the Allied forces from the peninsula would involve a higher casualty list than the April landings.

There were others who maintained that with the support of the ships' guns only a comparatively small rearguard need be sacrificed. Some argued that to leave Gallipoli would be a fatal blow to our prestige in the East—a weak contention, if the same troops were destined to pursue the Gallipoli objective, an attack on the Turks, in some other Near Eastern theatre. One school maintained with much force that it was a case of Hobson's choice. Winter was coming, when contrary winds would make the task of supplying the Gallipoli lines extraordinarily difficult. The Turks were about to receive from Germany a great new munitionment, and in that case we must decide between abandoning our positions and being blown out of them.

They did not minimise the difficulties of withdrawal, but they insisted upon the greater difficulties of remaining. On the purely military side, it was clear that if we were to fight a campaign in any part of the Balkans, and if speed was the essence of the undertaking, then the only troops which could be put in the field soon were those drawn from Gallipoli. But, on the other hand, it was urged that soldiers who had fought for months in cramped trench battles should not be forthwith used for a manoeuvre campaign in an open country. They must be given an interval for rest and reorganisation. Finally, there was a natural reluctance to leave the old battle-ground which had cost us so dear. This was especially felt by the Anzac corps, who regarded the Gallipoli heights as sacred ground, the burial-place of their friends which it was a point of honour to redeem from the enemy.

Such were a few of the difficulties to be faced in any decision. On 16th October Sir Ian Hamilton was recalled to London to "report," and General Sir Charles Monro, commanding the British Third Army, was appointed to the command of the Mediterranean Expeditionary Force. General Monro had won a great reputation in the West first in command of the 2nd Division, and then of the First Corps. He is a soldier somewhat after the peninsular type, with admirable nerve, great sagacity and judgment, and the gift of inspiring confidence in all who serve with him. No better man could have been found for this responsible and arduous task.

Meantime, about the middle of September two divisions were withdrawn from Gallipoli—the 10th British, under Sir Bryan Mahon from Suvla, and a French division from Cape Helles. This was the force whose landing at Salonika we have already seen beginning. It was destined to be placed under General Sarrail, who had formerly commanded the 3rd French Army at Verdun, and had been for some months the designated successor of General Gouraud in the command of the French Corps Expéditionnaire.

We must leave the military operations in the Balkans for later chapters, and consider here the general situation in the Near East. Assuming that in some way or other, with greater or lesser loss, the Gallipoli problem could be solved, what were the dangers to be feared from the new German and Bulgarian move? If it succeeded wholly, if Serbia were vanquished, and Germany won the river and railway routes to Constantinople, then, apart from the advantages she would gain in regard to her own supplies, she might be able to equip an offensive against Britain in two localities.

One was Egypt and the other Mesopotamia. It was unlikely that she could send troops of her own, but she could send officers and munitions, and do precisely what she had already done at the Dardanelles. If she were once placed firmly at Constantinople with an open road behind her, it was conceivable that she could inspire an offensive against Egypt more serious than the fiasco of the preceding February. Following Bismarck, who described Egypt as the "neck of the British Empire," German political thought had always looked to the banks of the Nile as the quarter where the power of England could be most vitally crippled. There was a railway from the Bosphorus to Aleppo, with two short breaks, and the roads of the Central Anatolian plateau were suitable in dry weather for motor transport.

From Aleppo the Syrian and Hedjaz railways would carry troops to within a short distance of the Egyptian frontier. Was not von Mackensen's force known in Germany as the "Army of Egypt"? She could also—-though here the transport problem was more difficult—send assistance to the hard-pressed Baghdad corps in Mesopotamia. These things were conceivable, but they involved a great effort, and at the time it was hard to believe that Germany, compelled in common wisdom to husband her strength, would regard such an effort as worth making. The approach to the Suez Canal was the most difficult conceivable, and Britain, with her command of the sea, could strengthen the defences of Egypt long before the threat materialized.

Again, even if reinforcements were sent to Baghdad, all that would happen would be that Sir John Nixon's advance would be stayed. The British there had the river and the sea behind them, and no immediate cause to be anxious about their communications. It seemed, therefore, fair to conclude that the German threat to Egypt and the road to India was a threat rather than a plan. She hoped to make Britain anxious for her Imperial communications, and thereby to distract her effort in more vital theatres. Too much, perhaps, was made at the time of the danger of Germany in Constantinople to our Eastern prestige.

Germany had in substance been for a year on the Bosphorus. The situation so far as that was concerned was in no way changed. All the prestige that she could gain from an alliance with the Sultan of Roum had already been won. A descent in force into Syria might increase it, but prestige is an incalculable thing, and the approach of Germany to the Holy Land of Islam might have an effect contrary to her anticipations. It was hard to resist the conclusion that at its inception the Teutonic *Drang nach Osten* had for its principal aim to raise doubt and hesitation in the Allies about the future developments of the war, and in particular to complicate for them the already difficult situation in the Aegean. It was also true that certain elements in Germany, which still believed that a crushing victory was possible, desired to "peg out claims" in the Near East against the day of peace. The Allies were rarely clear about their general plan, and there is no reason to believe that the German objective was always simple, luminous, and precisely calculated.

There was another factor in the situation—Russia. Apart from her main Eastern front, she had an army in Transcaucasia, and, till the unfortunate reappearance of the *Goeben* at the end of October, she had a virtual control of the Black Sea. We last saw her Caucasian Army in the spring faced with the remnants of three Turkish corps. Throughout the summer this wardenship of the marches continued, and there were many battles of which no news came to the West. In especial a brilliant action was fought in the beginning of May at Dilman, northwest of Lake Urmia, and inside the borders of the Persian province of Azerbaijan, which Russia had been compelled to occupy.

The better part of the 12th (Mosul) Corps, under Halil Bey—15,000 regular infantry and 5,000 Kurdish cavalry—attacked a weak Russian force of 3,000, supported by a few hundred Cossacks. After two days' heroic resistance on the Russian side the Turkish ammunition gave out, and Halil retired across the frontier with a loss of over 4,000. He was again in action later, and succeeded in reducing his army to a quarter of its strength. The Battle of Dilman was opportune, for it prevented the Turks in Mesopotamia receiving reinforcements which might have checked the British advance, and turned the tide at Kut-el-Amara five months later.

The Turkish military failure on the Transcaucasian border was followed by one of the most wholesale and cold-blooded massacres in the distracted history of Armenia. That unhappy race, industrious and pacific, had long been the whipping-boy on which Constantinople had taken revenge for its defeats and fears. This is not the place to discuss the causes of the Armenian persecutions. In the two years between 1895 and 1897 Abdul Hamid had destroyed little less than half a million. In 1909, the Young Turks, not to be outdone in this honourable activity, had instituted the Adana massacres. The atrocities which filled the first eight months of 1915 were carefully organised and represented the fulfilment of a long-cherished policy.

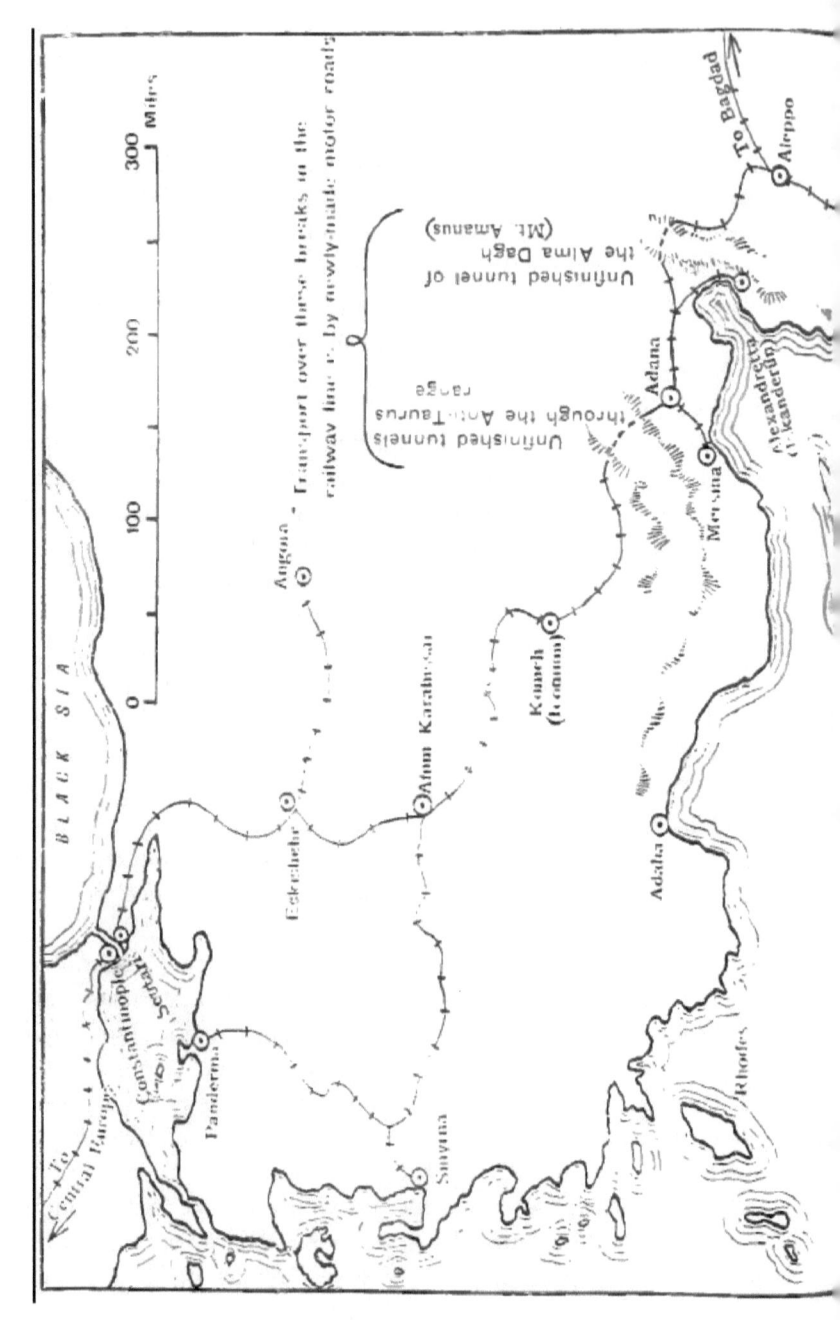

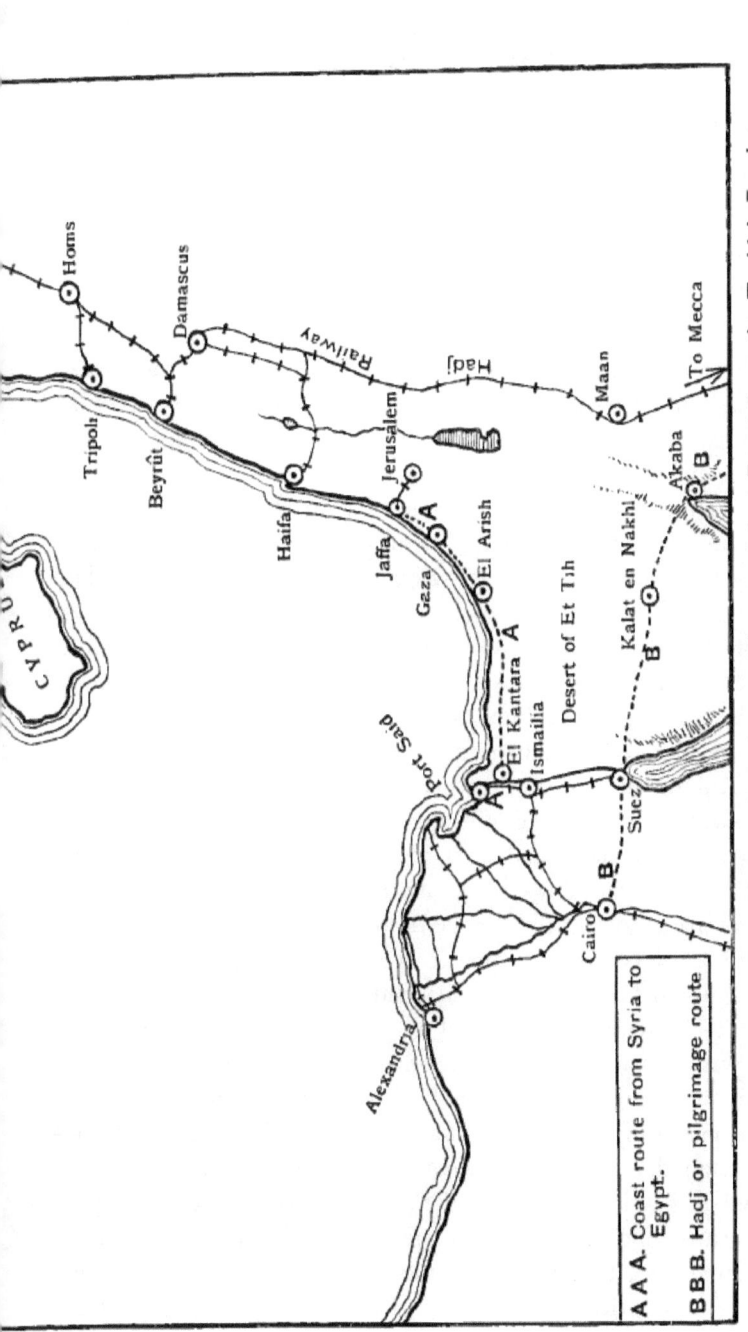

Routes and Railway Communications available for an Advance against Egypt from the Turkish Empire.

Their instigators were Enver and Talaat the Bulgarian Jew, ably seconded by the Jew Cavasso and by other members of the Committee of Union and Progress. Now that Turkey was a war with the West, she need listen to no more pratings about humanity, what the *grand vizier* described as "nonsense about Armenian reforms." She could make an effort to extirpate a race she had always detested. Talaat was perfectly frank. He told the American Ambassador at Constantinople:—

> I am taking the necessary steps to make it impossible for the Armenians ever to utter the word autonomy during the next fifty years.

He was as good as his word. In the early spring while the Turkish regulars seem to have behaved with some moderation, the irregular bands round Bayazid and Erzerum and on the Persian frontier slaughtered mercilessly, and drove the miserable remnants into Russian territory. From April onward the whole of Eastern Anatolia, from Trebizond to Alexandretta, was the scene of systematic massacres. In a military history it is needless to dwell on a tale of horror which had no military significance.

Not always was the attack unresisted. Ten thousand Armenians were serving as volunteers with the Russian Army of the Caucasus, and they gave a good account of themselves at Van. At Shaban Karahissar, near Trebizond, 4,000 Armenians held back the Turkish troops for a fortnight, till reinforcements reached the enemy and all were put to the sword. The same thing happened at Jebel Musa. West of Lake Van 15,000 Armenians banded together, and held out in the mountain tops. Near Antioch many of the Cilician Armenians withdrew to the hills, and made good their defence till they were rescued by a French cruiser. For the rest, about a quarter of a million refugees found haven in the Russian Caucasus, a few reached Bulgaria, and in one or two places the humanity of the local authorities gave them protection. But it was estimated that well over half a million perished, and great numbers of women and children were sold into slavery.

The protesting voices were few and ineffective. The Sheikh-ul-Islam resigned, and Ahmed Riza and Djavid declared their disagreement when it was too late. Only the Vali of Smyrna refused to be party to the crimes, and carried out his refusal by protecting the Armenians in his province. The Pope made remonstrances through the Latin Patriarch. The American Ambassador in Constantinople did his best, but his Austro-German colleagues declined to join him, declaring that they could not interfere in the internal affairs of Turkey, though on 31st August they made a half-hearted protest, and asked the *grand vizier* for a written guarantee that they had had no connection with the massacres. Meanwhile the German Baron von Oppenheim in Syria was openly preaching persecution, and Count zu Reventlow in Germany was defending Turkey's action, on the ground that Armenians were rebels who deserved all they had received.

The Turco-German pupils of Abdul Hamid were busy in another province. In Northern Persia they and their agents were carrying on what can only be described as a campaign of assassination. With wholesale bribery they tried to corrupt the *gendarmerie* and the Persian officials. The strange spectacle was seen of the stout and elderly ambassadors of Turkey and Germany hurried about the land in the company of the sweepings of two nations. There was small military significance in these escapades, but they contrived still further to unsettle a land which had never been very famous for peace. It seemed to be the aim of the Central Powers to kindle all the sporadic fires they could compass, in the hope that by some happy chance the smoke and sparks might incommode the enemies in the main theatres.

The only military question in Eastern Anatolia was the position of the Russian Army of the Caucasus. It had held the frontiers during the summer, and guarded Russia's south-eastern gate. But the accession of the Grand Duke Nicholas to its command in the beginning of September had suggested to observers in the West that a diversion might come from that quarter to ease the situation in the Aegean. Apparently, the Turkish Command shared the same view, for in September they did their best to increase their forces on the Transcaucasian borders. During that month they seem to have had not less than 200 battalions on the front from the Black Sea to the south of Lake Van—eighteen from the 1st, and, and 4th Corps north of the Chorak valley, one hundred and twelve from the 9th, 10th, 11th, and 12th Corps in the centre, and seventy from the 13th Corps north and south of Lake Van, where also they had the support of Kurdish irregulars.

These battalions were, of course, greatly depleted, and probably did not yield a fighting strength of more than 100,000 men, while, owing to the activities of the Russian Fleet in the Black Sea, they were poorly fed and badly supplied with clothing and munitions. Yet they represented a force by no means negligible, and the prospects of an advance westwards through the central plateau of Anatolia were not alluring. Unless it was made with large armies on a broad front,

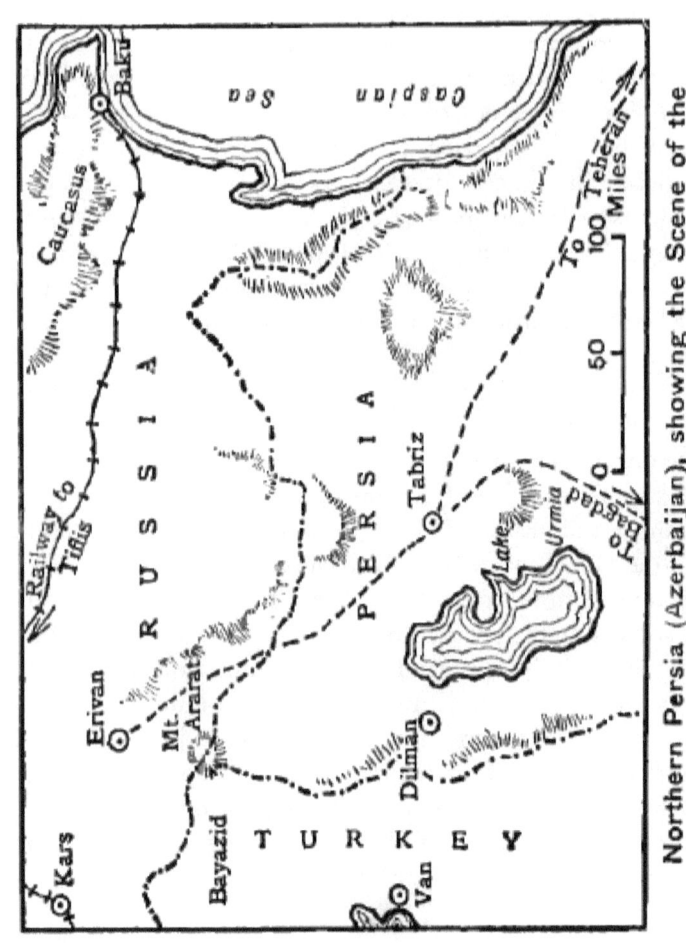

Northern Persia (Azerbaijan), showing the Scene of the Fighting near Lake Urmia.

it would be strategically dangerous, for an attack on the left flank and rear was always possible. Again, there were no railways on the Turkish side, and no possibility of striking a blow at a vital part till the shores of the Bosphorus were reached. The Russian commander would have his farthest railhead short of the frontier at Sarikamish, and that point was already many miles from his main bases of supply.

A move westward in force could scarcely be justified in the circumstances; it would be a subsidiary operation, which might presently develop into a difficult major operation. All that the Grand Duke would do was to detain as many Turkish troops as possible in that area to prevent reinforcements being sent to Baghdad or the Dardanelles. In the event of a Turkish embarrassment elsewhere, his Army of the Caucasus was well placed to strike a blow from behind.

The urgent question of the moment was the possibility of Russia moving a force from her southern Black Sea bases against Bulgaria. There was much talk of a landing at Varna, on the Black Sea coast, a step against which Bulgaria had prepared; but the Russian fleet, especially since the reappearance of the *Goeben*, was not in such a position of dominance as to make the naval side of the operation secure, and in any case recent experience of landings in the face of a prepared opposition had not been encouraging.

The real point was whether Russia could mass in Bessarabia an army strong enough to give adequate support to Rumania in the event of her entering the war on the Allied side. The situation of the latter power was one of immense and increasing difficulty. She had south of her a Bulgarian Army watching the Danube, and north the main Austro-German right wing in the Bukovina. If she entered the campaign unsupported she would be in danger of being caught between two fires. The western Bulgarian armies, with von Mackensen's assistance, would in all likelihood be able to crush Serbia and contain the small Franco-British force to the south; and though Ivanov was winning successes against von Pflanzer and von Bothmer north of the Dniester, he was still far from making that flank secure.

Two conditions seemed essential before Rumania could move. There must be an adequate Allied force on the shores of the North Aegean to occupy the attention of the main Bulgarian Army, and Russia must be able to send sufficient troops to counteract the danger of an Austro-German movement from the Carpathians. Of these two conditions the second was the more important. Rumania was at the moment neutral, with a leaning towards the Allies. But it was clear that

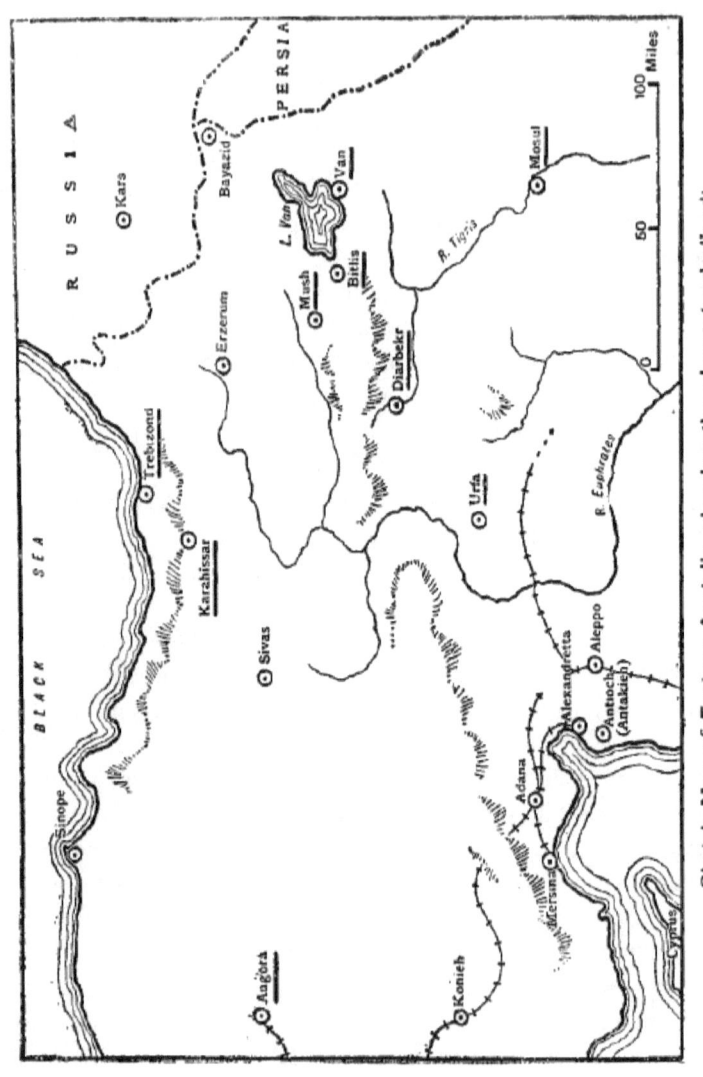

Sketch Map of Eastern Anatolia, showing the places (underlined)

in certain events she might be compelled, even against her will, to join the side of the Teutonic League.

There are three routes into Bulgaria from the northern Aegean. The most westerly runs from Salonika up the valley of the Vardar and down the Upper Morava to Nish, whence the valley of the Nishava takes it eastwards towards Sofia. It is throughout followed by a railway. Farther east the valley of the Struma is open to troops advancing from Kavala. It goes through the heart of difficult mountains, and has no railway and but one road suitable for heavy traffic in winter. The most easterly is the route by the Maritza valley from the port of Dedeagatch, which has a good railway, and turns the flank of the Rhodope range. It leads through Turkish territory by Adrianople.

If the Allies, assuming they were present in sufficient force, desired to strike at Bulgaria, the middle route by the Struma valley was clearly the worst. The best, so far as purely military considerations went, was probably that by the Maritza valley. The western route by the Salonika railway was long, and had the disadvantage that against it the enemy was massed in his chief strength. Had an advance there been possible before the end of September, while Serbia was still unbroken, it was obviously the best course, but if Serbia should be put out of action it had little to recommend it. The Allies' object was to cut the Austro-German communications with Constantinople, and it is common wisdom, if you are too late to cut a line some distance from its objective, to make an attempt on it, if possible, nearer the goal. These considerations seemed to point to a campaign in Western Thrace.

But no such simple solution was possible. In the first place, the Allies were already at Salonika, sent there for the reasons we have recounted. If they re-embarked, they left Greece open to the persuasions or the threats of the advancing Bulgarians and Austro-Germans, and the Greek situation at the moment was too delicate to take any risks. In the second place, an advance in Thrace demanded an army of at least 300,000 men, and that would not be forthcoming for weeks, probably months, unless the troops could be removed from Gallipoli.

We may therefore sum up the situation in the beginning of October somewhat as follows: Some 200,000 Austro-Germans and rather more Bulgarians were pressing in on Serbia with every chance of occupying that country and driving the remnants of the Serbian Army into the Albanian hills. A small force of 13,000 Allies was at Salonika, moving northwards against the Bulgarian left wing, but without any hope of succouring Serbia or stemming the tide of invasion. The most they

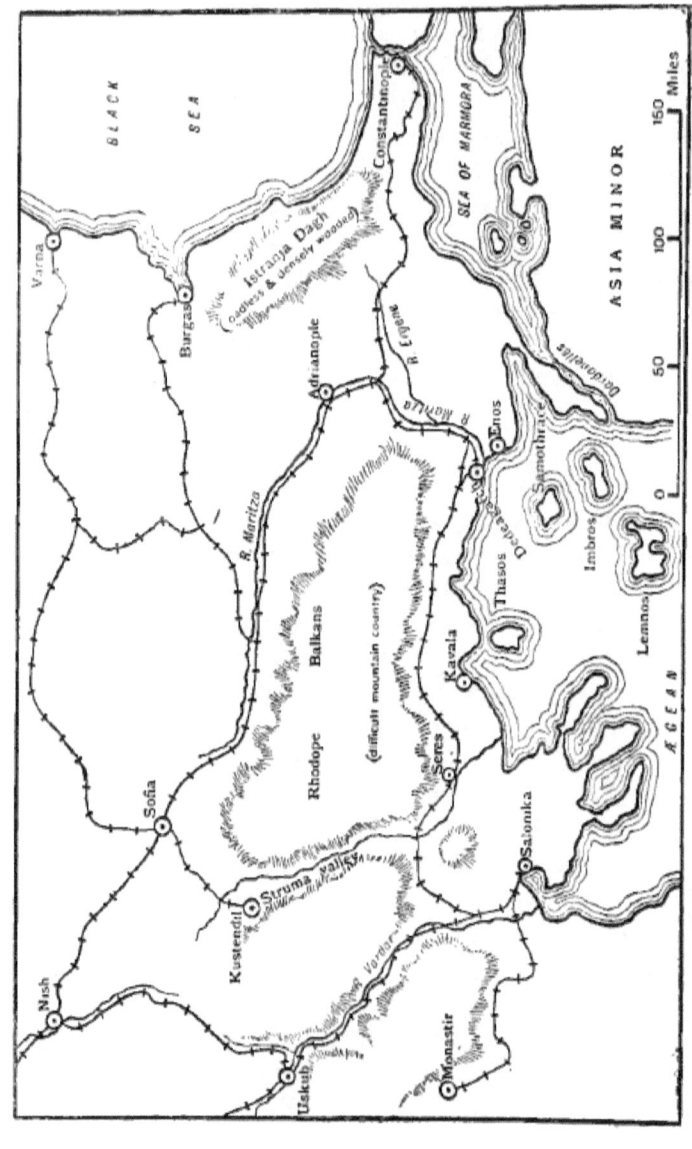

Sketch Map showing the Avenues into Bulgaria from the Ægean Coast.

(Vardar and Struma valleys to the west of the Rhodope mass, and east of it the fairly open country along the Lower Maritza and the Ergene and between the Rhodope and the Istranja Dagh.)

could do would be to protect the coast end of the Salonika railway.

In Gallipoli an Allied force of nearly a dozen divisions was held fast, and their future had not been decided. Greece and Rumania were mobilized and watching events, no doubt benevolent to the Allies, but waiting for some proof that the Allies had a chance of success. The one strategic plan which offered good hope was a joint attack from north and south on Bulgaria's rear—a plan of which we have outlined the difficulties. The two possibilities which might solve the puzzle were the ability of Russia to provide in Bessarabia an army sufficient to quiet Rumania's fears and encourage her to move against the Danube, and the providing by France and Britain, from Gallipoli or elsewhere, of an adequate field force to advance from the south by whatever route proved most practicable.

Such were the elements of the Allied situation in the Near East. The first act of the drama was played in Western Macedonia and Serbia, and closed, with the expulsion of a heroic army from its native land. The one blow struck elsewhere during October was the bombardment of the Bulgarian coast on 21st October (Trafalgar Day) by Admiral de Robeck's squadron. The whole enemy seaboard was shelled from Port Lagos to Dedeagatch, and at the latter place all the barracks and Government buildings were destroyed.

The troops took refuge in the neighbouring hills, the civilian population fled, and the British efforts were confined to the destruction of property. The railway station, the line, rolling stock, the harbour buildings, oil stores, coal depots, warehouses, and factories were methodically obliterated. As the campaign then stood, such a bombardment could have no serious strategical effect. It was rather to be regarded as a timely hint to other maritime nations that the British Navy was a factor to be reckoned with.

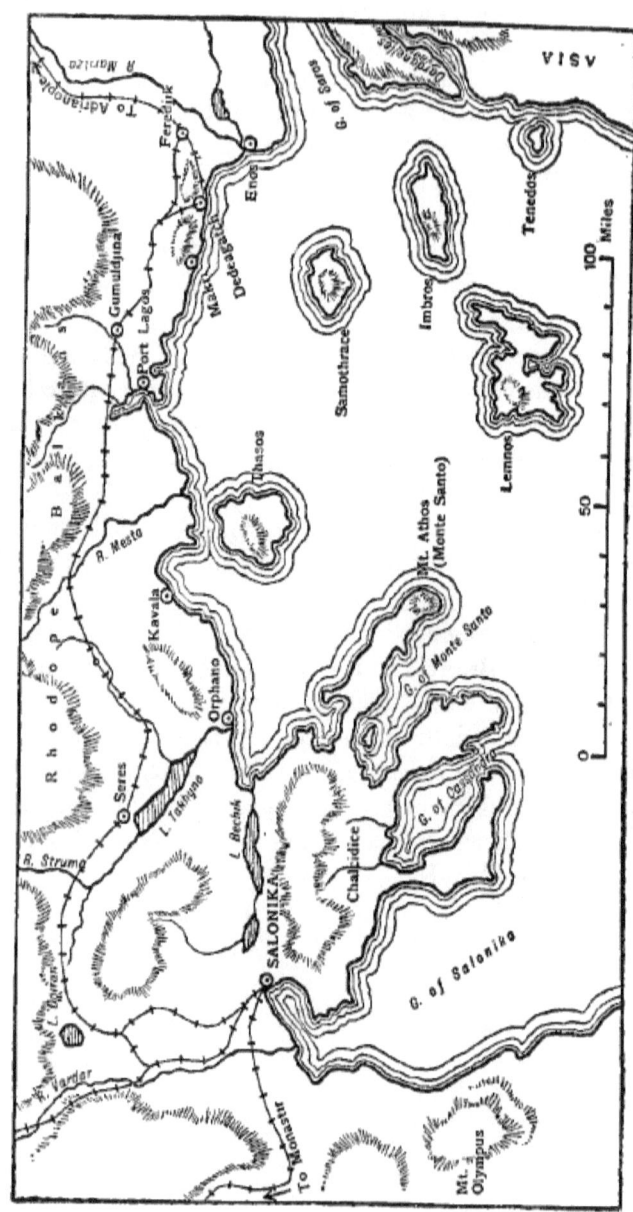

The Northern Coasts of the Ægean.

CHAPTER 12

The Baghdad Expedition

When, at the end of September, 1915, the Turkish defence was broken at Kut-el-Amara, the British force began its advance on Baghdad. General Townshend was now in the position in which many British generals have found themselves. He commanded little more than a single division, and was outnumbered by the enemy's forces directly opposed to him, and vastly outnumbered by their potential levies. He was well over three hundred miles from his base on the sea. He had a river for his sole communication, and, after our amphibious fashion, was assisted by armed vessels from the water; but that river was full of shallows and mudbanks more formidable than the cataracts of the Nile. All around him lay a country ill-suited for operations by European troops—sparsely-watered desert and reeking marshes, baked by the hottest of Asian suns, and brooded over by those manifold diseases which heat and desert soil engender.

The local tribes were either treacherous or openly hostile, and might at any moment strike at his long, straggling connections with the coast. Before him, a hundred miles off by the short cut across the loop of the Tigris, lay one of the most famous cities of the world. That a little British Army, wearied with ten months' incessant fighting, should advance to conquer a mighty province of a still powerful empire might well seem one of the rashest enterprises ever embarked upon by man. It was a war like that fought in the Sudan undertaken under far more difficult conditions, for the fall of Baghdad would not mean, like the fall of Khartum, the end of serious resistance, and no *Sirdar* had planned a Sudan railway to bring supplies and reserves more quickly than the route of the winding river.

It may well be asked why an advance was ordered. The Turkish Army which we had beaten at Kut-el-Amara could be readily reinforced. They had the Mosul Corps to draw upon; by the Tigris troops could be brought from Kurdistan; and from Damascus and Aleppo, by the caravan routes through the desert, reserves could be sent from the Army of Syria. Turkey had by no means used up all her supplies of men. The fronts in Gallipoli and Transcaucasia were stagnant, and the Allied embarrassments in the Balkans made any immediate pressure there unlikely. The British, on the other hand, could only add to their army by drafts from India or the Western Front, a matter of weeks in one case and months in the other. In the face of a demoralised enemy a bold dash for the capital might succeed. But the Turks, as we well knew, were not demoralized. If they had failed at Kut they had to all intents succeeded at Gallipoli, and there stood by their side their German taskmasters to keep them to their business.

Moreover, Baghdad was no easy problem. The Tigris for some miles below the town loops itself into fantastic whorls, which meant that at many parts any land force, whose aim was speed, would be deprived of the co-operation of its flotilla. Again, some twenty miles below the city, the River Diala, entering the main stream on its left bank, provided a strong line of defence. Finally, Baghdad was an open city, and, even if won, would be hard to defend. In fact, it was an impossible halting-place. Once there, for the sake of security we should have been compelled to go on seventy-five miles to Samara, on the Tigris, the terminus of the railway from Baghdad. We should also be obliged to occupy Khanikin, where the Diala crosses the Persian frontier. From Samara it would soon be necessary to advance another hundred miles to Mosul.

Indeed, there was no natural end, save exhaustion, to the progress which the need of security would impose on us. There was no attainable point where that security could be assured, for between the Tigris valley and the Russian front in Transcaucasia lay the wild mountains of Kurdistan. And all the while our communications would be lengthening out crazily. At Baghdad we should be 573 miles by river from the Gulf, and between 300 and 400 by the shortest land route. We should be hopelessly out of touch with our sea-power. On every ground of strategy and common sense the advance was indefensible.

On the other hand, it was undeniable that the conquest of Baghdad would have great political advantages—if it could be achieved. As we have argued in an earlier chapter, its fall would be a makeweight to the German domination at Constantinople. It would cut at their nodal point the principal routes of German communications with Persia and the Indian frontier. But even this success would not be

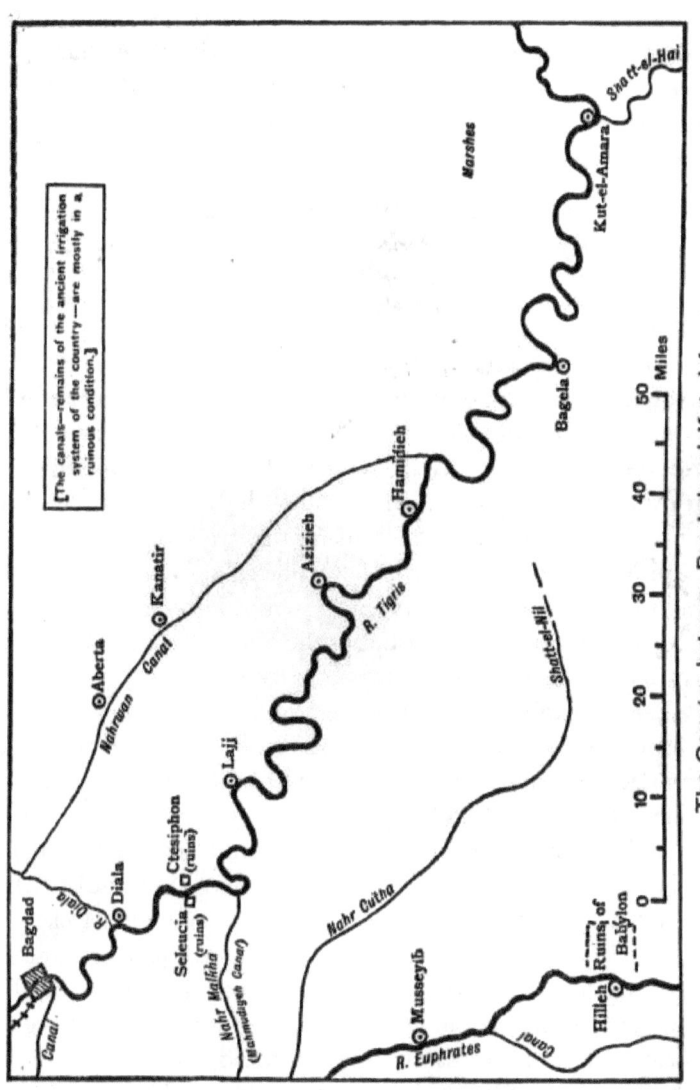

The Country between Bagdad and Kut-el-Amara.

final. There would remain the great caravan routes of the Northern Shammar desert, which followed the projected line of the Baghdad railway to Mosul, and thence to Rowandiz on the Persian frontier. Full success in our objective really demanded the control of the whole of Northern Mesopotamia. Such a control might have been won, but it required an adequate force—at least two army corps fully equipped, and not one weary division.

The British prime minister, in his speech in the House of Commons on 2nd November, defined the objects of the Mesopotamia Expedition as:—

> To secure the neutrality of the Arabs, to safeguard our interests in the Persian Gulf, to protect the oil-fields, and generally to maintain the authority of our flag in the East.

Of these aims the first may be dismissed as trivial. The Arab tribes of Mesopotamia were a much overrated folk, notable rather for low cunning than for military virtues. Their hostility and their friendship alike were worth little. The third we secured when we held Amara and the desert route to Ahwaz; the second when we won Basra. The fourth was a vague aspiration which did not involve any specific military operations, but which did demand that we should not get ourselves into impossible situations. All the objects defined by Mr. Asquith were, in fact, realised when General Townshend took Kut-el-Amara, and, by holding the northern end of the Shatt-el-Hai, prevented the enemy cutting his communications by a flank march.

At Kut the extreme purpose of the original expedition was fulfilled. The advance to Baghdad was a new scheme involving a new policy. If we remember the situation at the end of September, we shall find a possible clue to the reasons for the adventure. The great advance of the Allies in the West had reached its limit without a decision. The Balkan affair had gone from bad to worse, Serbia was about to be isolated, Bulgaria was entering the field on Germany's side, and von Mackensen's guns had begun to sound on the Danube. Our diplomacy, justly or unjustly, had suffered a serious loss of credit. Looking round the globe for something to restore our drooping prestige at the moment, the eyes of soldiers and statesmen naturally fell on Mesopotamia.

The expedition there had been up to date a brilliant success. No mistakes had been made. Miracles had been performed with a handful of troops. But the names of Kut-el-Amara and Nasiriyeh were not familiar to Europe. Now Baghdad was known to all the world. If the old city of the *caliphs* fell to British arms there would be a resounding success wherewith to balance our failure in the Aegean. Our much-tried diplomacy would have something to point to in its painful negotiations with suspicious neutrals. Therefore, let us make a dash for Baghdad, and trust to the standing luck of the British Army. It was commonly assumed in Britain at the time that the enterprise was primarily conceived by the politicians, and that we had embarked on a scheme politically valuable without counting the military cost. It was urged that we had forgotten one of Jomini's most pregnant aphorisms:—

> The choice of political objectives ought to be subordinate to the interests of strategy, at any rate until the great military issues have been decided by arms.

But for this most natural assumption there was in fact no warrant. The advance to Baghdad was advocated by the soldiers chiefly concerned, and on the information at our disposal we believed it to be a practicable undertaking. General Townshend was understood to have protested against an advance with such inadequate forces, but Sir John Nixon and the Indian military authorities thought differently.

In October Turkey had in the field as many men as the British Empire. She was fighting nominally in four theatres of war—Transcaucasia, the Egyptian frontier, Gallipoli, and Mesopotamia. Of her four theatres three were virtually in a state of stagnation. Probably not more than 150,000 men were mobilised along the Russian frontier; there was nothing doing on the Egyptian borders; the enemy in Gallipoli had shot his bolt; and in Mesopotamia alone was there any urgent question of defence. It was therefore open to Turkey, given a little time and some assistance from Germany in the way of supplies, to deploy on the Tigris little short of a quarter of a million men.

To meet this possibility Sir John Nixon had his Anglo-Indian division and an extra brigade—all told, perhaps, 15,000 bayonets. One-third of the force were British soldiers, including such regular battalions as the 2nd Dorsets, the 2nd Norfolks, and the 1st Oxford Light Infantry, and territorial battalions of the Hampshires and Sussex. The remainder were Indian troops, including a number of Punjab battalions, the 103rd, 110th, and 117th Mahrattas, the 7th Rajputs, two Gurkha battalions, and four regiments of cavalry.

The accompanying flotilla was composed of every conceivable type of boat, from ancient Admiralty sloops to Burma paddle-steamers, the river-boats of the firm of Lynch, motor launches, and the flat-bottomed native punts of the Delta. The whole British force was battle-worn and weary. Large numbers had contracted ailments and diseases, and all were jaded by the incessant struggle of the hot summer. But to cheer them they had a record of unbroken success. Wherever and in whatever numbers they had found the enemy they had soundly beaten him.

In Mesopotamia in October the days are bright and clear and the nights cold. It is the beginning of that bracing and clement winter which in subtropical deserts is the atonement for the arid summer. The normal period of floods was past, and the marshes were drying. It was the best season of the year for an advance, and no time was lost in making a start. After the victory of Kut the flotilla had pursued the enemy up the river, but the multitude of sandbanks made progress slow, and the chase was soon relinquished.

Our aeroplanes watched the retreating Turks, and reported that they were falling back in hot haste, and were not halting short of the Ctesiphon line, which was their last defence south of Baghdad. They seem to have moved at the rate of twenty-five miles a day, and, though they shed quantities of ammunition and rifles by the roadside, they got away all the guns which we had not captured on the field of Kut. Reconnoitring parties were sent forward on steamers by General Townshend. In the early days of October, the advance began, partly by land and partly by river. On 4th October there were troops already fifty miles upriver from Kut, and only sixty by road from Baghdad.

By 23rd October the bulk of the British force had reached Azizie, more than half-way to the capital. There had been a few skirmishes with raiding Arabs, but no serious rearguard fighting. At Azizie, however, we found the Turkish advanced guard in position, and for a few days our progress halted. Then by a flank attack we routed the 3,000 or 4,000 of the enemy, and pushed them back to their main Ctesiphon standing-ground. In the first week of November our movement began again. On the 12th General Townshend was encamped at Lajj, seven miles from Ctesiphon, and about thirty miles from Baghdad. His outposts were almost in touch with the prepared Turkish positions.

The map will show the nature of the ground. At Ctesiphon the Euphrates and the Tigris approach within twenty miles of each other. Such a position was obviously well chosen, for the Turks could bring reinforcements down the Euphrates from Aleppo and the Army of Syria. Had we been in sufficient force to send an expedition up that river, we should have won a double line of communications, and

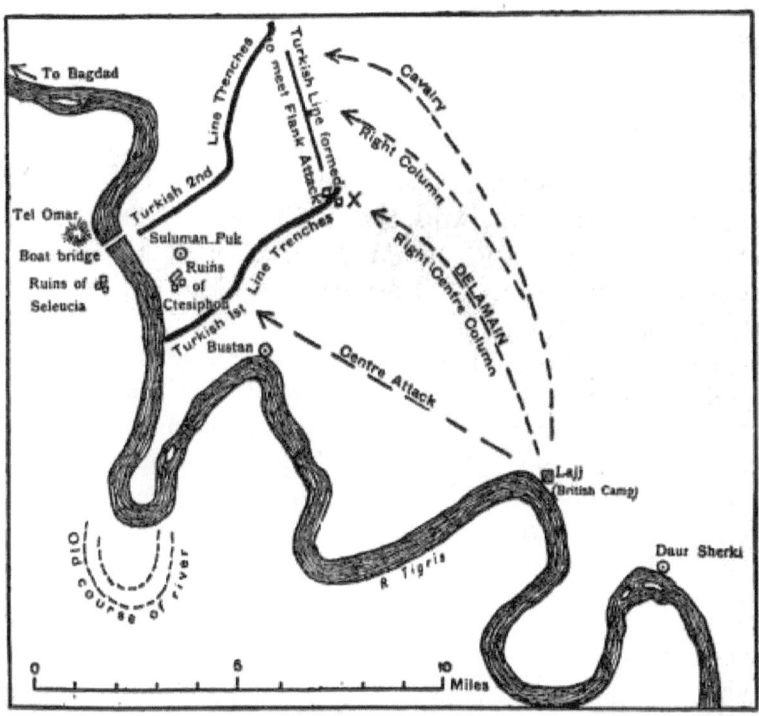

Battle of Ctesiphon.

been able to adopt an enveloping strategy. But the enemy was perfectly familiar with our numbers, and knew that of such a movement there was no possible danger. Ctesiphon, the old Sassanid capital, had been the battle-ground of Romans and Parthians, but only the massive brick shell of the "Throne of Chosroes," rising above the squalid Turkish village, remained to tell of its former grandeur.

Beyond the river lay the ruins of Seleucia, the old capital of the Seleucidae, for at this point Parthia and Syria had faced each other across the Tigris. The Turkish first position ran from the angle in the Tigris, with a second line about half a mile in the rear. The whole place had been strongly fortified according to the latest German fashion, and the wastes of old debris furnished admirable shelters for machine-guns, of the same type as the redoubts on the Western Front. The Turkish right wing was beyond the Tigris, but their centre and left, comprising three-fourths of their army, were on the left bank.

On the evening of 21st November General Townshend advanced from Lajj. His force, as at Kut, was divided into three columns. The tactical plan was almost the same as that at Kut. One column was to advance against the centre of the first Turkish position. A second column, under Delamain, was to envelop the left of that position; while a third was to make a wide detour, and come in on the left rear of the main Turkish force, and co-operate with Delamain in driving them back towards the river. We may call these columns the centre, the right centre, and the right. Behind the main Turkish position lay the village of Sulman Puk and the ruins of Ctesiphon.

On the right flank of the second Turkish position was a bridge of boats across the Tigris, and it was towards this bridge that our right centre and right columns were directed. The cavalry was sent round to the left of the Turkish reserve trenches in order to hinder any retirement. The scheme was an admirable one, but our numbers were barely adequate. All told we had, perhaps, 12,000 men. The Turks had the remains of the three divisions which had fought at Kut, little less than 20,000 men, and they had reinforcements at hand.

The British troops marched seven miles in the bright moonlight, till they saw before them the ruins of Ctesiphon casting blue shadows on the yellow plain. Before dawn the centre column had dug itself in in front of the main enemy line, Delamain's right centre had done the same on the flank, and the right column had covered ten miles and taken ground well to the left rear of the enemy. The cavalry had wheeled to the north-east, and hung on the flank of the Turkish re-

The British at Ctesiphon

serve trenches.

Dawn broke, and the enemy were aware of our advent. We could see bodies of Turks moving northward, and our first idea was that they were relinquishing Ctesiphon and falling back on the Diala. The cavalry and the British right promptly attacked the flank of the retreat, which formed in line to meet us, and revealed itself as a force several times our strength. The Turks were now drawn up along two sides of a square, of which the northern side was their reserve trenches, the western the Tigris, the southern their main position, and the eastern the force with which our right and our cavalry were engaged. At the point marked X in the map was a group of buildings, forming the junction of the eastern and southern sides.

About a quarter to nine the great attack began. Our centre moved against the main line, Delamain's right centre attacked at X, and the right and the cavalry assaulted the east side. The last, being greatly outnumbered, at first made no progress. Indeed, they lost ground, and Delamain was compelled to detach some of his battalions to support them. At eleven he carried X by artillery fire, and about half-past one the centre, with Delamain's assistance, succeeded in piercing the main Turkish front. These successes gave us the first position; but the Turks, assisted by their eastern flank, which defied our right and our cavalry, were able to retire in good order to their reserve lines. Our success so far had been brilliantly achieved, but there was to be no rout such as had followed the same tactics at Kut. Nur-ed-din had learned his lesson, and the real kernel of the position was the second line.

At half-past two in the afternoon we advanced against the second position. The eastern side of the former square was still intact, and our three columns drew together in an attempt to roll it up. But now we found out the true numbers of the enemy. Another division had joined him, and he counterattacked with such force that he recovered the guns he had lost, and before evening had driven us back to his old first trenches. Delamain, however, managed to hold the village of Sulman Puk in advance of these lines. Both sides were utterly wearied, and about 11.30 p.m. the battle died away.

Next day we saw fresh reinforcements arriving for the enemy, and all morning the two forces shelled each other. The Turkish attack came at three o'clock in the afternoon, and lasted till long after dark. It was now that they suffered their severest losses. Our men, being well-entrenched, beat them back time and again, but all night long there were intermittent assaults. Next day, the 24th, they fell back to their second line, and that day was filled with bombardments and counter-bombardments. Our force was badly disorganised, so we spent the day in consolidating our ground, and next day we received by river some much needed supplies. Our aeroplanes reported that reinforcements were still reaching the enemy. Obviously, we could now do nothing more.

Our casualties were about a third of our force—some 4,500, with 800 killed, and the losses among officers and staff had been specially heavy. We had handled the enemy severely, for the prisoners in our hands were over 1,300, and the killed and wounded we reckoned at some 10,000. But his strength was being replenished, and ours was waning. There was nothing for it but to fall back. We had won his first position and encamped on the battlefield, but we were very far from having broken his army. At midnight on the 25th we marched back to Lajj. Our wounded went by river, and reached Kut on the 27th. All the 26th we halted at Lajj to rest our men, and that evening we retreated twenty-three miles over a villainous road to Azizie. Four days later, on the 30th, we left Azizie and began to get news of the enemy.

Tidings travel fast in the East, and the word of our retirement encouraged the riverine Arabs to make an attempt on our communications between Kut and Amara, an attempt frustrated by a watchful gunboat. Early in the evening of 1st December General Townshend's little army reached camp ten miles below Azizie, where they were much sniped, and where next morning they saw the smoke of the Turkish fires all around them. The slowness of the enemy's pursuit is a proof of how severely he had suffered at Ctesiphon, for, had he been able to follow our trail at once, the whole British force must have perished.

We counterattacked and beat him off, losing only 150 men to the enemy's 2,500, but all that day we fought rearguard actions and marched twenty-seven miles before we dared to halt. We rested for three hours and then moved on for fifteen miles more. We were now only four miles from Kut, but we could not go a yard further. Both men and beasts were utterly leg-weary. Next morning, 3rd December, the remains of the Baghdad Expedition, which had set out with high hopes six weeks before, staggered into Kut. From north, east, and west the enemy closed in upon us, and the siege of Kut had begun. It had been a brilliant and memorable episode in the history of British arms, but, judged from the standpoint of scientific warfare, it had been no better than a glorious folly. Once again, as in the Nile Campaign, a beleaguered town far up an Eastern river became the centre of the anxious thought of our people.

British reserves were on the way. The two Indian divisions, which for a year had been on the Western Front, had reached Egypt *en route* for the Persian Gulf. By a wise decision Mesopotamia was selected as the terrain for the concentration of our Indian fighting strength. But Turkey was also awake, and her German masters saw in the check at Ctesiphon a chance for a blow which should drive the British from the Delta. The veteran Marshal von der Goltz had been for months in Constantinople, and had prepared the first Turkish armies for the field. He was now sent to take general charge of the Mesopotamia armies, a fitting honour for one who had been the chief military instructor of modern Turkey. On 24th November he was at Aleppo, and at a banquet given in his honour announced that in the appointment of so old a man to so great a command he recognised the hand of God.

> I hope that, with God's help, the sympathy of the Ottoman Empire and the friendliness of the whole people will enable me to achieve success, and that I shall be able to expel the enemy from Turkish soil.

Meanwhile things were going ill in northern Persia. The German Minister, Prince Heinrich XXXI. of Reuss, had won over to his side many of the Persian ministers, a number of the local tribes, and the 6,000 men of the *gendarmerie*, officered by Swedes, which had been established by Russia and Britain to police the country. The standstill of the Russians in the Caucasus and the British retirement from Ctesiphon brought these intrigues to a head. There were numerous local risings, and the British civilians at Yezd and Shiraz were made prisoners. In the capital, Teheran, things presently rose to the pitch of crisis. In the second week of November a detachment of the Russian Army of the Caucasus moved upon that city.

The German, Austrian, and Turkish *corps diplomatique* left on 14th November for the village of Shah Abdul Azim, on the Ispahan road, and frantic efforts were made to induce the *Shah* to accompany them, and so put himself into German hands. Prince Firman Firma and one or two of his advisers resisted the proposal, and after much wavering the boy-king resolved to remain. It was a difficult decision, for he had no troops to rely on against the *gendarmerie* and the Turkish irregulars except the Persian Cossack Brigade, which remained true to its salt.

Prince Reuss now showed his hand. He raised the standard of revolt, and with the 6,000 men of the *gendarmerie*, a number of tribesmen, and at least 3,000 Turkish irregulars from Mesopotamia—a total

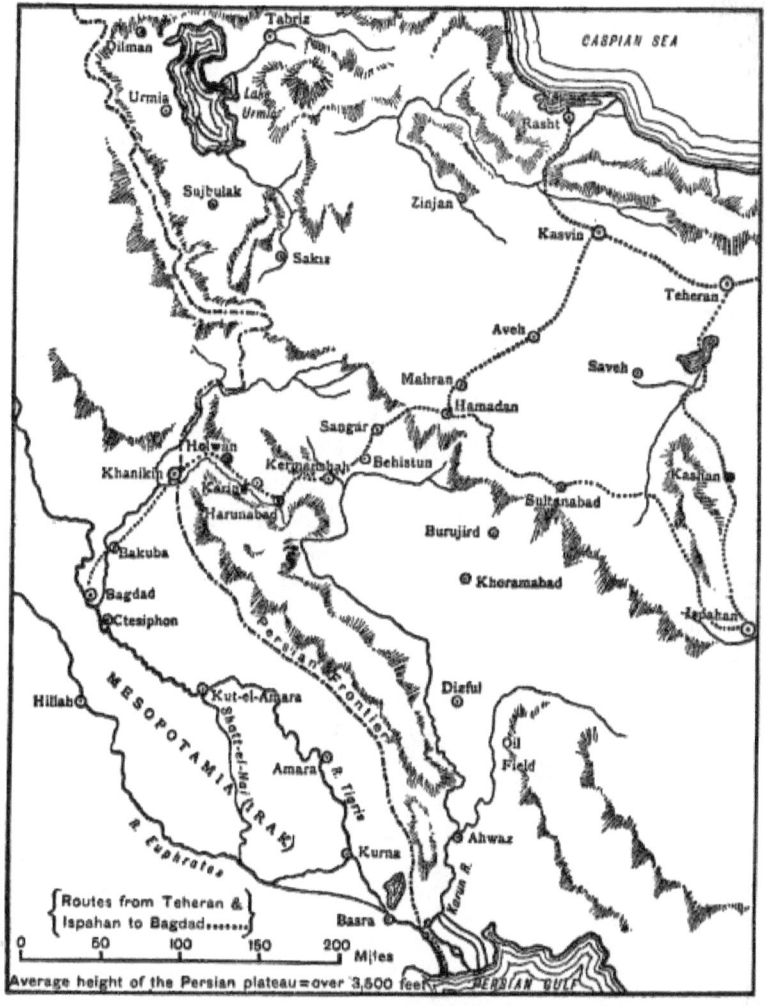

Map of the Scene of the Russian Operations in Persia, showing its relation to the Mesopotamian region.

strength of some 15,000— endeavoured to hold the key points, which would allow him to keep in touch with his friends on the Tigris. One was Kum, eighty miles south of Teheran, on the Ispahan road, which, being a telegraph junction, tapped all the communications with southern Persia. The other was Hamadan, near the ancient Ecbatana, two hundred miles from Teheran, on the Baghdad road. Prince Reuss divided his forces between these two places, and also held the pass which led to Hamadan from the north. By the end of November, the Russians were in Teheran. One detachment marched south towards Kum, but the main force was at Kasvin, moving on Hamadan.

On 7th December the rebels were driven out of Aveh, and two days later were routed at the Sultan Bulak Pass and forced back upon Hamadan. On the 11th Hamadan submitted, and on 17th December the Russians were pursuing the enemy through the mountains towards Kermanshah. The rebel strength at Hamadan was estimated at 8,000 irregulars and 3,000 *gendarmes*, all plentifully supplied with rifles and machine-guns. Prince Reuss departed for Kermanshah to take counsel with the emissaries of von der Goltz.

On the 20th the Russian left took Saveh and Kum, and put an end to rebel activity in that notorious centre of intrigue. Five days later the Persian Government fell, and Prince Firman Firma, a staunch friend of the Allies, was appointed Premier. For a moment the air was clear. But all Persia was in a ferment; the rebels who had been driven towards Kermanshah were in touch with the Turkish Army of Mesopotamia, and could call upon reserves which might gravely embarrass the far-flung Russian detachments. Germany had succeeded in one of her purposes. She had kindled a fire in the inflammable Middle East, and she was whistling for a wind to fan it.

CHAPTER 13

The Situation in Egypt

The situation in Egypt, since that day a year before when a British Protectorate had been proclaimed and Sultan Hussein placed on the throne of the deposed Khedive, had been one of internal tranquillity. Great masses of British troops had been under training, a Turkish force had reached the banks of the Suez Canal, and later the place had been the base for the Gallipoli operations; but these military doings had small effect on the serenity of the land. Nationalism, in the old bad sense, was quiescent. Its leaders were either in detention camps or in exile, and the attempts on the life of the *Sultan* and one of his ministers were the only flickering of what Germany had hoped would be a consuming fire.

The secret of this tranquillity is not to be sought only in the firm hand of the British Military Governor, but rather in the very real economic prosperity of the country. Egypt was in the rare position of being untouched, so far as her pockets were concerned, by the world-war. The presence of great armies brought money into the country, and provided an inexhaustible market for local produce. Her crops were good; even her cotton crop, which at one moment gave cause for disquiet, belied her fears. The peasant farmer of the Nile valley might owe a shadowy allegiance to the *khalif*, but he was first and foremost a man who had to get his living. Lord Cromer had long before discovered that the centre of gravity was economic, and that political stability would be assured if among the general population there was a straightforward security and comfort.

By the end of the year the German threats of invasion were very generally discounted. The so-called "Army of Egypt" was watching the Bulgarian frontier; and its former commander, von Mackensen, was at grips with Ivanov on the Dniester. Had Turkey been in earnest, preparations for the great assault should have been begun in early December. But in spite of rumours of pipe lines and light railways being built westward from Beersheba, it was clear that no serious effort was being made to prepare the ramshackle Syrian railways for the transport of a great army. The invasion could only succeed if it were conducted on a colossal scale with the most elaborate preliminaries, and these neither Djemal at Damascus nor Enver at Constantinople had seriously envisaged. Part of the Syrian Army had gone to reinforce Baghdad; part, it was clear, might soon be called for in Transcaucasia. The Turkish aims were distracted; and Germany, having locked up eight Allied divisions at Salonika, showed some disposition to rest on these laurels. The *Drang nach Osten* had not had the popular success which its promoters expected.

But it behoved the Allies to be ready for all emergencies. Their position in the Eastern Mediterranean was roughly that of an army holding interior lines, and, with the command of the sea, their communications were simple. From a proper base they could reinforce Salonika and Gallipoli at will. That base must clearly be Egypt, which had the further advantage that it was the most convenient base for the Mesopotamia campaign. Accordingly, the defence of the Nile valley could be combined with the provision of a base for all the other activities in the Near East. Egypt, said one of the characters in Mr. Kipling's stories, was "an eligible central position for the next row." Britain was fortunate in controlling a territory which was at once a training-ground and a starting-point.

The only cloud which threatened immediately—and it was a very small one—came from the west. The Western Frontier of Egypt, seven hundred miles long, adjoined the Italian possessions in Tripoli, and Italy was an ally. But the writ of Italy ran feebly in the interior. After the Tripoli war the Italian *suzerainty*, formally acknowledged in the Treaty of Lausanne, was not made effective beyond the coast-line. Turkish regulars and Turkish guns remained behind to help the Arab and Berber tribes to resist the alien rule. When Italy declared war on Austria the Italian force of occupation fell back to the coast, and the inland tribesmen were left to their own devices. Stirred up by German and Turkish agents, these tribesmen prepared for action. They hoped to gather to their standard the Bedouins of the Libyan plateau, and to win the support of the great Senussi brotherhood.

The Senussi form one of those strange religious fraternities common in North Africa. Their founder had been a firm friend of Britain,

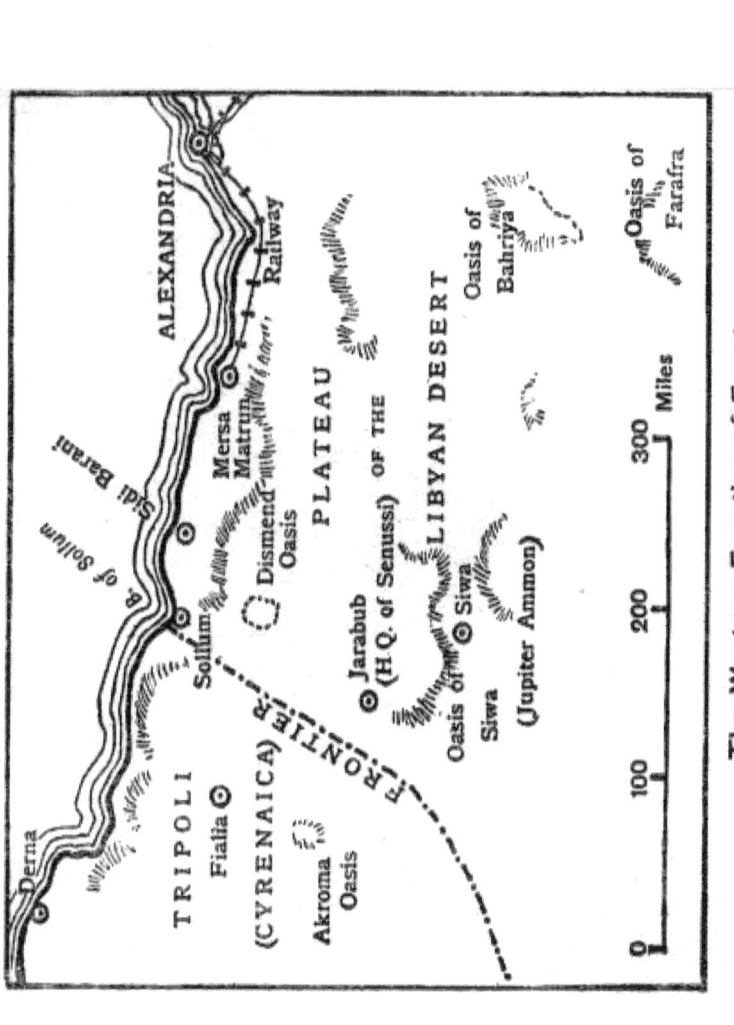

The Western Frontier of Egypt.

and had resisted all overtures from the Mahdi. He had preached a spiritual doctrine which Islam for the most part regarded as heterodox, and his followers were outside the main currents of the Moslem world. In especial they were untainted with Pan-Islamism, and had held themselves aloof from politics. Their headquarters were the oases of the North Libyan desert, and they had no fault to find with British rule in Egypt. Their Grand Sheikh, Ahmed Sherif, had given assurance of friendliness to the Anglo-Egyptian authorities, and his official representatives lived on the Nile banks in cordial relations with the government.

But a mass of tribesmen called themselves Senussi who were only loosely attached to the main organisation; and there was the danger that these, whatever the attitude of the *grand sheikh,* might join hands with the Tripolitan Berbers and the less reputable of the Bedouins in an assault from the west, which would disarrange our military plans.

It was only at the north end that the Tripoli frontier had to be guarded. South lay the endless impassable wastes of the Libyan desert. But along the coast ran the Libyan plateau, with many little oases linked up by caravan tracks. A railway runs from Alexandria as far as Mersa Matruh, a port on the coast, and beyond that were Egyptian forts at Sidi Barani and at Solium close to the Italian border. When trouble began to threaten, the posts at Solium and Sidi Barani were drawn in, and Matruh was held in some strength. With the railway behind it and the sea at its doors it was amply equipped to defend the marches.

The first hostilities began on 13th December, when 1,300 Arabs were driven back with heavy losses. Towards the end of the month a force of 3,000 gathered on the outskirts of Matruh. A British force, consisting of part of a new New Zealand Brigade then training in Egypt, the 15th Sikhs, and detachments of the Australian Light Horse and British Yeomanry, went out against this, the first invasion of Egypt from the west since the Fatimites in the tenth century. The enemy was located in a *donga* some eight miles from Matruh, and was completely routed by the British infantry with a loss of over 500 killed and prisoners. Our own casualties were inconsiderable. The mounted troops swept up most of the transport and supplies of the raiders.

The invasion was handicapped from the start. It had no sea bases by which to receive reinforcements from Turkey, and it was confined by the nature of the land to certain well-marked routes. There was another attempt on 13th January, and the tribesmen after their fashion still hung around our camp. On 23rd January our forces, under General Wallace, now increased by part of General Lukin's South African Brigade, marched out in two columns, fell on the tents of the enemy, now 4,500 strong, and drove them westward in utter rout, with losses of over 600. After this the attack languished. The eastern and western tribesmen took to quarrelling, refugees came in in starving mobs, and the tribes on the Egyptian side, notably the Walad Ali, petitioned the British Government and the *grand sheikh* of the Senussi for protection against their former allies.

The affair soon degenerated into little more than frontier brigandage. If Germany hoped to make of the Arabs and Bedouins of the Tripoli hinterland a fanatical horde which should sweep to the gates of Cairo, she had wholly misjudged their temper. To build up armies from such material was like an attempt to make ropes of desert sand.

Meanwhile, as this skirmishing proceeded, the troops in Egypt received a sudden accession. By one of the miracles of the war the forces in Gallipoli had been safely withdrawn from the peninsula, and with scarcely a casualty the wildest adventure of the campaign had come to a fortunate close.

SENUSSI PRISONERS

CHAPTER 14

The Evacuation of Gallipoli

While the Serbian Army were in retreat to the Adriatic and the Allies at Salonika were slowly falling back to the coast zone, the campaign at Gallipoli languished. Neither side had any inducement to a great attack. The Allies had shot their bolt and failed; the Turks were still awaiting the new munitionment which Germany's success in the Balkans had ensured to them. There were minor affairs on both sides which came to nothing, such as the attack on 15th November by the 156th Brigade of the 52nd (Scottish Lowland) Division—4th and 7th Royal Scots, 7th and 8th Scottish Rifles, and Ayrshire Yeomanry— which captured nearly 300 yards of front-line trench at the Krithia *nullah*. As November wore on it became apparent that the Turks were getting bigger guns and an ampler supply of shells.

New roads were being made, as we learned from prisoners, to facilitate the progress of the Krupp and Skoda monsters, and the six-inch batteries on the Asiatic shore became unpleasantly industrious in the bombardment of the Helles beaches. It must be remembered that the Turkish possession of the high ground forming the spine of the peninsula gave excellent observation posts, and in the circumstances, it was a miracle that their artillery did so little damage. But any increase in their batteries could not but be viewed by the Allied command with grave disquiet.

The weather of late autumn was mild and equable, but towards the end of November our men had a taste of an Aegean winter storm. On the 27th it rained without ceasing for twelve hours. The trenches became canals, the dug-outs cisterns, and every *nullah* held a raging torrent. Next day the wind shifted to the north, and there was a spell of bitter frost. This was followed by a snow blizzard, which recalled the worst days of the Crimea.

Frozen, buffeted by wind and sleet, with hardly a possibility of motion to keep the circulation alive, the men endured agonies. Sentries watching through the loopholes in the parapets were found dead at their posts when their turn came to be relieved, frozen solid, their stiff fingers still clutching the rifle in an ironfast grip, the blackened face still leaning under its sackcloth curtain against the loophole.

This weather bore especially hard on the Australian Corps, many of whom had never seen snow before, and who longed now for the dust and stifling heat of the August battles. The force of the storm was felt chiefly at Suvla, where there were over 200 deaths from exposure. Over 10,000 sick were evacuated in the succeeding week as a further consequence.

The gale lasted three days, and was followed by a spell of mild weather which gave us leisure to repair the damage. But the experience was ominous; the Dardanelles winter had scarcely begun, and the worst storms might be looked for in the first months of the new year. Our troops were dependent for every necessary of life and war on seaborne supplies, and it became a question how our ships could keep the water if the gales were frequent. Without the aid of the warships we had no real answer to the Turkish bombardment, and without the transports and cargo-boats we should certainly starve. The publication of the Gallipoli casualties up to 11th December enabled the world to judge of the cost of the enterprise. In seven months over 25,000 officers and men had perished, over 75,000 were wounded, and over 12,000 missing—casualties nearly twice the number of the force which landed on 25th April.

Sickness had been rife, and over 96,000 cases had been admitted to hospital. The chief causes were dysentery and paratyphoid, and the prevalent type of the former was one which demanded careful nursing and a long convalescence if it were not permanently to impair the constitution. An enterprise which had shown such unparalleled losses, and which, what with the probability of ill weather and the certainty of an increased enemy strength, boded so ill for the future, ought clearly to be relinquished, if relinquishment was possible.

The decision to evacuate Gallipoli was made in the course of November by the British Government in deference to the clearly expressed opinion of General Monro. It was not an easy decision. It meant in the view of all concerned a considerable loss, and even those who took the

Troops awaiting evacuation

optimistic side put that loss at not less than a division. Historical precedents were clear on the point. An embarkation in the face of the enemy had always meant a stiff rearguard fight and many casualties.

Corunna, (1809), was a typical case. There we succeeded well, but in most instances the cost had been far greater. Take, for example, an almost forgotten episode in the Seven Years' War. In 1758 a British expedition attacked St. Malo. The troops disembarked six miles west of the town and tried to cross the Rance to the south of the place. This movement was prevented by the numbers of the enemy, and we fell back on the bay of St. Cast, where we re-embarked after heavy losses. It was the accepted military doctrine that re-embarkation without disaster was only possible after a victorious battle with the enemy, and that even then a considerable price must be paid for getting away.

The difficulty was increased by the fact that the evacuation of Gallipoli must be lengthy and must be piecemeal. It was not a question of shipping a division or two, but three army corps. It was impossible to move them all at once with our existing transports. There must be a gap between the operations, and this meant that with regard to the later movements the enemy would be abundantly forewarned.

Moreover, a protracted embarkation put us terribly at the mercy of the winter weather. Even a mild wind from the south or south-west raised such a groundswell as to make communication with the beaches precarious. Those who looked for the loss of a third of our strength had good historical warrant for their pessimism. Few more anxious decisions have ever fallen to the lot of a British commander than that on which Sir Charles Monro was required to pronounce the final word.

The problem fell into three parts: Suvla, Anzac, and Cape Helles. From Suvla the 10th Division had already gone to Salonika, as well as one French division from Cape Helles, and the 2nd Mounted Division had left for Egypt. But in each zone, there remained a matter of three or more divisions to be moved. The whole thing was a gigantic gamble with fate, but every precaution was taken to lessen the odds. The plan, which was mainly the work of General Birdwood, was to remove the *matériel*, including the heavy guns, by instalments during a period of ten days, working only at night. A large portion of the troops would also be got off during these days, certain picked battalions being left to the last. New lines of trenches would be constructed to cover the embarkation points in case a rearguard action became necessary.

Everything must be kept normal during the daylight—the usual artillery shelling and spurts of rifle fire. Every morning before daybreak steps must be taken to hide the results of the night work. Any guns brought nearer the shore must be covered up so as to be unrecognizable by an enemy airplane. Success depended upon two things mainly—fine weather and secrecy. The first was the gift of the gods, and the second was attained by sheer bluff. It was a marvellous achievement, considering that every man in the British force had been talking for three weeks about the coming "rest camp."

Its success may have been due partly to the curious apathy which at the moment had seized the Turks and made them disinclined for the offensive. The new big howitzers were arriving and settling down on their concrete emplacements. Enver proposed to wait till these could be used to blow the British off the peninsula. Unfortunately for him these pledges of German friendship arrived too late for the fair.

Before the end of November, the battalions holding the firing lines were conscious of great nocturnal activity in their rear. Stores which had been accumulated at advanced bases were shifted nearer the coast, and at Suvla, especially on the two flanks, trenches and entanglements were being created which seemed irrelevant to any military purpose. On the 8th of December it was whispered that orders for the evacuation had arrived, and night after night our men watched the shrinking of their numbers. There was a generous rivalry as to who should stay to the last—a proof of spirit when we remember that every man believed that the rearguard was almost certainly doomed to death or capture. Presently only those in the prime of physical strength were left. All the weak and sickly had gone to the transports, which nightly stole in and out the moonlit bay.

Soon it became clear that the heavy batteries had also gone. To the ordinary observer in daylight they still appeared to be in position, but the guns in the emplacements were bogus. Then the field guns began to disappear, leaving only a sufficiency to keep up the daily pretence of bombardment. It was an eery business for the last battalions as they heard their protecting guns rumbling shorewards in the darkness. The hospitals were all evacuated, and their stores moved to the beach. New breakwaters had been built there, and all night long there was a continuous procession of lighters and motor boats.

Soon the horses and motorcars were also shipped, and by Friday, 17th December, very few guns were left. To the Turkish observers the piles of boxes on the beaches looked as if fresh supports had been landed, and we were preparing to hold the place indefinitely. These beaches were shelled all day, principally by the heavy howitzers be-

EVACUATING A FIELD GUN

hind the Anafarta ridge. But at night, fortunately for us, the shelling ceased.

The weather was warm and clement, with light moist winds and a low-hanging screen of clouds. No fisherman ever studied the weather signs more anxiously than did the British commanders during those days. Hearts sank when the wind looked like moving to the west. But the weather held, and, when the days consecrated to the final effort arrived, the wind was still favourable, the skies were clear, and the moon was approaching its full.

On Saturday, 18th December, only picked battalions held the front. The final embarkation had been fixed for the two succeeding nights, and it was believed that if the first night was successful the whole enterprise would go through. Evening fell in a perfect calm. The sea was as still as a quarry-hole, and scarcely a breath of wind blew in the sky. Moreover, a light blue mist clothed all the plain of Suvla, and made a screen against the enemy observers, while a haze also shrouded the moon. At 6 p.m. the crews of the warships went to action stations, and in the darkness the transports stole into the bay. Not a shot was fired. In dead quiet, showing no lights, the transports moved in and out. Every unit found its proper place. By 1 a.m. on the morning of Sunday, the 19th, all had gone, and the bay lay empty in the moonlight.

That Sunday was one of the most curious in the war. Our lines lay to all appearances as they had been for the past four months, but they were only a blind. We kept up our usual fire, and received the Turkish answer, but had any body of the enemy chosen to attack they would have found the trenches held by a handful. There were 20,000 Turks on the Suvla and Anzac fronts, and 60,000 in immediate reserve. Had they known it, they had before them the grand opportunity of the campaign. But our warships plastered their front and they "watered" our routes of transport as methodically as they had done since the August battles. Lala Baba came in for a heavy bombardment, but there was no longer a gun on the little hill.

An attack by our troops at Helles on that day distracted the enemy's mind from their immediate opponents. Night fell with the same halcyon weather. The transports—destroyers, trawlers, picket boats, every kind of craft—slipped once again into the bay, and before midnight the last guns had been got on board. At 1.30 a.m. on Monday morning the final embarkation of the troops began. Platoon by platoon they filed in perfect order down the communication trenches, a detachment occupying one of the new defensive positions till the other had passed. Strange receptions were provided for the first enemy who should enter the deserted trenches in the way of mines and traps and automatic bomb-throwers.

There were messages left, too, congratulating "Johnnie Turk" on being a clean and gallant fighter, and expressing hopes that we might meet him again under happier conditions. By 3.30 the last of the troops were on the beach, and long before the dawn broke all were aboard. One man had been hit by a bullet in the thigh; that was the only casualty. The Highland Mounted Brigade acted as the rearguard to fight the expected action which never came. Among the last to embark were 200 men who had been the foremost to land in August. They left from the very spot where they had first set foot ashore.

The operations at Anzac were conducted on the same lines. The beaches at Suvla were five miles or so from the enemy, and open to his observation. At Anzac they were less than two miles in places, but concealed from view under the steep seaward bluffs. But the intricate Anzac lines, and the exceeding precariousness of many of the positions, made the movement of guns and troops far more difficult. Some of our gun positions there were on dizzy heights, down which a gun could only be brought part by part. This work was brilliantly performed. Half the guns and half the men of the New Zealand batteries disappeared in a single night. As at Suvla, only picked battalions were left to the end, and there was desperate rivalry as to who should be chosen to act as rearguard. On the Saturday night three-fifths of the entire force was got on board the transports. On Sunday night the rest left, with two men wounded as the total casualties. By 5.30 a.m. on Monday morning the last transports moved from the coast, leaving the warships to follow.

Then on the twelve miles of beach from Suvla Burnu to Gaba Tepe began one of the strangest spectacles of the campaign. All the guns but four 18-pounders, two old 5-inch howitzers, one 4.7 naval gun, one anti-aircraft and two 3-pounder Hotchkiss guns had been removed, and these were rendered useless, (these were at Anzac; every gun, vehicle, and animal was got away from Suvla); ammunition and the more valuable stores had been cleared, but there was a quantity of supplies, chiefly bully-beef, which was not worth the risk of human life. These were piled in great heaps on the shores and drenched with petrol. Before the last men left parties of Royal Engineers set them on fire. About 4 a.m. on the Monday morning the bonfires began, blazing most fiercely near Suvla Point.

The Australians at Anzac about 3.30 had exploded a big mine on Russell's Top, and this called forth from the Turks an hour's rifle fire. As the beach fires blazed up the enemy, thinking that some disaster had befallen us, shelled the place to prevent our extinguishing the flames. The warships shelled back, and all along that broken coast great pharoses flamed to heaven. At 4.30 a.m. a motor lighter at Suvla, which had been wrecked some weeks before, was blown up, and added to the glare. Watchers on the Bulgarian coast, looking seaward, saw the peninsula wrapped in flames, as if its stony hills had become volcanoes vomiting fire.

It was not till dawn that the Turkish guns ceased. Even then they did not know what had happened. They shelled the bonfires still blazing in the bright sunrise; they searched the solitudes of Lala Baba and Chocolate Hill with high explosives, and the British warships fired a final volley. Picket boats at Anzac and Suvla up to eight o'clock were still collecting a few stragglers from the beaches. By 9 a. m. it was all over, and the last warship steamed away from a coast which had been the grave of so many high hopes and gallant men.

We were just in time. That night the weather broke, and a furious gale blew from the south, which would have made all embarkation impossible. Rain fell in sheets and quenched the fires, and soon every trench at Suvla and Anzac was a torrent. Great seas washed away the landing-stages. The puzzled enemy sat still and waited. They saw that we had gone, but they distrusted the evidence of their eyes. History does not tell what fate befell the first Turks who penetrated our empty trenches, what heel first tried conclusions with the hidden mines, or with what feelings they viewed the parting Australian message left on Walker's Ridge—a gramophone with the disc set to "The Turkish Patrol."

The success, the amazing success, of the Suvla and Anzac evacuation made the position at Cape Helles the more difficult. Few observers in the West believed that there was any chance of a similar operation there. At the most they looked to see a new Torres Vedras fortified at the butt-end of the peninsula, where, with the help of the ships, the enemy might be held off till the situation cleared. It was true that Helles was ill placed for such a policy. It was too well commanded by the heights on the European and Asian shores, and it was doubtful how the Torres Vedras plan would work in the face of the big Austro-German howitzers, of which the departing Australians at Anzac had seen the first shots. But there seemed no other way. The first bluff had worked to admiration; but it is of the nature of bluff that it can scarcely be repeated against the same opponent. Moreover, the Turkish aerial reconnaissance had now become active over all our positions.

Sunday, 19th December, the second last day of the Suvla and Anzac embarkation, saw a covering attack of the troops at Helles. At two in the afternoon the ships opened a bombardment of the enemy's front, which was soon taken up by all the land batteries, including those of the French, which had remained after most of their infantry had been withdrawn. Under this cover a brigade attacked up the Krithia *nullah*, and with some 250 casualties won 200 yards of trench, and left the Turks with an awkward salient to defend. After that came the storm, and then another spell of fine weather.

The Turks did not press their advantage, though they now outnumbered the British by more than three to one. They did not occupy the old Anzac lines, and men from Cape Helles made excursions there, and brought back among other things some welcome cases of champagne. Perhaps the enemy was still busy getting his new big guns in place. Perhaps he thought that he had us at his mercy, and could finish the business at his leisure. What is certain is that he never dreamed that the Suvla and Anzac enterprise could be repeated.

Towards the close of the year, in the first quarter of the new moon, guns and supplies and supernumerary troops were brought down to the beaches and quickly embarked.

******

In these days one of the most gallant of the actions which have earned the Victoria Cross was performed at Krithia by Second-Lieutenant A.V. Smith of the 1/5 East Lancashire Regiment on 22nd December. To quote the official account, "he was in the act of throwing a grenade when it slipped from his hand and fell to the bottom of the trench, close to several of our officers and men. He immediately shouted out a warning, and himself jumped clear and into safety; but, seeing that the officers and men were unable to get into cover, and knowing well that the grenade was due to explode, he returned without any hesitation and flung himself down on it. He was instantly killed by the explosion."

******

The French used S beach and the British used the famous landing-places of April. The French troops under General Brulard were now reduced to 4,000 men, and all except the gunners were embarked on the first night of January. On the last three days of the year the 52nd

Division made a demonstration, and during the first days of 1916 there was a good deal of artillery fire along our depleted front.

As at Suvla and Anzac, two nights had been allotted to the final evacuation, those of 7th and 8th January. New positions covering the landing-places were prepared, and an embarkation zone was created under the general commanding the 52nd Division, Major-General the Hon. H. A. Lawrence. There was no time to be lost, for all must be finished before the moon reached the full and while the fine weather held. It would appear that one interesting device, which had already been adopted at Anzac, was used to mislead the Turk, who was, of course, on the lookout for an attempt at withdrawal.

Our trenches would be perfectly silent for a day or two, but when the enemy made a reconnaissance they woke to aggressive life. The intention was to implant firmly in the Turkish mind the notion that quiet on our side did not mean that we had gone, in order that the real silence after the withdrawal might for a time pass undetected.

On Friday, 7th January, it looked for a moment as if a general action would have to be fought by way of farewell, a necessity which would have wrecked our carefully laid plans. From 1.30 to 3 o'clock in the afternoon all the front-line trenches held by the 13th and Royal Naval Divisions were continuously shelled, and the Turks opened a heavy musketry fire. At four they sprang two mines, and their parapets were manned with bayonets. But the infantry attack miscarried. We could see the officers trying to urge their men forward, but only at one point did a charge come; and then a battalion of the Staffords beat back the enemy. Our losses were six officers and 158 men—casualties which had nothing to do with the evacuation proper. That night the Scottish Lowland Division embarked, and rather more than half of the troops had left the peninsula.

Next day, Saturday the 8th, was calm and fine, the enemy were quiet, and all seemed in train for the final effort. But about four in the afternoon the weather changed. A strong south-westerly wind blew, which by 11 p.m. had increased to thirty-five miles an hour. This storm covered our retirement so far as the enemy were concerned, but it all but made it impossible. Hitherto, for example, our troops had been embarked in destroyers alongside the sunken ships at W beach, but the seas washed away the connecting piers, and lighters had to be used. At one beach, which felt the full force of the wind, shipment was impracticable, and the troops directed there had to march on to W beach. In one sense the weather was a blessing in disguise. An en-

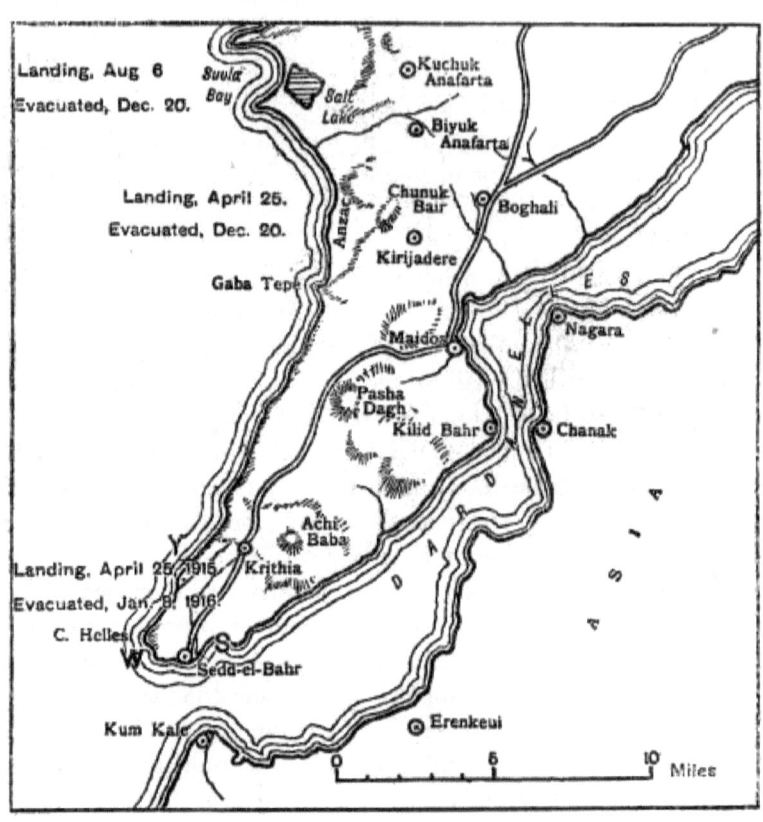

Evacuation of the Gallipoli Peninsula.

emy submarine had been reported off Cape Helles at 9 p.m., but the seas made its efforts futile. (H.M.S. *Prince George, en route* for Mudros, was struck about midnight by a torpedo which failed to explode.) By 2.30 a.m. on the morning of 9th January Y and W beaches had been cleared, and by 3.30 p.m. the last troops of the 29th Division were on board. An officer has described the final moments:—

> In the actual end, we said goodbye to our dug-outs after a last and very good dinner, and leaving the candles still alight in the banqueting-hall just for luck, we up-anchored and moved down to the water's edge, looking for all the world as if we were going to catch the 10.15 at Waterloo. I had on my best railway platform waddle, carrying, as I did, my helmet-case in a bucket, a loose blanket in one hand and my other blankets and waterproof sheet in the other. Strung all round me were the various impedimenta which a soldier has to carry about with him when he cannot avoid doing so. It was the funniest sight. And in the end, we just calmly stepped on the lighter and left Turkey-in-Europe, I suppose for ever. Practically nothing was left behind. No, I forgot. On our mess dug-out table we left the German book *J'accuse* for the edification of our successors there!

The Turks all night gave no sign. But when the transports had moved off, the stores, left behind were fired simultaneously by time fuses. Instantly red lights burned along the enemy lines, and heavy shelling began on the beaches and our empty support trenches. Till sunrise the red lights burned and the bombardment continued. When the enemy learned the truth, he made the best of the business, and proudly announced to the world that he had driven us from Seddel-Bahr, and that no Ally was left in the peninsula. He added that the retreat had been attended with desperate losses, and that he had made great captures of guns. The claim was untrue. We blew up and left behind the ruins of seventeen old worn-out pieces. Our total casualties amounted to one man wounded.

The evacuation of Gallipoli was a triumph of staff work, and of co-operation between the army and the fleet. To Sir Charles Monro, to Generals Davies, Birdwood, and Byng, to Admirals de Robeck and Wemyss, and not less to the divisional, brigade, and battalion commanders, the highest praise is due for an achievement which, in the words of the prime minister, was "without parallel in military or naval history." Nor must we forget the splendid discipline and stamina of their men. General Monro's special order, issued after the Suvla and Anzac evacuations, stated without exaggeration the difficulties surmounted:—

> The arrangements made for withdrawal, and for keeping the enemy in ignorance of the operation which was taking place, could not have been improved. The General Officer Commanding the Dardanelles Army, and the General Officers Commanding the Australian and New Zealand and 9th Army Corps, may pride themselves on an achievement without parallel in the annals of war. The Army and Corps Staffs, Divisional and subordinate Commanders and their Staffs, and the Naval and Military Beach Staffs proved themselves more than equal to the most difficult task which could have been thrown upon them. Regimental officers, non-commissioned officers, and men carried out, without a hitch, the most trying operation which soldiers can be called upon to undertake—a withdrawal in the face of the enemy—in a manner reflecting the highest credit on the discipline and soldierly qualities of the troops.
>
> It is no exaggeration to call this achievement one without parallel. To disengage and to withdraw from a bold and active enemy is the most difficult of all military operations; and in this case the withdrawal was effected by surprise, with the opposing forces at close grips— in many cases within a few yards of each other. Such an operation, when succeeded by a re-embarkation from an open beach, is one for which military history contains no precedent.
>
> During the past months the troops of Great Britain and Ireland, Australia and New Zealand, Newfoundland and India, fighting side by side, have invariably proved their superiority over the enemy, have contained the best fighting troops in the Ottoman Army in their front, and have prevented the Germans from employing their Turkish allies against us elsewhere.
>
> No soldier relishes undertaking a withdrawal from before the enemy. It is hard to leave behind the graves of good comrades, and to relinquish positions so hardly won and so gallantly maintained as those we have left. But all ranks in the Dardanelles Army will realise that in this matter they were but carrying out the orders of His Majesty's Government, so that they might in due course be more usefully employed in fighting elsewhere for their king, their country, and the Empire.

There is only one consideration—what is best for the furtherance of the common cause. In that spirit the withdrawal was carried out, and in that spirit the Australian and New Zealand and the 9th Army Corps have proved, and will continue to prove, themselves second to none as soldiers of the Empire.

The news was received in France and Britain with incredulity, which speedily changed to profound relief. To be sure, there was something shamefaced in our pride. We were celebrating a failure and a retreat. The gallantry of the wonderful April landings, the long struggle for Krithia, the heroic Australasian attack on Sari Bair had gone for nothing. We had spilled blood like water to win a mile or two of land, and now we had relinquished all. Fifty thousand Allied graves with their rude crosses passed under the sway of the Crescent. But these melancholy reflections properly belonged to the subject of the original Gallipoli adventure. Having failed, we had succeeded in escaping the worst costs of failure. We had brought off three Army Corps to be refitted and reorganised for use in more hopeful theatres. We had defeated the calculations of the enemy. We had stultified our pessimists and amazed even the most optimistic.

To frustrate the consequences of a disaster is, as a military operation, usually more difficult than to win a victory. There is less chance of the spirit of the offensive, for it is proof of the generosity of the human spirit that safety is less of an incentive to effort than the hope of victory. A retreat, on the confession of the greatest soldiers, is the most difficult task which a general can be called on to undertake. The evacuation of Gallipoli, in point of pure technical skill and soldierly resolution, deserves to rank in the story of the campaigns with the retirement of the Allies from Mons and the withdrawal of Russia from the Vistula to the Dvina.

We had upset every precedent in history. The impossible had been achieved by a series of incalculable chances. But for the two spells of fine weather and the unexplained preoccupation of the enemy the odds would have been crushingly against us. It is true that without a perfect organisation and discipline we should not have been able to take advantage of our good fortune, but no human merit would have availed had the fates been unkind. It was an instructive lesson in the folly of dogmatism. In the spring of 1915, our ships had attempted to beat down the forts of the Dardanelles without the assistance of a land army. That effort failed, and it was condemned as contrary to all the lessons of history.

The criticism was just; but those who claimed that precedents were not the whole of war were also justified. For in the evacuation of Gallipoli we saw an enterprise as flagrantly heterodox succeed. The "sporting chance" is not as a rule a desirable obsession for any commander. It is his business to use the accumulated experience of his predecessors, and to follow soberly the path of common prudence. But if some great end is to be won or some great misfortune avoided, there may come a day when it is his duty to defy precedents. For it should never be forgotten that the lost hope, the desperate remedy, and the outside chance may win. Across the ribbon of the Dardanelles, on the green plain of Troy, the most famous of the wars of the old world had been fought.

Appendix to Chapter 14

THE EVACUATION OF GALLIPOLI
Sir Charles Monro's Dispatch.
Headquarters, First Army, France,
March 6, 1916.

My Lord,—

I have the honour to submit herewith a brief account of the operations in the Eastern Mediterranean from the 28th October 1915, on which date I assumed command of the Mediterranean Expeditionary Force, until the 9th January 1916, when, in compliance with your directions, I handed over charge at Cairo to Lieut.-General Sir Archibald Murray, K.C.B., C.V.O., D.S.O.

On the 20th October, in London, I received Your Lordship's instructions to proceed as soon as possible to the Near East and take over the command of the Mediterranean Expeditionary Force.

My duty on arrival was in broad outline:—

(*a*) To report on the military situation on the Gallipoli Peninsula.

(*b*) To express an opinion whether on purely military grounds the peninsula should be evacuated, or another attempt made to carry it.

(*c*) The number of troops that would be required,

(1) to carry the peninsula,
(2) to keep the Straits open, and
(3) to take Constantinople.

Two days after my arrival at Imbros, where the headquarters of the M.E.F. was established, I proceeded to the peninsula to investigate the military situation. The impressions I gathered are summarised very shortly as follows:—

The positions occupied by our troops presented a military situation unique in history. The mere fringe of the coast line had been secured. The beaches and piers upon which they depended for all requirements in personnel and material were exposed to registered and observed artillery fire. Our entrenchments were dominated almost throughout by the Turks. The possible artillery positions were insufficient and defective. The Force, in short, held a line possessing every possible military defect. The position was without depth, the communications were insecure and dependent on the weather. No means existed for the concealment and deployment of fresh troops destined for the offensive—whilst the Turks enjoyed full powers of observation, abundant artillery positions, and they had been given the time to supplement the natural advantages which the position presented by all the devices at the disposal of the field engineer.

Another material factor came prominently before me. The troops on the peninsula had suffered much from various causes.

> (a) It was not in the first place possible to withdraw them from the shell-swept area as is done when necessary in France, for every corner on the peninsula is exposed to hostile fire.
>
> (b) They were much enervated from the diseases which are endemic in that part of Europe in the summer.
>
> (c) In consequence of the losses which they had suffered in earlier battles there was a very grave dearth of officers competent to take command of men.
>
> (d) In order to maintain the numbers needed to hold the front, the Territorial Divisions had been augmented by the attachment of Yeomanry and Mounted Brigades. Makeshifts of this nature very obviously did not tend to create efficiency. Other arguments, irrefutable in their conclusions, convinced me that a complete evacuation was the only wise course to pursue.
>
> (a) It was obvious that the Turks could hold us in front with a small force and prosecute their designs on Baghdad or Egypt, or both.
>
> (b) An advance from the positions we held could not be regarded as a reasonable military operation to expect.
>
> (c) Even had we been able to make an advance in the peninsula, our position would not have been ameliorated to any marked degree, and an advance on Constantinople was quite out of the question.

(*d*) Since we could not hope to achieve any purpose by remaining on the peninsula, the appalling cost to the nation involved in consequence of embarking on an Overseas Expedition with no base available for the rapid transit of stores, supplies, and personnel made it urgent that we should divert the troops locked up on the peninsula to a more useful theatre. Since, therefore, I could see no military advantage in our continued occupation of positions on the peninsula, I telegraphed to Your Lordship that in my opinion the evacuation of the peninsula should be taken in hand.

Subsequently I proceeded to Egypt to confer with Colonel Sir H. McMahon, the High Commissioner, and Lieut.-General Sir J. Maxwell, Commanding the Forces in Egypt, over the situation which might be created in Egypt and the Arab world by the evacuation of the peninsula.

Whilst in Egypt I was ordered by a telegram from the War Office to take command of the troops at Salonika. The purport of this telegram was subsequently cancelled by Your Lordship on your arrival at Mudros, and I was then ordered to assume Command of the Forces in the Mediterranean, east of Malta, and exclusive of Egypt.

Consequent on these instructions, I received approval that the two Forces in the Mediterranean should be designated as follows:—

(*a*) The original Mediterranean Expeditionary Force, which comprised the Forces operating on the Gallipoli Peninsula and those employed at Mudros and Imbros as the "Dardanelles Army," under Lieut.-General Sir W. Birdwood, K.C.B., etc., with headquarters at Imbros.

(*b*) The troops destined for Salonika as the "Salonika Army," under Lieut.-General Sir B. Mahon, K.C.B., with headquarters at Salonika.

The staff of the original M.E.F. was left in part to form the Dardanelles Army, and the remainder were taken to make a General Headquarter Staff for the increased responsibilities now assumed. Other officers doing duty in this theatre with the necessary qualifications were selected, and, with no difficulty or demands on home resources, a thoroughly efficient and adequate staff was created.

Mudros was selected as being the most suitable site for the establishment of headquarters, as affording an opportunity, in addition to other advantages, of daily consultation with the Inspector General,

Line of Communications. The working of the services of the Line of Communications presented difficulties of a unique character, mainly owing to

> (a) the absence of pier and wharfage accommodation at Mudros and the necessity of transferring all Ordnance and Engineer Stores from one ship to another;
> (b) the submarine danger;
> (c) the delay caused by rough weather. Close association with General Altham was therefore most imperative, and by this means many important changes were made which conduced to greater efficiency and more prompt response to the demands of fighting units.

A narrative of the events which occurred in each of the two Armies is now recorded separately for facility of perusal and reference.

SALONIKA.

Early in October the 10th Division, under Lieut.-General Sir B. Mahon, K.C.B., was transferred from Suvla to Salonika, and fully concentrated there. The dislocation of units caused by the landing on the peninsula and the subsequent heavy fighting which occurred prevented this division being dispatched intact. The organisation of the infantry and the Royal Engineers was not disturbed, but the other services had to be improvised from other divisions as found most accessible.

The arrival of the 10th Division had been preceded by two French Divisions under General Sarrail, whose Force was subsequently augmented by another division. These three divisions were then moved into Serbia under the understanding arranged between the Allies' Governments, which was to the effect that the French Forces were to protect the railway between Krivolak and Veles, and to ensure communication with the Serbian Army, whilst the British were to maintain the position from Salonika to Krivolak, and to support the French Right. If communication with the Serbian Army could not be opened and maintained, the Allied Forces were to be withdrawn.

With this object, two battalions of the 10th Division were moved from Salonika on 27th October, and took over the French front from Kosturino to Lake Doiran. The remainder of the division was sent to Serbia on 12th November and following days, and took over the French front eastwards from Kosturino.

The task of moving troops into Serbia and maintaining them there presented many difficulties. No road exists from Salonika to Doiran, a few miles of road then obtains, which is followed within a few miles by a track only suitable for pack transport. Sir B. Mahon had therefore to readjust his transport to a pack scale, and was dependent on a railway of uncertain carrying power to convey back his guns and all wheeled traffic in case of a withdrawal, and to supply his troops whilst in Serbia.

Very soon afterwards reinforcements commenced to arrive. The disembarkation of these new divisions was an operation which taxed the powers of organisation and resources of the staff at Salonika to the highest degree possible, and it speaks highly for their capacity that they were able to shelter and feed the troops as they arrived.

During November and the early part of December the 10th Division was holding its position in Serbia, and the disembarkation of other divisions was proceeding with difficulty.

In order to gain time for the landing of the troops, and their deployment on the positions selected, I represented to General Sarrail and Sir B. Mahon the urgent need of the divisions withdrawing from Serbia being utilised as a covering force, and retaining their ground as such until the Forces disembarking were thoroughly in a position to hold their front.

DIFFICULTIES OF OPERATIONS.

It had been evident for some time that the power of resistance of the Serbian Armies was broken, and that the Allied Forces could afford them no material assistance. It was also clear from all information received that the position of our troops was becoming daily more precarious owing to a large German-Bulgarian concentration in the Strumnitza Valley. I, therefore, again pressed General Sarrail to proceed with his withdrawal from the positions he was holding. The British Division, operating, as it was, as the pivot upon which the withdrawal was effected, was compelled to hold its ground until the French Left was brought back.

Before our withdrawal was completed the 10th Division was heavily attacked on the 6th, 7th, and 8th December by superior Bulgarian Forces. The troops had suffered considerably from the cold in the Highlands of Macedonia, and in the circumstances conducted themselves very creditably in being able to extricate themselves from a difficult position with no great losses. The account of this action was reported by wire to you by General Mahon on the 11th December: no further reference is therefore necessary to this incident.

As soon as I was informed that the 10th Division was being heavily pressed, I directed Sir B. Mahon to send a brigade up the railway line in support, and to hold another brigade ready to proceed at short notice. The withdrawal was, however, conducted into Greek territory without further opposition from the Bulgarians.

Meanwhile, the operation of disembarkation at Salonika was being carried out with all possible speed, and the Greek Authorities through their representative from Athens, Colonel Pallis, were informed by me that we intended to proceed to the defensive line selected. This intimation was received in good part by the Greek generals. They commenced to withdraw their troops further to the East where they did not hamper our plans, and they showed a disposition to meet our demands in a reasonable and friendly spirit.

Whilst dealing with the events above enumerated, I desire to give special prominence to the difficulties to which General Sir B. Mahon was exposed from the time of his landing at Salonika, and the ability which he displayed in overcoming them. The subjoined instances, selected from many which could be given, will illustrate my contention, and the high standard of administrative capacity displayed by the G.O.C. and his Staff:—

> (a) From the date on which the 10th Division first proceeded into Serbia until the date of its withdrawal across the Greek frontier, personnel, guns, supplies, and material of all kinds had to be sent up by rail to Doiran, and onwards by march, motor lorries, limbered wagons, and pack animals. This railway, moreover, was merely a single track, and had to serve the demands of the local population as well as our needs. The evacuation of the wounded and sick had to be arranged on similar lines, yet the requirements of the troops were fully satisfied.
>
> (b) The majority of the divisions were sent without trains to Salonika, most units without first line transport; in spite of this, part of the Force was converted into a mobile condition with very little delay.
>
> (c) The complications presented by the distribution and checking of stores, supplies, ammunition, etc., discharged from ships on to quays, with insufficient accommodation or storehouses, and with crude means of ingress and egress therefrom, and served by a single road which was divided between the French and ourselves, constituted a problem which could only be

solved by officers of high administrative powers. I trust, therefore, that full recognition may be given to my recommendation of the officers who rendered such fine service under such arduous conditions.

The Situation at Gallipoli.

On my arrival in the Mediterranean theatre a gratifying decline in the high rate of sickness which had prevailed in the Force during the summer months had become apparent. The wastage due to this cause still, however, remained very high.

The corps commanders were urged to take all advantage of the improved weather conditions to strengthen their positions by all available means, and to reduce to the last degree possible all animals not actually required for the maintenance of the troops, in order to relieve the strain imposed on the Naval Transport Service.

During the month of November, beyond the execution of very clever and successful minor enterprises carried out by corps commanders with a view to maintaining an offensive spirit in their commands, there remains little to record, except that an increased activity of the Turkish artillery against our front became a noticeable factor.

On the 21st November (27th?), the peninsula was visited by a storm said to be nearly unprecedented for the time of the year. The storm was accompanied by torrential rain, which lasted for 24 hours. This was followed by hard frost and a heavy blizzard. In the areas of the 8th Corps and the Anzac Corps the effects were not felt to a very marked degree owing to the protection offered by the surrounding hills. The 9th Corps was less favourably situated: the water courses in this area became converted into surging rivers, which carried all before them.

The water rose in many places to the height of the parapets, and all means of communications were prevented. The men, drenched as they were by the rain, suffered from the subsequent blizzard most severely. Large numbers collapsed from exposure and exhaustion, and in spite of untiring efforts that were made to mitigate the suffering, I regret to announce that there were 200 deaths from exposure and over 10,000 sick evacuated during the first few days of December.

From reports given by deserters, it is probable that the Turks suffered even to a greater degree.

In this period our flimsy piers, breakwaters, and light shipping became damaged by the storm to a degree which might have involved most serious consequences, and was a very potent indication of the dangers attached to the maintenance and supply of an army operating on a coast line with no harbour, and devoid of all the accessories such as wharves, piers, cranes, and derricks for the discharge and distribution of stores, etc.

SCHEME FOR EVACUATION.

Towards the latter end of the month, having in view the possibility of an evacuation of the peninsula being ordered, I directed Lieutenant-General Sir W. Birdwood, Commanding the Dardanelles Army, to prepare a scheme to this end, in order that all details should be ready in case of sanction being given to this operation.

I had in broad outline contemplated soon after my arrival on the peninsula that an evacuation could best be conducted by a subdivision into three stages.

The first, during which all troops, animals, and supplies not required for a long campaign should be withdrawn.

The second to comprise the evacuation of all men, guns, animals, and stores not required for defence during a period when the conditions of weather might retard the evacuation, or in fact seriously alter the programme contemplated.

The third or final stage, in which the troops on shore should be embarked with all possible speed, leaving behind such guns, animals, and stores needed for military reasons at this period.

This problem with which we were confronted was the withdrawal of an army of a considerable size from positions in no cases more than 300 yards from the enemy's trenches, and its embarkation on open beaches, every part of which were within effective range of Turkish guns, and from which, in winds from the south or south-west, the withdrawal of troops was not possible.

The attitude which we should adopt from a naval and military point of view in case of withdrawal from the peninsula being ordered, had given me much anxious thought. According to text-book principles and the lessons to be gathered from history, it seemed essential that this operation of evacuation should be immediately preceded by a combined naval and military feint in the vicinity of the peninsula, with a view to distracting the attention of the Turks from our intention.

When endeavouring to work out into concrete fact how such principles could be applied to the situation of our Forces, I came to the conclusion that our chances of success were infinitely more probable if we made no departure of any kind from the normal life which we were following both on sea and on land. A feint which did not fully fulfil its purpose would have been worse than useless, and there was the obvious danger that the suspicion of the Turks would be aroused by our adoption of a course the real purport of which could not have been long disguised.

Evacuation Ordered.

On the 8th December, consequent on Your Lordship's orders, I directed the General Officer Commanding Dardanelles Army to proceed with the evacuation of Suvla and Anzac at once.

Rapidity of action was imperative, having in view the unsettled weather which might be expected in the Aegean. The success of our operations was entirely dependent on weather conditions. Even a mild wind from the south or south-west was found to raise such a ground swell as to greatly impede communication with the beaches, while anything in the nature of a gale from this direction could not fail to break up the piers, wreck the small craft, and thus definitely prevent any steps being taken towards withdrawal.

We had, moreover, during the gale of the 21st November, learnt how entirely we were at the mercy of the elements with the slender and inadequate means at our disposal by which we had endeavoured to improvise harbours and piers. On that day the harbour at Kephalos was completely wrecked, one of the ships which had been sunk to form a breakwater was broken up, and the whole of the small craft sheltered inside the breakwater were washed ashore. Similar damage was done to our piers, lighters, and small craft at Suvla and Anzac.

The Withdrawal from Anzac and Suvla.

Lieutenant-General Birdwood proceeded on receipt of his orders with the skill and promptitude which is characteristic of all that he undertakes, and after consultation with Rear-Admiral Wemyss, it was decided, provided the weather was propitious, to complete the evacuation on the night of the 19th-20th December.

Throughout the period 10th to 18th December the withdrawal proceeded under the most auspicious conditions, and the morning of the 18th December found the positions both at Anzac and Suvla reduced to the numbers determined, while the evacuation of guns, animals, stores, and supplies had continued most satisfactorily.

The arrangements for the final withdrawal made by corps commanders were as follows:—

It was imperative, of course, that the front line trenches should be held, however lightly, until the very last moment, and that the withdrawal from these trenches should be simultaneous throughout the line. To ensure this being done, Lieutenant-General Sir W. Birdwood arranged that the withdrawal of the inner flanks of corps should be conducted to a common embarking area under the orders of the G.O.C., 9th Corps.

In the rear of the front line trenches at Suvla the General Officer Commanding 9th Corps broke up his area into two sections divided roughly by the Salt Lake. In the Southern Section a defensive line had been prepared from the Salt Lake to the sea and Lala Baba had been prepared for defence; on the left the second line ran from Kara Kol Dagh through Hill 10 to the Salt Lake. These lines were only to be held in case of emergency—the principle governing the withdrawal being that the troops should proceed direct from the trenches to the distributing centres near the beach, and that no intermediate positions should be occupied except in case of necessity.

At Anzac, owing to the proximity of the trenches to the beach, no second position was prepared except at Anzac Cove, where a small keep was arranged to cover the withdrawal of the rearmost parties in case of necessity.

The good fortune which had attended the evacuation continued during the night of the 19th-20th. The night was perfectly calm with a slight haze over the moon, an additional stroke of good luck, as there was a full moon on that night.

Soon after dark the covering ships were all in position, and the final withdrawal began. At 1.30 a.m. the withdrawal of the rear parties commenced from the front trenches at Suvla and the left of Anzac. Those on the right of Anzac who were nearer the beach remained in position until 2 a.m. By 5.30 a.m. the last man had quitted the trenches.

At Anzac four 18-pounder guns, two 5-in. howitzers, one 4.7 Naval gun, one anti-aircraft, and two 3-pounder Hotchkiss guns were left, but they were destroyed before the troops finally embarked. In addition, 56 mules, a certain number of carts, mostly stripped of their wheels, and some supplies which were set on fire, were also abandoned.

At Suvla every gun, vehicle, and animal was embarked, and all that remained was a small stock of supplies, which were burnt.

The Position at Cape Helles.

Early in December orders had been issued for the withdrawal of the French troops on Helles, other than their artillery, and a portion of the line held by French Creoles had already been taken over by the Royal Naval Division on the 12th December. On the 21st December, having strengthened the 8th Corps with the 86th Brigade, the number of the French garrison doing duty on the peninsula was reduced to 4,000 men. These it was hoped to relieve early in January, but before doing so it was necessary to give some respite from trench work to the 42nd Division, which was badly in need of a rest.

My intention, therefore, was first to relieve the 42nd Division by the 88th Brigade, then to bring up the 13th Division, which was resting at Imbros since the evacuation of Suvla, in place of the 29th Division, and finally to bring up the 11th Division in relief of the French. Helles would then be held by the 52nd, 11th, and 13th Divisions, with the Royal Naval Division and the 42nd Division in reserve on adjacent islands.

On the 24th December, General Sir W. Birdwood was directed to make all preliminary preparations for immediate evacuation in the event of orders to this effect being received.

On 28th December Your Lordship's telegram ordering the evacuation of Helles was received, whereupon, in view of the possibility of bad weather intervening, I instructed the General Officer Commanding Dardanelles Army to complete the operation as rapidly as possible. He was reminded that every effort conditional on not exposing the personnel to undue risk should be made to save all 60-pounder and 18-pounder guns, 6-inch and 4.5 howitzers, with their ammunition and other accessories, such as mules and A.T. carts, limbered wagons, etc.

In addition, I expressed my wish that the final evacuation should be completed in one night, and that the troops should withdraw direct from the front trenches to the beaches, and not occupy any intermediate position unless seriously molested. At a meeting which was attended by the vice-admiral and the general officer commanding Dardanelles Army, I explained the course which I thought we should adopt to again deceive the Turks as to our intentions.

The situation on the peninsula had not materially changed owing to our withdrawal from Suvla and Anzac, except that there was a marked increased activity in aerial reconnaissance over our positions and the islands of Mudros and Imbros, and that hostile patrolling of our trenches was more frequent and daring. The most apparent factor was that the number of heavy guns on the European and Asiatic shores had been considerably augmented, and that these guns were more liberally supplied with German ammunition, the result of which was that our beaches were continuously shelled, especially from the Asiatic shore.

I gave it as my opinion that in my judgment I did not regard a feint as an operation offering any prospect of success. Time, the uncertainty of weather conditions in the Aegean, the absence of a suitable locality, and the withdrawal of small craft from the main issue for such an operation were some of the reasons which influenced me in the decision at which I arrived. With the concurrence of the vice-admiral, therefore, it was decided the navy should do their utmost to pursue a course of retaliation against the Turkish Batteries, but to refrain from any unusually aggressive attitude should the Turkish guns remain quiescent.

General Sir W. Birdwood had, in anticipation of being ordered to evacuate Helles, made such complete and far-seeing arrangements that he was able to proceed without delay to the issue of the comprehensive orders which the consummation of such a delicate operation in war requires.

He primarily arranged with General Brulard, who commanded the French Forces on the peninsula, that in order to escape the disadvantages of divided command in the final stage, the French infantry should be relieved as early as possible, but that their artillery should pass under the orders of the General Officer Commanding 8th Corps, and be withdrawn concurrently with the British guns at the opportune moment.

On the 30th December, in consequence of the instructions I had received from the Chief of the General Staff to hand over my command at Alexandria to Lieutenant-General Sir A. Murray, who, it was stated, was to leave England on the 28th December, I broke up my Headquarters at Mudros and proceeded with a small staff, comprising representatives of the General Staff, the Quartermaster-General, and Adjutant-General branches, on H.M.S. *Cornwallis* to Alexandria. The rest of the staff were sent on in front so as to have offices in working order when my successor should arrive.

In the meantime, the evacuation, following the same system as was practised at Suvla and Anzac, proceeded without delay. The French infantry remaining on the peninsula were relieved on the night of the 1st-2nd January, and were embarked by the French Navy on the following nights. Progress, however, was slower than had been hoped, owing to delays caused by accident and the weather. One of our largest horse ships was sunk by a French battleship, whereby the withdrawal was considerably retarded, and at the same time strong winds sprang up which interfered materially with work on the beaches. The character of the weather now setting in offered so little hope of a calm period of any duration that General Sir W. Birdwood arranged with Admiral Sir J. de Robeck for the assistance of some destroyers in order to accelerate the progress of re-embarkation. They then determined to fix the final stage of the evacuation for the 8th January, or for the first fine night after that date.

Meanwhile the 8th Corps had maintained the offensive spirit in bombing and minor operations with which they had established the moral superiority they enjoyed over the enemy. On the 29th December the 52nd Division completed the excellent work which they had been carrying out for so long by capturing a considerable portion of the Turkish trenches, and by successfully holding these in the face of repeated counterattacks. The shelling of our trenches and beaches, however, increased in frequency and intensity, and the average daily casualties continued to increase.

The method of evacuation adopted by Lieutenant-General Sir F. J. Davies, K.C.B., Commanding 8th Corps, followed in general outline that which had proved successful in the Northern Zone. As the removal of the whole of the heavy guns capable of replying to the enemy's artillery would have indicated our intentions to the enemy, it was decided to retain, but eventually destroy, one 6-inch British gun and six French heavy guns of old pattern, which it would be impossible to remove on the last night. General Brulard himself suggested the destruction of these French guns.

The first step taken as regards the withdrawal of the troops was the formation of a strong Embarkation Staff and the preparation of positions covering the landings, in which small garrisons could maintain themselves against attack for a short time should the enemy become aware of our intention and follow up the movement.

Major-General the Hon. H. A. Lawrence, commanding the 52nd Division, was selected to take charge of all embarkation operations. At the same time the services of various staff officers were placed at the disposal of the general officer commanding, 8th Corps, and they rendered very valuable assistance.

The general officer commanding, 13th Division, selected and prepared a position covering Gully Beach. Other lines were selected and entrenched, covering the remainder of the beaches from the sea north of Sedd-el-Bahr to "X" Beach inclusive. Garrisons were detailed for these defences, those at Gully Beach being under the general officer commanding, 13th Division, and those covering the remainder of the beaches being placed under the command of a selected officer, whose headquarters were established at an early date, together with those of the general officer commanding, embarkation, at Corps Headquarters.

As the withdrawing troops passed within the line of these defences, they came under the orders of the general officer commanding, embarkation, which were conveyed to them by his staff officers at each beach.

In addition to these beach defences four lines of defence were arranged, three being already in existence and strongly wired. The fourth was a line of posts extending from De Tott's Battery on the east to the position covering Gully Beach on the west.

The time fixed for the last parties to leave the front trenches was 11.45 p.m., in order to permit the majority of the troops being already embarked before the front line was vacated. It was calculated that it would take between two and three hours for them to reach the beaches, at the conclusion of which time the craft to embark them would be ready.

The naval arrangements for embarkation were placed in the hands of Captain C. M. Staveley, R.N., assisted by a staff of naval officers at each place of embarkation.

On the 7th January, the enemy developed heavy artillery fire on the trenches held by the 13th Division, while the Asiatic guns shelled those occupied by the Royal Naval Division. The bombardment, which was reported to be the heaviest experienced since we landed in April, lasted from noon until 5 p.m., and was intensive between 3 p.m. and 3.30. Considerable damage was done to our parapets and communication trenches, and telephone communications were interrupted.

At 3.30 p.m. two Turkish mines were sprung near Fusilier Bluff, and the Turkish trenches were seen to be full of men whom their officers appeared to be urging to the assault. No attack, however, was developed except against Fusilier Bluff, where a half-hearted assault was quickly repulsed. Our shortage of artillery at this time was amply compensated for by the support received from fire of the supporting squadron under Captain D. L. Dent, R.N. Our casualties amounted to 2 officers and 56 other ranks killed, and 4 officers and 102 other ranks wounded.

The Last Days on Gallipoli.

The 8th January was a bright, calm day, with a light breeze from the south. There was every indication of the continuance of favourable conditions, and in the opinion of the meteorological officer, no important change was to be expected for at least 24 hours. The Turkish artillery were unusually inactive. All preparations for the execution of the final stage were complete.

The embarkation was fixed at such an hour that the troops detailed for the first trip might be able to leave their positions after dark. The second trip was timed so that at least a greater portion of the troops for this trip would, if all went well, be embarked before the final parties had left the front trenches. The numbers to be embarked at the first trip were fixed by the maximum that could be carried by the craft available, those of the second trip being reduced in order to provide for the possibility of casualties occurring amongst the craft required to carry them.

The numbers for the third trip consisted only of the parties left to hold front trenches to the last, together with the garrisons of the beach defences, the naval and military beach personnel and such R.E. personnel as might be required to effect the necessary repairs to any piers or harbour works that might be damaged.

About 7 p.m. the breeze freshened considerably from the southwest, the most unfavourable quarter, but the first trip, timed for 8 p.m., was dispatched without difficulty. The wind, however, continued to rise until, by 11 p.m., the connecting pier between the hulks and the shore at "W" Beach was washed away by heavy seas, and further embarkation into destroyers from these hulks became impracticable. In spite of these difficulties the second trips, which commenced at 11.30 p.m., were carried out well up to time, and the embarkation of guns continued uninterruptedly.

Early in the evening reports had been received from the right flank that a hostile submarine was believed to be moving down the Straits, and about midnight H.M.S. *Prince George*, which had embarked 2,000 men, and was sailing for Mudros, reported she was struck by a torpedo which failed to explode. The indications of the presence of a submarine added considerably to the anxiety for the safety of the troop carriers, and made it necessary for the vice-admiral to modify the arrangements made for the subsequent bombardment of the evacuated positions.

At 1.50 a.m., Gully Beach reported that the embarkation at that beach was complete, and that the lighters were about to push off, but at 2.10 a.m. a telephone message was received that one of the lighters was aground and could not be refloated. The N.T.O. at once took all possible steps to have another lighter sent in to Gully Beach, and this was, as a matter of fact, done within an hour, but in the meantime at 2.30 a.m. it was decided to move the 160 men, who had been relanded from the grounded lighter, to "W" Beach and embark them there.

From 2.40 a.m. the steadily increasing swell caused the N.T.O. the greatest anxiety as to the possibility of embarking the remainder of the troops if their arrival was much deferred.

At 3.30 a.m. the evacuation was complete, and abandoned heaps of stores and supplies were successfully set on fire by time fuses after the last man had embarked. Two magazines of ammunition and explosives were also successfully blown up at 4 a.m. These conflagrations were apparently the first intimation received by the Turks that we had withdrawn. Red lights were immediately discharged from the enemy's trenches, and heavy artillery fire opened on our trenches and beaches. This shelling was maintained until about 6.30 a.m.

Apart from four unserviceable 15-pounders, which had been destroyed earlier in the month, ten worn-out 15-pounders, one 6-in. Mark VII. gun, and six old heavy French guns, all of which were previously blown up, were left on the peninsula. In addition to the above, 508 animals, most of which were destroyed, and a number of vehicles and considerable quantities of stores, material, and supplies, all of which were destroyed by burning, had to be abandoned.

It would have been possible, of course, by extending the period during which the process of evacuation proceeded to have reduced the quantity of stores and material that was left behind on the peninsula, but not to the degree that may seem apparent at first sight. Our chances of enjoying a continuity of fine weather in the Aegean were very slender in the month of January; it was indeed a contingency that had to be reckoned with that we might vey probably be visited by a spell of bad weather which would cut us off completely from the peninsula for a fortnight or perhaps for even longer.

Supplies, ammunition, and material to a certain degree had therefore to be left to the last moment for fear of the isolation of the garrison at any moment when the evacuation might be in progress. I decided therefore that our aim should be primarily the withdrawal of the bulk of the personnel, artillery, and ammunition in the intermediate period, and that no risks should be taken in prolonging the withdrawal of personnel at the final stage with a view to reducing the quantity of stores left.

Skill and Good Fortune.

The entire evacuation of the peninsula had now been completed. It demanded for its successful realisation two important military essentials—*viz.*, good luck and skilled disciplined organisation—and they were both forthcoming to a marked degree at the hour needed. Our luck was in the ascendant by the marvellous spell of calm weather which prevailed. But we were able to turn to the fullest advantage these accidents of fortune.

Lieutenant-General Sir W. Birdwood and his corps commanders elaborated and prepared the orders in reference to the evacuation with a skill, competence, and courage which could not have been surpassed, and we had a further stroke of good fortune in being associated with Vice-Admiral Sir J. de Robeck, K.C.B.,Vice-Admiral Wemyss, and a body of naval officers whose work remained throughout this anxious period at that standard of accuracy and professional ability which is beyond the power of criticism or cavil.

The Line of Communication Staff, both Naval and Military, represented respectively by Lieutenant-General E.A.Altham, C.B., C.M.G., Commodore M. S. FitzMaurice, R.N., principal Naval Transport Officer, and Captain H.V. Simpson, R.N., Superintending Transport Officer, contributed to the success of the operation by their untiring zeal and conspicuous ability.

The members of the Headquarters Staff showed themselves, without exception, to be officers with whom it was a privilege to be associated; their competence, zeal, and devotion to duty were uniform and unbroken. Amongst such a highly trained body of officers it is difficult to select and discriminate. I confine myself, therefore, to placing on record the fine services rendered by—

Colonel (temporary Major-General) Arthur Lynden Lynden-Bell, C.B., C.M.G., Chief of General Staff, G.H.Q.;

Colonel (temporary Major-General) Walter Campbell, C.B., D.S.O., Deputy Quartermaster-General, G.H.Q., M.E.F.;

Lieutenant-Colonel (temporary Brigadier-General) W. Gillman, C.M.G., D.S.O., Brigadier-General, General Staff;

Brevet Major (temporary Lieutenant-Colonel) G. P. Dawnay, D.S.O., M.V.O., General Staff;

And whilst bringing to notice the names of these officers to whom

I am so much indebted, I trust I may be permitted to represent the loyal, cordial, and unswerving assistance rendered by General J. M. J. A. Brulard, commanding the French troops in the peninsula.

Before concluding this inadequate account of the events which happened during my tenure of command of the Forces in the Eastern Mediterranean, I desire to give a brief explanation of the work which was carried out on the Line of Communications, and to place on record my appreciation of the admirable work rendered by the officers responsible for this important service.

On the Dardanelles Peninsula it may be said that the whole of the machinery by which the text-books contemplate the maintenance and supply of an army was non-existent. The zone commanded by the enemy's guns extended not only to the landing places on the peninsula, but even over the sea in the vicinity.

The beaches were the advanced depots and refilling points at which the services of supply had to be carried out under artillery fire. The landing of stores as well as of troops was only possible under cover of darkness.

The sea, the ships, lighters, and tugs took, in fact, the place of railways and roads, with their railway trains, mechanical transport, etc., but with this difference, that the use of the latter is subject only to the intervention of the enemy, while that of the former was dependent on the weather.

Between the beaches and the Base at Alexandria, 800 miles to the south, the Line of Communications had but two harbours, Kephalos Bay, on the Island of Imbros, 15 miles roughly from the beaches, and Mudros Bay, at a distance of 60 miles. In neither were there any piers, breakwaters, wharves, or store houses of any description before the advent of the troops. On the shores of these two bays there were no roads of any military value, or buildings fit for military usage. The water supply at these islands was, until developed, totally inadequate for our needs.

The peninsula landing places were open beaches. Kephalos Bay is without protection from the north, and swept by a high sea in northerly gales. In Mudros Harbour, trans-shipments and disembarkations were often seriously impeded with a wind from the north or south. These difficulties were accentuated by the advent of submarines in the Aegean Sea, on account of which the vice-admiral deemed it necessary to prohibit any transport or store ship exceeding 1,500 tons proceeding north of Mudros, and although this rule was relaxed in the case of supply ships proceeding within the netted area of Suvla, it necessitated the trans-shipment of practically all reinforcements, stores, and supplies—other than those for Suvla—into small ships in Mudros Harbour.

At Suvla and Anzac, disembarkation could only be effected by lighters and tugs; thus for all personnel and material there was at least one trans-shipment, and for the greater portion of both two trans-shipments.

Yet notwithstanding the difficulties which have been set forth above, the army was well maintained in equipment and ammunition. It was well fed, it received its full supply of winter clothing at the beginning of December. The evacuation of the sick and wounded was carried out with the minimum of inconvenience, and the provision of hospital accommodation for them on the Dardanelles Line of Communication and elsewhere in the Mediterranean met all requirements.

The above is a very brief exposition of the extreme difficulties with which the officers responsible were confronted in dealing with a problem of peculiar complexity. They were fortunate in being associated in their onerous and anxious task with a most competent and highly trained naval staff. The members of the two staffs worked throughout in perfect harmony and cordiality, and it was owing to their joint efforts that the requirements of the troops were so well responded to.

Recommendations.

In accordance with the instructions received from Your Lordship by telegram on 10/1/16, I had the honour of telegraphing the names of the undermentioned officers who rendered most valuable and distinguished service in connection with the evacuation of Gallipoli, to be specially submitted for His Majesty's gracious consideration for promotion and reward, *viz*:—

> Colonel (temporary Major-General) Arthur Lynden Lynden-Bell, C.B., C.M.G., Chief of General Staff, G.H.Q., M.E.F.
> Colonel (temporary Major-General) Walter Campbell, C.B., D.S.O., Deputy Quartermaster-General, G.H.Q., M.E.F.
> Lieutenant-General Sir William Riddell Birdwood, K.C.S.I., K.C.M.G., C.B., CLE., D.S.O., Commander, Dardanelles Army.
> Major-General (temporary Lieutenant-General) Edward Altham Altham, C.B., C.M.G., Inspector-General of Communications, M.E.F.
> Major-General (temporary Lieutenant-General) Hon. Sir Julian Hedworth George Byng, K.C.M.G., C.B., M.V.O., Com-

mander, 9th Army Corps.

Major-General (temporary Lieutenant-General) Sir Alexander John Godley, K.C.M.G., C.B., Commander, A. and N.Z. Army Corps.

Major-General (temporary Lieutenant-General) Sir Francis John Davies, K.C.B., Commander, 8th Army Corps.

Brevet Colonel (temporary Brigadier General) George Fletcher MacMunn, D.S.O., R.A., D.A. and Q.M.G., Dardanelles Army.

Lieutenant-Colonel (temporary Brigadier-General) Hamilton Lyster Reed, V.C, C.M.G., R.A., Brigadier-General, General Staff, 9th Army Corps.

Lieutenant-Colonel (temporary Brigadier-General) Cyril Brudenel Bingham White, R.A., D.S.O., Brigadier-General, General Staff, Anzac.

Colonel (temporary Brigadier-General) Robert John Tudway, C.B., D.S.O., D.A. and Q.M.G., 8th Army Corps.

Brevet Colonel (temporary Brigadier-General) Harold Edward Street, R.A., Brigadier-General, General Staff, 8th Army Corps.

Major (temporary Brigadier General) Arthur George Preston McNalty, A.S.C., Acting D.A. and Q.M.G., 9th Army Corps.

Major (temporary Lieutenant-Colonel) Cecil Faber Aspinall, Royal Munster Fusiliers, Acting Brigadier-General, General Staff, Dardanelles Army.

Royal Navy.

Captain F. H. Mitchell, D.S.O., R.N., Naval Adviser at G.H.Q., M.E.F.

Captain Edwin Unwin, R.N., V.C, attached to Headquarters, Dardanelles Army.

French Army.

J. M. J. A. Brulard, Général de Division, Grand Officier de la Legion d'Honneur.

In the course of a few days I propose to forward recommendations for gallant and distinguished conduct performed by officers and men in the period under reference.

I have the honour to be.

Your Lordship's most obedient servant,

C. C. Monro,
General.

ALSO FROM LEONAUR
AVAILABLE IN SOFTCOVER OR HARDCOVER WITH DUST JACKET

THE FALL OF THE MOGHUL EMPIRE OF HINDUSTAN by H. G. Keene—By the beginning of the nineteenth century, as British and Indian armies under Lake and Wellesley dominated the scene, a little over half a century of conflict brought the Moghul Empire to its knees.

LADY SALE'S AFGHANISTAN by Florentia Sale—An Indomitable Victorian Lady's Account of the Retreat from Kabul During the First Afghan War.

THE CAMPAIGN OF MAGENTA AND SOLFERINO 1859 by Harold Carmichael Wylly—The Decisive Conflict for the Unification of Italy.

FRENCH'S CAVALRY CAMPAIGN by J. G. Maydon—A Special Correspondent's View of British Army Mounted Troops During the Boer War.

CAVALRY AT WATERLOO by Sir Evelyn Wood—British Mounted Troops During the Campaign of 1815.

THE SUBALTERN by George Robert Gleig—The Experiences of an Officer of the 85th Light Infantry During the Peninsular War.

NAPOLEON AT BAY, 1814 by F. Loraine Petre—The Campaigns to the Fall of the First Empire.

NAPOLEON AND THE CAMPAIGN OF 1806 by Colonel Vachée—The Napoleonic Method of Organisation and Command to the Battles of Jena & Auerstädt.

THE COMPLETE ADVENTURES IN THE CONNAUGHT RANGERS by William Grattan—The 88th Regiment during the Napoleonic Wars by a Serving Officer.

BUGLER AND OFFICER OF THE RIFLES by William Green & Harry Smith—With the 95th (Rifles) during the Peninsular & Waterloo Campaigns of the Napoleonic Wars.

NAPOLEONIC WAR STORIES by Sir Arthur Quiller-Couch—Tales of soldiers, spies, battles & sieges from the Peninsular & Waterloo campaigns.

CAPTAIN OF THE 95TH (RIFLES) by Jonathan Leach—An officer of Wellington's sharpshooters during the Peninsular, South of France and Waterloo campaigns of the Napoleonic wars.

RIFLEMAN COSTELLO by Edward Costello—The adventures of a soldier of the 95th (Rifles) in the Peninsular & Waterloo Campaigns of the Napoleonic wars.

AVAILABLE ONLINE AT **www.leonaur.com**
AND FROM ALL GOOD BOOK STORES

ALSO FROM LEONAUR
AVAILABLE IN SOFTCOVER OR HARDCOVER WITH DUST JACKET

OFFICERS & GENTLEMEN *by Peter Hawker & William Graham*—Two Accounts of British Officers During the Peninsula War: Officer of Light Dragoons by Peter Hawker & Campaign in Portugal and Spain by William Graham.

THE WALCHEREN EXPEDITION *by Anonymous*—The Experiences of a British Officer of the 81st Regt. During the Campaign in the Low Countries of 1809.

LADIES OF WATERLOO *by Charlotte A. Eaton, Magdalene de Lancey & Juana Smith*—The Experiences of Three Women During the Campaign of 1815: Waterloo Days by Charlotte A. Eaton, A Week at Waterloo by Magdalene de Lancey & Juana's Story by Juana Smith.

JOURNAL OF AN OFFICER IN THE KING'S GERMAN LEGION *by John Frederick Hering*—Recollections of Campaigning During the Napoleonic Wars.

JOURNAL OF AN ARMY SURGEON IN THE PENINSULAR WAR *by Charles Boutflower*—The Recollections of a British Army Medical Man on Campaign During the Napoleonic Wars.

ON CAMPAIGN WITH MOORE AND WELLINGTON *by Anthony Hamilton*—The Experiences of a Soldier of the 43rd Regiment During the Peninsular War.

THE ROAD TO AUSTERLITZ *by R. G. Burton*—Napoleon's Campaign of 1805.

SOLDIERS OF NAPOLEON *by A. J. Doisy De Villargennes & Arthur Chuquet*—The Experiences of the Men of the French First Empire: Under the Eagles by A. J. Doisy De Villargennes & Voices of 1812 by Arthur Chuquet.

INVASION OF FRANCE, 1814 *by F. W. O. Maycock*—The Final Battles of the Napoleonic First Empire.

LEIPZIG—A CONFLICT OF TITANS *by Frederic Shoberl*—A Personal Experience of the 'Battle of the Nations' During the Napoleonic Wars, October 14th-19th, 1813.

SLASHERS *by Charles Cadell*—The Campaigns of the 28th Regiment of Foot During the Napoleonic Wars by a Serving Officer.

BATTLE IMPERIAL *by Charles William Vane*—The Campaigns in Germany & France for the Defeat of Napoleon 1813-1814.

SWIFT & BOLD *by Gibbes Rigaud*—The 60th Rifles During the Peninsula War.

AVAILABLE ONLINE AT **www.leonaur.com**
AND FROM ALL GOOD BOOK STORES

07/09

www.ingramcontent.com/pod-product-compliance
Lightning Source LLC
Chambersburg PA
CBHW030216170426
43201CB00006B/106